FOODSERVICE FACILITIES PLANNING
PLANNING
Third Edition

FOODSERVICE FACILITIES PLANNING

Third Edition

Edward A. Kazarian Ph.D.

Professor Emeritus
School of Hotel, Restaurant and
Institutional Management
Michigan State University
East Lansing, Michigan

VNR VAN NOSTRAND REINHOLD
_____ New York

Library of Congress Catalog Card Number 88-5408
ISBN 0-442-20588-0

I(T)P Van Nostrand Reinhold is an International Thomson Publishing company.
ITP logo is a trademark under license.

Printed in the United States of America

Van Nostrand Reinhold
115 Fifth Avenue
New York, NY 10003

International Thomson Publishing GmbH
Konigswinterer Str. 518
5300 Bonn 3
Germany

International Thomson Publishing
Berkshire House,168-173
High Holborn, London WC1V 7AA
England

International Thomson Publishing Asia
38 Kim Tian Rd., #0105
Kim Tian Plaza
Singapore 0316

Thomas Nelson Australia
102 Dodds Street
South Melbourne 3205
Victoria, Australia

International Thomson Publishing Japan
Kyowa Building, 3F
2-2-1 Hirakawacho
Chiyada-Ku, Tokyo 102
Japan

Nelson Canada
1120 Birchmount Road
Scarborough, Ontario
M1K 5G4, Canada

16 15 14 13 12 11 10 9 8 7 6 5 4

Library of Congress Cataloging-in-Publication Data

Kazarian, Edward A.
   Foodservice facilities planning / Edward A. Kazarian.— 3rd ed.
      p.   cm.
   Includes bibliographies and index.
   ISBN 0-442-20588-0
   1. Food service management.   I. Title.   II. Title: Food service
facilities planning.
TX911.3.M27K398   1989
647'.95068'2—dc19   88-5408
                                                              CIP

Contents

11 Equipment and Facility Maintenance   **219**

12 Space Requirements   **238**

13 Layout of Facilities   **272**

Preface

The planning of foodservice facilities has become very complex with the increased competitiveness of the foodservice industry. Successful design can be attained only when all aspects of the foodservice operation have been evaluated and planned for accordingly. The menu offerings, arrangement of the dining areas, kitchen floor plan, and a myriad other details have to be effectively blended to create a facility that can achieve the goals of the owner or operator.

Within the relatively few years since the original edition of this text was published, several changes affecting the foodservice industry have taken place. Changes in consumer attitudes, consumer behavior, labor costs, energy costs, regulatory considerations, and the general business environment have created new and challenging problems for foodservice planners and designers.

Today's foodservice consumer shows a greater awareness of economic value and sanitary requirements and demands quality food at a reasonable price. These changing consumer characteristics require foodservice designs that can quickly adapt to new menu items, new methods of service, different atmospheres, or new operating procedures. A greater emphasis has to be placed on the marketing function as it relates to planning new facilities or in remodeling existing facilities.

Increasing labor costs have to be offset by increasing labor productivity through improved workplaces, working conditions, and using modern labor saving equipment. New approaches to planning are also needed in order to minimize energy costs and to meet the ever-increasing regulatory requirements imposed on the foodservice industry. Environmental concerns regarding air pollution, litter, traffic, signs, and waste disposal will continue to influence the planning function in the future.

These considerations place a greater emphasis on foodservice planning as a prerequisite to the success of foodservice operations. Only those facilities that are planned for flexibility, labor productivity, efficient use of energy, and managed accordingly will survive the competitive environment of the foodservice industry.

It is with these concepts in mind that this text was revised and expanded.

EDWARD A. KAZARIAN

1

Introduction to Foodservice Facilities Planning

Foodservice facilities vary from the simplest limited-menu snack bar to the multifaceted hotel foodservice that may involve public dining rooms, employee dining rooms, cafeterias, banquet service, and room service. Each type of foodservice facility is characterized by unique traits in the meals offered, type of service, operational methods, marketing approach, customers served, and atmosphere or ambience.

The foodservice industry has experienced tremendous growth and change in the last few years, which have created a need for foodservice facilities capable of providing the variety of meals prepared by different preparation techniques that will satisfy the changing desires of customers.

Each foodservice facility may be planned to meet different objectives. For example, the objective for a fast food facility may stress the speed of service, whereas the hospital foodservice has to stress the nutritional and therapeutic values of food. These variations indicate the complexity of planning foodservice facilities. However, there is one characteristic common to all foodservice facilities. Each is involved in the production and sale or distribution of meals. This common characteristic requires that foodservice facilities be planned for technologically modern production techniques and operated by modern management concepts.

The planning of foodservice facilities is usually a continuous process for those individuals and organizations engaged in the foodservice industry. The planning involved may be quite simple, as in the case of rearranging tables and chairs in an existing dining room or replacing equipment in production areas. In other cases, the planning may be a very complex problem such as the development of a completely new foodservice facility, which may involve considerations of land, building design, financing, management policies, and operating procedures. Regardless of the complexity of the project, satisfactory results can be obtained only when the planning is guided by the basic concepts and objectives of design and layout.

DESIGN AND LAYOUT

The terms "design" and "layout" are sometimes confused and should be clarified to simplify further discussion. Design refers to the broad function of developing the entire foodservice facility, including the original concepts of operation, site selection, menu development, equipment requirements, and all the other pertinent planning functions that are necessary to develop the concept into a structural and operational reality.

Layout is a more limited function of the planning process that deals with the arrangement of the physical facilities for the foodservice operation. Layout is one of the many tasks that have to be accomplished in the overall design of the facility. It is one of the most important aspects of design because it dictates to a great extent the operational efficiency of the facility.

The entire design of a foodservice facility includes many functions that are related to the layout function, as well as being related to each other. Some of these design functions can be identified as

conceptualization of the proposed project
market studies of a particular area or perhaps finding a
  suitable location
financial planning
location and site considerations
determining the overall size of the facility
feasibility studies
menu development
merchandising
service considerations
development of the dining atmosphere
organization
pricing considerations
food preparation and production techniques

selection of materials and methods of construction
layout of equipment, workplaces, and aisles

The design functions identified emphasize the importance of correlating the design and layout of the physical facilities with the operational characteristics of the foodservice facility. It is common to discuss and evaluate such areas as marketing, menus, labor availability, atmosphere, sales, and many others during the planning process.

The order of the functions is not intended to signify the sequence in which they are performed or their importance. For certain projects, some of these functions are very important to the successful planning of the facility; yet these functions may not be so significant in other types of projects. For example, the layout function for a drive-in chain that uses basically the same arrangements of equipment and spaces becomes a minor part of design after the first one is planned. In this case, location and site analysis or merchandising may be the more important design functions for the chain. On the other hand, the layout function for an institutional foodservice facility is very important because of its bearing on construction and operational costs. Food facility planners must sense the importance of the various design functions for each type of project and concentrate their efforts on the most relevant ones.

The design and layout of the workplaces, departments, storage areas, aisles, and other facilities should reflect the operational characteristics of the organization. Similarly, the existing facilities dictate to a great extent the operational characteristics of the foodservice enterprise. It is difficult to separate the concepts of design and layout of physical areas and facilities from the basic concepts of good operational procedures and policies. For example, one planning concept is to simplify the production of food items appearing on the menu. This concept is also a basis for the development of work procedures and training programs for employees. Another concept is to create a physical atmosphere that will attract and retain customers. The same concept is used to develop the merchandising aspects of the operation for purpose of generating sales. Thus it is easily seen that both planning and managing of a particular foodservice facility are guided by many identical concepts.

In reality, it would be impossible to plan a well-designed facility without a fundamental understanding of basic operational and management principles as they relate to foodservice operations. Since there is such a close relationship between the physical facilities and the operation of the foodservice, it is desirable for management personnel to understand the principles of planning, so that the functioning of the operation can be directed as conceived by the designer. Good management is obviously the key to the successful operation of a foodservice facility regardless of the physical facilities, since good management can overcome poor design and layout to a certain extent. However, a well-planned facility not only simplifies the managment of the operation but largely determines the success of the project.

PLANNING

Characteristics

The planning of foodservice facilities is characterized by some design and layout problems that are not commonly encountered in other types of planning projects. This uniqueness is partially caused by the great variety of foodservice operational concepts that may be used; the variety of customers and users to be served; the material choices available; the production methods possible; and the characteristics of the finished menu items. The fact that a typical foodservice facility is involved in the production, sales, and service of a highly perishable commodity to individuals who must be attracted and pleased contributes to these special problems of design and layout.

One specific problem that the food facility planner faces is the customer or user demand for foodservice at limited periods of time, which results in peak periods of activity in the facility. These peak periods are obviously the normal meal hours, and the planner must develop a design that will handle these periods with a minimum of effort and confusion. This problem is further compounded by having to plan for different menu items for each meal period during the day, and in some instances even a different type of service for different meal periods.

A related problem that must be solved by the food facility planner is that of efficiently and economically processing and producing all the various food items appearing on the menu in the quantities required. This is especially critical for those operations that have daily menu changes. Some food items on the menu may involve several different raw ingredients or materials that may be available in a variety of forms such as fresh, canned, frozen, or dried. The use of different forms of ingredients or materials will require different design decisions.

In addition to considering the menu items, beverages, and raw food ingredients involved, the planner is also faced with the design and layout of areas for processing nonfood items such as china, glasses, silverware, utensils, and linen, to name a few.

Food facility planning involves designing a system that will maintain the quality of the food items produced. Because of the perishability of many foods, the planner must be sure that appearance, taste, and palatability are not affected by the choice of process or equipment. This is especially critical when prepared foods must be held for a period of time before they are consumed. The design of holding systems for maintaining the desired temperature and moisture content of prepared foods is very important for cafeterias, banquet service, and catering operations.

The importance of good planning for foodservice facilities cannot be emphasized enough. Each new project that involves planning to any extent represents an investment in the physical structure, the equipment, the furnishings, and, most important, the continuing cost of the management and labor required to operate and maintain the facility. The result of poor planning is reflected daily in high costs for labor and maintenance and in poor worker morale.

A well-planned facility is developed by utilizing the basic principles from many areas of knowledge. The concepts of work analysis, time and motion studies, human engineering, management, economics, psychology, materials handling, and many other fields can be used advantageously to help plan a foodservice facility that will meet the objectives of the investors and operators.

In general terms, some of the identifiable characteristics of a well-planned foodservice facility include the following:

minimum investment in buildings, furnishings, and equipment
aesthetic appeal to customers and workers (pleasant dining and working areas)
maximum profit and return on investment
simplified production processes for food and nonfood items
efficient flow of materials and equipment that may have to be moved about
minimum employee travel
safe working areas
minimum waste of time, labor, and materials
sanitary conditions in all areas of the facility
minimum manpower requirements
low maintenance costs
ease of supervision and management

Much careful thought and planning are involved in developing a design that will meet the indicated criteria. This necessitates extra time spent in conferences, meetings, and research, and on the drawing board. The extra time spent in ironing out the problems of a new plan is probably the least costly investment of the entire project. Many of the characteristics of good design may also be considered as objectives of planning and will be discussed in detail later in this chapter.

Scope

The planning of foodservice facilities involves considerations of many diverse types of projects dealing with the development and arrangement of spaces, equipment, and work areas. The most complex situation is the planning required for the development of an entirely new facility. This type of project requires planners to utilize both their operational knowledge of the foodservice industry and their knowledge of the physical planning aspects as related to the facility. Planning a new facility may involve considerations of location and site selection that may not be involved in other types of projects. If the site is a variable in the planning of a new operation, the planner has an opportunity to do a thorough analysis of the potential market that will produce better decisions and ensure a successful operation.

The planning of a new facility also enables the planner to make the greatest use of new food products, new processing techniques, and new equipment. A more flexible operation can be planned if anticipated changes in products, market, or equipment are considered in the design. Planning a new facility also enables the planner to develop new and interesting concepts of foodservice merchandising more easily than one working within the restraints of an existing building or operation. Another aspect of planning a new facility is that it gives the designer the greatest freedom to make decisions regarding the operating characteristics and management policies that should be incorporated into day-to-day operation.

Although planning a new facility is complex, it is a desirable situation because of the many options available to the planner. Other types of projects usually have some type of restriction that the planner has to work around in order to arrive at a practical solution. These restrictions may take the form of existing buildings, which have walls, columns, and space limitations that have to be contended with. For example, remodeling of an existing facility is usually done within the confines of the exterior walls for purposes of economy and simplicity. Modernizing is required primarily because of the need for new or greater-capacity equipment to handle new foods, new processes, or new techniques of production. Occasionally, a modernizing project is undertaken in the public areas of food facilities to provide a different type of atmosphere or service.

Some remodeling projects involve major structural changes in the building, as when increasing the size of a dining area or when additional production facilities are needed. Projects involving major structural changes give the planner greater flexibility in design, but they do entail considerable cost and possible undesirable interruption of the operation. Whenever structural changes are involved in a project, it is desirable to anticipate any future changes so that provision for making these changes can be incorporated into the design. For example, planning a non-load bearing wall in the dining room is a good idea if it is anticipated that dining capacity will have to be increased in the near future.

Other types of projects that involve planning include the expansion of an existing production area or department. The expansion may be desired to increase the production capacity of the department or perhaps to provide faster service. Related to expansion projects are projects that will add new areas or new departments to an existing facility. The addition may be required in order to handle new menu items or a different production process. Sometimes additions are needed to provide a different type of service, such as carry-out or catering service.

Objectives

Every type of planning project regardless of size or complexity is best guided by well-defined objectives. These objectives may be determined by the owner or cooperatively by the owner and various consultants. Written statements outlining the objectives in detail are preferred, so that misunderstandings between owner and planner are avoided.

The general objective for all food facility planning is to make optimum use of money, materials, manpower, and equipment to provide the highest quality of food and service. Underlying this primary objective is the basic concept of assuring customer or user satisfaction. This means that the foodservice facility has to be designed so that foods can be freshly prepared and be appealing and tasty. More specific objectives of planning include areas relating to either the physical facilities or the operational concepts of the foodservice, and in many cases apply to both.

Facilitating Production.   As mentioned earlier, one objective common to all types of planning projects is identified as facilitating the food production function. The planner uses this objective to guide the arrangement and layout of spaces, workplaces, equipment, and aisles so there is a smooth flow of materials and employees. Management uses this same objective to direct employees in correct work procedures after the facility is built and put into operation.

Materials Handling.   Another objective of planning is to arrive at a design that will minimize the materials handling required in the facility. The planner will utilize many of the principles of materials handling as guides in achieving this objective. Wherever possible, the planner will visualize the flow of materials through the facility and evaluate many different alternatives for handling these materials. Materials flow in foodservice facilities includes not only food items but dishes, pots and pans, beverages, bottles, silverware, trash, paper, and linen as well. Regardless of the materials involved, it is best to be guided by the precept, "Don't handle materials by hand if they can be handled and moved by some other method." This implies that maximum use of carts, conveyors, and other mechanical aids is to be incorporated into the design of the facility. When materials have to be moved, they are best routed over straightline paths with a minimum amount of backtracking.

The food facility planner may use many aids, such as product process charts, flow diagrams, or string charts, to evaluate and plan for the efficient flow of materials. Some of the basic objectives that guide the design of a materials handling system are:

Minimize the cost of handling materials.
Minimize the time required to handle materials.
Miminize the inventory of materials required to meet the needs of the operation.
Safeguard the materials from deterioration and damage.
Simplify the control of materials used in the facility.

One of the most important aspects of materials handling deals with the standardization of equipment, containers, and utensils to be used in the system. Compatibility of sizes in the selection of these materials handling components will result in a simple and efficient system.

Space Utilization.   Because of the increasing costs of building materials, equipment, labor, and construction, the planner must utilize the objective of making economical use of space to develop a feasible plan. This objective refers to both horizontal and vertical spaces and is accomplished by using recommended space standards for workplaces, aisles, storage areas, ceiling heights, and shelving. The work area shown in Fig. 1.1 illustrates some of the concepts of space utilization. Different arrangements of equipment, storage areas, and aisle spaces should be evaluated to make certain that maximum use of space is achieved. This objective is not intended to create a facility that is too small and cramped, but to allow only the space needed to accomplish the essential functions and tasks. This objective is more important for the planning of processing and production areas than for planning for the dining or other income-producing areas. The space requirements for a facility can frequently be reduced by changing purchasing frequencies, type of raw materials, or production processes.

FIG. 1.1. Efficient use of horizontal and vertical space.
Courtesy of Keating of Chicago, Inc.

Maintenance and Cleaning. The provision for maintenance and cleaning ease in the foodservice facility is another objective of sound planning. The designer considers this objective when specifying materials for walls, floors, and ceilings and in the construction methods to be used. The design of equipment is also important in meeting this objective. Providing adequate space for maintaining and cleaning foodservice equipment is one thing that foodservice operators appreciate.

Flexibility.   Another objective that guides the planning of facilities is the concept that provides for flexibility and adjustment to change. In food facilities design, flexibility indicates that spaces and equipment can be easily changed, moved, or adjusted to make them more effective for the accomplishment of required tasks. Flexibility leads to better utilization of space and labor. Although this may be difficult to do in some cases, it is an indication of advance planning.

Most of the changes that may influence a foodservice operation can be fairly easily anticipated. In general, these changes will occur in the materials and products used or in the production techniques necessary to process these materials. The use of partially or fully preprocessed foods is the type of change that can easily be planned for if it is considered during the early stages of the project. Anticipation of changes in menus, portion sizes, or service methods can be envisioned in many cases, and appropriate provisions can be included in the final design of the facility. Many facilities are planned with expansion in mind and space for additional equipment can be provided.

Investment in Equipment.   Although maximum use of materials handling equipment satisfies the objective of minimizing the handling of materials, the planner should simultaneously consider another basic objective of planning—that the investment in equipment should be minimized. Thus the planner decides on the basis of economics whether or not it would be desirable to have certain types of materials handling equipment. The basic objective is related to all types of equipment to be used in the facility. Considerations of cost, type, size, and maintenance problems associated with equipment are all evaluated before a decision is made.

Labor Utilization.   A very important objective of planning is to develop a design that will promote the effective use of labor. This objective is accomplished primarily by the design of individual workplaces and work areas. The basic concepts of motion economy, human engineering, and work design are utilized by the planner to identify and visualize how the various tasks that have to be performed are to be done. Decisions are made as to the best and easiest way of accomplishing tasks, and from these decisions the appropriate workplaces are developed. Considerations of employee safety, comfort, and working conditions are also evaluated and provided for at this time. The physical factors of temperature and humidity control, lighting, noise, and air movement are considered as a part of the total design of workplaces. The design of the work area shown in Fig. 1.2 reflects many of these factors. Increasing labor costs demand that more time be allowed for planning efficient workplaces that result in greater employee productivity.

Supervision. An area that is related to the labor aspect is the consideration of supervision and development of employees. Anticipated methods of training, control, and evaluation of performance will influence the design of certain areas in the facility. Operations requiring

FIG. 1.2. Design with sufficient work table space for effective utilization of labor.
Courtesy of the Fresh Approach Handicapped Training Center and Hamill & McKinney, Architect-Engineers, Inc.

large numbers of employees may need special areas for meetings, orientation sessions, and training programs.

Cost Control. A foodservice facility designed with cost control as a basic objective will result in a more profitable operation. This, of course, assumes that management will operate the facility with the same objective. Food and beverage cost control is one area where the designer can incorporate many ideas that will keep costs to a minimum. The design of an adequate and properly equipped receiving area where incoming merchandise can be checked for weight, count, and quality is very important to this objective. Storage areas can be designed to simplify inventorying and keeping track of expensive food and beverage items. The design of issuing systems is also guided by this objective.

Another area of control that the designer will consider deals with portion control. Design for portion control is reflected by the selection of materials, equipment, utensils, and cooking processes that will be used. The availability of preportioned foods has done a great deal toward simplifying the design for portion control, especially for fast-food operations.

PLANNING IN THE FUTURE

The planning of foodservice facilities in the future will be influenced by a number of factors that are recognized as critical to the success of the operation. Such factors as customer appeal, labor costs, and management concepts must be evaluated and properly planned for. Although these factors were considered in the past, their importance was not stressed to the extent needed for designing the foodservice facility for the future.

Customer Appeal

The foodservice market of the future will be characterized by higher income levels, better education, and greater consumer awareness of products and services. For this highly competitive foodservice market projected for the years ahead, more emphasis must be placed on designing for customer or user appeal. Comfortable, pleasant dining areas, as illustrated in Fig. 1.3, will have to be planned in an attempt

FIG. 1.3. Attractive dining areas are important to the foodservice customer.
Courtesy of St. Clair's Crossing and Hamill & McKinney, Architects-Engineers, Inc.

to attract and retain a share of the market. Decor and atmosphere are becoming as important as the courteous serving of good food. Rest rooms, lounges, and other public areas are also going to be more important to customer reaction and should be planned accordingly. Fig. 1.4 shows rest-room facilities that are attractive and pleasant.

Other concepts dealing with the uses of colors, lighting, ventilation, and decor must be incorporated into the design of areas for customer use. The use of these factors in the design of a lounge area is shown in Fig. 1.5.

The future foodservice customer or user will undoubtedly be more insistent on clean and sanitary facilities; consequently designers should emphasize sanitation in the planning of the operation. There will also be increased restrictions in the sanitary and safety codes to be followed. Construction methods, equipment design, and ventilation requirements are being stressed more and more each year in city, country, and state building and sanitary codes. Local sanitarians will probably be more critical in their evaluation and approval of proposed foodservice facilities.

FIG. 1.4. Clean, pleasant rest rooms are required in modern foodservice facilities.
Courtesy of Kellogg Center, Michigan State University.

Labor Costs

In the past, poor design and layout in the production and service areas could be compensated for by adding whatever additional low-cost help was needed. The projected wage rates and fringe benefits for foodservice workers indicate that only the efficiently planned, highly productive facility will be able to survive this nemesis of high labor costs. Future foodservice facilities will have to overcome labor costs and decreased availability of labor by increased mechanization and automation; increased use of convenience foods; better arrangements of production areas; and greater improvements in employee working environment.

The incorporation of newly developed equipment such as silver sorters, conveying systems, change-makers, and continuous-process equipment into the planning of the facility will prove to be important labor-saving factors. Many facilities are using convenience foods to

FIG. 1.5.   Lighting used to create unusual and interesting decor.
Courtesy of The Henry Ford Museum, Dearborn, Michigan and The Hysen Group, Livonia, Michigan.

some extent to reduce labor costs. The improved quality and acceptability of convenience foods will result in increased use of these items in the future. The anticipated increase in the use of convenience foods will require changes in the design of areas for storage, production, and serving.

Probably the greatest change that will be evident in the future planning of foodservice facilities is the physical arrangement of spaces and equipment to increase the productivity of workers. A detailed analysis of the tasks to be performed, the best method of performing those tasks, and the planning of suitable layouts will result in the saving of time and labor. Many techniques for generating layouts with the aid of computers are being developed, and these will greatly aid the future planner. The use of computers will allow planners to evaluate many factors in great detail that time did not permit in the past.

PLANNING FOR ENERGY EFFICIENCY

The era of inexpensive energy is over, and energy conservation has now become one of the most important factors in the design of new foodservice facilities. Planners must consider all the areas that impact on energy usage and develop facilities that are energy efficient. The most important considerations in planning for energy efficiency include using new construction methods and materials that reduce heat loss or heat gain; using automated or computer-controlled equipment for heating, ventilating, and air conditioning the building; selecting energy-efficient equipment for preparation, cooling, cooking, and storing food; incorporation of energy recovery methods and the evaluation of using alternative energy sources such as solar or wind energy.

An example of an energy efficient building design is shown in Fig. 1.6, which features less window area and the use of double-pane windows to reduce the tremendous heat loss or heat gain associated with large single-pane glass areas. If large glass areas are to be used, as in the design of "solarium dining areas" or large glassed atriums, the consideration of the type of glass is critical to energy efficiency. Comparing the insulating ability using the "R" value shows the importance

FIG. 1.6. An energy-efficient building design.
Courtesy of RAX Systems, Inc.

of using double-pane insulating glass for these large glass areas. The typical "R" value for single-pane glass is approximately one. A sealed double-pane window has an "R" value of approximately two, which reduces heat loss through the glass area by 50%. Even double-pane glass, however, does not compare favorably with typical wall construction, which provides "R" values of ten or more depending on the construction materials and the amount of insulation.

Another option for large glass areas is triple-pane windows, which reduce heat loss by an additional 50% over the double-pane windows. Triple-pane windows, although energy efficient, are very heavy and may not be suitable for all types of design. Factors such as cost, type of construction, and severity of climatic conditions should be considered before deciding to use double-pane or triple-pane windows. These same factors may also affect decisions regarding the total amount of glass area to be used in the building. Increasing the thermal resistance of all exposed areas of the building in addition to the window area is an obvious requirement for the development of facilities that will achieve minimum energy consumption.

Some other specific ideas that may be used to guide the planning of an energy efficient facility are given below.

Consider the use of vestibules for entrances and exits.
Design the ventilation system for the minimum requirements.
Provide for the ventilation of attic spaces.
Consider designing for areas that may be closed off when they will not be used for extended periods of time.
Select colors that will reduce lighting levels.
Consolidate refrigerators and freezers.
Locate refrigerator compressors in cool areas.
Provide for adequate humidity control.
Use pipe and duct insulation.
All openings should be weatherstripped.
Exhaust hoods should be properly sized.
Incorporate the latest designs of make-up air systems for the exhaust hoods.
Select cooking equipment that will process food at low temperatures.
Provide lids and covers for cooking equipment where applicable.
Consider using timers or computer controls on equipment.
Develop plans that separate heating equipment from cooling equipment.
Consider the requirements for pollution control devices when selecting equipment.

Management Concepts

Managers will be a key to the efficient operation of future food facilities. They will be managing employees who have more intelligence and are better trained. Most employees will probably be tending equipment and controls rather than doing strictly manual tasks. They will also be demanding a much more pleasant place in which to work. The fields of human engineering and psychology will have to be used to a greater extent in the design of workplaces and work areas for these employees.

Another trend that management will be faced with in the future is increased union relations. Unionization of foodservice workers will probably continue to increase each year and require management to be more precise in setting standards of work and performance. More detailed job descriptions and other job-related documents will be necessary to minimize conflicts between labor and management. Careful anticipation of these factors during the planning phase can alleviate many of the problems that could arise after the facility is built and operational.

PROBLEMS AND EXERCISES

1.1. Distinguish between the terms "design" and "layout."

1.2. Briefly discuss why the concepts guiding the design and layout of foodservice facilities are similar to the operational procedures and policies of management.

1.3. Identify several special problems that a planner encounters in designing a foodservice facility.

1.4. Describe the advantages and disadvantages involved in planning and designing a new foodservice facility compared to remodeling an existing facility.

1.5. Identify the characteristics of a well-designed foodservice operation.

1.6. List three important concepts in materials handling for foodservice operations.

1.7. Identify and explain briefly the objectives involved in planning a foodservice facility.

1.8. Discuss the factors that will become more important in planning for facilities in the future.

1.9. List the ways a planner can reduce the reliance on labor, indicating future trends and innovations in the foodservice industry that will facilitate this process.

1.10. Describe five areas of design that can affect energy consumption and indicate how they might be modified to improve the energy efficiency of a facility.

1.11. Assume that you have to undertake the planning for each of the following four types of foodservice facilities: (a) a fast food franchise, (b) a moderately priced steak house, (c) an employee cafeteria at a manufacturing plant, and (d) a rooftop restaurant in a luxury hotel. Refer to the design functions identified at the beginning of this chapter and assess the relative importance of each of these functions to each of the foodservice facilities mentioned above.

BIBLIOGRAPHY

ANDERSON, H.W. 1976. The Modern Foodservice Industry. Wm. C. Brown Co., Dubuque, Iowa.

ANON. 1975. Guide to Energy Conservation for Food Service. Federal Energy Administration, Washington, D.C.

ASHRAE STANDARD 90–75. Energy Conservation in New Building Design. Am. Soc. Heating, Refrig., Air-Cond. Eng., New York.

AXLER, B.H. 1979. Foodservice: A Managerial Approach. Wm. C. Brown Co., Dubuque, Iowa.

DOERING, R.D. 1984. Food service facilities energy conservation projects. The Consultant *17* (4), 27–32, 44.

FARRELL, K. 1980. New dynamics in kitchen design. Restaurant Business *79* (4), 73–86, 118.

KAHRL, W.L. 1979. Planning and Operating a Successful Food Service Operation. Lebhar-Friedman Books, New York.

KAZARIAN, E.A. 1979. Work Analysis and Design for Hotels, Restaurants and Institutions, 2nd Edition. AVI Publishing Co., Westport, Connecticut.

KOTSCHEVAR, L.H. and TERRELL, M.E. 1985. Foodservice Planning: Layout and Equipment, 3rd Edition. John Wiley & Sons, New York.

KRAMER, A. 1980. Food and the Consumer. AVI Publishing Co., Westport, Connecticut.

LAWSON, F. 1973. Restaurant Planning and Design. Architectural Press Ltd., London.

MINOR, L.J. and CICHY, R.F. 1984. Foodservice Systems Management. AVI Publishing Co., Westport, Connecticut.

STOKES, J.W. 1977. How to Manage a Restaurant or Institutional Food Service. Wm. C. Brown Co., Dubuque, Iowa.

VAN KLEEK, P. 1981. Beverage Management and Bartending. CBI Publishing Co., Boston, Massachusetts.

2

The Planning Process

The planning of a complete foodservice facility requires the expertise of many individuals working cooperatively to gather and assimilate the information necessitated by the complexity of the project. It would be impossible to list chronologically all the detailed steps or phases included in the planning process, because many different approaches may be used. There are indeed certain steps that must be completed before further planning can proceed; however, some phases of planning can be accomplished simultaneously or in a few cases independently, depending upon the situation. Actually the planning process can have many starting points, or the various phases involved may be done in a different order.

The planning process usually begins when there is an idea generated, a desire to be fulfilled, or a pressing need for a foodservice facility. The project may originate in a market survey that indicates the need for a new restaurant in an area; or a land developer may have a particular location that may be suitable for a foodservice operation. Some planning projects are created by necessity because they are an integral part of a larger project where foodservice is desired. Examples include the building of new hospitals, schools, nursing homes, and office facilities. Other projects may be created because they are solutions to problems of high labor costs, lack of sales volume, or obsolescence in existing operations.

The various steps of the planning process will be outlined in this chapter, and detailed discussions of the more important steps will be presented in later chapters.

PRELIMINARY PLANNING INFORMATION

After the concepts or ideas for a proposed project have been formulated, the next logical step is to delineate the preliminary planning information and decisions that will characterize the foodservice facility. This information will be used to guide the overall planning of the project and therefore should be carefully considered. There should be enough detail so that the remaining steps of the planning process can be carried out smoothly. The following points should be considered when gathering and developing the preliminary planning information.

1. The information is to be used for guiding the overall design of the project, but it does not give all the final answers to all the problems of design.
2. Information should be general enough to allow for some flexibility in planning.
3. Information should be specific, on the other hand, on any aspects that are inflexible, such as a fixed site, a fixed budget, or a fixed size of building.
4. Some of the information gathered may be subject to change after further study and research are completed on the proposed project.
5. The information represents a comprehensive summary of the major objectives and requirements desirable for the project.

In these early stages of the planning process, the information gathered may be presented in outline form. A suggested form for indicating the desirable preliminary planning information is shown in Table 2.1. The form may be supplemented with additional information as required by the particular project to be planned. Some further information may also be gathered during the later stages of the planning process.

The accumulation of this preliminary planning information will help to ensure a more efficient, functional, and profitable final design for the foodservice facility.

PROSPECTUS

Using the preliminary concepts and information gathered in the previous step, the next stage of the planning process involves the de-

TABLE 2.1. PRELIMINARY PLANNING INFORMATION FOR FOODSERVICE
OPERATIONS

Type of Project		
New facility		
Remodeling of existing facility		_____
Expansion project		_____
Interiors only		_____
Production areas only		_____
Others (specify)		_____
Type of Foodservice Facility to be Planned		
University or college		
Public cafeteria		_____
Coffee shop		_____
Snack bar		_____
Catering		_____
Union building		_____
University club		_____
Residence halls		_____
Commercial restaurants		
Table service		_____
Cafeteria		_____
Coffee shop		_____
Drive in		_____
Take out		_____
Banquet		_____
Vending		_____
Others		_____
Hospital and nursing homes		
Patient service		_____
Snack bars		_____
Hotel, motel, motor inns, clubs		_____
Dining rooms		_____
Room service		_____
Other		_____
Employee foodservice		_____
Cafeteria		_____
Vending		_____
Executive dining rooms		_____
Other		_____
Location and Market Characteristics		
Type of clientele		
Medium income		
Upper income		_____
Lower income		_____
Location		
Urban		
Rural		_____
Suburban		_____
Size of Facility and Hours of Operation		
Number of seats, or	_____	
Total number of people to be fed		
Breakfast	_____	Hours _____
Noon	_____	_____
Evening	_____	_____
Other	_____	_____
Menu Characteristics		
Extent		
Limited		
Extensive		_____
Alcoholic beverages		_____

TABLE 2.1 Continued

Quality and pricing	
High	————
Medium	————
Low	————
Type of Service	
Table service	————
Booth service	————
Counter service	————
Self service	————
Take out service	————
Car service	————
Other	————
Standards of Service	
Speed	————
Linen	————
Paper	————
Other factors	————
Types of Atmosphere Desired	
Intimate	————
Subdued	————
Formal	————
Informal	————
Cheerful	————
Others	————
Future Plans	
Expansion capability	
Dining areas	————
Production areas	————
Special Features or Requirements	
Parking	————
Customer facilities	————
Employee facilities	————
Special functions	————
Banquet rooms	————
Party rooms	————
Others	
Service bars	————
Salad bars	————
Display cooking	————
Tableside cooking	————
Lobster tanks	————
Pastry carts	————

velopment of the prospectus. The prospectus is basically an operational model of the foodservice facility. This part of the planning process may be completed by the owner, or frequently a foodservice consultant will be retained to accomplish the task.

In the prospectus, the general and preliminary information regarding the proposed project is evaluated, and fairly detailed descriptions of how the food facility is to function are prepared. Considerable research into the areas of marketing, sales estimating, production techniques, control, and management is required to develop a well-prepared prospectus. A brief description of preparing the prospectus is presented here to show its relationship to the other steps in the planning process. This step is so important to the success of the planning effort that a detailed presentation of developing a complete prospectus is presented in Chapter 4.

Market

A detailed analysis and description of potential customers or users of the proposed foodservice facility is the first task to be accomplished in developing the prospectus. Desirable information regarding the market includes such items as occupation, age, sex, disposable income, social behavior, consumer behavior, and any anticipated changes in these characteristics. Actually, the more detailed the information regarding the customer or user, the easier it is to complete the other areas of the prospectus.

Menu

The next step in developing the prospectus is to determine the characteristics of the menu that best matches the market described. Menu characteristics regarding frequency of change, numbers of food items in each category to be offered, and the type of food item from the standpoint of a la carte versus complete meals are decided. Other factors include portion sizes, cooked-to-order versus prepared items, or items requiring batch preparation, and any other special features of the menu. Preparation of a typical menu with the suggested format, actual food entrées and portion sizes would be desirable at this stage, because the menu is the key to the development of the rest of the prospectus. All the decisions regarding the menu should correlate with the characteristics of the potential customer in order to maximize sales. The decisions regarding the menu are the most important aspect of preparing the prospectus, since most of the other decisions regarding the design of the foodservice facility are dictated by the menu.

Service

The next area to be considered in preparing the prospectus is determination of the type of service to be offered in the facility. This is decided by evaluating both the market and the menu in order to select the most appropriate type of service or combination of types of service, if more than one is desirable. Consideration of service standards is also appropriate at this time.

Type of Foodservice Facility

The decisions regarding the market, the menu, and the type of service can now serve to characterize the particular type of foodservice facility to be planned. The description can be stated in very general terms, such as cafeteria, coffee shop, specialty restaurant, or drive-in. The classification of the type of foodservice facility enables the planner to utilize specialized information available for such operations and simplifies completing the prospectus, as well as the remaining steps of the planning process.

Atmosphere

At this point in the development of the prospectus, the concept of the type of dining atmosphere to be developed for the facility is decided. The atmosphere is described in general terms that convey an image as related to the consumer, the menu, and the type of service. Foodservice atmosphere may be identified by such terms as formal, informal, cheerful, friendly, relaxed, or appealing. The creation of the dining atmosphere is accomplished by proper selection of colors, furnishings, wall and floor coverings, lighting, and by careful control of temperature, relative humidity, noise, and odors. Costuming and attitude of employees are also important to the development of a desirable dining atmosphere. A separate chapter is devoted to discussing the creation of atmosphere because it is so critical to the success of a food facility.

Operating Characteristics

The description of the market and the decisions regarding the menu and the type of service also lead to identifying the operating characteristics of the food facility, which is another component of the prospectus. Operating characteristics to be determined include days of operation per year, hours open per day, seasonal variations expected, and the expected meal loads per meal period and during peak periods.

Other operating characteristics described in the prospectus include the type of organization and management policies under which the food facility will operate. These can be briefly described by the type of ownership and an organization chart showing departmental breakdown. Control concepts and procedures, merchandising methods, public relations, maintenance, and personnel development are included in this part of the prospectus. Any special operational concepts that may be unique to a particular food facility should be adequately emphasized so that appropriate planning decisions can be made.

Feasibility Information

An essential part of the prospectus deals with the financial aspects of the proposed food facility. This obviously is a very critical point in the planning process and should be prepared as carefully as possible. In some instances, the feasibility study is done separately from the prospectus by a qualified consultant. The information pertaining to the market and the operational characteristics of the proposed facility are evaluated in relationship to a particular site or location. The concept of facility size in terms of number of seats or number of meals is determined as well as preliminary space estimates for the building. These are used to estimate income and costs. Seat turnover and check averages are used to develop sales volume for the foodservice facility.

Expected food and beverage costs are developed and estimates of labor, overhead, and other operational costs are prepared. A proposed budget, projected cash flow, return on investment, and other financial considerations are also estimated in order to evaluate the feasibility of the project. Chapter 5 is devoted to a detailed presentation of making the feasibility study because of the importance of this aspect of planning.

After the prospectus has been completed, it is reviewed to make sure that all the concepts are workable and that the information presented is as accurate as possible. If all aspects of the prospectus, especially the financial considerations, are satisfactory to the parties concerned and it appears that the proposed project can be economically undertaken, then the planning process can continue.

COMMISSIONING PLANNERS

Armed with the prospectus, the owner or the owner's representatives can approach and evaluate the individuals who will make up the planning team for the project. Hopefully, the selection of the architect, the foodservice consultant, and other members of the planning team will be based on their ability to develop the plans and specifications from the guidelines presented in the prospectus. Architects and consultants will show prospective clients completed projects they have done for others, so the owner can make an intelligent choice. After selection and commissioning of the architect and other consultants has been completed, the detailed planning of the proposed project can begin.

The key members of the planning team will meet with the owner or the owner's representatives to outline the necessary planning tasks. At this meeting, the prospectus is again reviewed to make sure it contains all the information necessary for the various members of the planning team. It is not uncommon for certain parts of the prospectus to be altered at this time to take advantage of ideas and concepts that may be presented by the planning group. Professional foodservice designers are usually the best source of advice and judgment regarding a proposed project because of their experience and knowledge about the foodservice field.

Whenever a group of individuals is involved in the planning process, some of whom work independently, it is advisable to have a written understanding of what functions each member of the group will undertake and be responsible for. This will eliminate duplicated effort and assures that the planning team will work effectively together.

DEVELOPING THE CONCEPT

This phase of the planning process involves identifying or visualizing the various functions and tasks that must be performed to meet the objectives of the foodservice facility. It is necessary, not only to develop detailed space and equipment requirements, but also to aid in the final arrangement and layout of the facility. Identification of the functions also simplifies the gathering of the data required for proper planning of the entire foodservice facility. The functions are determined by using the prospectus, especially the proposed menu, as a guide. Examples of common functions identified for food facilities are purchasing, receiving, storage, preparation, processing, and serving. These functions are related to the production of menu items and are easily identified. Auxiliary or supportive functions, such as warewashing, trash and garbage disposal, maintenance, and sanitation, should also be identified. Management functions of control, planning, supervision, and evaluation, to name a few, are to be included as well.

Requirements for both guest and employee convenience are also identified as necessary auxiliary functions; parking areas, waiting areas, washrooms, locker facilities, office space, and training facilities are examples of these.

A related step in this aspect of the planning process may be described as task analysis. For each function identified, there are certain basic tasks to be performed. An evaluation of these tasks generates the data needed to determine space and equipment requirements. To illustrate, consider the receiving function. The basic tasks involved include counting, weighing, determining quality, moving materials, and checking orders. These may be accomplished in different ways depending upon management policy and operational procedures. The method of performing each task is evaluated by considering the materials involved, type of equipment that may be used, and the skills required by the employees. This may require considerable data-gathering and research before deciding on the method of performing the task. The data are obtained and summarized so the planners can make appropriate decisions regarding the design of work areas to be developed.

EQUIPMENT REQUIREMENTS

Equipment requirements are best determined from a complete analysis of typical menus. For each food item on the menu, information regarding anticipated number of portions to be prepared, portion sizes, batch sizes, main ingredients, and the processes to be performed are indicated. Much of this information can be taken directly from the recipes for each of the menu items. If recipes are not available, the foodservice consultant will rely on a knowledge of production practices to generate the information.

From the production processes identified, the planner can then decide whether equipment is to be used to complete a particular process or whether it can be done manually. If equipment is to be used, the planner will then evaluate the type and capacity required. At the same time the various types of equipment are selected, the total time that the equipment will be used for each process is recorded. The specific time of day that each piece of equipment is to be used is also recorded. After this is done for each process, the equipment usage is evaluated and final equipment capacity can be determined.

At this point in the planning process, it may be found desirable to add, delete, or change some of the menu items or processing methods in order to achieve greater equipment utilization. For example, if a steam-jacketed kettle is required to process two menu items but is operated for a short period of time, additional menu items may be suggested to utilize the equipment more fully. Another solution would be to change or eliminate the two menu items, thus eliminating the need for the steam-jacketed kettle. In this manner the foodservice planner can maximize the usage of the equipment.

SPACE REQUIREMENTS

Another phase of the planning process deals with the determination of space requirements. This aspect is related to equipment selection because of the space needed for placement of equipment. Space requirements are also dependent upon the functions and tasks that have to be performed in the facility. The space required is best determined by considering all the factors involved, including the floor space needed for the employee; working surface space for manual tasks as illustrated in Fig. 2.1; aisle space for movement; equipment space; provisions for storage of hand tools and supplies; and provision for

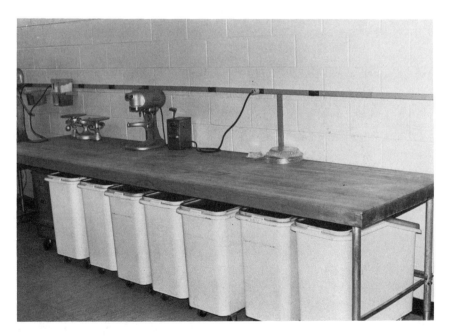

FIG. 2.1.   Sufficient working surface space for manual tasks.

storage of incoming and outgoing materials. This aspect of the planning process may be thought of as the development of workplaces or work areas for each task. As these workplaces are developed, the estimation of time requirements for each task may enable the designer to schedule several similar tasks to be performed at a given workplace. There are certain workplaces that can be used for only one task because of sanitary or other reasons.

As these individual workplaces are developed, consideration is given to the overall operation of the facility, so the grouping of individual workplaces into larger work areas or departments results in a feasible solution. Thus the planner is designing the individual workplaces and the total space for the facility simultaneously. This part of the planning process is completed when the space required for all the functions and tasks has been determined.

DEVELOPING PRELIMINARY PLANS

The next phase of the planning process involves preparation of preliminary sketches and drawings for the facility. This is referred to as the schematic design phase of the planning process. Ideas relating to the building structure, the site, and the location of various facilities, such as parking and receiving areas, as related to the building are developed and correlated with the arrangement of interior spaces. At this point, several feasible solutions may be generated, which are presented to the owner for approval or selection. Many planners use ideas and concepts from existing operations that they know are workable.

The preliminary plans usually include floor plans showing the general arrangement of equipment, aisles, and functional area locations. Frequently, pictorial views of selected areas are prepared, to provide a better grasp of the final design. Elevation views are used to depict size and shape of the building or to show cross-sections of parts of the building.

All drawings and sketches are prepared with the intent of conveying ideas and concepts, and therefore are quite tentative. There may be several changes made before a plan is acceptable to the individuals involved.

Cost Estimates

Although it is impossible to determine exact costs this early in the planning process, preliminary estimates should accompany the sketches. These include cost estimates for the building, site preparation, equipment, and furnishings. These costs are usually estimated on the basis of square footage or cubic footage of the building.

PREPARATION OF FINAL PLANS

Upon approval of the preliminary sketches and drawings, the next step of the planning process involves the development of the specifics of the design. The equipment capacities, workplace design, door sizes and locations, aisles, and other similar details are finalized and blended into a finished layout for the food facility. Many planners use templates or scale cut-outs of equipment and areas, as shown in Fig. 2.2, to evaluate possible arrangements and configurations. This is the phase of the planning process where the layout function is emphasized. Upon approval of the final layout, structural details, building materials, utility requirements and distribution, and a multitude of other details are decided upon and put into plans and specifications.

The final set of plans that are drawn are referred to as working drawings. They are drawn to scale and dimensioned to show sizes and locations of equipment and areas. These plans will be used for construction and installation purposes and must be accurately prepared.

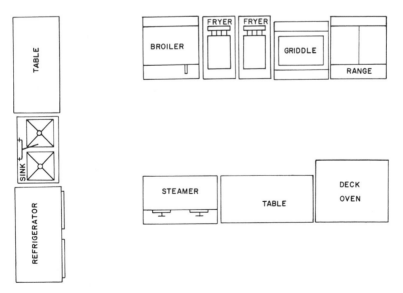

FIG. 2.2. Scale cutouts generate several alternative layouts.

Accompanying the working drawings are the written specifications for construction and installation.

PREPARING SPECIFICATIONS

Specifications are a written description of the proposed project. The specifications are intended to complement the working drawings and to clarify any items that may be questionable. To illustrate, the working drawings contain notations which are short, general, and describe a type of equipment or construction method. The specifications expand on the characteristics of the materials involved and the workmanship desired in installing them. A notation on a drawing may simply read "2-compartment stainless steel sink." The specifications will completely describe the sink and establish such details as type of stainless steel, construction of the joints, degree of finish, type of supports, and many other characteristics of design.

The specifications present a complete written description of the total project in an orderly and logical manner. They are used for estimating costs and for the preparation of bids by construction contractors. A complete set of specifications will expand and clarify the working drawings; define precisely the quality of materials, equipment, and workmanship; establish the scope of work to be performed; and spell out the responsibilities of the prime construction contractor. There are several types of specifications that may be written including performance, descriptive, reference, proprietary, and base-bid.

Performance Specifications

Performance specifications describe the work to be done by the results desired. For example, the performance specifications for a building roof will establish the following areas:

character and arrangement of the various components
materials and finishes
roof loads including wind loads to be supported
provision for expansion and contraction
allowable deflection
acceptable heat-loss coefficients

This type of performance specification allows the contractors enough freedom to employ their knowledge and experience to provide the desired results. They will design and select the various components, provide the necessary structural members and assemble the components to comply with the specifications.

As another example, foodservice consultants know that many manufacturers are capable of producing fryers with different characteristics. They may choose to write a performance specification that will establish the type, size, capacity, and output per hour that will meet their requirements. They may also require manufacturers to submit test data certifying the performance of their fryer. Now the manufacturers become responsible for the design of the fryer to ensure that it will perform as specified.

Descriptive Specifications

The most detailed type of specification is the descriptive specification. It describes the components of the building or piece of equipment and how these components are to be assembled. The specification identifies the physical properties of the materials, sizes of each component, spacing of supporting members, sequence of assembly, and many other requirements. The contractor has the responsibility of obtaining or constructing the work in accordance with this description. In this type of specification, the architect, engineer, or consultant assumes the responsibility for the performance of the final design.

Reference Specifications

Reference specifications employ standards of recognized agencies and authorities to specify quality. Some agencies and authorities frequently mentioned in specifications include Underwriters Laboratories, Inc., American Standards Association, American Society for Testing Materials, and the National Sanitation Foundation.

A portion of the National Sanitation Foundation Standard No. 2 for Foodservice Equipment is reproduced in Appendix A. The complete standard is available from the National Sanitation Foundation.

Many companies state in their literature and catalogs that their products or equipment conform to specific recognized standards. Most foodservice equipment, for example, is manufactured according to the standards set up by the National Sanitation Foundation. Electrical components are commonly built according to the Underwriters Laboratories' standards. The user is thus assured that such equipment will meet certain minimum requirements and that one can expect a certain degree of reliability and performance.

Reference specifications are generally used in conjunction with one or more of the other types of specifications. For example, in addition to specifying the performance of a fryer, a reference specification can be included that would indicate that the fryer has to conform to the National Sanitation Foundation standards.

Proprietary Specifications

Proprietary specifications call for materials, equipment, or products by trade name, model number, and manufacturer. This type of specification is the easiest to write because the commercially available

GN90 SERIES
GAS CONVECTION OVENS

HOBART
FOOD EQUIPMENT

SPECIFICATIONS Listed by National Sanitation Foundation. Certified by American Gas Association.

CONSTRUCTION: Outer shell is reinforced sheet steel furnished with stainless steel front and permalucent gray painted sides and top. Six sided insulation. Interior top, bottom, back and side inner panels are porcelain. Inner door liner is stainless steel. Five chrome-plated racks with positive stops are furnished. Vertical split doors (two per oven section) are full height with two double pane windows. Single handle opens both doors simultaneously. Doors swing 180°. Adjustable, mechanical spring-loaded door latch. Permanent stainless steel seal where cavity and doors join. Optional painted back. All stainless steel finish is optional with field-installable panels.

CONTROLS: Recessed controls located on right side. Line cord furnished for 115 volt models. ON-OFF switch energizes oven controls electrically. Infinite Load Control Switch varies input between 25% and 100%. Load control light indicates that the load control is functioning. Snap-action thermostat activates, deactivates burners and has a 200-500°F temperature range. Thermostat signal light indicates preheat and recovery. One-hour timer (settings from 0-60 minutes rings at end of preset time). A separate rocker switch controls the two cavity lights. Cool Down Fan Switch permits operation of fan only to cool down the oven when doors are open. Extremely accurate thermostat holds interior oven temperature within ± 10°F. Automatic interlock switch shuts off blower motor and burners when the doors are opened. Cool Down switch allows blower motor only to operate with doors open for rapid cooling of oven. Wire screen covers rear of motor. Motor has thermal protection against burnout.

CAPACITY: Oven cavity will accommodate eleven 27½" wide x 20" deep racks (5 furnished, 6 optional). Typical production per section: 385 3" sugar cookies in 15 minutes at 300°F; 120 well-done 3½" 2½ oz. hamburger patties in 7-10 minutes at 400-450°F; 560 ¾" x 3" 2 oz. fish sticks in 8 minutes at 350°F.

ELECTRICAL: ⅓ HP, 1725 rpm, permanently lubricated blower motor. Rated power input (for lights, blower motor and controls) is .6 KW per section. Wiring and connections are located behind the control panel and are accessible from the front. Each section has two interior lights. Connections are tension free and corrosion resistant. Units wired for 120 or 240 volts, 1-phase power supply (must specify voltage).

GAS: 60,000 BTU's; 30,000 per burner per hour. Designed for either natural or liquefied propane gas. Two tubular aluminized steel sheet metal burners operate in a combustion chamber insulated on top and side. The flame chambers, located directly above the combustion chamber, collect heat from the burners and direct it into the heat exchanger tubes located in the cooking compartment sides. The collection chamber, located above the oven compartment collects the heated flue products. A recycler tube, extending from the collecting chamber to the front of the blower, directs already heated air from the collection chamber to the blower wheel. The blower then recirculates heated air through the cooking compartment. The recirculated air is exhausted through the flue. Gas supply line must be equivalent of ¾" NPT. A pressure

regulator is set for 3.7" water column is standard for natural gas; pressure regulator for LP gas set for 10" water column. Standard design of this oven is for natural gas having the following characteristics; 1000 BTU per cubic foot, .64 specific gravity. **Please specify:** type of gas and altitude of location of equipment when installed.

ACCESSORIES:

Set of four 6" stainless steel adjustable legs for open stand

Set of four 25¾" adjustable tubular legs for GN901

Leg and stack set (includes set of 4-6" legs)

Set of four 6" adjustable tubular legs; (part of leg and stack set)

Open stand

Back panel, stainless steel

Back panel, painted

Right panel, stainless steel

Left panel, stainless steel

Top panel, stainless steel

Single extra rack

Six extra racks

Drip pan, stainless steel

WEIGHTS: (Approximate)

	SHIPPING	NET
GN901	560	510
GN904	590	665
GN902	1000	1130

As continued product improvement is a policy of Hobart, specifications are subject to change without notice.

FIG. 2.3. Manufacturer's specifications for a convection oven.
Courtesy of The Hobart Corporation.

products and equipment set the standard of quality acceptable to the specification writer. One disadvantage of proprietary specifications is that they may permit the substitution of alternative products and equipment that may not be exactly the same. Under a proprietary specification, the designer is responsible for the performance of the products and equipment.

An example of manufacturer's specifications for a convection oven is illustrated in Fig. 2.3.

Base-Bid Specifications

The establishment of acceptable materials and equipment by naming one or more manufacturers and fabricators is referred to as a base-bid specification. The bidder, under the specifications, is required to prepare the bid with prices submitted from the suppliers mentioned. The base-bid specification will usually permit a bidder to substitute for the specified materials or equipment providing this is acceptable to the architect or owner.

Base-bid specifications provide a great degree of control over the quality of the materials and equipment.

Regardless of the type of specification to be used, this difficult and time-consuming task is the most important aspect of preparing documents that guide the construction of the proposed facility.

BIDDING AND AWARDING CONTRACTS

On large projects involving building construction, the final drawings and written specifications are made available to contractors who are interested in submitting bids. On smaller projects, different arrangements for the work to be done can be made. For any project to be put out for bids, a standard set of documents, including bid forms, forms for bonds, insurance requirements, instructions to bidders, and legal considerations, is available. Most architects use the documents entitled "The General Conditions of the Contract for the Construction of Buildings" prepared by the American Institute of Architects as a guide for preparing these forms. Separate bids may be taken for food-service equipment.

When bids are received, the architect and other consultants involved in the planning will review them and make recommendations for the awarding of the contract for construction. If the drawings, specifications, and bidding documents are complete, the lowest bidder will usually get the recommendation. This does not have to be true in cases where the bidder has made exceptions to the specifications in preparing the bid.

After the construction contracts are signed, the contractor will make detailed roughing-in drawings for all utilities to be used in the facility. These drawings are referred to as shop drawings and are checked against the architect's mechanical and electrical drawings. The shop drawings are approved before actual construction begins.

CONSTRUCTION

During construction, the architect and foodservice consultant periodically check and evaluate the progress of the project. The completed building is accepted only after the architect has made a final inspection and is satisfied that all work has been completed as specified.

The finished facility (Fig. 2.4) will reflect the pains taken during the planning phases. If the planning was done carefully, the result will be functional, productive, and aesthetic. Careless or haphazard planning, on the other hand, usually results in a facility that will be inadequate for efficient foodservice operations. It is too late to think about the importance of good planning after construction has been completed.

FIG. 2.4. Careful planning results in functional and aesthetic design.
Courtesy of The Hysen Group, Livonia, Michigan and Hansen Lind Meyer, P.C., Architects.

PROBLEMS AND EXERCISES

2.1. Identify some reasons that new foodservice facilities may be established in a given area. Consider operations with which you are familiar and try to relate them to the reasons identified.

2.2. Fill in Table 2.1 for the four types of operations given in Problem 1.11 from Chapter 1.

2.3. Describe the prospectus, indicating its value to the various people involved in planning a foodservice facility.

2.4. Indicate the points in the planning process where the prospectus might be changed.

2.5. Discuss the importance of developing time requirements for the various tasks performed in a foodservice operation.

2.6. List and describe the various types of specifications that may be used for food-service equipment.

2.7. Arrange the following steps in the planning process in chronological order:

   a. Determining the proper size of oven
   b. Determining the proper type of oven
   c. Setting the hours of operation
   d. Reviewing the bids
   e. Hiring an architect
   f. Locating the parking lot
   g. Estimating check averages
   h. Determining characteristics of potential customers
   i. Task analysis
   j. Determining approximate cost of dining room furnishings
   k. Emphasizing the layout function

2.8. Briefly discuss the difference between working drawings and shop drawings.

2.9. Consider each of the four types of facilities identified in Problem 1.11. Analyze each with respect to the planning process described in this chapter, indicating what problems may be encountered with each type of facility.

BIBLIOGRAPHY

DYER, D.A. 1981. So You Want to Start a Restaurant. CBI Publishing Co., Boston, Massachusetts.

DUKAS, P. 1973. How to Plan and Operate a Restaurant, 2nd Edition. Hayden Book Co., Rochelle Park, New Jersey.

LAWSON, F. 1974. Designing Commercial Food Service Facilities. Whitney Publications, New York.

LIVINGSTON, G.E. and CHANG, C.M. (Editors). 1979. Food Service Systems: Analysis, Design, and Implementation. Academic Press, New York.

PHILIS, G. 1980. Planning and designing hotel food facilities, Lodging 5 (10), 24–29.

VASTANO, J.F. 1978. Elements of Food Production and Baking. Bobbs-Merrill Educational Publishing Co., Indianapolis, Indiana.

WILKINSON, J. (Editor). 1975. The Anatomy of Food Service Design I. Cahners Publishing Co., Boston, Massachusetts.

WILKINSON, J. (Editor). 1978. The Anatomy of Foodservice Design II. Cahners Publishing Co., Boston, Massachusetts.

The Planning Team

MEMBERS

Most large foodservice construction projects are planned by a team of individuals working cooperatively to achieve the final plan. All members of the planning team supply their own area of expertise to the project. The typical primary members of the planning team for a large project include the owners or their representatives (such as managers), an architect and various staff members, and a foodservice consultant. In some projects, additional members, such as interior designers or landscape architects, may be involved if there is need for their specialized services. Some architects who do a lot of foodservice projects will have foodservice consultants and other types of consultants on their staff. However, the owner is free to use an independent foodservice consultant or other outside consultants if desired.

In some cases, special consultants may be included on the planning team to handle problem areas of planning. These consultants may specialize in accounting methods, marketing, legal aspects, lighting systems, colors, acoustical methods, or structural design. The work of any of these special consultants is generally coordinated by the architect.

Smaller planning projects that do not involve major construction or structural building changes can be handled without the services of an architect. The remodeling of dining areas or production facilities, for example, may be entirely handled by a foodservice consultant. Some large foodservice organizations have their own planning department and do not require outside architects and consultants.

Regardless of the nature or size of the planning team, each member has certain tasks and areas of responsibility. These may be undertaken by the team members themselves, or they may assign or arrange for others to do the actual work under their supervision. For example, architects frequently will hire lighting engineers to plan and design the lighting system for the facility. However, the architect, who is responsible for this area of planning, must approve the work of the lighting engineer.

Owner

The owner or the owner's representative is a key individual in the planning team, since basically all design and planning decisions must be approved by the owner. The owner is usually responsible for seeing to the completion of the planning functions outlined next. (Frequently the owner will rely on others to do the actual work involved, but must still approve and bear the responsibilities for these areas.)

1. Develop statements of basic goals and objectives for the project.
2. Develop the basic operational concepts for the foodservice facility.
3. Assure that all legal and other regulatory restrictions that may influence the project have been checked out or cleared before too much time in planning is committed. This includes the areas of deed restrictions, codes, zoning ordinances, and licensing that pertain to the construction and operation of the food facility.
4. Complete the market analysis (frequently done by outside consultants hired by the owner).
5. Decide or approve all financial matters such as procurement of investment capital, financing methods, interest rates, and payment schedules.
6. Complete and approve the feasibility study. Feasibility studies are often done by accounting firms specializing in foodservice operations.
7. Develop policies regarding standards of operation for the food service facility. The owner may rely on a foodservice consultant's advice on this matter.
8. Select the architect and/or other members of the planning team.
9. Select and approve designs and plans submitted by the various members of the planning team.
10. Approve and sign contracts. Services of a legal advisor may be used here.

Architect

The architect is another key individual in food facility planning and coordination. All projects involving the new construction of public spaces have to be planned or approved by a licensed architect. The complexity of planning a new food facility has cast the architect in the role of an editor who has to coordinate, develop, select, and supervise all the various phases of planning. Some of the areas of responsibility of the architect, with a staff of engineers and other supporting individuals, are the following:

Site planning considerations such as building orientation, traffic patterns, parking areas, service areas, and the location of entrances and exits

Topographical changes required for drainage

Building design from the standpoint of shapes and configurations

Structural design of floors, walls, roofs, and ceilings

Exterior treatment of walls, windows, entrances, exits, and roofs (Fig. 3.1)

Interior treatment of floors, walls, windows, doors, and ceilings

Selection of building materials

Determination of construction methods to be used

FIG. 3.1. Exterior design is important for creating first impressions of a facility. *Courtesy of St. Clair's Crossing and Hamill & McKinney, Architects-Engineers, Inc.*

Checking building and construction codes for acceptable materials and
  construction methods
Design of the central heating system
Design of the ventilation system
Design of the plumbing and water system
Design of the air-conditioning system
Design of the lighting system
Coordinating the work of foodservice consultants, interior designers,
  and any other consultants working on the project
Preparing plans and blueprints for the facility (The foodservice con-
  sultant usually prepares the plans and blueprints for the kitchen
  and dining areas only. See Fig. 3.2 for a typical floor plan.)
Writing specifications for materials and construction methods
Developing cost estimates
Preparing bid documents
Analyzing bids for construction
Checking shop drawings provided by contractors
Inspecting construction of the building and installation of equipment
Acting as owner's representative when there are questions regarding
  construction and/or equipment

Selection of Architects. Early in the planning process, the owner
will select the architect to perform the just-mentioned tasks of planning. Selection of the architect is a very important matter, which must
be done carefully if the owner expects to get the type of facility desired. The selection of an architect usually begins with a list of prospects, whose names may be obtained from various sources. It is best
to seek out architects who specialize or do a good portion of their work
in the foodservice field. Checking with other foodservice operators who
have used the services of architects is one way of developing a list of
prospects. Another source is the local chapter of the American Institute of Architects. Before deciding upon an architect to do the planning, the owner will want to consider a number of points relating to
the ability of the architect. The following areas are sometimes used
as a basis for selection:

The design philosophy and creative ability of the architect to develop
  an aesthetic facility
The engineering design philosophy that the architect follows
Experience and reputation for designing foodservice facilities
Professional ethics
Size and type of staff

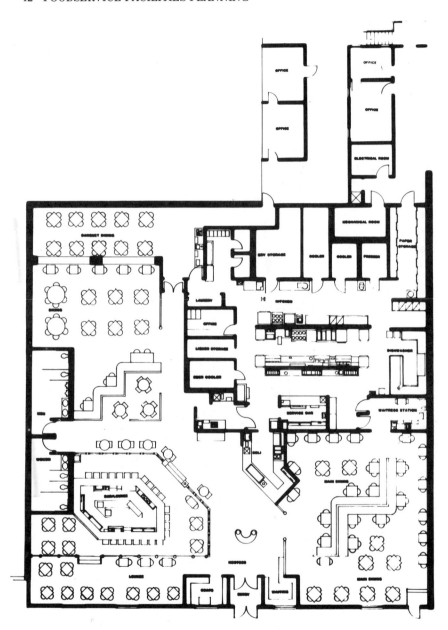

FIG. 3.2.   Preparation of floor plans is an important part of planning.
Courtesy of St. Clair's Crossing and Hamill & McKinney, Architects-Engineers, Inc.

Reputation for completing scheduled work on time
Methods of researching and specifying new materials and equipment
Cost consciousness
Accessibility to specialized consultants
Recommendations of satisfied clients
Ability to work with other consultants

The matter of fees is also important in the selection of an architect. Architectural fees are usually quoted on one of three different bases:

A percentage of the total construction cost
A lump sum, for which the project scope must be clearly defined
Cost plus a percentage fee

Architects charge additional fees for extra services, such as conducting feasibility studies, changes in plans after they have been approved, or special drawings and models. They may also add a fee for the coordination of outside consultants that are brought into the project.

Foodservice Consultant

The foodservice consultant is an individual who is familiar with all aspects of foodservice operation. The foodservice consultant is especially knowledgeable in the areas of menu planning, service, food merchandising, and the handling of food through the various storage, preparation, processing, and cooking steps. The foodservice consultant should also be familiar with management principles and the design of foodservice equipment and have a general knowledge of architecture, engineering, and interior design.

The foodservice consultant is responsible for the design of all aspects of the foodservice operation and consequently must work closely with the architect. Obviously, the owner and the architect together should select a foodservice consultant that is satisfactory to both. The best time for this selection is when the architect is commissioned.

The foodservice consultant may advise both the owner and the architect on certain aspects of the total design of the facility. They specifically, however, are involved in the following areas of responsibility:

Development of the menu including food items, portions, prices, and format
Determining methods of service for food and beverages
Creation of the dining atmosphere (usually with the help of interior designers)

Determining functions and tasks to be performed in the food facility, including the selection of materials and processes

Development of control procedures for food, beverages, cash, linen, and other materials

Preparation of potential profit and loss statements and budgets for the foodservice based on projected sales and costs

Advising the owner on preferred operating policies

Determining specific items of foodservice equipment to be used in the facility

Determining adequate space requirements for all the foodservice functions to be performed

Developing efficient space arrangements and layouts for the facility including dining areas, as illustrated in Fig. 3.3

Development of operational instructions for the use of the food facility and especially for the use of the foodservice equipment

Preparation of cost estimates for the foodservice aspects of the facility

Preparation of all plans required for installation of equipment in the dining and production areas

Checking equipment design for safety features and ease of cleaning

Writing specifications for all items of foodservice equipment, furnishings, and supplies

FIG. 3.3.   Arrangement of tables and chairs is a part of the foodservice consultant's responsibility.

Determination of utility connections and capacity required for the foodservice equipment

Checking contractors' shop drawings for all foodservice equipment installations

Inspection of equipment installation

Coordination with architect on information required for preparation of the bid documents

Helping in the analysis of bids

In general, the foodservice consultant deals with all aspects of design except the architectural, structural, and general mechanical work done by the architect. The close cooperation needed between the architect and the foodservice consultant is evident in the overlapping of their respective responsibilities in the design process. The wise owner pays as much attention to selection of the foodservice consultant as to choosing the architect.

The services of a foodservice consultant may be obtained from independent consultants or from individuals associated with manufacturers or suppliers of foodservice equipment. Many of the independent foodservice consultants are identified by their membership in the Foodservice Consultants Society International.

Foodservice consultants generally work under one of three payment methods. One method is based on a percentage of the cost of food preparation and service equipment; this cost is based on all equipment that is specified by the foodservice consultant only, and does not include any items specified by the architect. The second payment method is a cost-plus arrangement where the consultant will provide services on the basis of a multiple of the actual costs involved. A third possible payment method is a per diem arrangement where the consultant is paid for the total number of working days devoted to the project.

SPECIALISTS ON THE PLANNING TEAM

The owner, the architect, and the foodservice consultant are the main members of the planning team, and most foodservice projects are completely planned by these individuals. In projects where special requirements are needed or where special emphasis is to be placed, other individuals may be called in as members of the planning team. Some of these, and the contributions they can make toward the planning of the food facility, are indicated next.

Interior Designers

The services of interior designers are required when special emphasis is to be placed on creating a unique building interior. Interior designers will usually work with architects in developing the following areas:

Selection of furniture for the facility

Selection and coordination of interior wall and floor coverings (see Fig. 3.4)

Development of the color scheme for all interior surfaces

Treatment of windows (drapes, shades, and curtains)

Selection of lighting fixtures

Selection of decorator items, including items for dining tables such as tablecloths, china, and silver

Creation of special lighting effects

Development of shapes and sizes for areas and rooms by the use of dividers, plants, balconies, etc. (Figure 3.5 shows the use of a partial divider to create an intimate dining space)

Selection of uniforms for employees

FIG. 3.4. Selection of wall and floor coverings is an important aspect of interior design.
Courtesy of Houlihans.

FIG. 3.5. Use of partial walls can improve the design of large dining areas.

Landscape Architects

A landscape architect may be needed for projects demanding special treatment of the grounds surrounding the foodservice facility. Among the services that are contributed by landscape architects are the following:

Development of the total landscape plan for the facility
Selection and arrangement of trees, shrubs, and flowers
Development of lawn and garden areas
Design and placement of exterior lighting
Development of exterior pathways
Enhancement of desirable exterior building features

Although a landscape architect may be selected after the building has been constructed, it is desirable to hire one at the same time other consultants are retained to contribute to the overall planning of the facility.

Land Developers and Realtors

Land developers and realtors are involved in those projects that require the acquisition of land or space for the proposed food facility. Foodservice facilities are frequently a part of a larger development, such as shopping malls, apartment complexes, or office buildings, and land developers will sometimes seek out foodservice operators to install and operate these facilities.

The land developers and realtors are well versed in zoning ordinances and can be valuable in selecting sites or spaces for a food facility. Their knowledge of land values, future developments, and identification of growth areas of a community is useful in making decisions regarding a particular project.

CONTRACTING FOR SERVICES OF PLANNERS

Formal agreements are usually made between the owner and the other members of the planning team. In most cases, a single contract between the owner and the architect is sufficient. Under a single contract the architect will assume responsibility of all aspects of planning regardless of the members involved. Architects may have other consultants on staff who would be covered under the single contract, or may subcontract the services of other consultants. In projects where an architect is not required, the owner may work through a foodservice consulting firm and sign formal agreements with it.

The usual architect's contract calls for the architect to prepare and submit to the owner for approval all preliminary studies, sketches, drawings, and specifications. Architects are also expected to assist in the selection and procurement, at the most economical cost, of all equipment required for the foodservice facility. Architects will help in the selection of bidders, prepare bid documents, and be the general guardian of the owner's interest in obtaining all necessary permits and licenses. Filing of plans with appropriate authorities is also a part of the architect's responsibility.

The contract stipulates the architect's fees and the method of payment. Payments are usually spread over the duration of the project, a lump sum becoming payable when the drawings and specifications have been completed. The remainder of the fee is paid in installments as the project progresses. A set sum in the neighborhood of 10% is held out for a specified period of time after the completion of the building. This is not paid until all approvals of the project have been obtained from the public authorities having jurisdiction. The contract also contains a provision for the situation where the project is cancelled or abandoned by the owner, and for the payment to the architect in such cases. It is also desirable to have provisions for arbitration of any dispute that may arise between the owner and the architect.

Relationships Between Planners and Contractors

Although the general contractor who will construct the foodservice facility is not considered a member of the planning team, an understanding of the contractor responsibilities and relationship to the architect and the owner is helpful in discussing a total project.

The owner will carefully study the complete set of bid documents before requesting bids from contractors for the construction of a new facility. These include all the working plans, drawings, and specifications prepared by the architect, the foodservice consultant, and other consultants involved in the project. The owner should check them against the concepts and ideas developed during the preliminary phase to see if they will result in the type of facility desired. The owner is also advised to consult with a lawyer regarding the legal aspects of submitting the project for bids from a number of contractors. After the owner is satisfied with the bid documents, the job will be put out for bids with hopefully the lowest bidder being selected to construct the facility.

There are several types of contract arrangements that can be made between the owner and the contractor. Some of the more common arrangements for the construction of buildings are as follows:

A lump sum contract
A fixed ceiling price based on time and materials plus a fixed fee
A fixed ceiling price based on time and materials plus a percentage fee
Time and materials plus a fixed fee

Each type of contract has its advantages and disadvantages. However, under a detailed set of plans and specifications, there will not be a great deal of difference between them. Under all the time and materials contracts, all the labor and materials used in the construction of the facility should be audited by both the contractor and the owner or the owner's representative.

Standard agreement forms for the construction of buildings are available from the American Institute of Architects and are recommended for all large projects. The forms available include the following:

The standard form of agreement between owner and architect

The standard form of agreement between contractor and owner for construction of buildings

The general conditions of the contract for the construction of buildings

Under a construction contract, the general contractor is required to accomplish and be responsible for the following areas:

Performing the work and furnishing the materials and equipment as defined in the plans and written specifications

Complying with the regulations and ordinances of public authorities having jurisdiction over the project

Obtaining all necessary permits and all certificates showing satisfactory completion of the work

Furnishing the required public liability and compensation insurance

Completing the construction of the building on or before a predetermined time, or paying a penalty for failing to do so

Guarding against charges for extra work, labor, and materials (such charges should be authorized only by the architect or the owner)

Removing all trash and rubbish caused by the contractor's work from the premises

Maintaining adequate protection of all work from damage and protecting the owner's property from injury or loss

Payment to the contractor is made in installments as the work progresses. As with the architect, a certain sum is withheld for a specified period of time to assure that the project has been completed in accordance with all plans and specifications and has been fully approved by all parties concerned.

In summary, the planning and construction of a new foodservice facility involves many individuals who have to work very closely to enable the project to progress satisfactorily. Unnecessary delays by certain members of the planning team will in turn delay the completion of the plans and specifications. Likewise, delays in construction are also undesirable and should be avoided whenever possible.

PROBLEMS AND EXERCISES

3.1. Identify the primary members of the planning team who would be involved in designing a new foodservice facility.

3.2. Describe the general working relationships between the architect and the foodservice consultant.

3.3. Indicate the possible financial arrangements that may be made between the owner and the members of the planning team.

3.4. Describe the general duties and responsibilities of the following members of the planning team: (a) owner, (b) architect, and (c) foodservice consultant.

3.5. Identify the members of the planning team who would be referred to as specialists and briefly describe their particular roles in the design process.

3.6. Refer to the restaurant models described in Problem 1.11 and analyze and compare the composition, duties, and contractual relationships that would exist in a planning team for each of these facilities.

BIBLIOGRAPHY

AIA. 1977. Standard Form of Agreement Between Owner and Architect. Am. Inst. of Architects, Washington, D.C.

COHEN, G. and COHEN, N.E. 1982. Food Service Sanitation Handbook. Hayden Book Co., Rochelle Park, New Jersey.

DELUCA, M. 1980. Food facility planning: the design team. Restaurant Hospitality *16* (7), 85–86.

KAHRL, W.L. 1976. Introduction to Modern Food and Beverage Service. Prentice-Hall, Inc., Englewood Cliffs, New Jersey.

NSF. 1978. Sanitation Aspects of Food Service Facility Plan Preparation and Review. National Sanitation Foundation, Ann Arbor, Michigan.

POPLAI, B. 1978. Planning a new foodservice facility. Restaurant Business *77* (9), 260–262, 264.

ROBERTSON, B.E. 1968. The kitchen planner as a systems analyst. Kitchen Planning *5* (2), 37–39.

STEWART, A.J. 1986. Kitchen design. The Consultant *19* (1), 43–44.

4

Preparing the Prospectus

IMPORTANCE

The preparation of the prospectus or operational model is one of the first important steps to be completed in a planning project. A carefully prepared prospectus defines what the owner desires and expects in the foodservice facility. It enables the architect, the foodservice consultant, and other planning team members to plan and design the facility efficiently. The prospectus will include management objectives as well as decisions that will affect the operation of the foodservice facility. Experience has shown that the more detail there is in the prospectus, the easier the remaining planning steps become.

The prospectus should reflect the conceptual strategy for a particular project. The various ideas relating to marketing, financing, operational policies, and other characteristics that make the project unique are included in the prospectus. Development of the prospectus allows a systematic approach to identify all the component parts and their interrelations as they affect the total design concept. This systematic approach to planning leads to a design that meets the goals and objectives of the proposed facility.

Since the prospectus is the guide to planning, it is possible and sometimes even desirable to change the information or decisions as planning proceeds. Changes may be made that reflect new ideas or concepts that are developed as more information is gathered for the project. These changes should always be made with the objective of improving the final design.

The suggested areas of information to be included in the prospectus will be presented in outline form. The outline is primarily intended for commercial foodservice facilities; however, it may be used for other types of operations. It is important to indicate that there is considerable interrelationship between the various factors included in the prospectus.

CUSTOMER AND USER CHARACTERISTICS

A preferred method of starting the prospectus is to investigate and describe the potential customer or user that the foodservice facility will be designed for. The desirable information to be gathered and identified is indicated by the following categories.

Occupation

Identification of customer or user occupation is important to many of the planning decisions that are to be made for other parts of the prospectus. This information is also used in some of the later stages of the planning process. Development of the menu, portion sizes, method of service, pricing, and type of dining atmosphere to be created are all dependent upon adequate identification of the occupation of the potential customers or users. Occupational data for a given area may be obtained from census reports or from local chambers of commerce. A suggested listing of descriptive occupations commonly used to describe customers or users of foodservice facilities follows:

> business people, including manufacturers and retailers
> clerical workers and office workers
> craftsmen
> homemakers
> laborers
> professionals
> retired individuals
> sales personnel
> service workers
> students

Most planning projects will be designed to attract a particular occupational group. There may be certain foodservice projects that have to be designed for more than one occupational group. In this case, a percentage breakdown of occupations can be estimated to show the distribution.

Income Level

Information on annual income levels can also be obtained from census and chamber of commerce reports. In addition, several periodicals including *Sales and Marketing Management* devote an issue annually to market information that includes either total income or disposable income. The information from these various sources is usually expressed as per capita income or as family income. Needless to say, the higher the income level, the more there is available for eating out. Foodservice facilities designed for high income level customers can obviously be more elaborate and of higher quality.

Income data for the prospectus may be expressed as a percentage of individuals or families who fall in given ranges or groups. A typical breakdown of income ranges or groups is shown below.

Under $10,000	$30,000–34,999
$10,000–14,999	$35,000–39,999
$15,000–19,999	$40,000–44,999
$20,000–24,999	Over $45,000
$25,000–29,999	

The foodservice facility to be developed in a particular location has to be correlated to the income levels present.

Age

Knowledge of the ages or age groups of potential customers and users is needed for the development of the menu and dining atmosphere. The type of food items to be placed on the menu, the portion sizes, and prices must be matched to the particular age groups, to ensure attraction and retention of customers. Teenagers and young adults are very atmosphere-conscious, and this is frequently the influencing factor in deciding where to dine.

Census reports can be used to gather age data for particular locations. Suggested age categories for use in foodservice planning are as follows:

Under 5	27–39
6–12	40–52
13–19	53–65
20–26	Over 65

The age information can be expressed as percentages or numbers of people in each age category.

Sex

The foodservice facility that is designed primarily for one sex or the other will have a distinct character. For example, facilities designed for female clientele would be characterized by pleasant atmosphere, large and comfortable rest rooms, unique decorations, and menus that feature specials, salads, and sandwiches. Portion sizes can be smaller also.

Facilities designed primarily for males will be less formal and feature different menu offerings in larger portion sizes. The design of food facilities that cater to both sexes will necessarily blend these characteristics.

Education

The educational level of the potential customer has been identified as an important factor in dining-out habits. Generally speaking, the higher the educational level, the greater the frequency of dining out. Education also appears to be a factor influencing the variety of menu items desired and the willingness to try new or different foods.

Motivation

Knowledge of the motivation people have for dining out can aid planners and managers to develop and operate a successful food facility. Some of the motivating factors are listed here:

Change in routine (a favorite of housewives)
Necessity due to time or distance limitations
Convenience
Business reasons
Social, such as meeting or entertaining friends
Special occasions, birthdays, anniversaries
Adventure
Entertainment and enjoyment
To obtain special kinds of meals that are not usually available to the home market

These motivational factors for dining out are used to develop and guide the overall merchandising and public relations programs for the food facility.

Spending Habits

The spending habits for dining are related to occupation, age, income, and other factors and are very difficult to measure accurately. An analysis of spending for other items such as cars, appliances, and luxuries of life will be indicative of how much people will spend for dining out. In general, the amount of money spent on meals away from home is increasing in all segments of the population. This is especially true of the younger generation.

Activities That Relate to Dining Out

Another important guide to the overall design of the food facility is found by determining the activities that potential customers will be involved in. Only those activities that relate to dining out need be considered. Many of these activities reflect a particular location or area and may not be meaningful until a definite site for the foodservice facility is being considered. The typical activities that can be related to dining out are:

shopping
traveling or touring
attending conventions
visiting
business meetings
entertainment events (sports, shows, theaters)
organized group meetings
meetings of social groups

Evaluation of these activities will determine the desirability of designing special facilities such as banquet rooms, cocktail lounges, and meeting rooms for the proposed foodservice operation.

Arrival Patterns

The size of dining tables, seating arrangements, and serving times are among the design considerations determined by arrival patterns of potential customers. Arrival patterns will influence the design of the facility from the standpoint of peak periods of operation. An estimate of the numbers or percentages of each of the groups indicated is needed for these purposes.

singles	men groups
couples	women groups
families	mixed groups

Additional information in terms of arrivals per unit time can sometimes be estimated and are of great help in planning. Knowing the number of people to be fed per hour or per minute will pinpoint many of the design decisions needed to plan the food facility. Arrival patterns may also be estimated by statistical characteristics such as the Poisson distribution.

Miscellaneous Factors

For any given project, there may be other factors of customer or user knowledge that can be useful for design purposes. Their importance and need are best determined by the owner or the foodservice consultant. Some of these additional factors are identified as follows:

    ethnic background
    food preferences or types of meals desired
    eating habits
    service preferences
    marital status
    means of transportation
    preferred meal periods for dining out
    preferred days for dining out

Much of this information regarding the customer is used to develop the remaining parts of the prospectus. The information is critical to proper development of the menu, the type of service, the atmosphere, and the operating characteristics of the food facility. The development of these other areas of the prospectus should be closely correlated with the characteristics of the market to be served.

DEVELOPMENT OF THE MENU

The menu for the food facility should be developed carefully because it is the foundation upon which the layout and other design functions are based. The menu serves as the source of information for the various food items to be prepared and consequently the processes required for their preparation. The processes, in turn, determine the space and equipment requirements for the facility. In addition, the menu guides the decisions that are made regarding the merchandising policy developed for building and maintaining sales.

The owner or foodservice consultant will develop the menu by keeping in mind the effect it has on other design decisions. In essence, the development of the menu evolves from considerations of the market, ease of production, and the layout required. These areas are then used to arrive at the final decisions regarding the planning of the total facility. The menu also has a bearing on the type of personnel, their training, and the supervision needed to produce the various food items.

A brief discussion of the basic considerations for developing the menu for a proposed facility will be presented. The prospectus should not be considered complete unless it includes a sample menu.

Frequency of Change

The first decision to be made in developing the menu is to determine the frequency of change. This may vary from a completely fixed menu to one that changes daily. Considerable thought has to be given to this decision because of its relationship to the remaining phases of the planning process. Planning a facility for a fixed menu is much simpler than for a daily-change menu. Daily-change menus are required for many types of institutional food services; however, commercial operations are free to develop any type of menu characteristics desired. It is possible to have an operation that has a fixed menu for one meal and changing menus for the other meal periods. A common arrangement is to have a fixed menu for breakfast and changing menus for lunch and dinner. Some of the categories of frequency of change for menus are described in the following list.

1. *Completely fixed menu.* Many fast food and specialty operations use completely fixed menus. The only changes that are made occur when a menu item is added or dropped for popularity, profitability, or production considerations.

2. *Fixed menu with seasonal changes.* This variation of the fixed menu is used to accommodate the availability of seasonal food items. Most operations using this type of menu will change twice a year, a few making as many as four changes a year. This is not usually a complete change of menu items but primarily those items that have seasonal popularity.

3. *Fixed with changing specials.* This is also a variation of the fixed menu. The specials may be changed daily and are indicated clearly on the menu. This type of menu is used when the simplicity of a fixed menu is desired but consideration of repeat business leads to changing special food items.

4. *Complete daily changes.* This type of change is best for an operation that has decided upon offering a very limited number of food items on the menu and has heavy repeat business. This type of menu is also desirable for operations catering to captive customers, as in some resort or camp operations. This concept may be used by seasonal foodservice operations that are open for a limited period of time during the year.

5. *Cyclical daily changes.* This type of menu change is used in op-

erations catering to repeat or captive customers as exemplified by employee cafeterias, educational feeding operations, and institutional foodservices. The cycle is usually from two to six weeks in length. Seasonal variations can also be incorporated into this type of menu.

6. *Daily changes with standard items.* This is basically a daily change or cyclical daily change concept with the addition of some popular short-order items. Steaks and chops are common standard items with this type of menu.

Type of Menu Offerings

Another consideration in developing the menu is to decide on the type of menu offerings. The usual choices are a la carte items or complete meals. Most individuals prefer a la carte offerings although some market segments are inclined to favor the complete meal. A happy medium is to have the combination of a la carte and complete meals. Another possibility is to offer complete meals for one meal period, perhaps breakfast, and a la carte for the other meal periods.

Extent of Menu Offerings

A very critical decision regarding the menu is determining how extensive the menu offerings should be. In the total foodservice market, there is a place for all types, from the very limited offerings of small operations to the extensive choices available in deluxe table service operations.

A limited menu is desirable from many standpoints, including simplified planning for the facility and simplified production of the few items. The limited menu will require less equipment and space in the facility. Its drawback is that it may not attract enough customers to make the operation profitable.

The more extensive menus require more precise planning and are more difficult from the standpoint of production; they also result in slower service and require more equipment and space in the facility. They do attract a larger segment of the market and are desirable for this reason. Fortunately, many areas can support foodservice facilities of both types.

The extensiveness of the menu items can be modified somewhat after the operation is opened and a better feel for the customers' desires is obtained. It is better to avoid drastic changes in the menu after the facility has been planned.

The suggested offerings shown in Table 4.1 for each category of foods for a dinner menu may be useful in deciding how extensive a menu to develop. Similar tables of foods may be developed for other meal periods.

After deciding how extensive the menu offerings should be for each meal, the next step is to select the particular food items that will appear on the menu. The following factors are considered in selecting a particular food item.

1. *Popularity or sales appeal.* As related to the identified market, this area is very critical to the success of the operation. Food items

TABLE 4.1. SUGGESTED FOOD ITEMS FOR MENU DEVELOPMENT

Appetizers	Beverages
Canapes	Coffee
Cheeses	Fruit drinks
Cold cuts	Hot chocolate
Egg rolls	Milk, chocolate
Fruit cocktail	Milk, whole or skim
Marinated herring	Shakes and malts
Pickles	Soft drinks
Relishes	Tea, hot
Shrimp	Tea, iced
Bread and Rolls	Desserts
Biscuits	Brownies
Bread, rye	Cakes
Bread, white	Cheesecake
Corn bread	Cookies
Hard rolls	Fruit
Hot rolls	Gelatin desserts
Muffins	Ice cream, sundaes
Packaged crackers, garlic toast, etc.	Pies
Sandwich buns	Puddings
Toast	Tarts
Entrees	Potatoes
Beef	American fried
Chicken	Au Gratin
Chili Con Carne	Baked
Chopped beef	Boiled
Eggs	French fried
Entree salads	Hashed brown
Fish	Mashed
Frankfurters	Scalloped
Ham	Sweet potatoes
Macaroni and cheese	
Meat balls	
Meat loaf	Salads
Noodles	Cole slaw
Pot roast	Cottage cheese
Pork	Fruit
Shrimp	Gelatin
Spaghetti	Lettuce
Turkey	Tomato
Veal	Tossed salads

(continued)

TABLE 4.1 (*Continued*)

Sandwiches	Soups
Bacon-lettuce-tomato	Bean
Barbecue	Beef bouillon
Cheese	Celery, cream
Cheeseburgers	Chicken
Chicken salad	Chili
Club	Clam chowder
Corned beef	Consomme
Egg salad	French onion
Fish	Minestrone
Grilled cheese	Mushroom
Ham	Potatoe
Hamburgers	Tomato
Hero	Vegetable
Hot dog	
Roast beef	
Steak sandwich	
Turkey or chicken	
Tuna salad	
Vegetables	
Asparagus	Green beans
Baked beans	Lima beans
Beets	Onions
Broccoli	Peas
Brussels sprouts	Rice
Cabbage	Squash
Carrots	Spinach
Corn	Tomatoes

that are proven sellers should be selected, but not exclusively. Some variety of foods is desirable so that customers are not subjected to menu monotony and fatigue.

2. *Profitability of the foods.* This requires an analysis of the foods that would yield the greatest net profit after food, labor, and other costs are considered. Profitability and popularity are not necessarily found in the same foods and the menu should reflect a balance between them. A menu composed entirely of highly profitable items would certainly not be the most popular.

3. *Method, ease, and speed of production.* How smoothly a kitchen functions is a direct result of this factor. Foods that are easily processed require less time, labor, and equipment. Fully preprocessed and portioned food items represent one way of achieving the same result for foods that are difficult to process. Another alternative that leads to simplified production is to select short-order items processed on only one piece of equipment.

4. *Sources of supply and variations in supply.* A constant source of supply is desirable for all food items that will appear on the menu, but this may not always be possible for certain foods. If source and

reliability of supply appear to be a problem for a particular food item, it is best not to include it on the menu. Each food item that is put on the menu affects some aspect of design, and wise decisions at this point of the planning process will simplify later planning steps.

5. *Personnel required to produce the food item.* Considerations of skill, training required, and the availability of qualified personnel to prepare food items should be evaluated. It makes little sense to put a food item on the menu that cannot be produced with consistent high quality.

6. *Equipment requirements and usage.* A set of food items appearing on the menu that meet most of the mentioned criteria and still balance equipment workloads is an ideal situation. This can only be achieved by a careful analysis of the type of equipment required by each food item and the usage time needed to process the number of portions to be prepared. This analysis can be done after the menu has been developed to see if full equipment utilization has been achieved. Many food items can be modified slightly to make better use of equipment.

7. *Portion size.* Portion sizes are determined from the standpoint of appearance, cost, price, and variety. Some portion size variation among the food items appearing on the menu is desirable to satisfy those who are inclined to be small or big eaters. Visual appearance of the food item is the main consideration in determining portion sizes. The portion size and the number of portions to be prepared are needed before equipment capacity can be determined. Typical portion sizes for a variety of food items are given in Appendix B.

8. *Compatibility.* Food colors, textures, aromas, and visual appeal are important factors in evaluating food items for compatibility. Foodservice operations offering complete meals should be particularly careful to choose food items that go well together.

9. *Pricing.* Customers like to be given a sense of menu range and value. This can be accomplished by adding a lower-priced item or two to the menu. This tends to suggest fairness and the excellence of higher-priced menu items. It is also important to consider pricing in relation to consumer spending patterns.

The importance of carefully developing the menu cannot be stressed enough. The menu sets the character of the foodservice facility. It influences the size, design, layout, equipment, merchandising, operating procedures, and, most important, the projected profits. Since the menu is also the key to equipment utilization and balanced work scheduling, its influence is felt long after the facility has been planned and built.

SERVICE

The type and standards of service for the food facility are determined in the light of the potential customer and the menu offerings. The service has to be compatible with these factors in order to create a unified design. Although there is room for considerable variation in types of service, most individuals quickly relate certain menu offerings to service expectations.

Types

Generally, there are two basic methods of service to consider for food facilities. These are referred to as service units and self-service units. Service units provide waiters or waitresses or other personnel to serve the food directly. The principal types of service units are table service, counter service, booth service, tray service, and room service. The design and operational considerations related to each type of service unit are evaluated before a decision is made.

Table service operations with waiters or waitresses are preferred by those who wish to relax and enjoy a leisurely meal. The general table service operation as shown in Fig. 4.1 requires more square feet of space per seat than the other types of service units.

Counter service is suited to individuals who want a quick meal with a minimum of fuss. It is ideal for breakfast and luncheon operations that have a limited menu and desire a high turnover of customers. Counter service operations require a minimum of space because the preparation and service of food is done in the same area.

Booth service operations are usually preferred by teenagers, young workers, and travelers who want some privacy while eating. The use of booth service is recommended for medium-priced facilities that hope to cater to a large segment of the market. Both limited as well as fairly extensive menus can be used with this type of service.

In an attempt to appeal to a greater variety of people, combinations of table, counter, and booth service units may be used in a single facility. The number of seats to provide for each type of service is dependent upon the arrival patterns of customers. Counter and booth service units are not used for larger groupings of customers.

Tray service units are used primarily in hospitals, for airline feeding, and for drive-in operations. Special design is required for the assembly, holding, and distribution of foods in these types of facilities.

Room service is a specialty type of service unit for hotels, motels,

FIG. 4.1. Table service restaurants require ample space for the service function.

motor inns, and resorts. Facilities for this type of service require separate areas for loading the room-service carts.

The principal types of self-service units are cafeteria service, buffet service, take-out service, and vending units. Self-service units are selected when quick service to a large number of people is required.

Cafeteria service units are suited to busy shoppers, business people, and families. Low- to medium-priced prepared meals are usually featured, although cook-to-order sections can be provided.

Buffet service can be combined with other types of service units or used by itself. Some operations may decide to use buffet service for a particular meal, such as breakfast or lunch, and another type of service for the other meals. Buffet service is very suitable for special days or occasions where larger than normal crowds are anticipated.

Take-out service has become very popular with low-priced, limited-menu operations. It is appealing to a large segment of the market because it fills the need for a quick meal. This is evident by the growth of franchised take-out operations.

Vending units are ideal for between-meal snacks or for limited-time meals in schools, institutions, and industrial plants.

Selecting the type of service unit for the facility should be done carefully since, like the menu, it influences many design decisions. The type of service to be provided will determine the type of serving equipment and serving personnel required. The planner will also have to evaluate the flow of service personnel in the serving or dining areas.

Provisions for the service of beverages may also be evaluated in this part of the prospectus. This is important if it is anticipated that alcoholic beverages will be sold.

Other aspects relating to service that are identified at this time include the standards of service desired in the food facility. The selection of table coverings, dishware, glassware, and flatware should reflect the menu and the method of service. The decisions regarding these items should be made early in order to provide a simple and unified design.

ATMOSPHERE

Another important facet of preparing the prospectus is to identify the desired dining atmosphere for the food facility. For planning purposes, a brief description of the type of atmosphere as related to the customer, the menu offerings, and the method of service should be given. In a sense, the menu offerings and the method of service will characterize the atmosphere to some extent. These two factors, when matched to the expectations of the potential customers, will provide the clues as to the type of atmosphere to be planned. For example, if the prime customer group consists of women shoppers, offering a medium-priced menu with cafeteria service is a natural. The provision of a dining area that is quiet, colorful, and attractively decorated will complete the bill.

Since many factors make up the dining atmosphere, probably the easiest way to identify it at this stage of the planning process is by descriptive characteristics. Common terms used include formal, informal, quiet, rushed, noisy, cheerful, pleasant, relaxing, colorful, festive, and intimate. If any special feature such as the location, a unique building shape, or a theme is to be emphasized, it should also be identified as contributing to the desired atmosphere. Early identification

FIG. 4.2.   Exterior design is an integral part of the creation of a particular atmosphere.
Courtesy of Mother Lode Restaurant.

of the atmosphere is helpful to all members of the planning team
since it can affect all aspects of design and layout. Exterior design, as
illustrated in Fig. 4.2, is important in conveying a quick impression
of atmosphere to the customer.

Planning the atmosphere varies with each type of foodservice facility. Generally the atmosphere planned for a hotel dining room is more
lavish than for other types of operations. The frequency of redesign of
the atmosphere is an important consideration in modern planning
concepts. Many foodservice operators believe that the dining environment should be changed periodically to match the changing desires
of consumers. A redesign frequency of five years may be desirable to
maintain the competitive advantage of a foodservice facility. Thus the
original development of the atmosphere should include factors that
would simplify redesigning in the future. For example, a minimum
number of built-in features should be used if periodic changes in the
atmosphere are expected. This will allow for changes with a minimum of expense.

OPERATIONAL CHARACTERISTICS

The operational characteristics of the proposed foodservice facility
are identified by many items of information. Most of the operational

characteristics are determined by the foodservice consultant and are based on experience and a knowledge of successful methods of operation. Among the items of information required for completing the prospectus are the following:

Ownership
Legal organization
Days and hours of operation
Expected numbers of customers
Procedures for purchasing, production, service, warewashing, waste disposal, trash disposal, customer ordering, waitress ordering, maintenance, and cleaning
Control methods for costs, purchasing, receiving, storage, issuing, portions, cash, payroll, and security
Personnel requirements and policies
Accounting practices
Special functions for training, supervision, and management
Employee and guest facilities

Regulatory Considerations

The regulatory considerations are also included in this part of the prospectus because many of them have a direct bearing on how the facility is to be designed and operated. Examples of items that have to be checked to see how they might influence the proposed project are listed here:

1. *Zoning ordinances.* Most zoning ordinances will dictate the locations where commercial foodservice facilities may be built and operated within a community. Although variances to zoning requirements are available, they frequently are time consuming and may delay a project. Zoning ordinances may control such items as parking requirements, yard requirements, minimum building size, building height, and limitations on the use of signs.

2. *Building codes* (including electrical and plumbing codes). These codes cover every aspect of construction and specify in detail the design strength and types of construction materials allowable. Also covered are construction techniques, requirements for ventilation and lighting, design and installation of the electrical and plumbing systems, number of building exits, fire protection systems, and numerous other areas pertaining to the safety of public buildings. Planners must be knowledgeable of building code requirements prior to planning a

facility in order to avoid costly changes that may be needed to satisfy the codes.

3. *Sanitary codes.* State and local sanitary codes relate primarily to food safety and hygiene and thus influence both the planning and the operation of a foodservice facility. Typical areas covered by sanitary codes include (a) room finish schedules; (b) location, number, and type of plumbing fixtures; (c) handwashing facilities; (d) specifications relating to hot water supply; (e) type and location of refuse disposal and/or storage equipment; (f) type of lighting and levels of illumination; (g) ventilation equipment to be used in conjunction with cooking, frying, and dishwashing equipment; (h) type, make, model, and size of foodservice equipment; (i) method of hot, dry, and cold food storage; and (j) the nature, scope, and mode of operation of the facility. (See Fig. 4.3.)

Some states require that plans for new foodservice facilities be approved for compliance with sanitary codes before construction can begin. In such areas it is prudent to check with the local authorities prior to planning, especially if new or different concepts relating to foods are being considered. A typical plan specification and review form used for foodservice operations is shown in Appendix C.

4. *Deed restrictions.* Although not a frequent problem, deeds should be checked to assure there are no restrictions that may limit the use and occupancy of a piece of property or give easements to persons, utility companies, or other agencies.

5. *Lease restrictions.* For foodservice projects involving the leasing of building space such as in shopping centers or in office buildings, hours of operation, and other operating procedures may be specified and have to be considered prior to developing the prospectus.

6. Other regulatory areas include (a) labor laws, (b) licensing requirements, (c) OSHA requirements, (d) smoking ordinances, (e) pollution control ordinances, and (f) requirements for handicapped individuals.

Some of these items will directly affect the design and layout of the facility while other items apply primarily to the operating procedures. It is desirable to evaluate both areas carefully because of their relationship to the success of the proposed facility.

Since the development of the prospectus is deemed so important an aspect of the planning process, a suggested format for recording the information is given in Appendix D. This format can be used for most projects; however, additional data may be required for very special cases, which can be gathered as needed.

FIG. 4.3. A mobile food merchandiser also has to conform to regulatory requirements.
Courtesy of Cres-Cor/Crown-X, Crescent Metal Products, Inc.

PROBLEMS AND EXERCISES

4.1. Define the prospectus and discuss its value to the planning of a foodservice
facility.

4.2. List and briefly discuss the various customer characteristics important for planning a foodservice facility.

4.3. Identify the six types of menu frequencies and associate each type with a food-service facility where it would most likely be found.

4.4. Briefly discuss the advantages and disadvantages of using a limited menu for a restaurant.

4.5. From the sources listed in this chapter and others that may be available, define the customer characteristics of the potential market for a fast food operation.

4.6. The selection of particular foods for the menu was defined as a critical step in the planning process. Using the nine items listed in this chapter, identify the potential problems or costs associated with the failure to adequately consider each of these factors.

4.7. Considering each of the activities that relate to dining out, describe their relationship to the type of service and atmosphere required in a restaurant.

4.8. Referring to the four different foodservice facilities identified in Problem 1.11, relate the various customer and user characteristics described in this chapter to each of these facilities.

4.9. Select a particular type of foodservice facility and complete the information required for the prospectus outline shown in Appendix D.

BIBLIOGRAPHY

CHIFFRILLER, Jr., T.F. 1982. Successful Restaurant Operation. CBI Publishing Co., Boston, Massachusetts.

COURNOYER, N.G. 1978. Hotel, Restaurant and Travel Law. Wadsworth Publishing Co., Belmont, California.

DYER, D.A. 1981. So You Want to Start a Restaurant. CBI Publishing Co., Boston, Massachusetts.

ECKSTEIN, E.F. 1983. Menu Planning, 3rd Edition. AVI Publishing Co., Westport, Connecticut. In press.

GOODMAN, R.J., Jr. 1979. The Management of Service for the Restaurant Manager. Wm. C. Brown Co., Dubuque, Iowa.

GREEN, E.F., DRAKE, G.G. and SWEENEY, F.J. 1978. Profitable Food and Beverage Management: Planning. Hayden Book Co., Rochelle Park, New Jersey.

ROBBINS, C. 1982. So You Want to Open a Restaurant. Harbor Publishing Co., New York.

SEABERG, A.G. 1983. Menu Design, Merchandising and Marketing. CBI Publishing Co., Boston, Massachusetts.

WOODMAN, J.G. and LOEB, J.G. 1979. The IFMA Encyclopedia of the Food Service Industry, 3rd Edition. The International Food Service Manufacturers Assoc., Chicago, Illinois.

The Feasibility Study

IMPORTANCE

The feasibility study is essentially an analysis of the market information, the operational concepts, and the financial considerations that have been gathered for a particular project. The objective of the feasibility study is to determine whether the proposed project should be undertaken or abandoned. The decision is based on the economic factors involved. Owners, investors, or lending agencies are not likely to commit funds for a project until enough information is gathered and analyzed to assure them of a reasonable rate of return. The data must indicate a fairly high probability of success.

The feasibility study identifies hidden factors or hazards that may not be readily seen by a cursory description of the project. Some reasons for abandoning a proposed foodservice project include inadequate financing, anticipated changes in the market, inadequate profit potential, poor location, or excessive competition. Occasionally, the feasibility study will show areas where changes are needed to make the project acceptable to investors.

It is difficult to present a definite format for conducting the feasibility study because of the diversity of the types of foodservice projects that may be undertaken. Each feasibility study will reflect an analysis of the special requirements of the project under consideration. This indicates that some aspects of the feasibility study may involve greater research efforts in order to adequately guide the decisions that are to be made. For example, one type of project may require an in-depth analysis of the financing required, while for another project the marketing aspects may be more important. In any case, the data gathered and analyzed must be realistic so that the conclusions drawn from the study will be valid.

Each feasibility study has to be tailored to fit the project at hand. The suggested format and list of data requirements to be presented are generally applicable to most investigations of proposed new foodservice facilities. These items serve as a guide and in real practice the study is adapted to the requirements of the project under consideration. Feasibility studies are best conducted by professionals who specialize in this area. Many architects, foodservice consultants, and accounting firms provide this service.

Before a feasibility study can be made, the analyst should be provided with some preliminary plans and have some information regarding the menu and prices that are proposed. The days and hours of operation are also required before a projection of total anticipated sales can be made. For general foodservice operations, the sales estimates are based on seating capacity, seat turnover, and check averages. These data are usually obtained from the prospectus prepared for the project.

THE MARKET SURVEY

The market survey for the feasibility study may be accomplished for two different situations. In one case, a particular site may be under consideration for the proposed facility. In this situation, the market survey serves to characterize the immediate area of the site. In the other case, there may not be a particular site under consideration and market surveys of several localities may have to be made before deciding upon a site. In either case, the marketing data to be gathered are limited to the needs of the project. Only those areas of market information that relate directly to the demand for foodservice operations need be considered. Some of this information is obtained during the development of the prospectus. Additional market information required to complete the feasibility study is now gathered and summarized. The types of marketing data that may be gathered for a particular project are outlined in the categories shown here:

1. Potential customers
   location   ages
   number   sex
   types   occupations
   income levels   spending habits

2. Historical data
   attractions   types of businesses
   types of industries   climatological data

3. Growth characteristics
   population   transportation
   bank deposits   labor force
   telephones   government units
   utility connections   taxes
   building permits   recreation

4. Competition
   number and type of food-   turnover rates
     service facilities   sales volume
   number of seats   quality of facilities
   check averages   type of service

5. Sales generators
   conventions   residential developments
     size   homes
     types   apartments
     facilities   shopping areas
   lodging facilities   educational institutions
   office buildings   recreational facilities

Marketing data for a particular locality may be obtained from many sources. A partial list of these sources and the data available are indicated here.

General Data *

County and City Data Book. Bureau of Census, Department of Commerce, GPO. A total of 195 statistical items tabulated for the U.S., its regions, and each county and state; 190 items for each city; and 161 items for 277 standard metropolitan statistical areas. Information is derived from latest available censuses of population, housing, governments, mineral industries, agriculture, manufacturers, retail and wholesale trade, and selected services. Also includes data on health, vital statistics, public assistance programs, bank deposits, vote cast for President, and crime.

* Small Business Bibliography, No. 12. 1981. U. S. Small Business Administration, Washington, D.C.

Statistics for States and Metropolitan Areas. (A preprint from County and City Data Book.) Bureau of Census, Department of Commerce. $2.75. GPO. Presents data for 195 statistical items for the U.S., its regions, and each state, and 161 items for 277 standard metropolitan statistical areas.

Statistical Abstract of the United States. Bureau of Census, Department of Commerce. GPO. Includes many consumer market statistics such as income, employment, communications, retail and wholesale trade and services, housing, population characteristics by state and for large cities and standard metropolitan areas. The 1977 edition carries 131 new tables on such topics as gambling, daytime care for children, households with TV sets, Federal R&D obligations for energy development, franchised businesses, among others. Includes 56 maps and a glossary of terms.

A Guide to Consumer Markets. Annual. $30.00. The Conference Board, Inc., Information Services, 845 Third Ave., New York, N.Y. 10022. Presents a detailed statistical profile of U.S. consumers and the consumer market. Contains data on population growth and mobility, employment, income, consumer spending patterns, production and sales, and prices.

E&P Market Guide. Published annually in Fall. $30. Editor & Publisher Company, 575 Lexington Ave., New York, N.Y. 10022. Tabulates current estimates of population, households, and retail sales for nine major sales classifications, income for states, counties, metropolitan areas, and 1,500 daily newspaper markets. Also lists specific information on major manufacturing, retailing, and business firms, transportation and utilities, local newspapers, climate and employment, for newspaper markets. Includes state maps.

S&MM's Survey of Buying Power. Revised annually in July. $30. *Sales and Marketing Management,* 633 Third Ave., New York, N.Y. 10017. Information includes current estimates of population and households by income groups, total effective buying income, retail sales for major retail lines, and market quality indexed; given for all regions, states, counties, and metropolitan areas.

S&MM's Survey of Buying Power—Part II. Revised annually in October. $15. *Sales and Marketing Management,* 633 Third Ave., New York, N.Y. 10017. Gives population, income, retail sales, and buying income figures for television and newspaper markets in the United States and Canada. The data for television markets outlines the areas of dominant influence, while the newspaper market information identifies both dominant and effective coverage areas.

Specific Data for the Foodservice Industry

Institutions/Restaurants Magazine. Special issue (March 15). Gives projections of the size of the foodservice industry by segments. Also analyzes developments and trends in the industry.

Hospitality Magazine **(September issue).** Presents data on the commercial foodservice market.

Restaurant Business Magazine **(September issue).** Provides a segment analysis with growth projections. Includes a Restaurant Growth Index for metro markets and states.

National Restaurant Association. Provides periodic projections of food and beverage sales.

Many local chambers of commerce maintain a supply of marketing data for their particular locality and are a good source of information.

SITE ANALYSIS

In the case where a particular site is to be evaluated for the proposed foodservice facility, considerable additional information is gathered and correlated with the market data. Because of the great variety and types of foodservice facilities, the site analysis has to be done specifically for the type of operation proposed. A site which may be ideal for a table-service operation may be very poor for other types of facilities. Chain operations have considerable background information on their customers and will try to find locations where they will attract the same type of customers.

Zoning

The best situation for a potential site is to have definite commitments on the use, restrictions, and permits required for the proposed foodservice facility (Fig. 5.1). Otherwise, considerable time and money

FIG. 5.1.   Many cities have restrictions on the size and location of signs.

can be expended in trying to change the zoning or in obtaining the necessary permits.

Area Economics

Data on the growth of business activity in the immediate vicinity of the site are gathered and evaluated. This may be done by types of businesses to get a feel of the direction of growth areas. A pattern of economic growth over several years is obviously preferred.

Competition

The evaluation of competition may be considered in two separate categories. Foodservice facilities that offer the same type of meals and service as the proposed facility will offer direct competition and are considered a negative factor. Indirect competition includes foodservice facilities that offer a different menu and method of service. These may be a desirable factor since they are activity generators for a particular area. A lack of any type of competition near the proposed site should be carefully analyzed; it could mean a potentially excellent site or it could indicate a very poor site.

Information regarding existing foodservice facilities for a particular area can be obtained from travel guides, vacation guides, and tour books.

Physical Characteristics

Top soil and subsoil conditions, slopes, and surface drainage characteristics of a site are important from the standpoint of actual placement and construction of the building. Soil borings are desirable to determine the bearing capacity of the soil and to locate possible high water-table areas.

Facilities that will have to use septic tanks for waste disposal require percolation tests of the soil before county sanitarians will approve such systems.

Size and Shape

The potential site for the foodservice facility must be large enough to allow efficient placement of the building, parking areas, entrances, and other exterior areas required. The preferred shape of the site for most facilities is square or rectangular. Triangular and other odd-shaped sites cannot be efficiently used unless they are very large. Possibilities of future expansion are considered when evaluating the size and shape of the site.

Land Costs

A potential site that has many desirable characteristics may have to be eliminated from contention because of excessive costs. Land costs, improvement costs and taxes are evaluated in light of the total project cost to make sure they are not out of line. This factor is evaluated in the financial part of the feasibility study.

Availability of Utilities

The availability or cost of obtaining gas, water, sanitary sewer, electricity, storm sewer, and possibly steam at the proposed site are to be checked. Many urban locations present no problem; however, it may be quite costly to run utilities to remote locations.

The quality and capacity of the utilities should also be evaluated. Water quality is extremely important for foodservice facilities. Separate water treatment facilities may have to be provided in some instances.

Positional Characteristics

The positional characteristics indicate the location of the site in relationship to activity generators. Distances and directions to shopping centers, commercial areas, recreational areas, and so on are evaluated. Activity generators several miles away from a site can still generate sales for certain types of foodservice facilities.

Street Patterns

This factor is analyzed to determine whether street and traffic patterns tend to draw people to the site area or if they tend to diffuse the population as they travel to activity generators. Proposed new traffic routes or proposed changes in routes can be obtained from highway departments.

Traffic Information

Traffic information for streets surrounding the proposed site may be obtained from highway departments or local governmental agencies. If a traffic count has not been taken fairly recently or is not available, then sample counts may be taken at significant times during the day. Traffic counts are usually taken at noon-hours, weekend evenings, and Sundays. Counts taken over a period of several days should be used to eliminate biased results. Dinner-hour counts may be influenced heavily by commuter traffic and can be used for evaluating sites for take-home food facilities. They may not, however, be significant for other types of foodservice operations.

Visibility

The visibility of the site is evaluated by taking tours by auto or by foot from all directions. A good view of the facility is desirable even though signs are to be used for identification. This is most important for sites that are located on high speed routes that have heavy traffic.

Accessibility to the site and proposed parking areas should also be checked at the same time.

Services

Police and fire protection, garbage and trash pickup, and other desired services are included in this factor. Availability, cost, and quality of required services at the proposed site should be evaluated. This information can be obtained from city or municipal offices.

Availability of Local Labor

Considerations of the type of labor skills, ages, and availability of personnel to staff the proposed facility are involved in this factor. Of special importance to the success of the facility is the availability of management talent that will be required to operate it.

These are some of the major factors involved in the early considerations of site selection for a new foodservice facility. Some analysts find a form such as the one illustrated in Table 5.1 a great help in gathering site information.

The techniques used in site analysis for foodservice operations are very changeable. It pays to be very careful for this part of the feasibility study since the future of the foodservice facility is largely affected by the site. The problem of correctly selecting a site can only be solved by an intuitive analysis of the key factors involved.

The experienced market and site analysts, in addition to collecting and analyzing the facts and figures, will personally tour the area within a reasonable radius of the site. They may also visit all nearby competitive facilities to get a better "feel" for the area. Interviews may also be a part of the analyst's procedure to see how local businessmen and potential clientele feel about the proposed foodservice facility.

The market data and site analysis enables the analyst to advise the owner or investor in the following areas:

Seating capacity
Most desirable type of service unit
Expected seat turnover by days of the week and by months of the year
Expected check average for each meal period
Expected alcoholic beverage sales if a bar is to be included in the food facility

The analysis of the market and site data is one of the points in the feasibility study where a decision to continue the project can be made. A keen analyst will recognize when the facts indicate a negative de-

TABLE 5.1. SITE ANALYSIS FORM

(1) Zoning
    Current zoning of site   _____
    Use permits needed   _____
    Height restrictions   _____
    Front line set back   _____
    Side yard requirements   _____
    Back yard requirements   _____
    Restrictions on signs   _____
    Parking requirements   _____
    Other restrictions   _____
(2) Area Characteristics
    Type of neighborhood   _____
    Type of businesses   _____
    Growth pattern   _____
    Proposed construction   _____
    Other available sites   _____
    Zoning of adjacent sites   _____
(3) Competition
    Number of food facilities in drawing
        area of site   _____
    Number of seats   _____
    Type of menu offered   _____
    Method of service   _____
    Check averages   _____
    Number of cocktail lounges   _____
    Quality of drinks   _____
    Bar service available at tables   _____
    Annual sales   _____
(4) Physical characteristics
    Type of top soil   _____
    Type of subsoil   _____
    Depth of water table   _____
    Presence of rocks   _____
    Load-bearing capacity   _____
    Direction of slopes   _____
    Surface drainage   _____
    Percolation test results   _____
    Natural landscaping   _____
    Other features   _____
(5) Size and Shape (Including sketch)
    Length   _____
    Width   _____
    Total square feet   _____
    Square footage needed for building   _____
    Square footage needed for parking   _____
    Space for other requirements   _____
(6) Costs
    Cost per front foot   _____
    Cost per square foot   _____
    Total cost of site   _____
    Cost of comparable sites nearby   _____
    Costs for land improvements   _____
    Real estate taxes   _____
    Other taxes   _____
(7) Utilities
    Location, cost, and size or capacity of:
        Storm sewer   _____

TABLE 5.1 (*Continued*)

Sanitary sewer			_____
Gas lines			_____
Water lines			_____
Electricity			_____
Steam			_____
(8) Streets			
Basic patterns			_____
Width or lanes			_____
Paved			_____
Curbs and gutters			_____
Sidewalks			_____
Lighting			_____
Public transportation			_____
Grades			_____
Hazards			_____
(9) Positional Characteristics			

	Distance	Driving Time
Distance and driving time to:		
Central business district	_____	_____
Industrial centers	_____	_____
Shopping centers	_____	_____
Residential areas	_____	_____
Recreational areas	_____	_____
Sporting events	_____	_____
Educational facilities	_____	_____
Special attractions	_____	_____
Other activity generators	_____	_____

(10) Traffic Information
Distance to nearest intersection _____
Traffic characteristics

	Day	Time	Count
Traffic counts:			
Site street	_____	_____	_____
	_____	_____	_____
	_____	_____	_____
Adjacent streets	_____	_____	_____
	_____	_____	_____
	_____	_____	_____

Anticipated changes _____
(11) Visibility
    Distances of sight from:
      Left _____
      Right _____
      Across _____
    Obstructions _____
    Location of signs _____
(12) Availability of local labor _____
(13) Services
    Quality of police protection _____
    Quality of fire protection _____
    Location of hydrant _____
    Availability of trash pick up _____
    Availability of garbage pick up _____
    Other services required _____
(14) General Recommendations
    Suitability _____
    Desirability _____
    Other recommendations _____

cision. If it appears at this point that the proposed project has insufficient potential for success, it must be terminated before additional funds are spent. If the data indicate a potential success for the project the feasibility study is continued.

FINANCIAL ASPECTS

After completion of the market study and selection of a site for the proposed facility, the financial aspects of the feasibility study are considered. Two important areas are evaluated. First, preliminary estimates must be made of the costs of land, building, equipment, furnishings, and the amount of working capital needed. The second area deals with the projected income and expenses of the foodservice facility. These are usually prepared in the form of a tentative operating budget. Both these areas are of concern to the owner or investor because they indicate how soon one can expect to get an investment back and how much profit might be made. If the preliminary cost and profit estimates are not very encouraging, the owner should either modify the basic scheme of the project or abandon it completely.

Land and Construction Cost Estimates

The cost of land for the proposed facility can be obtained from realtors or by a real estate appraisal. The site development costs for excavating, removing rocks, and grading for driveways and parking areas are estimated by the architect.

The architect will prepare estimates of construction costs, including building equipment and utilities. These preliminary cost estimates can be made in different ways. One method, which is fast but may not be too accurate, is to use "rules of thumb" based on studies of actual costs of existing foodservice facilities. These costs are generally expressed in terms of the cost per seat. The cost per seat figures have to be used carefully because they can vary a great deal depending upon the size and style of facility involved. Typical cost per seat figures range from $2000 to $4000 or even higher, depending on the elaborateness of construction and furnishing.

Preliminary cost estimates may also be arrived at by using local construction costs per square foot or per cubic foot for similar types of buildings. Many construction contractors maintain up-to-date costs per square foot or per cubic foot of building space. The estimates should be obtained for approximately the same size building because size is an important variable of construction costs.

Another method of obtaining preliminary cost estimates is to analyze costs of similar types of foodservice facilities that have recently been built. Most operators will willingly give out the costs they have incurred in building their facility.

Regardless of the method used, the preliminary costs for maximum investment are needed in order to arrange the necessary financing.

Costs of Furnishings and Equipment

Cost estimates for furnishing and equipping the facility are determined by the interior designer and the foodservice consultant. These are estimates for equipment and furnishings in the kitchen, dining, and public areas and do not include building equipment, such as heating and ventilating equipment. The building equipment costs are included in the construction estimates. The furnishings and equipment category does include items of office furniture, office machines, linen room equipment, and furniture for employee and guest areas. (See Fig. 5.2.)

FIG. 5.2.   Cost estimates are based on types and models of equipment to be used in the facility.
Courtesy of The Hysen Group, Livonia, Michigan.

Operating Equipment

The cost estimates for furnishings and equipment do not include operating equipment. Operating equipment encompasses such items as china, glassware, silverware, utensils, linens, and uniforms. The cost estimate for operating equipment is generally based on the starting inventories required of each of the items. These costs can be obtained from local suppliers.

Planning Costs

Estimates for planning costs have to be determined separately. Planning fees for members of the planning team can be estimated at 7–10% of the total construction costs, including equipment and furnishings. Land costs are not included when determining this estimate.

All these various cost estimates are added together to develop a figure for the total amount of money needed to build and equip the facility.

OPERATING CAPITAL

Operating capital refers to the money required to finance the foodservice operation until some inflow of cash begins. The money is needed for house funds, payments for supplies, hiring and training employees, payroll expenses, and other current bills as they become due. Operating capital requirements may be broken down into the following categories.

1. *Cash on hand.* This is for the cashiers who will handle the cash transactions. The total amount needed will vary with the size of the operation and with the expected sales volume.

2. *Cash on deposit.* Includes funds to meet current payrolls, utility bills, materials, and supplies. The total amount on deposit will vary with the owner's desire to maintain a good financial position in meeting current obligations. Some funds for emergency expenditures should also be included.

3. *Accounts receivable.* The increasing popularity of credit cards requires some money to handle the accounts receivable. This may be determined by estimating the volume of charge business anticipated and the time required to collect the accounts. Those operators who will handle cash sales only do not have to consider this category.

4. *Inventories.* This category is to handle the beginning inventories of food, beverages, and supplies. The food inventory may be estimated

at 1% of the total annual food sales expected. Beverage inventories are frequently estimated at 5% of the expected annual beverage sales. Inventories of supplies vary with the type of operation; a rough estimate of 0.5–1% of annual sales can be used.

5. *Prepaid expenses.* Prepaid expenses include such items as insurance premiums, licenses, and interest payments. These may be estimated by contacting the appropriate agencies involved.

The accounts receivable and inventories are considered as current assets and are to be offset by the current liabilities in estimating the amount of working capital needed.

Current liabilities may be estimated for the following items. Accounts payable are usually on a monthly basis and any accounts can be estimated at one-twelfth of the annual cost of sales and services expected to be supplied by purveyors. Payroll and payroll taxes can be estimated for one week's time. The utility bills, local taxes, and other accrued expenses may be estimated at 1% of total sales volume. Any mortgage and other note obligations should also be included in the current liabilities category.

PROJECTED INCOME

The next step involved in the feasibility analysis is to determine the projected earnings for the food facility. A suggested format for estimating sales is shown in Table 5.2. Usually estimates for each of the first three years of operation are made. This results in a more realistic estimate.

Estimating Food Sales

Estimates of food sales for a proposed foodservice facility are usually based on the market research data and are made for each meal period. Anticipated between-meal period sales or late night sales are

TABLE 5.2. FORMAT FOR ESTIMATING INCOME FOR THE PROPOSED FACILITY

Meal period	Number of seats	Estimated turnover	Total meals	Estimated check avg.	Estimated daily sales	Annual operating days	Estimated annual sales
Breakfast	_____	_____	_____	_____	_____	_____	_____
Lunch	_____	_____	_____	_____	_____	_____	_____
Dinner	_____	_____	_____	_____	_____	_____	_____
Other	_____	_____	_____	_____	_____	_____	_____
						Total	_____

included where appropriate. Typical computations based on the number of seats, seat turnover, and check average for daily sales are made and projected for the estimated annual sales.

The estimates of seat turnover are critical to accurate projections of income. Seat turnover will vary with the type of operation, the menu, the method of service, type of clientele, and type of location and should be estimated by an evaluation of all these factors. Seat turnover will probably vary for each meal period and in some instances may vary for different days of the week. If daily variations are anticipated, a summary for each day of the week should be prepared. For example breakfast turnover may be two or three on weekdays but only one on Saturdays and Sundays. In this case the format shown in Table 5.2 is expanded to show the days of the week.

Check averages may be based on a popularity forecast of menu items as reflected by current consumer desires. Recent surveys of popular foods may be used to develop the forecast for a given menu. This method of determining check averages requires that the total menu for each meal period and the selling prices for all menu items be established. Additional food sales from special functions such as banquets, parties, or increased business due to holidays are incorporated into the final food sales estimates.

Estimating Alcoholic Beverage Sales

Sales of alcoholic beverages, where applicable, may be estimated as a ratio of total food and beverage sales. In most table service operations, an estimate of 25% of the total sales is used for alcoholic beverages. Since this is a general rule of thumb, it should not be used where a different pattern of alcoholic beverage consumption is anticipated.

An alternative method of estimating alcoholic beverage sales is to forecast the number of customers who might order drinks or wine for each meal period. Then the number of each type of sale would be multiplied by the selling price per drink and added to the forecasted food sales. Sales of alcoholic beverages for lounge or bar areas are usually estimated on a per day basis and extended to an annual basis as a separate category.

Projected Expenses

The expected annual expenses are also developed, in a similar manner. Although many percentage figures are reported in publications for various categories of expenses, these should only be used as a guide.

TABLE 5.3. ESTIMATED EXPENSES FOR FOODSERVICE OPERATIONS

Expenses	% of total sales	
Cost of Sales		
Food	38	
Beverage	30	
Total food and beverage costs		36
Operating expenses		
Payroll	28	
Employee benefits	3.5	
Laundry	1.5	
China, glass, silver, utensils	2.5	
Utilities	5	
Supplies	2	
Advertising	2	
Insurance	1.5	
Licenses	0.5	
Telephone	0.3	
Administrative	3	
Miscellaneous expenses	0.2	
Total operating expenses		50
Total costs and expenses		86
Estimated profit before occupancy costs and income taxes		14

These expenses can vary widely from operation to operation. Table 5.3 identifies the typical expense items with suggested costs expressed as a percentage of total food and beverage sales.

Estimating Food and Beverage Costs

Expected food costs may be determined by using the same popularity forecasts that were used to estimate check averages. This requires that each menu item be evaluated using standard recipes and identifying costs for each ingredient. After each menu item is costed, the popularity forecasts are used to determine the expected food cost. Food cost percentage is then computed by dividing the annual food cost estimate by the sales expected for the year.

Alcoholic beverage costs may be estimated in a similar manner and expressed as a percentage of total projected sales. Estimated food and beverage costs may be compared to industry averages for the type of foodservice facility being planned.

Estimating Controllable Expenses

The most critical item under controllable expenses is payroll, and accurate estimates are very important. The best estimates of payroll expense are obtained by taking the time to prepare a staffing schedule for the proposed facility. The staffing has to be correlated to the expected sales volume and should include all labor hours required for each job classification. Current wage rates for each job classification are used to obtain total payroll expense expected for the year.

Some items of controllable expenses are estimated by using industry averages. For example, employee benefits and employee meals may be estimated as a percentage of payroll cost. If industry averages are not thought to be applicable for a particular project, then estimates based on the proposed operational characteristics have to be developed.

Other items of controllable expenses are estimated by evaluating the pertinent factors involved. Some types of projects may anticipate large expenditures for advertising or for music and entertainment and are estimated accordingly. In many instances it is desirable to obtain projected energy usage from engineering data to determine accurate estimates of the costs of utilities.

Projected Earnings

The estimated income and expenses are used to project the potential earnings for the foodservice facility. The rate of return on the investment can be calculated and will be the determining factor in deciding whether or not the project is justified as conceived. If the proposed facility is deemed feasible, the planning process is continued by commissioning the planners. The planners are given the general requirements for the project as determined by the feasibility study. These requirements include total building size, number of seats and dining room square footage, number of parking spaces, bar space, and any other space needed for special functions.

PROBLEMS AND EXERCISES

5.1. Define and describe the importance of a feasibility study for a new foodservice facility.

5.2. Identify some categories of marketing data that might be gathered for a particular project. Indicate the types of information that would be included in each of the categories identified.

5.3. List several of the factors that are taken into account during the site analysis. Describe why each factor listed is important.

5.4. Gather the information required for the site analysis form in Table 5.1 for a specific site to be considered for a foodservice facility.

5.5. Describe each of the cost estimation methods discussed in the chapter, indicating the advantages and disadvantages of each method.

5.6. Considering the four foodservice models described in Problem 1.11, discuss why expenses would vary for each type of operation.

5.7. Determine the estimated income for a fast food operation using the format shown in Table 5.2.

5.8. Discuss the advantages and disadvantages of using industry average percentage of sales figures for cost estimates.

5.9. Determine the estimated dollar amounts for each item shown in Table 5.3 for a foodservice facility that is projected to have a total annual sales volume of $2,000,000.

BIBLIOGRAPHY

CASE, D.R. 1968. Food service site selection. Cornell Hotel Restaurant Admin. Q. *9* (3), 21–24.

CELLA, F.R. 1968. Computer evaluation of restaurant sites. Cornell Hotel Restaurant Admin. Q. *9* (3), 25–37.

COLTMAN, M.M. 1979. Financial Management for the Hospitality Industry. CBI Publishing Co., Boston, Massachusetts.

DARLEY/GOBAR ASSOCIATES. 1969. Restaurant site selection. Cornell Hotel Restaurant Admin. Q. *10* (3), 61–69.

FARRALL, K. 1980. Insight into site selection. Restaurant Business *79* (9), 115–123.

GREEN, E.F., DRAKE, G.G. and SWEENEY, F.J. 1978. Profitable Food and Beverage Management: Planning. Hayden Book Co., Rochelle Park, New Jersey.

KAHRL, W.L. 1977. Advanced Modern Food and Beverage Service. Prentice-Hall, Inc., Englewood Cliffs, New Jersey.

KALT, N. 1971. Legal Aspects of Hotel, Motel and Restaurant Operation. ITT Educational Services, Inc., New York.

KATSIGRIS, C. and PORTER, M. 1983. The Bar and Beverage Book: Basics of Profitable Management. John Wiley and Sons, New York.

POLEDOR, A.P. 1977. Determining the Feasibility of a Total Convenience Food System. CBI Publishing Co., Boston, Massachusetts.

6

Functional Planning

FUNCTIONS

The main concept of planning deals with functions. All foodservice facilities perform various functions in their day-to-day operation. General functions common to most operations include receiving, storage, preparation, production, service, warewashing, and waste disposal. These functions can easily be related to the materials and products involved in the food facility. Other functions that are performed but are not easily related to materials or products include accounting, purchasing, management, and communications. Typically, each function can be broken down into more specific items. For example, the general storage function may be subdivided into storage of meats, dry foods, beverages, linens, dishes, silver, supplies, and trash.

The functional planning for the various areas of foodservice facilities may be accomplished in different ways. Experienced foodservice consultants have developed their own techniques of planning and can plan areas fairly rapidly. In order to develop the basic concepts of functional planning, a detailed presentation will be given. In actual practice, much of this planning is done in the designer's mind before any sketches or plans are developed and drawn.

The first step in functional planning is to visualize all the necessary functions to be performed in the proposed foodservice facility. This obviously comes easily to experienced planners, but persons unfamiliar with planning may find it helpful to make a list of the functions. The more detailed the list, the easier the remaining steps of the planning process become.

Each function consists of a number of tasks. For example, the tasks involved in the preparation function may include weighing, cutting, mixing, blending, panning, moving, and judging quality. These tasks vary from one facility to another depending upon the method of operation desired by the owner or manager.

The method of performing the tasks also depends on the type and form of materials involved, the kind of equipment to be used, the quality of finished products, and the skill of the persons involved. The evaluation and selection of these variables that affect the tasks are a part of the designer's responsibility. Hopefully, the best choice of materials, equipment, and processes will be made, to facilitate performance of these tasks. Thus functional planning begins with identification of functions and visualization of the tasks to be performed for each function. A comprehensive list of tasks for foodservice operations is given in Appendix E. The tasks are listed by functional categories and may be used as a check list for this part of the planning process.

CONCEPTS OF FLOW

The identification and visualization of the functions and their associated tasks makes it easier to discuss the concepts of flow. Flow is identified as the movement of materials, workers, guests, equipment, forms, or any other element involved in the operation of the food facility. The most important concept of flow, as related to planning, is to minimize the amount of movement required for efficient operation. As functions and tasks are visualized, planning for the methods of performing them should be guided by this concept of minimum movement.

There are many aids that can be used to plan the facility so that flow is minimized. The most common of these is the flow diagram. The flow diagram is developed by showing the flow of materials between the various functions that relate to a particular project. A simple flow diagram for foodservice operations is shown in Fig. 6.1. Flow diagrams show the flow of primary materials only. The functions shown on the diagram are connected by arrows that indicate the direction of flow. Different types of arrows may be used to identify the flow of different materials. The flow diagram aids the planner in physically locating the areas where the functions will ultimately be performed. The flow diagram does not have to be developed at this stage of the planning process, but may be done later when specific aspects of flow will be considered.

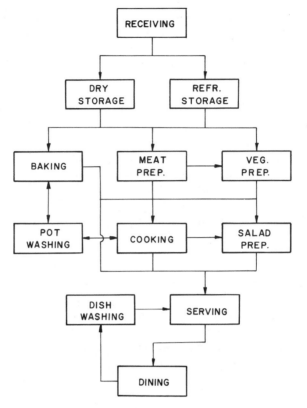

FIG. 6.1. A typical flow diagram for a foodservice facility.

FUNCTIONAL REQUIREMENTS

Another reason for identifying the functions and tasks is to develop the various physical requirements needed to perform them. The basic requirements considered are equipment and space. For each function or task, the planner will determine the type of equipment to be used, and this in turn leads to the development of space requirements. The capacity of the equipment is not usually determined at this time because a careful analysis of the menu and scheduling are required. The determination of equipment capacity will be discussed in detail in Chapter 9.

In the development of equipment and space requirements, the planner has to decide how each of the tasks for a particular function is to be performed in terms of the materials and processes involved. To illustrate, consider the task of making a stew as one of the components of the cooking function. Some of the variations of the materials that may be used in making the stew are:

1. Entirely from fresh raw ingredients, both meat and vegetables
2. Partially fresh vegetables and partially canned (i.e., fresh potatoes and other canned)
3. Partially fresh vegetables and partially frozen vegetables
4. All canned vegetables and fresh meat
5. All frozen vegetables and fresh meat
6. Fully processed canned stew
7. Fully processed frozen stew

It can be seen that each of these variations in the ingredients will require different tasks and different processes for production. This in turn leads to different equipment types. The planner will evaluate the menu items to be produced and make the decisions regarding the type of production equipment to use. This same concept is used for all the other functions and tasks required to operate the facility.

Considerations of space requirements are also evaluated in a similar manner. The mere identification of the functions and tasks alerts the planner to the fact that some kind of space will be needed. The planner does not necessarily need to determine the final square footage of space now, but does consider whether a particular task requires floor space, work space, and/or storage space. The designer is essentially developing the basic concepts for the operation of the facility. This is done prior to the planning of the actual physical areas. In other words, the planning of the operational methods is the key to the functional planning for the facility. A short discussion of some of these functional areas will illustrate and clarify the concept.

RECEIVING

The receiving function is very similar for most foodservice operations. The receiving of incoming foods, beverages, and supplies is planned according to the types and volumes of different materials handled. The frequency of deliveries and the type of delivery service are considered for each type of material to be received. For large facilities, materials-handling systems may be utilized to simplify the movement of materials into and out of the receiving area. Many suppliers offer their products in palletized form, which simplifies the movement. The use of carts, trucks, and conveyors will solve most materials-handling problems.

Planning of the materials-handling system for the receiving area is only a part of the total system for the entire facility, and the planner should consider all the various components of the handling system before making a final decision. Some may decide to use a single type of handling equipment for everything from the initial receiving to final service. Other planners may conceive a system which uses several types of equipment, each selected for its characteristics for handling certain types of materials. For example, mobile carts and trucks may be selected for handling food items, while conveyors may be chosen to handle dishes and other nonfood items. The availability of a wide variety of materials-handling equipment enables the designer to develop many different systems.

Some temporary storage in the way of floor space and table space is required to check deliveries for quantity and quality. This space is designed on the basis of the larger amounts of frequently delivered materials. Additional space is planned for scales, storage of skids and hand trucks, and for other necessary equipment for the receiving function.

Consideration of waste disposal is also a factor in planning for the receiving function, since some partial trimming and cleaning of materials may be needed before they are placed in storage. Disposal of boxes, cartons, and other packaging materials removed during the receiving function is also involved.

Architectural features, including the size and location of unloading docks and doors, may be developed at this time.

STORAGE

Planning for the storage function in food facilities includes dry storage, refrigerated storage, freezer storage, beverage storage, and storage for nonfood supplies.

Dry Storage

The dry storage function, like other storage functions, is necessary for the on-the-site storage of frequently used materials. Storage requirements will depend upon the types of materials, frequency of delivery and the volume of each delivery. These variables are evaluated before functional planning of the storage area begins.

Dry storage areas for food items are planned to maintain temperatures between 50° and 70°F (10° and 21.1° C). The desired relative humidity is approximately 50%. For this reason, heat-generating equipment, such as motors and compressors, should not be planned for this area. Pipes carrying steam or hot water are insulated to minimize heat gain of the storage area. Protection against moisture from sweating cold water or refrigerant lines is also important. Planning for protection of the foodstuffs from insects and vermin is required for sanitary reasons.

Some space for storage of frequently used dry items can be provided in various work areas of the facility. This concept will reduce the amount of movement required to obtain the materials.

Refrigerated Storage

Refrigerated storage areas maintaining temperatures of 32°–37° F (0.0°–2.8° C) are required for fresh meats, vegetables and fruits, dairy products, beverages, and carry-over foods. Many planners are specifying smaller but more numerous reach-in refrigerators strategically located throughout the facility instead of one large walk-in storage. The use of reach-in units as shown in Fig. 6.2 minimizes employee movements in obtaining items. A combination of walk-in and reach-in refrigerators seems to be a good design for many types of foodservice facilities. The reach-ins are usually located adjacent to preparation and production equipment or may be built-in under tables and counters.

The design of walk-in refrigerated areas is similar to the dry storage areas except for the refrigeration system required to maintain the desired temperature. The size and type of foodservice operation and the frequency and volume of deliveries will determine whether a walk-in refrigerated space is needed. It is thought that a walk-in refrigerator is feasible for operations serving over 300–400 meals per day. Reach-in refrigerators are generally designed to store for a shorter period of time and are ideal for smaller operations. Pass-through refrigeration units may be specified where their use will simplify the storage and movement of foods.

The increased use of frozen foods necessitates planning refrigerated space for thawing purposes. Requirements will depend on the volume and type of frozen foods to be used in the operation. Thawing space is generally designed to handle one day's production. Refrigerated space

FIG. 6.2. Reach-in refrigerators and freezers minimize employee travel.
Courtesy of the Fresh Approach Handicapped Training Center and Hamill & McKinney, Architects-Engineers, Inc.

for finished items, including salads, desserts, and appetizers, is planned accordingly.

Freezer Storage

Temperatures of $-10°$ to $-15°F$ ($-23.3°$ to $-26.1°$ C) are needed to safely store frozen foods. Designers are aware of the increased use of frozen foods that are partially or fully preprocessed, and plan accordingly. Some operations have gone almost exclusively to frozen foods. Freezers may be walk-in or reach-in, and requirements are dictated by several factors including the availability of seasonal items. The possibility of buying seasonal items in volume lots should be evaluated before the design of freezer storage is finalized.

Storage of Nonfood Items

The design of storage areas for nonfood items like dishes, glasses, flatware, utensils, paper goods, linen, cleaning supplies, and furniture

FIG. 6.3. Storage for utensils can be provided by shelving units.

can take many different forms. They may be stored in rooms, on shelves, in cabinets, or on specially designed racks. Figure 6.3 shows a utensil storage unit. In smaller operations, some items may be incorporated in the dry food storage area, but separate areas are best for larger operations. All chemicals, soaps, sanitizing compounds, and other cleaning supplies should be stored separately because of their danger to foods. Separate areas are also desirable for cleaning equipment such as brooms, mops, pails, scrubbers, and polishers.

In-process storage of items may be accomplished by special equipment such as self-leveling dispensers. The self-leveling dispensers shown in Fig. 6.4 are a very satisfactory method of providing storage for dishes.

PREPARATION

The preparation functions for a foodservice facility are meat/fish/poultry preparation, vegetable preparation, salad preparation, and sandwich preparation. Specialty restaurants may have different or

FIG. 6.4. Self-leveling dish dispensers are ideal for convenient storage.

additional functions depending on their menu items. An example is the fish and shellfish preparation function for seafood operations. The various preparation functions are sometimes combined and performed in one area. Smaller facilities frequently combine the salad and sandwich preparation areas. Combined vegetable and salad preparation areas are also common.

Meat/Fish/Poultry Preparation

The meat/fish/poultry preparation function consists of cutting, chopping, grinding, and portioning of these items and their products to ready them for further processing. The preparation function has changed drastically over the years with the advent and increasing use of fully preportioned products. Some operations may have minimal meat/fish/poultry preparation areas where the only tasks involved are the opening of packages and the panning of the items. Larger operations and commissary operations may still require a full meat/fish/poultry preparation function.

The planning for the meat/fish/poultry preparation function varies with the amount of preparation that will be done on the foodservice premises.

Vegetable Preparation

The vegetable preparation function historically involved preparing primarily fresh vegetables for cooking and salad production. Typical tasks associated with fresh vegetable preparation are trimming, peeling, washing, cutting, and chopping. As with meat preparation, the vegetable preparation function can be minimized by utilizing various types of preprocessed vegetables. Canned and frozen items are generally used as alternatives to fresh vegetables.

Design and planning for the vegetable preparation function depends on the state of the raw materials and the subsequent tasks to be performed. Large operations choosing to use fresh vegetables will require the use of cutters, choppers, slicers, peelers, and similar equipment. Type and capacity will be designed to handle the volume of vegetables to be prepared. Holding refrigerators are used if the preparation is done a day prior to usage.

Waste disposal is another aspect in planning for the vegetable preparation function. Mechanical waste disposal units are commonly used where permitted.

Salad Preparation

The function of salad preparation is that of combining and assembling ingredients prepared in the vegetable preparation area, or obtained from fruit and vegetable areas, into finished salads. Various quantities of meat, fish, and dairy products are used in certain salads. The preparation of some appetizer items may also be a part of this functional area.

Design for the salad preparation function will depend upon the type and volume of salads to be produced. As indicated earlier, salad and vegetable preparation functions are frequently combined in smaller facilities. Another alternative is to combine the salad preparation with the sandwich preparation function.

Large foodservice operations, especially those serving banquets, will design for a separate mass production salad area as shown in Fig. 6.5. In this situation, assembly line concepts and related equipment can be utilized.

The perishibility of salads necessitates planning of refrigerated holding facilities. Mobile refrigerated carts are selected by some designers as a method of transporting and holding the finished salads. Pass-through refrigerators are frequently specified for cafeteria operations. Fig. 6.6 illustrates a reach-in unit designed for holding items on trays and other containers.

FIG. 6.5.   Mass assembly of salads is required in large
foodservice operations.

Sandwich Preparation

The design of the area for sandwich preparation is based on the
need for fast and efficient work methods. The work areas are planned
to provide ample space for the ingredients used in the sandwiches,
hand tools, and a normal flow of work. Custom-designed sandwich
preparation areas are used for operations handling a large volume of
sandwiches. In some cases the sandwich preparation area may be in
a part of the serving area, as in cafeteria or counter-service operations. Assembly-line techniques and automatic wrapping machinery
are typical designs found in institutional and in-plant feeding operations.

COOKING

The heart of all foodservice facilities is the main cooking function,
and special care in planning for it is required. In addition to cooking
all meat and vegetable items, the cooking area serves as the hub between the production and service functions. In many table-service op-

FIG. 6.6.   Storage for finished items in a reach-in unit.
Courtesy of The Hobart Corporation.

erations, for example, the pick-up of food for serving is directly adjacent to the main cooking area.

The design of cooking areas varies from very limited facilities, as in fast-food and limited-menu operations, to the very extensive facilities of luxury table-service operations or in large institutional foodservices. In all cases, the design of cooking area is closely correlated with the various menu items to be processed. Considerations of cooked-to-order and batch cooking are important in arriving at the final design.

BAKING

Except in a relatively few cases, foodservice operations will not be involved in the production of a full line of baked goods. Even many large institutional operations in universities and hospitals confine their baking function to cakes, cookies, and pastries, other items being obtained from commercial bakeries. Even the operations that do a good portion of their own baking will use basic mixes that simplify the tasks of the baking function. Full bakeries are occasionally planned for commissaries or central kitchens that supply several outlets. These may be planned to handle the conventional tasks of formulation, scaling, mixing, handling, and makeup.

The advent of high-quality preprepared unbaked goods that require only thawing and baking has also had an impact on the design of baking areas. Many of the preprepared items can be processed in the main cooking area, eliminating the need for a separate baking area completely. A study of the quality and availability of these items and their scheduling into the cooking area should be made before a final decision is reached. An economic analysis of the cost of full baking on the premises versus the use of preprepared baked goods may also influence the design of the baking system.

SERVING

The different ways of performing the serving function result in a variety of serving facilities that may be planned. Basic table-service operations require pick-up areas immediately adjacent to the cooking battery. Separate pick-up areas are used for salads, beverages, and desserts. Some items, including rolls, bread, butter, and water, are stored at waiter or waitress stations located in dining areas.

Serving-line facilities are planned for cafeterias, employee feeding, and school or university feeding operations. Several configurations of serving lines can be used, depending on the total number of people to be served and the time allowed for serving. Straight-line configurations, as shown in Fig. 6.7, are the most basic and are characterized by easy access and well-defined traffic flow. The major problem with the straight-line configuration is its limited serving capacity per line.

Variations of the straight-line include the U-shaped counter and the herringbone design (Fig. 6.8). These configurations give more linear space and increase serving-line capacity. The shopping center or scramble serving line system is characterized by an open-square con-

FIG. 6.7. Straight-line cafeteria counters give a well-defined flow of traffic.
Courtesy of Martin Marietta Aerospace, Orlando, Florida and The Hysen Group, Livonia, Michigan.

figuration of counters at the perimeters that allow traffic to flow freely in the center. Total serving capacity of the shopping center or scramble system is much greater than that of the basic straightline configurations.

Other types of serving functions that may be planned are tray make-up conveyors for hospitals, cart assembly areas for banquets, and room service facilities for hotels. Each of these has special requirements and should be planned for efficient handling of the food to be served.

DISHWASHING

The dishwashing function is usually performed in a separate room or area that has to be well ventilated and illuminated, as shown in Fig. 6.9. Acoustical tile and noise-absorbing materials are used to aid in lowering the high noise levels associated with this function. Modern dishwashing machines can be obtained to handle any volume of dinnerware.

FIG. 6.8. An example of the herringbone or sawtooth type of cafeteria line.
Courtesy of The Hysen Group, Livonia, Michigan and Hansen Lind Meyer, P.C., Architects.

Glass washing, which used to be a major problem in food facilities, is now better accomplished through the control of washing, rinsing, and water additives. In many cases it is possible to wash glasses satisfactorily if they are washed shortly after the water has been changed. Other operators may prefer to have a separate glass washer.

Large hotel foodservice operations find it desirable to provide a separate silver room where silverware can be cleaned and polished. The separate silver room provides a better means of control over the expensive silverware.

The design of the dishwashing area is dependent upon the total volume of dinnerware to be washed and the time required to accomplish the washing. Some operations may prefer to carry a large dinnerware inventory in order to spread the washing over a long period of time. This usually occurs between the meal periods. Others may decide to carry a minimum dinnerware inventory and must therefore wash the items as soon as they are soiled so they can be returned to

FIG. 6.9. Dishwashing areas are planned with sufficient space for easy handling of dinnerware.
Courtesy of The Hysen Group, Livonia, Michigan.

service immediately. Regardless of the system to be used, the designer will provide methods of sorting, soaking, washing, and drying of the various dinnerware items. Appropriate handling and storage methods are also devised for both soiled and cleaned dinnerware.

POT AND PAN WASHING

The pot- and pan-washing function is also preferably done in a separate area instead of combining it with other areas as some small operations may be inclined to do. The basic pot- and pan-washing function can be handled with a three-compartment sink and sufficient space for storing the soiled utensils. A typical pot- and pan-washing area is shown in Fig. 6.10.

In some operations, a large storage area for soiled utensils may be required because they are not washed as soon as they are received. This occurs when the same personnel who wash dishes also wash the pots and pans. Pot-washing machines are considered for large food facilities if they can be economically justified.

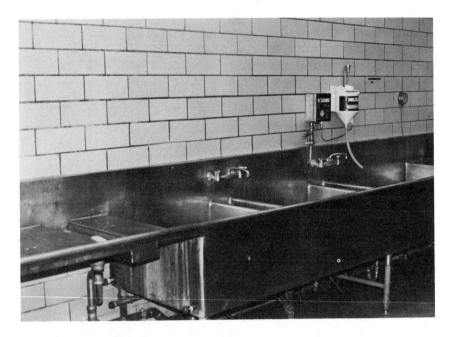

FIG. 6.10. A typical pot- and pan-washing area.

WASTE DISPOSAL

Every foodservice operation has different requirements for waste disposal and many factors should be evaluated before designing a system to handle this function: amount of waste generated, type of waste (paper, plastic, garbage, cans, etc.), cost of hauling and dumping, frequency of pickups, and stricter air and water pollution laws. Some of the waste disposal systems that may be used are described as follows.

1. *Compaction.* The use of compactors is usually considered where large volumes of disposables are to be handled. Compactors quickly reduce the volume of waste so that it can easily be handled in smaller units. The weight of the compacted waste should preferably be less than 50 lb. (22.7 kg) for convenience in handling.

2. *Incineration.* Incinerators can be used to some advantage if the cost of equipment needed to comply with local codes is not prohibitive. Pollution ordinances should be checked for requirements.

3. *Grinding.* Garbage grinding is generally allowed in areas with municipal sewerage systems. However, some communities may not

allow garbage grinding if they experience problems with nonbiodegradable materials such as completely plastic or plastic coated materials.

4. *Pulping.* Waste pulping creates a liquified waste by using heavy-duty rotary grinders with a recirculating water system. The liquified waste is then processed through a water extractor where it is reduced to a semi-dry pulp and then stored in bins. The semi-dry material has very little odor and is trucked away periodically. Metal or glass cannot be handled by a waste pulping system and therefore these materials have to be disposed of separately.

In many cases, different systems for different types of waste will have to be designed. For example, incineration may be used for paper, disposal units for food wastes, and a dumpster for cans, bottles, and other trash.

OTHER REQUIREMENTS

The functional areas discussed can be easily related to space and equipment requirements because of their identification with the flow of materials. Other functional areas that should be considered may not necessarily involve material flow, but are important from the standpoint of total planning. These areas include facilities for guests and employees and special areas such as equipment rooms and maintenance rooms.

The functional planning for a food facility is completed when all the functions and their related tasks have been identified and provisions for efficiently performing them have been outlined. The remaining steps of the planning process will be easier if the functional planning has been correctly and thoroughly accomplished.

PROBLEMS AND EXERCISES

6.1. Prepare a list of functions that are common to foodservice operations performed on a daily basis. Then subdivide each function into more specific areas; for example, the general storage function may be subdivided into storage of meats, dry foods, beverages, linens, silver, and trash.

6.2. Describe the concepts of flow and discuss their importance to a foodservice facility.

6.3. From the list of tasks shown in Appendix E determine the equipment needed for each task that would be performed in the cooking area of a cafeteria operation.

6.4. Select one main entree item from a menu and determine the possible variations of the food materials that may be used in preparing the item.

6.5. Indicate the characteristics of an efficient receiving area for a foodservice facility.

6.6. Discuss the possible differences and similarities between the storage facilities for a fast-food restaurant as compared to a full-service luxury restaurant.

6.7. Select a dinner menu including a meat, vegetable, potato, salad, and dessert and identify the preparation functions involved with each item.

6.8. Determine the advantages and disadvantages of the following types of serving line configurations: (a) straight line, (b) U-shaped, (c) herringbone, and (d) scramble.

6.9. Discuss the requirements of the dishwashing and pot- and pan-washing areas for a table-service restaurant.

BIBLIOGRAPHY

BORSENIK, F.D.   1979.   The Management of Maintenance and Engineering Systems in Hospitality Industries. John Wiley & Sons, New York.

FRESHWATER, J.F. and STECKLER, D.M.   1973.   Evaluation of Dishwashing Systems in Food Service Establishments. Agric. Res. Service, USDA, Beltsville, Maryland.

GRAHAM, H.D.   1980.   The Safety of Foods, 2nd Edition. AVI Publishing Co., Westport, Connecticut.

GUTHRIE, R.K.   1980.   Food Sanitation. AVI Publishing Co., Westport, Connecticut.

HERDMAN, W.E.   1975.   Designing for solid waste disposal: some reminders. Architectural Record 157 (5), 141–144.

KAZARIAN, E.A.   1979.   Work Analysis and Design for Hotels, Restaurants and Institutions. AVI Publishing Co., Westport, Connecticut.

KNIGHT, J. and KOTSCHEVAR, L.H.   1979.   Quantity Food Production, Planning and Management. CBI Publishing Co., Boston, Massachusetts.

MARTIN, L.F.   1982.   Foodservice waste material handling. The Consultant 15 (1), 24–27, 34.

TERRELL, M.E.   1979.   Professional Food Preparation, 2nd Edition. John Wiley & Sons, New York.

THORNER, M.E. and MANNING, P.B.   1983.   Quality Control in Foodservice, Rev. Ed. AVI Publishing Co., Wesport, Connecticut (in press).

TOLVE, A.P.   1984.   Standardizing Foodservice. AVI Publishing Co., Westport, Connecticut.

Planning the Atmosphere

ATMOSPHERE AND MOOD

The atmosphere of foodservice facilities is considered to be the total environment to which customers or users are exposed. Atmosphere is sometimes described as everything that makes an impression on people. It involves more than just the physical environment and decor created by the architect, the foodservice consultant, and the interior designer. Contributing to the concept of atmosphere may be physical aspects such as unusual location, a spectacular view, the method of pouring a drink, or a combination of interior colors, fabrics, spaces and textures, as well as such nonphysical aspects as the attitude of service personnel as exhibited in courtesy, ability, pleasantness, and promptness. The architect, consultants, and designers can develop the physical components of the atmosphere, but it is up to management to provide and maintain its nonphysical components.

Mood is best described as the response of an individual to the various components that make up the atmosphere. Every individual experiences some type of reaction to the atmosphere that may be desirable or undesirable. If the individual response to the foodservice facility is favorable, the atmosphere has served to put that person into a good mood.

Importance

Atmosphere has been identified as one of the inducements for people to dine out. Many people like to be in different surroundings to enjoy the dining experience. In addition to good food and courteous service, the diner is looking for a restaurant that offers luxury or excitement, or at least something pleasant. If customers experience a desirable dining atmosphere, they are more likely to come back because they remember that experience. Atmosphere is one of the prime generators of repeat business and is an important aspect in the successful planning of foodservice facilities.

In the highly competitive commercial restaurant field, the planning of the atmosphere for new facilities is going to be more important. The coming generation of potential customers is growing up in an environment that associates dining out with more than just good food. They will be expecting to experience a variety of feelings, and these feelings will be a direct result of the atmosphere. The planning of atmosphere may well include specialized audiovisual equipment and other electronic devices to help create a particular mood.

Relating Atmosphere to the Customer

Many factors have to be taken into account when planning the atmosphere for a food facility, and they must be considered in light of the clientele who constitute the market. Just as food choice is a matter of individual preference, social custom, income level, needs of time, and so on, the individual's choice of atmosphere is related to many of these same factors. People from varying backgrounds and engaged in different activities will seek out different dining atmospheres. The atmosphere has to be planned to appeal to the particular segment of the market that the foodservice facility wishes to attract. A well-planned restaurant is characterized by both the right menu offerings and the right atmosphere. The most efficiently planned production areas are of little use if there are no customers to serve.

Atmosphere and Marketing Concepts

The foodservice industry continues to be more and more competitive, and the integration of marketing concepts into the creation of the atmosphere is desirable from the standpoint of increasing sales. One approach to this integration is to use attractive displays of food and beverages in the dining areas or lobby and lounge areas. Displays of wines, salads, desserts, or baked goods lend to the creation of a pleasing dining atmosphere as well as help increase the sales of these items. The use of salad bars, dessert carts, carving carts, and refrigerated display cases are some of the methods used to accomplish this integration.

Developing the Atmosphere

Among other things, the atmosphere to be developed for a food facility should attract attention, be pleasing to the eyes, and provide an interesting change of pace (see Fig. 7.1). For example, an intimate, peaceful dining room provides welcome relief from noisy offices and industries. Likewise, a noisy cafeteria may actually be refreshing to students who are in quiet surroundings most of the day. The warmth and glow of a fireplace provides a welcome change in cold weather.

The development of the physical and psychological aspects of the

FIG. 7.1. An appealing atmosphere enhances the image of a foodservice operation.
Courtesy of Multicare Medical Center, Tacoma General Hospital, Tacoma, Washington and The Hysen Group, Livonia, Michigan.

atmosphere depends in great part upon the planners selected to design the facility. They must have a clear understanding with the owner of the particular needs and goals to be accomplished in developing the atmosphere. In addition to knowledge of the functional operation of the facility, the planners should be keenly aware of the type of clientele to be attracted. Only then can they come up with a suitable design that will be attractive as well as functional. It is then up to management to develop the nonphysical aspects of the atmosphere to complete the total concept.

Perceptions of Atmosphere

Comfort is one of the key considerations in atmosphere planning. If individuals do not feel comfortable in their surroundings, the atmosphere has not been properly designed. Comfort is created when individuals feel secure and at ease. Security may be psychologically imposed by the use of red and orange colors and by privacy, which can be provided by booths and partitions. Figure 7.2 shows one way of using dividers to create private areas in the dining room. Dining rooms which have an expensive look may create feelings of insecurity because individuals feel status-conscious in such surroundings.

Atmosphere planning is dependent on an understanding of the perceptual awareness of individuals as sensed through sight, touch, hearing, smell, temperature, and movement. The primary considerations of these perceptions as related to a dining experience are summarized as follows.

Sight.   The perception of visual space involving lighting levels, colors, eye contact with fixtures and decorator items, and the use of mirrors and screens to expand or contract the visual space.

Touch.   Perception of seat comfort, body contact, and contact with floor, tables, tableware, and upholstery fabrics.

Hearing.   Perception of noise levels of conversation, kitchen sounds, outside sounds, and music.

Smell.   Perception of cooking aromas, body odors, and material odors from fabrics such as linen and leather.

Temperature.   Perception of air temperature, relative humidity, body heat, cooking heat, radiant heat, and heat of cooked foods.

FIG. 7.2.   Some individual booths in dining areas provide space for those
seeking privacy.
Courtesy of Pistachios.

Movement.   Perception of muscle activity required for access to tables and chairs, movement of servers and other customers, movement
outside as viewed through windows.

It is important not to think of atmosphere as simply a combination
of colors, lights, and spaces, but how the individual is affected by those
factors. It is the perceptual concepts that should be kept in mind when
developing atmosphere. To clarify the concept of perceptual environment, consider the matter of space. A person's perception of space is
measured more in terms of freedom of movement than in terms of
physical dimensions of feet and inches. A dining room one hundred
feet long means very little to diners. If persons can walk across a
smaller room without encountering obstacles, it will be perceptually
large. On the other hand, if they must make their way around closely

placed tables and chairs, it will be perceptually smaller. This is due to the feeling of crowding when their movements are restricted.

Temperature works in much the same way. It is measured in terms of contrast rather than by degrees on a thermometer. An individual just coming in from the cold will require less heat to perceive a feeling of warmth than someone who has been exposed to a heated room for a long time. The body heat of others is also an interrelated factor in how an individual perceives a crowded condition. Individuals who are in a cooler room may be seated closer together than those who are in a warmer room.

A person's eyes are probably the most important yet deceptive tools of measurement in perceiving feelings. The structure of the eye exaggerates activity or movement that takes place on the periphery of vision. Consequently, individuals can be in an uncrowded room, yet feel as if it is crowded if there is a great deal of action or movement around them. When obstructions are used to block out the activity or movement on the periphery of their vision, they will perceive the area as uncrowded.

Thus, individuals measure the atmosphere with their senses and evaluate it as desirable or undesirable. The atmosphere must be planned so that the individual's perceptions result in a feeling of comfort, ease, and acceptability. With these concepts as a guide, the food facility planner should evaluate the many physical components of atmosphere that can be manipulated and arrive at a combination that will give the desired sensations. Table 7.1 identifies the physical components that affect the perception of atmosphere. Many of these components will be discussed in detail to show their relationships to the design of dining areas.

TABLE 7.1. PHYSICAL COMPONENTS AFFECTING PERCEPTION OF ATMOSPHERE

(1) Colors
(2) Illumination
(3) Noise
(4) Ambient temperature, relative humidity, odors
(5) Type of seating (tables, booths, counters)
(6) Furnishings; floor and wall coverings, drapes
(7) Table appointments; dishware, silverware, napkins
(8) Shape and size of rooms
(9) Layout of tables
(10) Appearance and dress of employees
(11) Menu design
(12) Sanitary conditions
(13) Exterior design
(14) Landscaping
(15) Age and dress of customers

COLOR

Color is one of the visual aspects of the atmosphere as perceived by individuals; it is also one of the best tools that planners have to create a variety of moods. Most people make a number of choices based on color; they select their clothes, cars, houses, paints, and even foods by color. Color can be used to induce a feeling of happiness, to promote serenity, or to stimulate hunger. It can attract people to one type of dining room and drive them out of others. Certain colors are especially important to the development of dining areas.

Effects on Individuals

Many experiments have shown that certain colors have a very strong emotional effect on most individuals. It is known that blue reduces excitability and therefore helps one to relax. Blue is also considered to be cooling and is "easy" on the eyes. Green is a color that acts as a sedative. Yellow, on the other hand, is cheery, stimulating, and attention-drawing. On dull, sunless days, people exhibit mental and physical sluggishness which is partially attributed to the absence of yellow, red, and other stimulating colors. Red is associated with excitement and violence. Gray suggests coldness and is very depressing unless it is combined with livelier colors.

Color sensations can sometimes produce physical reactions that are not just of the visual system but affect the entire body. For example, persons exposed to predominately red colors exhibit increased blood pressure, quickened muscular reactions, and greater emotions. Red also tends to produce restlessness and makes time seem to pass very slowly. In comparison, persons exposed to predominately blue and green colors have been found to exhibit slower muscle response and quicker mental and conversational response. Blues and greens also make time seem to go faster. Some of the common emotional responses caused by exposure to various colors are summarized in Table 7.2. These may be used to develop the type of response desired in

TABLE 7.2. EMOTIONAL RESPONSES TO COLORS

Color	Effect
Red	Excites, stimulates
Orange	Exhilarates
Yellow	Stimulates, boosts morale
Green	Imparts serenity and tranquility
Blue	Lends liberation and leisure
Purple	Creates graciousness and elegance
Brown	Relaxes

various areas of the food facility. The colors have to be predominant in an area and individuals must be exposed to them for a period of time.

Color Characteristics

Because of the strong effect colors may have on individuals, care should be taken in selecting them to achieve the desired result. One of the aspects of good color planning deals with contrast. A single predominant color, no matter how pleasing, cannot function alone. A restful green that is predominant would strain the part of the eye susceptible to it and eventually lead to eye and body fatigue. With a single predominant color individuals would have to look harder to distinguish objects because of the lack of contrast. Extreme contrast between very light and dark colors is also undesirable since they too result in eyestrain.

In general, the desired degree of contrast can be obtained by using the following guides.

Use a light color with a darker version of the same color. Pink and red result in a desirable contrast that is not fatiguing.

Use a weak chroma of a color with a stronger chroma of the same color. A pale blue and a royal blue illustrate this combination of colors.

Use a warm color with a cool color.

Use complementary colors such as peach and gray-blue or pale pink and dull green.

Achieving the right amount of contrast along with maintaining the desired emotional responses is necessary to the creation of a pleasing environment for dining. Many of these color recommendations can be used in other areas of the facility.

Color Classifications

Red, yellow, and blue are the primary colors. They are referred to as primaries because other colors are derived from them. In their pure form the primary colors are too strong to use on large areas and therefore are used as accents.

The secondary colors are green, orange, and violet and are mixtures of two of the primary colors. Green is obtained by mixing blue and yellow, orange by mixing red and yellow, and violet by mixing red

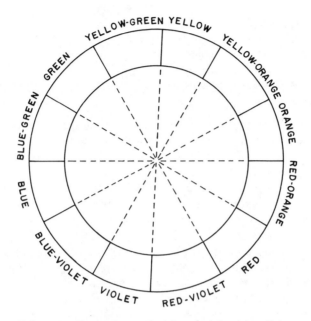

FIG. 7.3. The color wheel is used for identifying primary, secondary, and intermediate colors.

and blue. Mixtures of primary colors and secondary colors result in the intermediate colors. Examples of intermediates are red-orange, yellow-green, and blue-violet. The primary, secondary, and intermediate colors are shown on a color wheel, as illustrated in Fig. 7.3.

Colors are also classified as warm or cool. Red, orange, and yellow are the warm colors; they seem to advance and convey a feeling of warmth. The cool colors are blue, green, and violet; these are retracting colors and are cooling and relaxing. A combination of one warm color and one cool color results in the complementary colors used in color planning.

Color Harmonies

The problem of selecting colors that go well together or harmonize is solved by using one of five rules. These rules are related to harmonies and are identified as monochromatic, analogous, complementary, split complementary, and triad.

Monochromatic harmony uses a single color and is the simplest of color schemes. The single color can be expressed in the following ways.

As the pure color itself

As a tint of the pure color (a tint is the pure color mixed with white)

As a shade of the pure color (a shade is the pure color mixed with black)

As a tone of the pure color (a tone is the pure color mixed with both black and white).

Analogous harmony is obtained by using any three or four consecutive colors on the color wheel. Examples of analogous harmony are red-orange, orange, and yellow-orange; or red, red-orange, orange, and yellow-orange.

Complementary harmony results by using any two colors that are directly opposite each other on the color wheel. Red and green, red-orange and blue-green, or yellow and violet are examples of complementary harmony.

Split complementary or near complementary harmony involves three colors. Any one of the two complementary colors and two colors adjacent to the omitted complementary color are used. On the color wheel, the split complementaries are in the form of a Y. Examples of split complementary colors are yellow, blue-violet, and red-violet; green, red-orange, and red-violet; and red, blue-green, and yellow-green.

Triad harmony also involves three colors. These are selected by taking every fourth color on the color wheel. Two examples of triads are red, yellow, and blue; and yellow-orange, red-violet, and blue-green.

After a particular harmony is selected, then a decision regarding the tints, shades, or tones of the colors is made. One or two of the colors selected will be used for the walls and other major surfaces. The other colors will be used as accents on smaller objects like drapes, table cloths, and dinnerware.

The important points in color selection are as follows:

Pure colors are usually too strong and brilliant when applied to large areas or surfaces.

Colors should be selected under the kind of lighting that they will be used under. Colors selected under fluorescent lighting will appear different under incandescent lighting.

Colors selected from a small sample will appear brighter when applied to large areas.

Complementary, split complementary, and triad harmonies always result in a combination of warm and cool colors. The desired atmosphere will dictate which color is to predominate.

Black, white, brown, and gold usually go well with any of the color harmonies.

Texture is closely related to color application and usage is best considered at the same time the color choices are made.

Lighting and Color

As light modifies colors in many ways, the type of light source and systems of lighting should be considered when selecting colors. Pink lights, for example, have been shown to pale lipstick colors. Green lights have a tendency to show up wrinkles and should not be used in an atmosphere where a feeling of well-being is to be created. Another problem is the use of amber lights which tend to wash out colors. A well-chosen color scheme can be easily spoiled by poorly selected lights.

Lights and colors for work areas are quite different from those desirable for dining areas and should be planned separately.

Color Planning for Food Facilities

The uses of color in foodservice facilities are so numerous that space will not allow a complete presentation of all of them. Therefore, a guide to the uses of color is presented in Table 7.3. Note that many of the uses of color are related to other factors that affect an individual's perception of atmosphere.

TABLE 7.3. GUIDE TO COLOR USAGE IN FOODSERVICE FACILITIES

(1) The use of warm reds, browns, yellows, golds, and oranges enhances the appearance of foods.
(2) Where emphasis is to be placed on fast service and high turnover, warm colors should dominate the major areas.
(3) Use colors in dining areas that are flattering to people. Colors that tend to make people look pale (green and grey) should be avoided.
(4) Use light colors in small areas to create the impression of size.
(5) Use warm colors in rooms that are windowless.
(6) High ceilings can be made to appear lower by using dark colors.
(7) Emphasizing horizontal lines by dark colors will make a ceiling appear lower.
(8) Low ceilings can be overcome by emphasizing vertical lines with dark colors.
(9) The end walls of long narrow rooms should be a warmer or deeper hue than the other walls to make them approach and make the room seem squarer.
(10) Undesirable features of a room can be painted the same color as their background so as not to emphasize them.
(11) Each room or area should have a mixture of warm and cool colors.
(12) Adjoining rooms or areas are best painted in harmonious colors.
(13) Avoid using too many different colors in one room or area.
(14) Use light colors to make objects appear larger if they are to be emphasized.
(15) Use dark colors to make rooms appear smaller.
(16) Use brilliant colors to bring attention to signs or other features.
(17) Dark-colored objects appear to be smaller than they really are.
(18) Maintain proper contrast to permit differentiation of objects from their backgrounds.
(19) Avoid highly reflective colors that tend to tire the eyes.

The selection of colors is a very difficult task that requires skill, taste, and experience. Color scheming does not end with the blending of wall colors with upholstery, fabrics, and carpets, but includes the considerations of menus, dinnerware, uniforms, and even the type of decorations. Just as the right colors can be used to make a food facility more attractive, the wrong colors can focus attention on features that should not be accented. Also, since color is so influenced by fashion and trend, these factors must be considered in the color scheme chosen.

LIGHTING

As mentioned previously, color and lighting are interrelated and it is difficult to discuss them separately. It is therefore important to recall some of the fundamentals of color when thinking in terms of lighting. As with color, proper planning of lights can achieve dramatic effects and aid in the creation of the desired atmosphere.

Both sexes enjoy a type of lighting that makes them look their best. This factor is of great importance in the planning and design of lights for dining areas, bars, rest rooms, and other public spaces.

The best system of lighting for restaurants appears to be a combination of indirect, direct, and spot lights. These lights can be arranged to accomplish the desired flexibility required for the various meal periods. Areas should be well lit for breakfast and lunch, while less lighting is desired for evening meals. The installation of rheostats will provide this flexibility.

In considering the lighting system, the amount of daylight entering an area should be considered. Total glass area can be specified by the architect to adjust for this factor. The use of tinted glass may be considered for some situations.

Type of Lighting

The ultimate type of lighting for dining areas has traditionally been considered to be candlelight. The reddish flame of candlelight is flattering to people and to most foods. The flickering of the flame adds to the creation of a desirable atmosphere.

Alternatives to candlelight are incandescent and fluorescent lights. The economy of operation of fluorescent lights favors their installation in large areas. Incandescent lights would be the best choice in dining areas because of their red color enhancement. Properly selected fluorescent lights may also be used in dining areas if sufficient red tones are used in the color scheme. The deluxe warm white fluorescent tubes are the closest in color tint to incandescent bulbs and would be recommended.

Uses of Lights

As with color, lighting can do much toward creating atmosphere by correcting spacial deficiencies and accenting desirable areas. To illustrate, a low ceiling can be made to appear higher if it is well-lit; high ceilings will appear lower if they are dimly lit. Care should be taken not to light the long walls brightly in a narrow room since it will appear to be even narrower. Dark walls will show up better with bright lights, and if the color is to be accented, the illumination level has to be high. Bright lights are placed above normal eye levels to minimize glare. The same concept applies to candles since they too can create glare. Candles may be placed in frosted globes if they are at eye level or slightly below.

In dining areas, it is best to concentrate illumination on the seats and tables and perhaps on special design features. The ceilings and walls should not be so brightly lit that they detract attention from the room.

Bright lights may be used to create a brisk atmosphere which, if service is fast, results in a high turnover of customers. Serving areas, as illustrated in Fig. 7.4, should be well-lighted. Some operations may use full lighting for a high turnover at lunch and then dim the lights for evening meals in hopes of attaining higher check averages.

Colored Lights

A popular design trend is to use various-colored lights for foodservice facilities. Careful selection of colored lights will enhance the total atmosphere. The first consideration is to coordinate the colored lights with other colored objects and color schemes used in the room. This is important, since certain colors will take on strange off-colors when subjected to colored lights. Red colors will appear very dark under blue or green lights and olive-green colors look brown under yellow lights.

Colored lights affect the appearance of the faces and clothes of people. Red lights have the advantage of flattering complexions and tend to enhance the color of fabrics. Red lights also have a good effect on most foods.

FIG. 7.4.   A well-lit serving area helps increase the serving rate.
Courtesy of The Ford Motor Company, Dearborn, Michigan and The Hysen Group, Livonia, Michigan.

Green and blue lights are undesirable for illuminating areas where people will be present. These lights tend to distort the red hues and are unflattering because of this. Green and blue lights may be used for inanimate objects that serve as accent pieces.

The use of pink, ivory, or amber lights is suggested for areas where skin tone is important, as they are warm and impart a friendly and inviting feeling. It is better to use tints of colors rather than strong hues.

Lighting Levels

Lighting should not only provide atmosphere but should reach a satisfactory level of illumination from a practical standpoint. If the lighting level is too high, individuals will have a feeling of exposure; or if too dim, they may feel fearful. For these reasons, there should be enough light so persons can see, yet not so much that they feel uneasy. One method of attaining such an arrangement is to lower the height of ceiling fixtures, as shown in Fig. 7.5. This provides a suffi-

FIG. 7.5. Lowering ceiling fixtures enables people to see their food without significantly increasing the general lighting level.
Courtesy of Sheraton Inn, Lansing, Michigan.

cient amount of light and at the same time results in a comfortable soft effect.

Foodservice lighting levels typically will range between 5 and 50 foot-candles (53.8–538 lux), with 30–50 foot-candles (323–538 lux) usually used for breakfast and lunch. A level of 5–30 foot-candles (53.8–323 lux), depending on the atmosphere desired, is used for evening meals. Public traffic areas and stairs, as shown in Fig. 7.6, will require a minimum of 30 foot-candles (323 lux).

The lighting level in all areas must be sufficient to make the other elements of the atmosphere visible. It is senseless to spend a great deal of time and money creating a striking color scheme and then ruin it with poor lighting. Any area with less than 5 foot-candles (53.8 lux) of illumination may as well be colorless.

Placement of Lights

The light most complimentary to human faces is from a source that is at eye level or slightly below. High light angles produce grotesque facial shadows by deepening eye sockets and showing every wrinkle and hollow in the skin. The traditional table lamp and table candles

FIG. 7.6. Lighting levels at stairways are important in preventing accidents.
Courtesy of Riverside Methodist Hospital, Columbus, Ohio and The Hysen Group, Livonia, Michigan.

are recommended because their position as a light source is ideal. The light source should not be bright enough to cause glare.

One misconception about lighting is that it should be shadowless. In reality, the excitement of good lighting comes largely from its shadows and variations in brightness. Flat, shadowless lighting is dull and monotonous. The general lighting system for an area needs the accents of bright areas which come from direct light sources. These may take the form of wall brackets, chandeliers, downlights, or spot lights. Recessed ceiling downlights of low intensity are very satisfactory for lighting dining areas. They emphasize the table areas and are very pleasant to the eyes.

ACOUSTICS, NOISE, AND MUSIC

Other physical components of atmosphere are the level of noise and type of sounds present. The acoustical environment for the facility should be planned so the individual is not aware of noise. Aside from dinner music, sounds are to play a passive role and never attract attention. The design goal is to create a balance between quiet and noise. Many people are uncomfortable in a room which is very quiet. A noisy room creates tension and irritability. For dining rooms, a satisfactory acoustical environment has a reverberant sound level that is high enough to be heard, but not so high that individuals at nearby tables can distinguish what is being said.

Correct planning for the acoustical environment contributes to the development of the desired atmosphere. The sensitivities of individuals to various sounds require control of undesirable noise and maintenance of desirable sounds at an acceptable level.

Sound Characteristics

Sound may be considered to be a pressure wave and is compared to the ripples spreading out from a pebble dropped in water. If the sound is not restricted, it will spread out in all directions. The speed of sound in air is about 1100 feet per second (335 meters per second). Any sounds produced in open air will travel directly from the source to the listener. In a room, however, sound is reflected from the walls, floor, and ceiling and can build up a general sound level much greater than that which results from the same source in open space. Sounds that are repeatedly reflected become noise or unwanted sounds. Noise at a high enough level causes irritation and fatigue. It can interfere with communication and concentration and become very distracting and disturbing.

The intensity of sound is measured by the decibel. A sound intensity of one decibel is at the threshold of audibility for the normal human ear. A sound intensity of 20 decibels may be compared to a whisper. The normal speaking voice has an intensity of about 60 decibels. Any sound intensities over 100 decibels for any length of time are undesirable, and constant exposure can cause partial loss of hearing.

When there is a source of sound in a room, the level of noise at any position is made up of two parts. The first part is the direct sound traveling straight from the source to the position under consideration. The second part is the reverberant sound, which is the sound reaching the position after multiple reflection from the room surfaces. Fig. 7.7 illustrates these two different parts of sound.

The intensity of direct sound falls off as the distance from the source increases. Direct sound is reduced by about 6 decibels each time the distance from the source is doubled. Reverberant sound levels will generally be at a uniform intensity throughout the room. Direct sounds

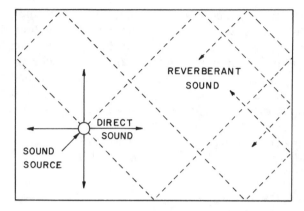

FIG. 7.7. Direct and reverberant sound in a room.

are predominant at positions close to the source, while reverberant sounds will dominate positions remote from the source.

Noise Control

The problem of controlling noise levels is basically a matter of suppressing the sounds from the source or reducing the amount of reverberant sounds. Sound-absorbing materials are used to minimize both types of sounds. In some instances, the source of the sounds can be isolated by coverings or baffles. Kitchen areas are very difficult to sound-proof because of the materials used in the construction of the room and the large amount of metallic equipment present. Hard, dense materials, like quarry tile or clay tile used for kitchen floors and tiled wall surfaces, reflect a large portion of the sound striking them. Stainless steel surfaces actually act as sound surfaces much like a drum. In these areas, it is desirable to increase the amount of sound-absorbing materials as much as possible to overcome the severe noise problem.

Service doors leading to the kitchen can be vestibuled to reduce the noise level before reaching the dining room. This is a compromise between the additional square footage needed for the vestibule and the desirability of reduced noise levels. Thus a facility designed for professionals may include a vestibule while a facility to be designed for other segments of the market may not consider one.

Additional things that can be done to minimize noise from the kitchen include the following:

1. Selecting mechanical equipment such as fans and compressors for quiet operation.
2. Using installation techniques that minimize duct noises, the sound of water flow, and water hammer.
3. Using silent closing devices on doors and drawers.
4. Providing rubber bumpers for mobile equipment.
5. Soundproofing walls between kitchen and dining areas.
6. Placing a service station between the entrance to the kitchen and the dining room.
7. Creating a quiet work environment to reduce employee noise.
8. Using the spread load dishwashing concept where an adequate inventory of china, silverware, and glassware are maintained to handle the entire meal period. Dishwashing begins after the meal period to clean the dinnerware for the next meal period. This concept has several ramifications in terms of soiled and clean dish storage requirements, dishwasher size, impact on employee scheduling, and the total size of the dishwashing area.

In addition to acoustical treatment of walls and ceilings, carpeting where permitted will also help. Local sanitarians should be consulted before specifying carpet for production areas. The sound-proofing of metal surfaces by undercoating will reduce the noise created. One method of handling noise problems in dining areas is to vary the spacing of tables. The distance between diners at one table should be appreciably less than the distance to diners at adjoining tables. If a greater density of seating is desired, the use of screens or partial partitions will reduce the sound levels. Bar areas tend to be noisy and can be partially partitioned.

Music

The use of music as a desirable sound is one way of enhancing the audible environment. Music has a direct effect on the mood of individuals. Background music should be selected so it does not attract attention. It should be soft, inoffensive, and as characterless as possible. The correct use of background music can put customers in a good mood for dining.

CLIMATE CONTROL

Climate is another facet of atmosphere planning that merits careful consideration. It is one of the important factors affecting the comfort of people. Most individuals are very sensitive to thermodynamic phenomena and variations from an ideal climate are easily noticed and quickly lead to discomfort. Customers will quickly respond to environmental conditions that are too hot, too cold, too drafty, too stuffy, or too damp.

The ideal climate for dining consists of temperatures between 70 and 75°F (21.1 and 23.9°C) with a relative humidity of 50%. Thermodynamic comfort is a function of activity and other factors such as age, sex, and the amount of clothing worn. Needless to say, the climate should be designed for the particular type of patron that the facility is to be planned for. Higher-priced operations will usually attract people who are accustomed to slightly higher temperatures. Women prefer higher temperatures than men, and children require less heat than both men and women. People who are in active occupations prefer lower temperatures.

The amount of clothing worn during the different seasons reflects the needs of different temperatures. People will be wearing lighter clothing in the summer; therefore, slightly warmer than normal temperatures would be appreciated. Clothing worn in the winter is heavier and temperatures should not be allowed to get too high. The effects of colors and lighting are evaluated before a particular temperature level is decided upon.

Temperature can be used to some extent to affect a desired turnover of customers. Many fast-food operations may want lower temperatures to keep the customers on the move and thereby increase the turnover rate. The opposite is true in more luxurious dining rooms where turnover is not stressed. Customers are inclined to be more relaxed in a higher temperature, and the warmth is conducive to a leisurely meal of several courses. The ideal design is to have a system where the temperature can be precisely adjusted for the particular situation.

Climate control in most regions requires both heating and air conditioning. The systems should have sufficient capacity to maintain the desired temperature and relative humidity. Air inlets and outlets should be placed to avoid drafts.

Odors

Climate control also includes the control of odors. Odors are an important part of the atmosphere, because smell usually evokes much deeper memories in individuals than either vision or sound. People are often uncomfortable in odor-free surroundings, and pleasant odors can contribute to the desired atmosphere. The popularity of display cooking areas in the dining room is partially caused by the cooking aromas that are emitted.

Odors have to be controlled or they will blend and can become quite offensive. This is very noticeable in dining areas where the air circulation system may bring in varied kitchen odors. Mixing the odors of fish and steak, for example, is not at all appealing to the person eating the steak. Odors are very disturbing to individuals when dining because taste is largely a matter of smell. If the odors cannot be controlled and separated, or if they are undesirable, they should not be allowed to seep into the dining room. One method of accomplishing this is to maintain the air pressure in the dining room at a higher level than the air pressure in the kitchen.

Exhaust systems designed to rid the interiors of smoke, fumes, and odors should be positioned to avoid affecting the immediate exterior environment. This is especially important for exterior walks and entrances into the public areas.

FURNISHINGS

Furnishings for the dining area are also correlated to the type of atmosphere to be planned. The first thing that an individual does upon entering a dining room is to look for a place to sit. Therefore, arrangement of tables, chairs, and auxiliary furnishings does much to affect the initial impression of customers. Many people do not like to sit at exposed tables because they feel observed. This problem is overcome by the use of booths or by planters that act as partitions. Changes in elevation, as illustrated in Fig. 7.8, can also be planned to break up large exposed areas.

Tables and Chairs

Tables, chairs, and banquettes should be large enough to seat diners comfortably without crowding. Distances between tables are sized to enable waiters or waitresses to move through the area while serving and allow diners to eat and converse without being distracted.

Selection of chairs is critical since the greatest body contact is made with them. Chairs must have suitable shape, angle of seat and back, size, relationship to table, and tactile qualities to be comfortable. The chairs shown in Fig. 7.9 are suited for luxurious dining. The essential dimensions for comfortable chairs are shown in Fig. 7.10.

FIG. 7.8.   Large areas can be broken up by changes in elevation.
Courtesy of Kellogg Center, Michigan State University.

Table space of at least 26 in. (660 mm) should be allowed for chairs without arms to provide elbow room. Armchairs require a minimum table space of 28 in. (711 mm) for comfort. The preferred height of chair seats is 17 to 18 in. (432 to 457 mm), for adults. A minimum of 12 in. (305 mm) of space is needed between the top of the chair and the bottom of the table.

The shape of the table should be considered in relation to the dining mood to be created. Round tables, for example, tend to promote communications among the diners and may result in a lower turnover but higher check averages. Square or rectangular tables tend to increase turnover and are more efficient in the use of dining space.

Counter seating can be used to accommodate single customers and also increase turnover rates. Combinations of tables, booths, banquettes, and counters are frequently planned to appeal to a variety of market segments.

Cashier areas should be placed for ease of access and in consideration of flow patterns. Bars, buffets, wine displays, or other merchan-

FIG. 7.9.   Comfortable chairs and tables contribute to a pleasant dining atmosphere.
Courtesy of Imperial Garden.

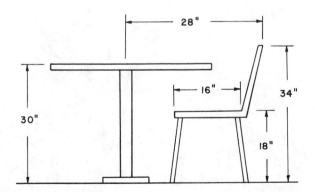

FIG. 7.10.   Basic dimensions for comfortable seating.

dising setups are placed for maximum visibility and exposure to the customers.

Drapes and Fabrics

The selection of drapes, carpeting, and fabrics is guided by the need for variations in textures, colors, and shapes. These materials may be chosen to blend with or contrast with the architectural features of the building (see Fig. 7.11).

Drapes and floor coverings are selected to give an overall appearance of unity and balance. Various fabrics are selected to add warmth and coziness to a room and to relieve any monotony in the shape of the room. Fabrics contribute not only by their visual impact, but by the fact that they are more pleasant to touch than hard surfaces. Designers may use grass wallpapers, ceramic tile, cork, linen, silk, brick, and other materials that are textured and appealing for wall coverings. Carpeting adds a feeling of intimacy and comfort because it is a point of contact.

FIG. 7.11. Blending design elements with architectural features.
Courtesy of Rita St. Clair Assoc., Inc.

Pictures

Pictures and prints used to decorate wall areas add considerably to the atmosphere. An advantage in using these items is that they can be easily changed. The pictures selected should not clash with the decorative scheme. The shape and size are correlated to the walls on which they will be placed. Colors within the pictures or on frames should blend with the overall scheme of the room to give a coordinated appearance.

Table Settings

Table settings can enhance the appeal of the dining atmosphere. Customers notice the tableware they are using and will thus form an impression of the restaurant. Each item placed on the table is selected to add to the feeling and mood to be created in the room. This pertains to dishes, glasses, silver, napkins, and tablecloths.

EXTERIOR DESIGN

The term exterior, as used in food facilities design, is taken to include signs, landscaping, parking areas, building structure, doors, and windows. The objective of exterior design is to attract customers. To perform this function effectively, the exterior must convey the correct impression of the type of food facility into which the customer is being invited. Exterior design, as illustrated in Fig. 7.12, has to be coordinated with interior design to provide the total atmosphere.

Visibility

One problem to be dealt with in exterior design is the matter of attracting initial attention. This is a problem of visibility as seen through the eyes of pedestrians and people in slow- or fast-moving cars. An attractive sign, large enough for the situation, is generally accepted as the best method of attracting attention. The placement of the sign must ensure that drivers are aware of the facility before it appears in view. In some locations, signs may have to be placed at considerable distances from the building. The most effective signs are those that are short and to the point.

Attraction is also gained by the exterior treatment of the building.

FIG. 7.12.   Design of exterior areas has to be coordinated with the interior design of the foodservice facility.
Courtesy of Imperial Garden.

This includes the size, shape, colors, and materials used in construction. The first impression of an interior of a facility is gained from the exterior. This impression is derived not solely by the exterior design but from glimpses of the interior that are provided by windows. Windows are so located as to frame the parts of the interior that they expose.

Exterior Color and Lighting

The aspects of color and lighting were discussed earlier in connection with creating the interior atmosphere. They have as great an importance in the design of the exterior of the facility. Color and lights can be used in signs, facades, building elements, and landscaping.

Color usage on the exterior can follow the same general guidelines presented for interior use. An additional consideration is to let any natural landscaping provide much of the color. In this case, the building elements can be finished as plainly as possible so as not to compete.

Floodlighting is frequently used with success when the architectural features of the exterior are appealing or dramatic. Care must be used in sizing and placing windows in floodlighted areas to prevent glare into the building.

Decorative Detail

The amount and kind of decorative detail used on the building exterior is chosen to reflect the total atmosphere concept of the foodservice facility. Some designers may prefer to rely on the elegance of simplicity and use little, if any, decorative detailing. On the other hand, facilities with perhaps a national theme may require carefully selected exterior details to complete the concept of total atmosphere.

Parking Areas

The planning of parking lots and areas is important in creating the right impression with the customers. The ease of entering and leaving the parking lot as well as the individual parking space is critical to good design. Consideration should also be given to the placement of walkways from the parking lot to the building.

The locations of exterior trash and garbage containers have to be selected carefully. It may be desirable to sacrifice a parking space or two to give special treatment to these undesirable areas. The customers' first impression of a foodservice facility as they leave their cars should not be the sights and smells of trash and garbage. Management should stress the cleanliness of exterior areas at all times.

Entrances

The entrance door to the facility can form the climax of the exterior attractiveness. It should be selected in accord with the overall design of the building exterior. Doors may be all glass, half glass, wood, or metal, plain or with panels. Separate entrances to the bar are provided if the bar will be used by nondiners. Entrance doors are located for easy access from streets or parking areas.

Whether to provide an entrance area or not is largely a matter of choice. An entrance area can have several desirable functions: it can convey a sense of spaciousness and enhance the atmosphere. Entrance areas also provide a meeting place for people and can be used as waiting space during rush hours.

Landscaping

Although maintenance of landscaped areas is costlier than of blacktop or gravel, a well-landscaped exterior may overcome the added cost by attracting more customers. Landscaping provides the setting for the facility. Another use of landscaping is to hide undesirable service areas or views from dining areas that are not pleasant.

The landscape architect may use contours, plant textures, heights, rocks, pathway surfaces, or garden furniture to achieve the desired exterior appearance. In laying out the landscape, important views are selected and foregrounds and backgrounds are developed for them. The landscaping must harmonize with the exterior features of the building so that a good impression is created from all angles of view.

PERSONNEL

The atmosphere for foodservice facilities is created for people who want to be satisfied by that environment. In the long run, people will be more influenced by the employees that they come in contact with than by anything else. The importance of retaining good employees and keeping them in a pleasant mood cannot be underestimated as a vital part of the atmosphere. A cold welcome, poor service, or indifferent attitude can ruin all the friendliness which the color, lighting, decor, and furnishings have created. These physical components of the atmosphere are ineffective unless they are complemented by the human components.

The projection of atmosphere is carried to the point of selecting uniforms for waitresses, bartenders, bus boys, and other personnel. The style and colors of uniforms are an integral part of the decor and add a touch of personality.

ADVERTISING AND PUBLIC RELATIONS

The atmosphere created for a facility is reflected by its name, the advertising, public relations efforts, brochures, signs, and menus. Choosing a name is important to promotional materials to be used. The name and design concepts should be interrelated. The best names to use are those that are simple, easy to remember, easy to spell and pronounce, and are distinctive and reflective of the character of the food facility. The name will logically be the main feature in advertising and public relations.

The importance of menu design as a component of the atmosphere is frequently overlooked. The menu is the silent salesman for the restaurant and is designed to reflect many aspects of atmosphere. The descriptions of foods, lettering style, arrangement, colors, materials, and size are involved in menu design. The design of display menus as shown in Fig. 7.13 is a part of the development of the atmosphere.

The design of the atmosphere for a successful restaurant is a very complex problem involving many factors. The additional efforts taken

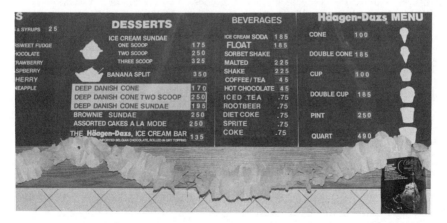

FIG. 7.13.   Design of display menus is a part of planning the atmosphere.
Courtesy of Häagen-Dazs, East Lansing, Michigan.

to develop the right atmosphere are justified by customer reaction and acceptance of the facility.

PROBLEMS AND EXERCISES

7.1. Identify some of the nonphysical aspects of the atmosphere for a foodservice facility.

7.2. Compare and contrast the specific aspects of what the perceived atmosphere should be for (a) a fast-food restaurant, (b) a luxury table-service restaurant and (c) an employee cafeteria.

7.3. Give two examples of each of the following color harmonies: (a) monochromatic harmony, (b) analogous harmony, (c) complementary harmony, (d) split complementary harmony, and (e) triad harmony.

7.4. Describe the color combinations and lighting that would be used to decorate a fast-food restaurant.

7.5. Indicate the color combinations and lighting that would be used to decorate a lounge.

7.6. Discuss how acoustics, noise, and music may affect the perceived atmosphere of a formal table-service restaurant.

7.7. Discuss why the exterior design of a foodservice facility is equally as important as the interior design.

BIBLIOGRAPHY

BACKUS, H.　1977.　Designing Restaurant Interiors: A Guide for Foodservice Operators. Lebhar-Friedman Co., New York.

DAVERN, J.M.　1976.　Places for People. McGraw-Hill Book Co., New York.

GIAMPIETRO, F.N.　1977.　Shed some light on your illumination. Restaurant Business 76 (7), 79–83.

HALSE, A.O.　1978.　The Use of Color in Interiors. McGraw-Hill Book Co., New York.

HOPKINS, R.　1983.　Light. The Consultant 16 (4), 34–37.

KAZARIAN, E.A.　1984.　Color. Independent Restaurants 46 (3), 40–42.

KAZARIAN, E.A.　1984.　Controlling noise helps create a pleasant dining atmosphere. Independent Restaurants 46 (4), 28.

MOTTO, M.　1970.　Profit by design. Cornell Hotel Restaurant Admin. Q. 11 (1), 113–117.

LIBSCOMB, D.M. and TAYLOR, A.C. (Editors).　1978.　Noise Control: Handbook of Principles and Practices. Van Nostrand Reinhold Co., New York

PLANK, R.W.　1978.　Design: the new ingredient in foodservice. Restaurant Hospitality 14 (7), 41–46.

VILADAS, P.　1981.　Interiors Book of Shops and Restaurants. Watson-Guptill Publications, New York.

WEXLER, D.　1978.　Feast for the eyes: visual marketing pays off. Institutions 83 (3), 15–20.

WILKINSON, J. (Editor).　1972.　Special Atmosphere Themes for Food Service. Cahners Books, Boston, Massachusetts.

YERGES, L.F.　1978.　Sound, Noise and Vibration Control. Van Nostrand Reinhold Co., New York

8

Workplace Design

DEVELOPING WORKPLACES

One of the steps in planning a foodservice facility for maximum efficiency and productivity is the design of the workplaces. Workplaces are identified as the location and facilities where one or more employees can perform their respective tasks. The design of workplaces includes determining the necessary floor space, work surface space (see Fig. 8.1), storage space, and necessary equipment. As emphasized earlier, identification of the tasks that must be accomplished is one of the first steps in planning a restaurant. At this point in the planning process, a further evaluation of the tasks is needed. Decisions regarding the specific materials required and the work methods to be used are finalized. Questions to be resolved include the following.

Who will do the task?
Will the task be done manually?
Where will the task be done?
What are the form, shape, and characteristics of the materials?
What hand tools will be required?
What kinds of utensils will be used?
What type of equipment is needed?
What is the best work pattern to use?
How will the materials be brought to and removed from the workplace?
What must be stored at the workplace?

One method of systematically deciding some of these questions is by a detailed analysis of the menu. This involves taking a typical menu and evaluating each of the items listed. The menu analysis may

FIG. 8.1.   Work surface space for certain tasks involved in baking requires special design.

be done by using the format illustrated in Table 8.1. The use of standard recipes for each menu item is very helpful in completing this analysis.

The menu analysis will identify the workplaces needed to produce the food items only. Workplaces for processing nonfood items are developed by a similar analysis of the tasks required for processing the various items. This will enable the planner to develop workplaces for dishwashing, pot and pan washing, linen sorting, and can washing,

TABLE 8.1.   MENU ANALYSIS FOR WORKPLACE DESIGN

Menu item	Portion size	Total portions	Materials req'd.	Process req'd.	Utensils needed	Hand tools	Work surface	Equipment req'd.
1.								
2.								
3.								

to name a few. Similarly, the processing of paperwork will lead to the development of workplaces for purchasing, inventorying, personnel management, and cost control tasks.

Having accumulated the desired information, the designer will develop the workplaces by providing for the following areas:

Adequate floor space for the worker to move around in.

Working surface space for the task; this may take the form of a work table, a counter surface, or in some cases a piece of equipment used for working surface space.

Space for temporary storage of incoming materials. Incoming materials may be placed on tables or carts, in tote pans, or on specially designed equipment. Soiled dish tables are illustrative of the type of space needed.

Space for temporary storage of finished products. Examples of this type of storage are salad carts, hot food-holding equipment, mobile shelf units, and even conveyors. A mobile cart for holding trays of salads as shown in Fig. 8.2 is a versatile piece of equipment.

FIG. 8.2. Mobile carts provide storage for food items.
Courtesy of Martin Marietta Aerospace, Orlando, Florida and The Hysen Group, Livonia, Michigan.

Space for storage of frequently used minor materials and ingredients. Seasonings, condiments, dressings, and sauces may be stored in special containers at the workplace.

Space for hand tools required for the task.

Space for the floor-mounted or free-standing equipment required for processing.

A brief description with recommendations for designing the workplaces for general foodservice operations will be given. Different designs may have to be developed for special operations that have special requirements.

Floor Space

The floor space required for a worker to accomplish manual tasks is frequently referred to as work aisle space. Work aisles are separated from traffic aisles as much as possible to assure minimum interference with the worker. The amount of space required for a single-person work aisle varies from 24 to 36 in. (610 to 914 mm). A 24 in. (610 mm) work aisle is the bare minimum and would not be suitable for tasks that require bending and stooping, or where equipment components like doors and controls extend into the aisle. A 30 in. (762 mm) work aisle is desirable, since this allows freedom of movement for the worker. When oven or steamer doors extend into the aisle space, additional room is alloted as needed for the situation. For example, an aisle space of 36 in. (914 mm) would be used when employees work with ovens.

For situations where two workers will be working back-to-back, the recommended minimum work aisle space is 42 in. (1067 mm). This figure does not include the allowance for equipment projections into the aisle space. In most cases, an allowance of 6 to 12 in. (152 to 305 mm) is sufficient.

Work Surface Space

Requirements for work surface space are dependent upon the materials used and the types of hand and arm actions needed to work on the materials. The workers' hand and arm movements should be confined to the normal and maximum work areas as much as possible. The normal work area for a work surface is defined as the space enclosed within the arc scribed by pivoting the forearm in a horizontal plane at the elbow. The worker should be in a typical working stance.

The arc scribed on the working surface will have a radius of 14 to 16 in. (356 to 406 mm) for most people. The area within the arc scribed by each hand describes the normal work area for each hand. Where the arcs overlap in front of the body is the normal work area for two-handed tasks. Hand actions for such tasks as cutting, slicing, mixing, or assembling are best performed within the normal work area.

The maximum work area is defined in a similar manner except that the entire arm is pivoted at the shoulder. Figure 8.3 illustrates the normal and maximum work areas in the horizontal plane. Locations outside the maximum work area require bending of the body to reach them and therefore movements to these locations should be kept to a minimum.

In consideration of the normal and maximum work areas, the work surface for most tasks performed in food facilities can be done within a space 2 ft. (0.61 m) deep and 4 ft. (1.22 m) in width.

Height

The height of the work surface will vary with the type of task. Tasks involving small, light-weight materials can be easily done at a surface height which is about 2 in. (50.8 mm) below the height of the worker's elbow. The makeshift work surface shown in Fig. 8.4 is too low for comfortable work.

As the materials involved in the task become larger or heavier, the height of the work surface can be lowered. The lowest workable sur-

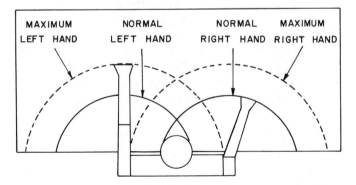

FIG. 8.3. Normal and maximum work areas for the horizontal plane.

FIG. 8.4.   Work surfaces that are too low will lead to back muscle tension and fatigue.

face is at the point where the wrist bends when the arms are extended at the worker's sides. This height allows workers to use their shoulder and back muscles in handling the heavier materials.

General recommendations for work surface heights for light tasks are 37 to 39 in. (940 to 991 mm) for women and 39 to 41 in. (991 to 1041 mm) for men. Work surfaces for heavy tasks are usually 34 to 36 in. (864 to 914 mm) high. Adjustable work-surface heights to fit both worker and task are the ideal design; however, an adjustable chair may be used to give the needed adjustment at lower cost.

Material, Tool, and Utensil Storage

The materials, tools, and utensils frequently used for tasks may be located in various places at the workplace. Overshelves, undershelves, bins, drawers, and cabinets can all be incorporated into the design. The ideal location for storage facilities at workplaces is between waist and shoulder height. Items that have to be stored below waist level can be put on pull-out or swing-out shelving. Cabinets with fixed shelves below waist level are not easy to use. For the same reason, shelves and cabinets are not placed more than 6 ft. (1.8 m) above the floor. Self-closing cabinet doors and drawers are desirable. Mobile bins or carts may be used adjacent to the workplace if additional storage is needed.

A definite fixed location for all materials and tools to be stored at the workplace is good design. The locations are selected in accordance with easy work patterns and help employees to develop good work methods. Designers can often dictate a particular pattern of desirable motions and actions by their strategic placement of materials and tools at the workplace.

Mounted Equipment

Equipment that is to be mounted at a workplace should also be designed with the worker in mind. Slicers, mixers, kettles, grinders, and similar equipment may be mounted on tables or carts at a height that will make them easy to use. Feeding and working height is important from the standpoint of safety. If the feeding or working level is too high, the worker will be forced to use awkward motions that can be hazardous.

Built-in sinks are required at many workplaces and should be placed at convenient heights. Sinks that are placed too low will require bending, and sinks placed too high are difficult to use. Preparation sinks used for light work are designed so the bottom of the sink is 10 to 12 in. (254 to 305 mm) below the worker's elbow. Sinks for heavier tasks, such as pot and pan washing, generally require a bottom depth of 16 to 18 in. (406 to 457 mm) below elbow height. As with other components of the workplace, sink heights should be designed to fit the worker and the task.

Free-standing Equipment

The use of larger pieces of foodservice equipment that will be free-standing or mounted to the floor deserves special attention (see Fig. 8.5). Some equipment, ranges and griddles, for example, can be considered as a separate workplace for certain types of cooking tasks. In other cases, additional work surface space may be required, and the

FIG. 8.5. Floor-mounted equipment has to be planned for ease of use and convenience.
Courtesy of The Hysen Group, Livonia, Michigan.

combination of the equipment and a work table are considered as the workplace. Other combinations of equipment can be developed to meet the requirements of the tasks to be performed. The description of a workplace for one food facility does not necessarily apply to all facilities. An oven may be described as a separate workplace for a larger operation yet may only be one component of a workplace for another operation. The planner designs workplaces for the project at hand, which usually results in different combinations of equipment and work surfaces.

Regardless of the type and number of major items of equipment in the work area, the recommendations related to height and ease of use apply. Ranges, for example, may be set down into the floor so that pots placed on top of them are low enough to see into and stir easily. Similar recommendations apply to free-standing kettles, ovens, griddles, fryers, broilers, and other items of preparation and production equipment.

Workplace Seating

Chairs are desirable at workplaces where the tasks require only hand and arm movements and are repetitive in nature. Seat heights between 24 and 30 in. (610 to 762 mm) will be suitable for most variations of workers and tasks. Adjustable foot rests are recommended so that leg circulation in shorter people will not be impaired when their legs dangle without support. Wherever chairs are to be used, the tables are designed to allow sufficient space for positioning the legs and feet. A minimum of 25 in. (635 mm) of clearance under the table is recommended.

After all the components of the workplace have been determined, they are arranged into a final design based on a normal flow of work. Symmetry in arranging the components of the workplace is important in conveying a sense of order. Most workers respond extremely well to an orderly environment and will work more productively under these conditions.

WORKPLACE ENVIRONMENT

The design of the environment where workers will perform their tasks is just as important as providing them with the required space, tools, and equipment. Although certain tasks may require special environmental conditions, most workplaces are designed for the maximum performance of the worker. The concepts of environmental design are drawn from the field of human engineering. In the broadest sense, human engineering deals with the design of human tasks and the working environment that maximizes a worker's output with the least amount of input. Of the many areas encompassed by the field of human engineering, only those that pertain to the design of work environment will be highlighted.

Many of the factors affecting the environment were discussed earlier in relation to development of the dining atmosphere. These factors are now presented in the light of a worker's requirements. The differences between a dining and working environment are caused by the different objectives involved. There are, of course, several similarities in both environments.

Thermal Comfort

Workers are very aware of the factors that influence their sense of thermal comfort. Continuous exposure to high temperatures, high relative humidities, and radiation effects from hot equipment cause most of the feelings of discomfort. Most workers perform best when these factors are within a fairly limited range of values. For example, effective temperatures between 65° and 70°F (18.3° and 21.1°C) in winter and 69° to 73°F (20.6° and 22.8°C) in summer are recommended for most tasks. These recommendations may be modified somewhat depending on the age and sex of the workers. Older people, especially women, prefer slightly higher temperatures. Some people can adjust to temperatures outside the recommended range without too much difficulty.

Radiation effects result when a worker is exposed to extremely hot or cold surfaces even though the air temperature around the body is at a comfortable level. Working near ovens, broilers, fryers, and other high-temperature equipment illustrates this effect. Continued exposure to high-temperature surfaces causes increased body and skin temperature that leads to thermal discomfort. Exposure to extremely cold surfaces results in heat loss from the body, which produces the sensation of coldness.

Relative humidity recommendations call for a range of 40 to 60%. Higher humidities cause thermal discomfort, and lower humidities result in the drying of skin and nasal passages.

Control of the worker's thermal environment is basically incorporated into the heating, cooling, and ventilating system of the building. Special consideration has to be given to kitchen areas because of the large number of heat- and moisture-producing pieces of equipment present. The amount of heat and moisture added to the kitchen environment from equipment can be minimized by selecting equipment that is well-insulated or by specifying additional insulation. All pipes carrying steam or hot water to equipment should also be insulated. Proper venting of equipment is important, especially for mechanical dishwashers.

Lighting

Lighting recommendations for workplaces are determined by the amount of visual effort needed to accomplish a particular task. Obviously, tasks requiring greater visual effort, as reading or bookwork, will require a higher lighting level. The recommended lighting level for general areas of a kitchen that are nonwork areas is 15–20 foot-candles (161–215 lux). Working surfaces require 30–40 foot-candles (323–430 lux) for most tasks. Tasks that involve reading and working with figures should have a minimum of 50 foot-candles (538 lux).

Either incandescent or color-improved fluorescent lamps may be used for work areas. General white fluorescent lamps are not desirable because of poor color perception that results with many foods. Incandescent lamps are available in a variety of types and permit flexibility of design. Fluorescent lighting systems are more expensive to install but operate more efficiently than incandescent systems.

Brightness ratios between the work and adjacent areas are considered in the design of the lighting system. Current lighting practice indicates that best results are obtained when the brightness ratio does not exceed 3 to 1, the work itself being the brighter.

Special care is required in planning the lighting system for workplaces to eliminate both direct and reflected glare. Direct glare is the result of locating the luminaire, or light source, near the line of sight. Any luminaire that is placed within 30 degrees above the line of sight of the worker should be screened. Reflected glare occurs when highly polished surfaces in the line of vision reflect the light striking them. Stainless steel tables and equipment, being especially good reflectors, cause many of the glare problems in foodservice facilities. Glare is highly disturbing to workers and leads to discomfort and fatigue.

A well-planned lighting system for workplaces should provide enough brightness for the worker to see everything that must be seen to perform the task efficiently. This includes light for seeing into drawers, shelves, cabinets, and equipment. Light sources are spaced and arranged in a manner that will illuminate the workplace uniformly, without shadows or dark spots.

Color

Colors are used to enhance the workers' feeling of well-being and consequently their work performance. Since the psychological aspects of color were described in Chapter 7, only general comments on the use of colors at workplaces will be made.

As indicated earlier, color and illumination are closely related. However, certain aspects of color deserve separate attention because of their interesting effect on human beings. Colors, used alone or in combination, can create conditions that can reduce fatigue, improve morale, and even increase productivity. Good color planning can also reduce accidents.

The use of color to achieve certain physical and mental effects is very complex. However, it is possible to achieve the desired conditions with some basic knowledge of the functions of color.

Color and illumination combine to give us the perception of contrast. Contrast is desirable from the standpoint of reducing eye fatigue and making objects easy to see. When objects and their surroundings are the same color or the same shade, a person is forced to look harder to separate the object from its surroundings. The use of a single color, or color monotony, as it is known, is one of the primary reasons why such areas have high accident rates and low employee morale.

Desirable contrasts can be achieved by one of the following methods: 1) using a light color with a darker version of the same color; 2) using a warm color in combination with a cool color such as ivory and medium blue; or 3) using a color with its complementary color—for example, peach and gray blue or pale pink and light green.

Too much contrast is just as hard on the eyes as not enough contrast. For this reason, the contrast between walls and the equipment or other objects in the work area should be kept at a moderate level.

The use of warm colors is discouraged for general painting of workplace areas because they tend to tire the eyes after a period of time. Blue and green are much easier on the eyes. Pure colors are also hard on the eyes and should be toned down, especially in areas where a lot of close work is to be done. The use of pure white in any area along the worker's line of sight is discouraged because of its reflectance quality.

Another use of color in work areas is for color-coding. Red can be used to identify moving parts of equipment or other dangerous components. Green is commonly used for first aid equipment. Steps, landings, and platforms coded with yellow paint can reduce tripping and falling. Color-coding of various forms helps in identification and minimizes errors.

Noise

Noise levels of 50 decibels or less are recommended for work areas. Somewhat higher levels may be tolerated for a short period of time but continued exposure to high noise levels leads to short-tempered, quarrelsome, and dissatisfied workers. Most sources of noise can be prevented or controlled at acceptable levels by proper design and management. Sources of noise are classified as follows:

1. Impact noises resulting from contact between hard objects, such as metal utensils banged against metal sinks, or pieces of china banged against each other

2. Gear noises caused by the contact of moving parts of equipment and machinery
3. Fluid-flow noises of air, water, or gases produced by fans, pumps, and compressors
4. Combustion noises resulting from the burning of fuels, as in gas cooking or heating equipment
5. Magnetic noises produced by transformers and electric motors used for foodservice equipment.

Effective noise control is achieved by reducing the transmission of air-borne and structurally transmitted noises. Air-borne transmission of noise can be controlled by placing silencing enclosures around the noise source or by using sound-absorbing surfaces to reduce the amount of reverberation. Silencing enclosures must be constructed in such a way that the enclosed piece of equipment or machinery can be operated and maintained. Unfortunately, silencing enclosures cannot always be built for all the noise-producing sources in work areas.

When complete isolation is not possible because of required air circulation or for maintenance or inspection reasons, baffles of sound-absorbing material can be placed above or partially around the equipment. This solution is not as good as isolation but will reduce the general noise level in the area.

A common noise control technique that is used when many noise-producing sources are present is to place acoustical materials on the ceiling, walls, and floors. Acoustical materials absorb a portion of the sound hitting them, therefore reducing the amount that is bounced back into the space. The selection, design, and placement of acoustical materials is best left in the hands of the acoustical engineer.

Structurally transmitted noises can be minimized by installing equipment on vibration-isolating mounts. Using plastic dishracks and other containers will reduce both the creation and transmission of noise.

Music

The use of music to stimulate or create certain moods in people has been employed for many years. However, the greatest strides in scientifically providing music for certain effects have been made during the last twenty years. Properly programmed music has proved to be a good morale booster that results in increased employee production.

The benefits of music are the greatest when persons are engaged in physical tasks. The music has to be patterned to fit the efficiency curve of employees. Most people are highly efficient 2 to 2½ hours after they start work. Then their performance drops off and continues at a lower level for a period of time. There usually is some increase in performance as the meal period is approached. This same pattern usually exists after the meal period with the performance hitting lower levels than before the meal period.

Thus the music provided should be moderate and cheerful during high efficiency periods and more pronounced with increased tempo and rhythm during low efficiency periods. Mild and restful music should be provided during the meal period.

Ventilation

Adequate ventilation of work areas is necessary to remove smoke, odors, moisture, and grease-laden vapor and to bring in fresh air. A well-planned ventilating system can reduce the amount of general cleaning and maintenance.

A general recommendation for ventilation of foodservice work areas is to supply 5 cubic feet per minute of fresh air per square foot (0.142 cubic meters per minute per square meter) of floor space. This recommendation assumes the presence of heat- and moisture-producing equipment in the area. Air vents for the ventilating system are sized and placed to obtain maximum effectiveness without causing drafts. Fresh air should be tempered by air make-up systems based on outside air characteristics. Make-up air can sometimes be drawn from dining areas if a suitable design can be worked out.

Air-conditioning

In warmer climates, air-conditioning of work areas is needed to maintain the desired environmental conditions. The design of air-conditioning systems for food facilities is very complex because of the special requirements of the cooking process. On one hand, heat-producing equipment is used for cooking which introduces unwanted heat into the general work areas. The air-conditioning system, on the other hand, is used to cool the same general work areas. In a sense, the work areas are being heated and cooled at the same time. The air-conditioning system has to be designed with sensitive controls to maintain the desired environmental conditions without causing an overload for cooking equipment. The rapid cooling of cooked foods exposed to air-conditioned spaces must be taken into account in the design of the system.

CONCEPTS OF MOTION ECONOMY

The principles of motion economy are used in the development of work methods, the workplace, and the tools and equipment needed to complete an operation. The studies of the motions of the human body members indicate there are five characteristics of easy movement: simultaneous movements, symmetrical movements, natural movements, rhythmical movements, and habitual movements.

Simultaneous Movements

Movements of the hands that begin and end at the same time are easier than movements where one hand requires a longer or shorter time to complete the motion. Simultaneous movements are best accomplished when both hands are doing identical work. If each hand is doing different work, the tendency is to have the right hand (for a right-handed person) work faster and thus violate the concept of simultaneous movements. The work of each hand should be planned so they take the same amount of time to complete. If this is difficult to do, individuals can be trained to balance the time required for each hand to do the different tasks.

Symmetrical Movements

Movements of the hands are easiest if they are symmetrical about the center line of the body. Symmetry indicates that the right hand moves to the right of the center line, while the left hand moves to the left of the center line. Movements that cause both hands to move to the right or left of the center line at the same time are not symmetrical. Movements directly forward from the body should start with both hands at the body and move forward at the same time and return at the same time. The difficulty of performing nonsymmetrical motions can be shown by attempting to draw simultaneously a square with one hand while the other hand draws a circle. Examples of nonsymmetrical movements are shown in Fig. 8.6. Symmetrical movements are easiest when the hands move in the same plane.

Combining symmetry with simultaneous movements creates a time balance and sense of equilibrium for the entire body. When a choice between symmetry and simultaneity has to be made, it is more important to maintain simultaneity of movements.

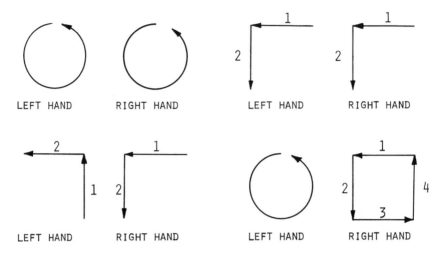

FIG. 8.6.   Examples of nonsymmetrical hand movements.

Natural Movements

Movements that correspond to the physical structure of the body are easiest. For example, the movement of the extended arm will result in an arc. This indicates that curved movements are more natural than straight movements of the arm. The same is true for movements of the forearm pivoted at the elbow or the movements of the hands and fingers.

Natural movements are also the fastest to make. Movements along an arc are faster than movements along a rectangular pattern. The movements along the rectangular pattern involve acceleration, deceleration, and a change in direction, which account for the longer time.

Consideration should also be given to the natural shape and position of the hand and fingers. It is much easier to grasp an object suspended with the long dimension in a vertical plane compared to suspension with the long dimension in a horizontal plane. The exertion of force is also associated with the shape and position of the body members. The greatest force that fingers can achieve are when the movement of the fingers is toward the palm. The arms exert the greatest force when the bicep muscle is used.

The various types of natural movements are classified according to the muscle system involved. These classes of movement are:

Class 1. Finger movements
Class 2. Finger and wrist movements

Class 3. Finger, wrist, and forearm movements
Class 4. Finger, wrist, forearm, and upper arm movements
Class 5. Finger, wrist, forearm, upper arm, and shoulder movements

The first class movements (finger movements) require the least amount of time and effort to perform and are also the weakest type of movement. Fifth class movements are the least efficient, but can exert the greatest force. The design of methods should consider the speed and force limitations of the various classes of motion. Levers and controls, for example, should be designed so the amount of force required to turn or move them matches the appropriate classification of motion.

Rhythmical Movements

The simultaneous, symmetrical, and natural movements are descriptive of parts of the total motion pattern needed to accomplish a task. A total motion pattern that creates a rhythm when repeated frequently is the easiest to perform. Rhythm indicates that the last part of the cycle should flow smoothly into the first part of the next cycle. Rhythm can be improved by minimizing the changes of direction involved in the motion pattern.

Habitual Movements

The creation of rhythmic patterns of simultaneous, symmetrical, and natural movements leads to the development of habitual movements. With habitual movements, the cycle of movements is made in exactly the same way each time the cycle is repeated. Movements become automatic or habitual after a period of time, eliminating much fatigue and strain.

The principles of motion economy are devoted to accomplishing the five basic characteristics of easy movements. The principles may be divided into three groups: (1) those pertaining to the use of the human body, (2) those pertaining to the design and layout of the workplace, and (3) those pertaining to the design of tools and equipment.

The principles of motion economy that pertain to the human body are specifically aimed at reducing the physical effort or energy required to perform work. Some of these principles are self-explanatory or were discussed earlier. Additional discussion should clarify and point out the importance of the principles.

The use of both hands to do work seems to be a logical principle leading to increased productivity. Studies have shown that working with both hands instead of one hand at a time results in less fatigue even though the same amount of work may have been accomplished. Greater effort is required when one hand is working under load while the other hand is idle because the body tries to put itself in balance. Obviously the time required to do the work with both hands is about 50% shorter. Thus using both hands to accomplish work is not only productive but also less fatiguing.

Momentum of body members is developed when the body members are put into motion. Since effort is required to start and stop the motion, the developed momentum should be put to effective use. This is done by using continuous instead of stop and start movements and by beginning or ending activities while the body members are in motion.

Many tasks require close coordination between the movements of the hands and the eyes. When the work requires the concentrated use of the eyes, it should be arranged so the number of eye movements is minimized.

Highly repetitive tasks using short movements are conducive to monotony and fatigue. Some of the monotony and fatigue can be alleviated by using occasional longer movements during the task. Care should be taken not to carry this mixing of short and long movements too far since it may result in extra effort. Since exact ratios of the various types of movements are not available, judgment has to be used. The individual differences among workers will also have an effect on

TABLE 8.2. CONCEPTS OF MOTION ECONOMY PERTAINING TO THE DESIGN OF WORKPLACES

(1) Materials, tools, and equipment are best located within the normal working area of the worker (see Fig. 8.7).
(2) Tools and frequently used materials should have a fixed location at the workplace.
(3) Work requiring the use of the eyes should be done within the normal field of vision.
(4) Prepositioning of tools and materials to facilitate the picking-up actions of hands is desirable.
(5) Gravity-feed bins or chutes should be used to deliver incoming materials to the workplace.
(6) Gravity can also be used to deliver outgoing materials.
(7) The height of the work surface that allows either a standing or sitting position is preferable.
(8) The physical environment of the workplace should be conducive to productive motions.
(9) Tools and equipment controls should be designed for easy grasp.
(10) Jigs, fixtures, or foot-operated devices should be used to relieve the work of the hands.
(11) Two or more tools should be combined where possible with due regard for the quality of work.
(12) Tools and materials should be so located as to promote good motion patterns of body members.
(13) Equipment should be designed so the inherent capabilities of the body members are fully utilized.

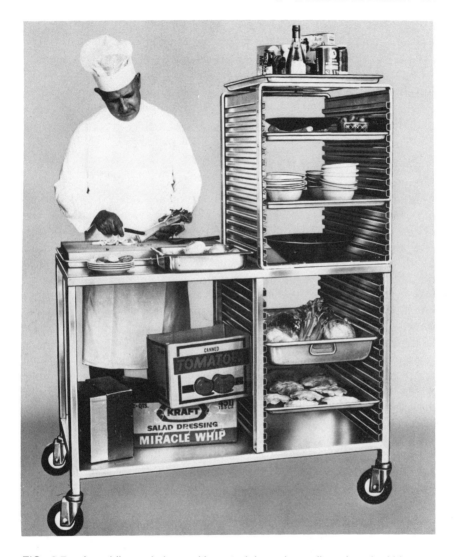

FIG. 8.7. A mobile workplace with materials and supplies placed within easy reach of the employee.
Courtesy of Cres-Cor/Crown-X, Crescent Metal Products, Inc.

this problem. A motion pattern that feels comfortable for one worker may feel awkward for others.

The principles related to the design of the workplace and tools and equipment primarily involve creating situations that lead to easy body member motions. Locating tools within the normal working area forces the motions of the hands to stay in the area. Placing objects in fixed positions leads to the development of habitual motions and using gravity flow minimizes the total number of motions required.

Planners should frequently check their design against these well-known concepts and make changes as needed. The important concepts of motion economy as they pertain to the design of the workplace are given in Table 8.2.

MATERIALS HANDLING

Materials handling refers to the movement and storage of materials and products as they proceed through the work system. Of all the activities associated with materials and products, materials handling often accounts for a greater portion of labor costs than any of the other activities such as operations or inspections. Materials handling does not add appreciable value to the product and therefore is considered as an undesirable activity. The primary objective of materials handling is to eliminate the movements and storages of materials and products. Movements and storages that cannot be eliminated should be done as easily and economically as possible.

Materials handling in restaurants and other foodservice operations involves such items as food, beverages, dishes, luggage, linen, empty bottles and trash, garbage, silverware, mobile equipment, pots and pans, paperwork, banquet tables, and cleaning supplies. These materials are frequently moved from one location to another by hand or by trucks or carts pushed by employees.

The amount of materials handling involved in a given work system is dependent upon the location and arrangement of storage areas, workplaces, and equipment. Therefore the first prerequisite to a good materials-handling system is a good layout. Conversely, a good layout is characterized by a minimum amount of materials handling. After the layout has been determined, materials handling can be improved to some extent by good planning and using the principles of materials handling.

Good design requires a system of materials handling that is desirable for each individual workplace, which in turn makes up the materials-handling system for the entire foodservice facility. Systems for the handling of food, utensils, garbage, dishes, tools, etc., at the workplace can be guided by the principles identified in Table 8.3.

The principles of materials handling should be used to develop the system for moving materials from workplace to workplace as well.

TABLE 8.3. PRINCIPLES OF MATERIALS HANDLING

---

(1) Minimize all material movements and storages.
(2) Use the shortest and straightest routes for the movement of materials across the workplace.
(3) Store materials as close to the point of first use as possible.
(4) Minimize handling of materials by workers unless absolutely necessary.
(5) Preposition all materials at the workplace as much as possible to reduce handling effort.
(6) Handle materials in bulk if at all possible.
(7) Provisions should be made to remove scrap, trash, and other wastes at the point of creation.
(8) Take advantage of gravity to move materials when feasible.
(9) Use mechanical aids to lift heavy materials that are frequently used at workplaces.
(10) Built-in leveling devices can be used to keep materials at a convenient working height.
(11) Use mechanized conveyors to move materials that follow a fixed route across the workplace if they do not interfere with the work.
(12) Use well-designed containers and tote pans that are easy to pick up and move.
(13) Consider the use of interlocking containers for moving greater loads with ease and safety.
(14) Consider changing the design of the products involved to improve their materials-handling characteristics.

The total design of the system for the entire facility has to be unified in order to achieve maximum efficiency of movement.

DESIGNING SAFE WORKPLACES

Some aspects of workplace safety are dictated by ordinances and codes such as the OSHA guidelines. Good design, however, results only when all areas relating to a safe environment are considered. The most frequent types of accidents in the foodservice area, their causes, and the recommended remedies to provide a safer work environment are summarized below.

1. *Falling.* Falling may be caused by slippery floors, highly polished floors, steep stairways, or obstructions in aisleways. Areas that are constantly wet or greasy should be equipped with nonskid flooring. Carpeting is also a possibility. All stairways should conform to specified tread and riser dimensions and should be equipped with sturdy hand rails. All work and traffic areas should be kept clean. Suitable storage areas should be provided for equipment, and supplies and employees must be required to put items in their designated storage places as soon as they are through using them.

2. *Bumping*. Bumping frequently occurs in areas where there is not ample clearance overhead or between objects. Narrow aisleways, low-hanging shelves, protruding levers, or square corners on tables or equipment lead to bumps. Congestion may also cause workers to bump into one another and consequently lead to an accident. All sharp corners and protrusions should be eliminated or at least rounded or shielded. Color coding may be helpful in drawing the employee's attention to protruding objects.

3. *Snagging*. Exposed gears, belts, and other moving parts of machines and equipment can snag clothing, hand-held objects, or even the hands. All moving parts should be completely enclosed to prevent employees from coming in contact with them. Guards should be kept in place and correctly adjusted. Interlocks that stop the machines when guards are removed should be installed where feasible. Special guards should be provided where it is possible for the hands to come close to moving parts.

4. *Cutting*. The improper use of equipment and hand tools and poor guarding of moving edges are the causes of cutting. Many of the machines used in foodservice operations do not have sufficient guarding of cutting edges. In such cases, additional guarding should be installed and kept in place.

5. *Burning*. Hot grease, steam, hot water, or hot pipes cause most of the burns in foodservice operations. Proper training in the use of fryers, kettles, and steamers is essential in preventing burns. All steam and hot water lines should be placed where they present no hazard. If this is not possible, the lines should be fully insulated so employees cannot be burned by making contact with them.

6. *Electrical shock*. Most electrical shocks are caused by improper grounding of equipment and machines and by frayed wires or deteriorated electrical insulation on wires. All electrical equipment should be properly installed in accordance with electrical safety codes. Only equipment that bears Factory Mutual approval or is listed by Underwriters Laboratories should be used. Periodic inspections should be made to assure the safety of electrical equipment. Built-in ground wires with three-prong plugs should be used for portable equipment. Grounding outlets should be provided where such equipment is frequently used. Heavy duty water-proof wiring should be used.

7. *Pinching or mashing*. The exposed moving parts of equipment, heavy portable equipment that is moved about the kitchen, and falling lids may result in pinched or mashed fingers and feet. The heavy lids of steam kettles can be counterbalanced to keep them from falling on the fingers.

8. *Dropping.* Dropping is primarily caused by sweaty or greasy hands or by stiffness of fingers resulting from exposure to the cold. Employees should be trained to keep their hands dry. Frequently carried objects such as tote pans should be equipped with adequate handles. The wearing of gloves by employees is recommended when the hands contact hot or cold objects for a long period of time.

9. *Falling objects.* Improperly placed objects on shelves, falling equipment and hand tools, or tipping of equipment result in many injuries. Suitable storage facilities for supplies, tools, and minor equipment should be provided to prevent falling of these items. Tables that support equipment should be sturdily built and large enough to keep the weight of the equipment from tipping them over. Portable equipment carts should have casters that lock to prevent movement when the equipment is in use.

10. *Physical strain.* Physical strain is caused by lifting heavy objects, using improper lifting methods, or working in awkward positions. Mechanical lifting aids should be used for heavy objects. Using portable carts will minimize the strain caused by carrying heavy objects. Tables and work areas should be of proper dimensions so workers do not have to stretch or bend extensively.

A workplace safety check list such as that shown in Table 8.4 may be helpful in the development of safe workplaces. Designing safe work-

TABLE 8.4. WORKPLACE SAFETY CHECK LIST

1. Provide storage for knives and other cutting tools to protect the cutting edges.
2. Provide cutting boards for tasks involving slicing, cutting, dicing, or mincing of food items.
3. Pot holders or gloves should be provided where hot utensils will be handled.
4. Provide floor mats or boards where permissible to prevent slipping and sliding on wet floors.
5. Space for incoming hot foods should be provided so that they are not placed in aisleways.
6. Provide space for waste removal.
7. Locate electrical outlets where they cannot be splashed with water or other liquids.
8. Provide adequate lighting at the working surface.
9. Provide easy access to controls for water, steam, electricity, or gas that must be used at the workplace (see Fig. 8.8).
10. Use sturdy equipment stands where needed.
11. Provide suitable safety equipment such as hand protection, aprons, or eye protection where needed.
12. Locate equipment handles to prevent their catching on employees' clothing.
13. Assure that the vision of the employee is not obscured by equipment or materials at the workplace.
14. Use color coding to designate dangerous areas.
15. Provide pushers, plungers, or feeders for mechanical chopping and cutting equipment.
16. Specify raised edges on tables where liquid spillage is anticipated.
17. Provide adequate shielding or guarding for all hot surfaces, including steam lines.

FIG. 8.8.   Placement of controls that are easily used is illustrated by this serving station.
Courtesy of The Hysen Group, Livonia, Michigan and Hansen Lind Meyer, P.C., Architects.

places is reflected in a reduction of accidents and may result in reduced insurance premiums after a foodservice facility is operational. Safe areas also lead to improved employee morale and increased productivity.

SUMMARY

The design of the individual workplaces for the foodservice facility is one of the keys to good overall design. As each workplace is developed, planners must continually relate their ideas to the operation of the entire facility. The design of a particular workplace is dictated by the movement of workers and materials to and from other workplaces adjacent to or near it. Even though only one workplace at a time is planned, it is a part of the total design concept that has to be developed.

PROBLEMS AND EXERCISES

8.1. Choose a food item that has to be prepared in volume and develop a workplace specific to that item. Do the same for a nonfood item.

8.2. Complete Table 8.1 for a luncheon menu at a country club.

8.3. Identify several tasks that are performed in a foodservice operation and determine whether they should be performed standing up or sitting down.

8.4. Indicate the importance of controlling such factors as temperature, lighting, noise, and ventilation at workplaces.

8.5. Using Table 8.2, give an example of each concept of motion economy pertaining to the design of workplaces for a foodservice facility.

8.6. Using Table 8.3, give an example of each principle of materials handling that may be found in a commissary operation.

8.7. Evaluate the safety of a workplace at a local foodservice operation by using Table 8.4 as a guide.

8.8. Plan a materials-handling system for moving tableware for a large dormitory cafeteria. Identify the type of equipment that would be used in the system.

8.9. Identify several pieces of equipment whose design is based upon a principle of materials handling or a principle of motion economy.

BIBLIOGRAPHY

BENDER, F.E., KRAMER, A. and KAHAN, G. 1976. Systems Analysis for the Food Industry. AVI Publishing Co., Westport, Connecticut.

HEATON, H. 1978. Productivity in Service Organizations: Organizing for People. McGraw-Hill Book Co., New York.

KAZARIAN, E.A. 1979. Work Analysis and Design for Hotels, Restaurants and Institutions. AVI Publishing Co., Westport, Connecticut.

KOTSCHEVAR, L.H. and TERRELL, M.E. 1985. Foodservice Planning: Layout and Equipment, 3rd Edition, John Wiley and Sons, New York.

MUNDEL, M.E. 1978. Motion and Time Study. Prentice-Hall Inc., Englewood Cliffs, New Jersey.

NADLER, G. 1970. Work Design: A Systems Concept. R.D. Irwin Co., Homewood, Illinois.

PEDDERSEN, R.B., AVERY, A.C., RICHARD, R.D., OSENTON, J.R. and POPE, H.H. 1973. Increasing Productivity in Foodservice. Cahners Books, Boston, Massachusetts.

TOURISM EDUCATION CORPORATION. 1976. A Hospitality Industry Guide for Writing and Using Task Unit Job Descriptions. CBI Publishing Co., Boston, Massachusetts.

WEST, B.B., WOOD, L., HARGER, V. and SHUGART, G. 1977. Food Service in Institutions, 6th Edition. John Wiley and Sons, New York.

Equipment Requirements

METHODS

Determining the specific equipment requirements for the proposed foodservice facility is one aspect of design on which considerable time can be spent. During this part of the planning process, the foodservice consultant has to estimate accurately the capacity of each of the various types of foodservice equipment to be used. If these capacity estimates are too low, the result will be delays and bottlenecks in the production process. Estimates that are too high will result in an expensive and inefficient piece of equipment. The foodservice consultant must be careful to take into account any projected increases in business volume that would require increased equipment capacity, and plan accordingly. Additional decisions regarding the equipment that may be made at this time include the manufacturer, the model number or designation, attachments, and other special accessories needed to process the food items.

A systematic method of determining equipment capacity required is to analyze each food item appearing on the menu. If daily-change menus are used, a sampling of typical menus may be sufficient. The first bit of information needed is an estimate of the number of portions that have to be prepared for a particular meal period. This estimate is made for every menu item requiring equipment, including appetizers, entrees, desserts, breads, salads, and beverages. Next, the portion size of each of the menu items is identified. (Typical portion sizes are given in Appendix B). Multiplying the estimated number of portions by the portion size will give the total volume of food to be prepared.

The capacity of equipment should be determined with future changes anticipated. Trends can be studied, and then any anticipated changes in foods, sales volume, or meals offered can be projected to see if drastic changes in equipment will be necessary. For example, perhaps no freezer space will currently be required, but if the need for freezer space is highly probable in 5 or 10 years, space can be left to add it then conveniently and economically.

The method of preparation and production for each item is then evaluated. Possible alternatives may include items individually prepared to order; items prepared in small batches in anticipation of orders; items prepared in large batches; and items that are partially batch-prepared and finished when orders are received. The batch size is next determined for those items that are to be prepared in batches. The selection of batch size is one way that the foodservice consultant can control the capacity of the equipment. Smaller and more frequently prepared batches are desirable because they require less equipment capacity and the foods are fresher when served. Some items that can be held well after cooking can be made in larger batches.

For those items to be prepared and cooked to order, the maximum number of portions to be made at one time is estimated on the basis of the number of customers, their menu preferences, and their arrival patterns. Some projects may require estimates of portions to be prepared per time unit. For example, the number of hamburgers per hour would be estimated for high-volume operations that utilize continuous processing instead of batch processing.

The capacity of some types of equipment is designated by the number of pans they can hold. In those cases, the designer will have to convert the total number of portions into number of certain-size pans. Ovens may be selected by the number of 18 by 26 in. (457 by 660 mm) bake pans they can hold. There are other methods of designating capacity for certain types of equipment, and the foodservice consultant has to convert the portion calculations accordingly.

After determining portions, equipment catalogs may be consulted to match the capacity needed for production with the available sizes of standard equipment. The designer is also careful when sizing some equipment that may have a usable capacity that is somewhat less than the stated capacity. Appropriate adjustments are made in the computations to allow for this discrepancy.

Other data required include the total processing time needed for each menu item for a particular piece of equipment and the time of day that the processing can be done. This information is useful in anticipation of possibly scheduling those items that require the same type of equipment through one piece of equipment instead of two or more. Duplication of equipment is avoided unless there is a need for it, such as having separate deep fryers for fish and chicken, or having one slicer in the preparation area and one in the cooking area if the volume of work to be done in each area warrants it.

EQUIPMENT CHECKLIST

The equipment required for foodservice facilities varies from one type of operation to another depending on the menu offerings, the nature of the food materials, the chosen method of preparation and service, and the personal desires of owners, managers, or chefs. The following list of equipment is presented so planners may evaluate the choices available and select the equipment that would be most appropriate for their particular project. The listing is grouped by typical functional areas.

Receiving Area

Air curtain	Dollies	Platform truck
Chute	Dumbwaiter	Receiving table
Conveyor	Elevator	Scales
Dock/leveler		

Dry Storage

Desk	Platform truck	Storage cabinets
Dunnage rack	Portable bins	Utility carts
Pallets	Shelving	Table

Refrigerated Storage

Carts	Fish refrigerator	Salad refrigerator
Compressor	Freezer (holding)	Shelving
Dairy refrigerator	Freezer (sharp)	Thaw refrigerator
Dunnage racks	Meat rail	Vegetable refrigerator
Evaporator	Meat refrigerator	

Meat and Seafood Preparation

Boning table	Meat saw	Slicer
Breading machine	Patty machine	Sterilizer
Can opener	Reach-in freezer	Tenderizer
Disposer	Reach-in refrigerator	Tilting kettle
Food shaper	Sausage stuffer	Tool and knife racks
Knife rack	Scales	Utility cart
Meat block	Shrimp peeler and deveiner	Vertical cutter/mixer
Meat chopper	Sink and drainboard	Wrapping table
Meat rail		

Vegetable and Salad Preparation

Can opener	Mixer	Salad/dessert rack
Cutting board	Peeler	Sink and drainboard
Dicer	Preparation table	Slaw cutter
Dish storage	Reach-in freezer	Slicer
Disposer	Reach-in refrigerator	Vegetable cutter
French fry cutter	Roll-in freezer	Vertical cutter/mixer
Grater	Roll-in refrigerator	

Sandwich Preparation

Bread cabinet	Griddle	Sandwich unit
Bread dispenser	Microwave oven	Sink and drainboard
Cutting board	Preparation table	Slicer
Dish storage	Reach-in refrigerator	Toaster
Food freshener		

Cooking

Au gratin oven	Food warmer	Refrigerated table
Bain marie	Fry pan, tilting	Reach-in freezer
Braising pan	Fryer	Reach-in refrigerator
Broiler	Griddle	Roll-in freezer
Broiler-griddle	Grill	Roll-in refrigerator
Can opener	Ingredient bins	Revolving tray oven
Cereal cooker	Kettle	Salamander
Char broiler	Knife rack	Scales
Chinese range	Lavatory	Sink and drainboard
Condiment cabinet	Microwave oven	Slicer
Cooker/kettle	Mixer	Spice cabinet
Cooker/mixer	Pizza oven	Steam cooker
Cooks' table	Portable table	Steam jacketed kettle
Deck oven	Pot and pan rack	Toaster
Disposer	Pot filler	Utensil rack
Egg boiler	Pot stove	Utility cart
Exhaust ventilator	Quartz oven	Vertical cutter/mixer
Fat filter	Range	Work table
Food rack		

Baking

Bakers table	Cooling rack	Dough sheeter
Bread molder	Convection oven	Dough trough
Bread slicer	Deck oven	Doughnut dropper
Bread wrapper/sealer	Disposer	Doughnut fryer
Bun slicer	Dolly	Divider/rounder
Can opener	Dough divider	Egg wash applicator
Condiment cabinet	Dough mixer	Exhaust ventilator
Cookie dropper	Dough retarder	Fat filter
Cooker/mixer	Dough rounder	Flour sifter and scale

Baking (continued)

Food pump	Pastry filler	Revolving oven
Grater/shredder	Pastry glazing machine	Roll divider
Icing machine	Pastry table	Scale
Ingredient bins	Pie cabinet	Shelving
Kneader	Pie filler	Sink and drainboard
Lavatory	Proofing box	Spice bins
Mixer, horizontal	Proofing cabinet	Tilting kettle
Mixer, vertical	Proofing rack	Utensil rack
Mixing bowl truck	Range	Utility cart
Pan rack	Reach-in freezer	Vertical cutter/mixer
Pastry board	Reach-in refrigerator	Work table
Pastry cutter		

Serving, Pick Up

Bain marie	Dessert cart	Linen cart
Banquet carts	Dish storage	Malted milk dispenser
Barbecue grill	Food warmer	Microwave oven
Beef cart	Fudge warmer	Milkshake machine
Butter chip dispenser	Hot chocolate dispenser	Order wheel
Catering supplies	Hot plate	Roll warmer
Coffee maker	Ice cream cabinet	Room service carts and supplies
Coffee range	Ice dispenser	Service stand
Coffee urn	Ice maker	Shake maker
Coffee warmer	Infrared heater	Sink
Cutlery box	Juice extractor	

Short Order, Fountain, Snack Bar

Back counter	Dipper well	Hot plate
Beverage dispensers	Dish storage	Ice cream cabinet
Blender	Display case	Ice dispenser
Bread dispenser	Disposer	Ice maker
Broiler	Drive-up unit	Ice shaver
Butter dispenser	Egg cooker	Iced tea dispenser
Can opener	Exhaust ventilator	Juice dispenser
Cash register	Fat filter	Lavatory
Char broiler	Food freshener	Malted milk dispenser
Coffee maker	Food warmer	Menu board
Coffee range	Freezer	Microwave oven
Coffee urn	French fry bagger	Milk dispenser
Coffee warmer	Fryer	Milkshake machine
Condiment dispenser	Fudge warmer	Mixer
Condiment pump	Glass washer	Pastry cabinet
Condiment stand	Griddle	Refrigerator
Cold pan	Grill	Roll warmer
Corn popper	Hot chocolate dispenser	Rotisserie
Cream dispenser	Hot dog and hamburger broiler	Sandwich grill
Creamer	Hot dog steamer	Sandwich unit

Short Order, Fountain, Snack Bar (continued)

Sink	Soup dispenser	Utility cart
Slicer	Table	Waffle maker
Slush machine	Take out section	Water dispenser
Soda fountain	Toaster	Waste receptacle
Soft ice cream machine		

Cafeteria, Buffet, Self-Service

Buffet unit	Tray slide	Ice cream display cabinet
Butter dispenser	Tray stand	Ice dispenser
Cafeteria counter	Utility section	Infrared heater
Beverage section	Coffee urn	Milk cooler
Bread and roll section	Coffee warmer	Milk dispenser
Cashier stations	Cold pan	Menu board
Dessert section	Condiment stand	Napkin dispenser
Dinnerware dispensers	Dish storage	Salad bar
Hot food section	Display case	Tea maker
Ice cream dispenser	Food warmer	Water dispenser
Salad section	Hors d'oeuvres cart	Waste receptacle
Soup section		

Tray Service

Beverage dispenser	Food warmer	Plate cover dispenser
Bread table	Hot food table	Roll warmer
Conveyor	Ice dispenser	Salad table
Dessert table	Menu holder	Toaster
Dish storage	Pellet heater	Tray cart
Elevator		

Dining

Banquettes	Food conveyor	Settees
Booths	Ice bin	Stools
Bus stand	Lobster tank	Tables
Cash register	Pastry cart	Tray stand
Chairs	Restrooms	Utility cart
Coat rack	Salad bar	Water station
Counter	Service stand	Wine rack
Dish conveyor	Serving cart	

Dishwashing

Blower dryer	Compactor	Dishwashing racks
Booster heater	Detergent dispenser	Disposer
Bowl dispenser	Dish cart	Exhaust ventilator
Bussing conveyor	Dish dispenser	Glass dispenser
Clean dishtable	Dishwasher	Glass washer

Dishwashing (continued)

Landing conveyor	Racking table	Soak sink
Lavatory	Rinse injector	Soiled dish table
Prerinse faucet	Scrap trough	Storage cabinet
Prerinse sink	Shelving	Supply cabinet
Rack dollies	Silver baskets	Tray dispenser
Rack return conveyor	Silver burnisher	Utility cart
Racking bridge	Silver sorting table	Waste pulper
Racking shelf	Silver washer	Waste receptacles

Pot Washing

Booster heater	Pot rack	Sink heater
Cart washer	Pot scrubber	Soiled pot table
Clean pot table	Pot washer	Steam injector
Disposer	Prerinse faucet	Storage cabinet
Drying rack	Shelving	Water agitator
Exhaust ventilator	Sink	

Cocktail Bar

Back bar	Bottle disposal system	Glass chiller
Bar workboard	Bottle rack	Glass washer
Beer cooler	Bottle trough	Ice bin
Beer dispenser	Cash register	Ice maker
Beer system	Cocktail mix section	Portable bar
Blender	Condiment section	Refrigerator
Bottle cart	Drink dispensing system	Sink
Bottle cooler	Drink mixer	Stools
Bottle chute		

Management Facilities

Bookcase	Desk	Table
Calculator	File cabinets	Typewriter
Chairs	Photocopier	Typewriter stand
Coat rack	Safe	Wastebasket
Computer	Storage cabinet	

Employee Facilities

Bulletin board	Hand dryer	Time card holder
Benches	Lavatories	Time clock
Chairs	Lockers	Towel dispenser
Cot or couch	Mirror	Urinals
Dining room	Soap dispenser	Waste receptacles
Drinking fountain	Shower	Water closets
First aid supplies		

Sanitation and Maintenance

Detergent storage	Mop rack	Vacuum cleaner
Floor scrubber	Mop sink	Shelving
High pressure washer	Mop truck	Utility sink
Linen hamper		

Trash and Garbage, Utility

Bottle breaker	Cleaning cart	Storage rack
Bottle crusher	Disposer	Trash receptacles
Can storage	Garbage receptacles	Water extractor
Can washer	Incinerator	Water heater
Compactor	Pulper	

A complete discussion of selecting and sizing all the different types of foodservice equipment is beyond the scope of this book. A brief discussion of frequently specified major items of equipment will serve to illustrate this part of the planning process.

BROILERS

Broilers are classified as equipment that utilizes intense radiant heat for rapid cooking of foods. The two common types are the overhead broiler and the underfired broiler. Other types of specialty broilers and combinations are available. Broilers are available in either gas or electric models.

Overhead Broilers

Heavy-duty overhead broilers have a large grid area and are equipped with large burners for fast broiling. They may be used individually or incorporated into a heavy-duty range section. Three common methods of incorporating the broiler into the range section are:

Having the broiler at the same height as the range tops

Having the broiler as an integral unit with an overhead oven that is heated by the burners in the broiling compartment

Having the broiler mounted on a conventional range-type oven with or without an overhead oven

A small broiler referred to as a salamander can be mounted above the top of a heavy-duty range or above a spreader plate as part of a back-shelf assembly. The broiling capacity of the salamander is not as great as that of the regular overhead broiler. It is primarily used for small operations with light broiling loads or as an auxiliary broiler during off-peak hours in larger operations when the main broiler is not in use.

Modern overhead broilers, as shown in Fig. 9.1, usually will heat to broiling temperatures in a short time and have pull-out grids for easy loading and unloading. Adequate venting of broilers is required to remove smoke and odors.

FIG. 9.1. High capacity broilers are used for rapid cooking.
Courtesy of The Hobart Corporation.

Underfired Char Broilers

Char broilers use pieces of ceramic or other refractory materials to form a radiant bed above the burners. The food items are placed on a grate located directly above the radiant bed. While cooking, the juices from foods drip directly on the hot bed and burn, which gives the typical charcoal flavor and appearance. Since a great deal of smoke is given off by char broilers, they must be used under an efficient exhaust hood.

Char broilers are available in multiple sections that increase the grid area for high-capacity broiling. A two-section char broiler is shown in Fig. 9.2.

Approximate cooking times for typical items processed on broilers are given in Table 9.1. These times are used for estimating the grid area of the broiler that is required for the food facility. Cooking times vary with many factors, including initial temperature of the food and closeness to the heat source. Consequently these times should be used only for estimating equipment capacity.

To determine the broiler capacity required for a particular menu item, the designer will estimate the total number of portions that

FIG. 9.2. An underfired char broiler.
Courtesy of The Hobart Corporation.

TABLE 9.1. APPROXIMATE COOKING TIMES FOR BROILING

Item	Thickness (in.)	Approximate cooking time (min)		
		Rare	Medium	Well-done
Beef				
Steaks	1	15	20	30
	1½	25	35	
	2	35	50	
Ground Beef	1	15	20	
Lamb				
Chops and Steaks	1		12	15
	1½		15	20
	2		20	25
Ground Lamb	1		20	22
Poultry				
Chicken parts				20
Half chickens				30
Pork				
Ham, uncooked	½			15
	1			20
Ham, cooked	½			6
	1			10
Seafood				
Fish, fillets	½			8
	1			12
Fish, whole	2			20
	3			25
Lobster tails				12

would have to be placed on the broiler grid at one time. Knowing the approximate area per portion, the total area required can be computed. If more than one type of food item is to be processed, then each type is checked to see which item will generate the greatest demand on the broiler. If the production estimates are in terms of portions per hour, the average cooking time is considered and the capacity of the broiler is based on this factor.

Deep Fryers

Deep fat fryers are available in a variety of types, capacities, and degree of automatic operation desired. Computer monitoring and control are available for the optimal frying of foods. The productive capacity of a fryer is related to the pounds of fat in the fry kettle, the heat input, and the cooking time required for various foods. Typical designs of fryers are based on a fat-to-food ratio of 6 to 1. This indicates that each pound of food to be fried requires 6 lb. (2.7 kg) of fat in the kettle. The size designation for fryers is indicated by pounds of fat. Fat capacity designations for conventional fryers vary from 15 to 130 lb. (6.8 to 59 kg). Conventional fryers, as shown in Fig. 9.3, may

FIG. 9.3. Conventional fryers for deep frying.
Courtesy of The Hobart Corporation.

be free-standing or can be built-in. Counter models are available for small requirements.

Pressure fryers make up another category of deep fryers. Those fryers, as shown in Fig. 9.4, are equipped with lids that can be sealed to permit steam pressure to build up between the lid and the fat surface. The steam is generated from the foods fried or by water injectors. The pressure fryer minimizes the loss of moisture from foods. Heat transfer in a pressure fryer is greater than in a conventional fryer and consequently the cooking time is shorter. This is also accomplished at a lower fat temperature, which does not break down the fat as rapidly. Most foods that are pressure fried are crispy and

FIG. 9.4. Pressure fryers are
frequently used for specialty
items.
Courtesy of the Broaster® Co.

brown on the outside and moist and juicy on the inside. This type of
fryer is ideal for certain specialty items such as deep-fried chicken.

The last category of deep fryers is the continuous-type fryer. These
fryers are equipped with a screw conveyor or belt that continuously
moves the product through the fat.

Fryer capacity is sometimes estimated by assuming that a fryer can
process from 1.5 to 2 times its weight of fat per hour. For example, a
50 lb. (22.7 kg) fryer should be able to fry from 75 to 100 lb (34.7 to
45.4 kg) of food per hour. An alternative method of determining fryer
capacity is to determine the actual weight of the food item to be fried
per hour and compare this figure with capacity specifications provided
by the manufacturer. Most manufacturers will supply capacity information for a variety of food items such as potatoes, chicken, and
shrimp.

Typical frying times for conventional deep fryers are shown in
Table 9.2. These times may be used to estimate the number of batches

TABLE 9.2. APPROXIMATE FRYING TIMES FOR
CONVENTIONAL FRYERS

Food item	Frying time (min)
Chicken	
Raw pieces	10–15
Fritters	3–4
Sea foods	
Fish fillets	3–5
Clams	3–4
Scallops	3–5
Shrimp	3–4
Oysters	3–5
Vegetables	
Potatoes, ¼ in. cut	4–6
Potatoes, ⅜ in. cut	5–7
Potatoes, ½ in. cut	6–8
Cauliflower	2–4
Eggplant	5–7
Onions	2–3
Miscellaneous	
Doughnuts	2–3
Corn on the cob	3–4
Meat turnovers	5–7
French toast	2–3

per hour that can be produced. Times for loading, draining, and un-loading are estimated and added to the cooking times to obtain the total batch time.

Since the frying time for many items is quite short, an automatic basket-lift or at least a timer bell is desirable. This allows cooks to attend other needs without consistently having to check the fryer.

Tilting Fry Pan

The tilting fry pan is one of the most versatile pieces of cooking equipment. Its design is such that it can be used to boil, simmer, braise, grill, saute, fry, and even steam a variety of foods. For some items such as stews all the preparation steps can be done in the tilting fry pan with some savings in time that would normally be spent transferring foods and cleaning other utensils and equipment.

Tilting fry pans may be free-standing, wall mounted, or counter mounted and are available in either gas or electric models. A free-standing tilting fry pan is shown in Fig. 9.5. The fry pan is tilted by a worm and gear assembly operated by a hand wheel. Typical capacities range from approximately 10 qt (9.46 liter) for the table top models to 40 gal (403 liter) for the floor models.

FIG. 9.5.   The tilting fry pan is used for a variety of cooking processes.
Courtesy of Groen Division/Dover Corporation.

GRIDDLES

Griddles are flat-top pieces of equipment heated from beneath (see Fig. 9.6), as compared to grills which have heating sources both above and beneath. Griddles are used for high-production foodservice and fast-food operations. Grills are more of a specialty piece of equipment.

Griddles are available in a variety of sizes from as small as 7 in. (178 mm) wide and 14 in. (356 mm) deep to as large as 72 in. (1829 mm) wide and 24 in. (610 mm) deep. Both gas-fired and electric models are suitable for most purposes. Typical foods and the approximate cooking times on griddles are given in Table 9.3.

Griddle capacity is designated by the physical dimensions of the cooking surface. Griddle capacity required is determined by the same

FIG. 9.6. Griddles are popular for cook-to-order items.
Courtesy of The Hobart Corporation.

FIG. 9.7. A combination griddle-grill featuring a chromium plated surface.
Courtesy of Keating of Chicago, Inc.

method suggested for broilers. Manufacturers will frequently have production capacity stated in terms of certain food items.

Griddles can be free-standing, counter-mounted, mobile, or built-in as the situation demands. Thermostatic controls which maintain constant surface temperatures are necessary for proper operation of the griddle. The height of splash guards and the location and width of grease troughs should be considered when specifying griddles.

Combination griddle-grills are available as shown in Fig. 9.7. This provides greater flexibility for the preparation of different menu items.

OVENS

Ovens are available in a great variety of types, sizes, and methods of operation. Different types may be used to bake, roast, oven-broil, oven-fry, cook casseroles, and reconstitute frozen foods. The capacities of ovens are stated in terms of the cooking chamber dimensions or by the number of bake or roast pans that can be placed in the oven at one time. Some operations may require more than one oven to handle the different temperature and time requirements of their menu items.

Deck Ovens

Deck ovens, as the name implies, can be decked or stacked to increase capacity without using additional floor space. Deck ovens may be either roasting or baking ovens. Roasting ovens have chambers that are 12–15 in. (305–381 mm) high while baking decks are usually 8 in. (203 mm) high. Both types of ovens are available in a wide range of chamber lengths and widths. The approximate roasting times for

TABLE 9.3. APPROXIMATE COOKING TIMES FOR GRIDDLING

Food item	Cooking time (min)
Bacon	5–6
Beef tenderloin	6–8
Bologna	2–3
Grilled cheese	1–2
Eggs	2–3
Fried potatoes	3–4
Hamburgers	2–5
Ham loaf	2–3
Ham steak	8–10
Minute steak	3–5
Pancakes	2–3
Sausage	3–5

TABLE 9.4. APPROXIMATE ROASTING TIMES
FOR MEATS

Meat	Approximate cooking time per lb (min)
Beef	
Rare	20–30
Medium	24–40
Well-done	28–50
Veal	25–35
Lamb	30–35
Pork, fresh	30–50
Ham, uncooked	20–25
Ham, cooked	15–18

meat items are given in Table 9.4. Cooking times are used to estimate the oven capacity required by computing the number of batches per hour that can be handled. Baking times for typical baked goods are shown in Table 9.5.

Baking and roasting decks may be combined in any desired arrangement. For best performance, each deck can be equipped with its own burner and thermostat. Less expensive arrangements using one burner and thermostat for two or more decks are available.

The two-deck oven is preferred for ease of use and safety. The top deck of a three-deck arrangement is usually too high for safe and easy reach, while the bottom deck requires considerable bending to load and unload.

TABLE 9.5. APPROXIMATE BAKING
TIMES

Food item	Baking time (min)
Bread	30–35
Cakes	20–25
Cookies	15–20
Pastry	
Pie shells	20–25
Puff pastry	25–30
Eclairs	25–30
Turnovers	25–30
Pies	
Fruit	50–60
Meringue	15–20
Pumpkin	30–35
Custard	30–35
Rolls	15–20
Buns	20–25

Convection Ovens

Convection ovens differ from other ovens in that a fan is used to provide rapid circulation of heated air within the chamber. This permits foods to be cooked on multiple racks instead of on a hearth; consequently almost the entire volume of oven space can be utilized. This results in an increased production capacity. Rapid air circulation also maintains an even temperature in all parts of the oven chamber.

Since heat transfer into the food products is increased by the forced convection, a lower temperature and shorter cooking time may be used. Lower temperatures will minimize the shrinkage of roasts.

Convection ovens, as illustrated in Fig. 9.8, are usually more energy efficient than other types of ovens, especially if they are well insulated and used properly.

Revolving-Tray Ovens

Revolving-tray ovens use flat trays suspended between two reels that rotate the trays. Food items to be roasted or baked are loaded on the trays as they appear opposite the door opening. The ovens are designed to prevent the escape of hot air when the door is opened for loading or unloading. One advantage of the revolving-tray oven is that its high capacity allows several menu items to be cooked simultaneously.

Most ovens are built with 4 to 7 trays, the tray sizes varying from as little as 18 by 30 in. (457 by 762 mm) to as much as 26 by 108 in. (660 by 2743 mm). The larger capacities are best suited to institutional or commissary-type operations. Capacity is designated by the total number of pans that can be loaded into the oven at one time.

Microwave Ovens

Microwave ovens cook foods by converting microwave energy into heat energy within the food. The energy is created by electronic microwave tubes placed in the cooking chamber. As the microwave energy is emitted, it is absorbed by the foods and converted into heat. Characteristics of various foods dictate how long it will take to fully cook them. Cooking time is reduced considerably in comparison to other types of ovens. The quick heating capacity of microwave ovens makes them ideal for reconstituting frozen foods.

As with other ovens, capacity is dependent upon the volume of the cooking chamber and the cooking time required. With the shorter cooking time, microwave ovens have a higher output per hour than

FIG. 9.8. Convection ovens feature a faster rate of heat transfer than conventional ovens.
Courtesy of The Hobart Corporation.

other similar-sized ovens. Microwave ovens are available in a number of compartment sizes and in a continuous type. Typical processing times for a variety of food items are given in Table 9.6.

Infrared Ovens

Infrared ovens (Fig. 9.9) operate on a principle somewhat similar to microwave ovens. The basic difference is that the infrared oven uses infrared energy waves, which have shorter wavelengths than

TABLE 9.6. APPROXIMATE PROCESSING TIMES FOR
MICROWAVE OVENS

Food item	Processing time (min)
Meat, precooked and cooled	
Ham steaks	3
Short ribs of beef	2
Poultry, precooked and cooled	
Fried chicken, disjointed	2½
Fried chicken, half	2½
Seafood, raw to done	2
Vegetables, canned	
Corn, green beans, peas	½
Baked beans	¾
Potatoes	1¼
Vegetables, fresh	
Corn on the cob	2
Broccoli	8
Spinach	3
Asparagus	9
Potatoes	5
Vegetables, frozen	
Corn	5
Asparagus	7
Cauliflower	12
Casseroles, precooked and cooled	
Chicken a la king	1½
Stuffed cabbage	2
Macaroni and cheese	1¾
Spanish rice	1½
Spaghetti	1½
Beef stew	2
Ravioli	2
Chili con carne	1¾
Meat pie	1¾
Chop suey	2

microwaves. In an infrared oven, the energy waves are directed to the food, where they are absorbed and converted into heat. The penetration of infrared energy into the food is not very deep and consequently the cooking process is similar to conventional ovens. Microwaves penetrate much deeper into the food than do infrared waves. An advantage of both infrared and microwave ovens is that the air enclosed in the oven chamber is not heated by the radiant energy. This characteristic of introducing energy into the food directly without heating the air makes it a highly efficient method of heat transfer.

The characteristics of the infrared oven make it suitable for both regular cooking of raw foods and for reheating or reconstituting frozen items. The time required for cooking raw items in an infrared oven is less than in conventional ovens. Reconstitution of frozen foods in infrared ovens takes somewhat longer than in microwave ovens.

FIG. 9.9. Infrared oven with a temperature range of 200 to 850° F.
Courtesy of Groen Division/Dover Corporation.

Conveyor ovens are very suitable for peak period production of a variety of foods. Figure 9.10 shows a conveyor oven equipped with infrared emitters. The production capacity of this type of oven is very high.

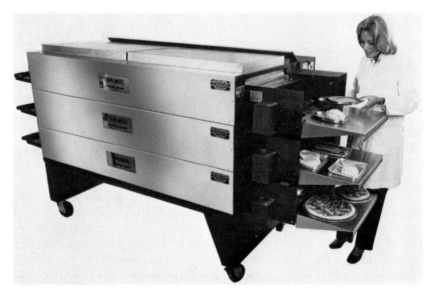

FIG. 9.10. Conveyor oven equipped with infrared emitters.
Courtesy of CTX Products, Pet Corporation.

PREPARATION EQUIPMENT

Food Cutters

Food cutters are versatile pieces of equipment than can handle meats, vegetables, and fruits. The food cutter can cut, dice, shred, and almost liquefy foods, depending upon the amount of time the food is left in the cutter. The foods to be size-reduced are placed in a bowl which rotates and exposes them to high-speed rotating blades. The capacity of cutters is measured by the size of the bowl or by the amount of food that can be processed per minute. Both bench and floor models are available. Some cutter models are equipped with an attachment hub for accepting various attachments.

Slicers

The basic design of food slicers includes a circular knife blade and a carriage that passes under the blade. Foods to be sliced are placed on the carriage and are either hand-fed or automatically fed. A very close adjustment and consequent control of thickness of the slices can be obtained with slicers. The food cutter and slicer shown in Fig. 9.11 are excellent labor-savers for foodservice operations.

Mixers

The primary function of a mixer is to mix; however, it can perform a variety of other functions by using accessories and attachments. Mixer capacity is indicated by the capacity of the bowl. Bench models are sized from 5 to 20 qt (4.73 to 18.9 liter); larger floor models as shown in Fig. 9.12 range from 30 to 400 qt (28.4 to 378 liter) capacity. Most mixers have adapter rings enabling them to handle different-sized bowls. Larger models can be obtained with bowl-raising and lowering mechanisms to simplify handling large bowls.

Mixers are designed to operate at a variety of rotational speeds, depending on the job. Accessories available include various whips, beaters, and knives attached directly to the drive shaft. Attachments, which permit the mixer to perform other functions, are adaptable only to the mixers that have an attachment hub. Available attachments include a food chopper, dicer, slicer, juice extractor, tool sharpener, and a variety of shredder and grater plates.

FIG. 9.11. Food cutters and slicers speed up many preparation tasks.
Courtesy of The Hobart Corporation.

Vertical Cutter/Mixer

The vertical cutter/mixer is basically a stationary bowl with horizontal blades that rotate at high speed. The capacity of a vertical cutter/mixer is much greater than the typical food cutter and is suitable for large-volume operations. Capacity is designated by the bowl size and ranges from 25 to 60 qt (23.7 to 56.8 liter).

Vertical cutter/mixers, as illustrated in Fig. 9.13, operate at a very high speed and can be used for cutting, blending, chopping, mixing, grating, crushing, and stirring many different food items.

Vegetable Peelers

Vegetable peelers are cylindrical tanks that have a revolving disc at the bottom. The tank is equipped with two openings, one above the disc for loading vegetables and one below it for removing the peels.

FIG. 9.12. Floor model mixers are commonly used in baking areas.
Courtesy of The Hobart Corporation.

Depending upon the model, the disc or the walls, or in some cases both, are coated with an abrasive. As the disc revolves, the vegetables are thrown against the abrasive, which peels the skin. Water is introduced to keep the abrasive surface clean and to carry away the peeled skins to the lower opening. Peeling time varies with the type of vegetable and may be from 30 seconds to 4 minutes.

Capacity of peelers is designated by the quantity of vegetables that can be placed in the peeler. Capacities from 15 to 70 lb (6.81 to 31.8 kg) are typical. Some manufacturers designate capacity by relating it to the horsepower rating of the electric motor.

FIG. 9.13. The vertical cutter/mixer is used for
high speed size reduction of foods.
Courtesy of The Hobart Corporation.

RANGES

The advent of new processed foods and new equipment, coupled with
the shortage of skilled chefs, have relieved the need for a large battery of ranges for many types of foodservice facilities. The range is
still a favorite for operations that feature cook-to-order items and
homemade menu items. A solid top range with an oven underneath is
illustrated in Fig. 9.14.

Heavy-duty ranges are designed to meet the requirements of continuous high production volumes. Restaurant-type ranges are of lighter
construction and do not have the durability for continuing heavy production requirements; they are suggested for smaller operations or for
limited-use applications.

FIG. 9.14.   Closed top range with oven.
Courtesy of The Hobart Corporation.

A variety of range designs are available, including solid tops, open tops, and griddle tops. Most ranges will have ovens under, although models with shelves or storage cabinets under are used in some cases.

Range sections are usually 29–37 in. (737–940 mm) wide and from 34 to 42 in. (864 to 1067 mm) deep. Sections are joined to give any desirable range top area to meet the requirements of the food facility.

STEAM-JACKETED KETTLES

Steam-jacketed kettles are constructed of two bowls sealed one within the other, with about 2 in. (51 mm) of space between them for the introduction of steam. The amount of steam surface between the bowls is referred to as jacketing, and models from half-jacketed to full-jacketed types are available. The operation of steam-jacketed kettles utilizes steam, which is condensed back to water in the jacket to provide the heat for the inner kettle. A condensate line is provided to remove the water that accumulates. The amount of heat input is dependent upon the pressure and amount of steam allowed to enter the jacketed area.

Smaller steam-jacketed kettles may be mounted on tables or counters; larger models are mounted to the floor or wall. Many models can be tilted for easy removal of contents. Figure 9.15 shows a tilting steam-jacketed kettle mounted on a pedestal base, which makes it easy to use. Capacity designations are in quarts for smaller models and gallons for larger models. The usable capacity of steam-jacketed kettles is generally figured to be 75% of stated capacity.

STEAMERS

Steamers are basically sealed compartments where steam is allowed to come in direct contact with the food for cooking. Conven-

FIG. 9.15. A tilting steam-jacketed kettle simplifies removal of contents.
Courtesy of Groen Division/Dover Corporation.

tional steamers operate with steam at a pressure of 5 psi (34.5 kPa), which corresponds to a temperature of 227°F (108.3°C). These steamers are referred to as large-compartment steamers and are capable of producing large volumes of food.

High-pressure steamers, sometimes called speed-cookers, are smaller units that operate with steam at a pressure of 15 psi (103 kPa). The resultant temperature in the high-pressure steamer is approximately 250°F (121.1°C).

Pressureless steamers operate at zero psi, which corresponds to a cooking temperature of 212°F (100°C). The obvious advantage of the pressureless steamer is the ability to open the door during the cooking process, which cannot be done with either the low-pressure or the high-pressure steamers. The convection pressureless steamer depicted in Fig. 9.16 may be used for quick cooking vegetables and other items. Some models of pressureless steamers, as shown in Fig. 9.17, have the boiler that creates the steam housed underneath the steamer compartment.

The capacity of a steamer is designated by the number of steamer

FIG. 9.16. Convection pressureless steamers are ideal for quick preparation of vegetables and other foods.
Courtesy of Southbend Escan Corporation.

pans that can be placed in it at one time. Usual capacities range from units that can hold three 12 by 20-in. (305 by 508 mm) pans to those having a capacity of 18 pans. An unusual designation of bushels is sometimes used to indicate steamer capacity; this implies the bushels of vegetables that can be cooked at one time in the steamer.

Typical processing times for some foods for conventional and high-pressure steamers are given in Table 9.7. These times may be used to determine the number of batches that can be processed per hour.

Steamers are ideal for vegetable cookery because they retain the color and textures without undue shrinkage. Both fresh and frozen vegetables may be steamed.

WAREWASHING EQUIPMENT

Dishwashers are the major item of equipment for warewashing and are generally classified by the number of tanks. A single-tank dishwasher is the smallest-capacity machine and is used for limited facilities. Counter-service operations frequently use single-tank dishwashers that are either bench-mounted or placed under counters or work tables. Most single-tank dishwashers have only a wash-and-rinse cycle. Figure 9.18 illustrates a single-tank dishwasher.

TABLE 9.7. APPROXIMATE PROCESSING TIMES FOR STEAMERS

	Approximate processing time (min)	
Food items	Conventional steamer	High-pressure steamer
Vegetables, fresh		
Asparagus	6–8	1–1½
Beans, green	20–25	2–3
Beans, lima	10–12	1–2
Broccoli	7–10	1–3
Carrots, sliced	12–15	2–5
Cauliflower, pieces	8–10	2–3
Corn, kernel	6–8	2–3
Peas	4–5	1–1½
Potatoes, quartered	18–24	5–10
Tomatoes	4–5	½–2
Vegetables, frozen		
Asparagus	4–6	2–3
Beans, green	15–18	2–3
Beans, lima	8–10	1–2½
Broccoli	4–6	1–2
Carrots, sliced	10–12	2–3
Cauliflower	6–8	1½–2½
Peas	3–4	1–1½
Seafood, frozen		
Shrimp		10–12
Lobster tails		7–8
Poultry, fresh		
Chicken, pieces		4–5

FIG. 9.17. Pressureless steamers can be opened during the cooking process.
Courtesy of Groen Division/Dover Corporation.

Two-tank dishwashers are used for greater loads and are available in rack or rackless models. They usually have a power wash cycle, a power rinse cycle, and a final rinse cycle. Some models may omit the power rinse and have a pre-wash cycle instead. The discharge sections are designed to allow sufficient drying of dinnerware before it is handled. Larger three-tank dishwashers have power pre-wash, wash, and rinse sections.

Dishwasher capacity is stated in terms of numbers of pieces of dinnerware that can be washed per hour. Some manufacturers also have recommendations of size based on the number of meals to be served per meal period. For example, a single-tank dishwasher will be suitable for washing dinnerware from 50 to 600 meals per meal period. Two-tank machines are capable of handling dinnerware from 1500 to 2000 meals per meal period. Three-tank dishwashers are usually rated for 2500 meals. These recommendations are guides, and the actual capacity required for a particular operation will depend on the number of each type of dinnerware to be washed and the time allowed for washing.

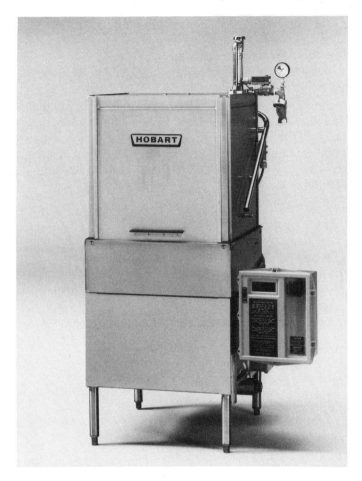

FIG. 9.18.   Door type dishwasher for smaller warewashing
needs.
Courtesy of The Hobart Corporation.

Some operations may prefer separate glasswashers, especially if
large numbers are to be washed daily. Small glasswashers are frequently located in bar areas and in counter units.

WASTE DISPOSALS

Most waste disposal units operate by using water to carry the waste
into shredders that cut it into small pieces. As the size of the pieces

is reduced to about one-eighth inch, they are flushed into the sewer. Some large disposals have a screw-type shaft that forces the waste into the shredders. Waste disposals are sized according to the horsepower of the motor. Typical sizes available range from 0.33 to 5.0 horsepower.

Waste disposal units are frequently installed at points where garbage and wastes are generated. Locations such as soiled dish tables, pot- and pan-washing areas, and preparation areas are usual waste-disposal installation points. Optional accessories for the disposal units include silver trappers and overhead spray units for washing waste directly into the disposal.

EQUIPMENT CHOICES

Selecting a particular make and model of any type of equipment is the final step in determining equipment requirements. Foodservice consultants will prepare a "schedule of equipment" that will list the specific equipment to be used for the facility. The following points are considered in deciding the make and model of equipment to specify:

    simplicity of operation
    sanitary design
    modular sizes to fit standard-sized pans
    ease of installation
    cost of operation
    ease of repair and maintenance
    durability
    compatibility with other equipment

The design of the equipment should be simple, functional, and attractive. Maximum utility at a reasonable cost is to be sought for all types of equipment.

DISPLAYS

One of the most important aspects of equipment design deals with the details of conveying information to the operator (referred to as displays), the controls for adjusting the equipment, and the physical limitations of the human body.

Displays should be designed so that optimum operator efficiency is present regardless of the type of activity required. There are three types of activity usually associated with the display-operator system:

watching, which occurs when the operator is waiting for something to happen; warning, when the operator is aware that something in the equipment is not functioning properly; and action, when the operator takes steps to correct the condition by using a control. These three activities may be illustrated by a fry cook using a deep fat fryer equipped with an indicating thermometer and a temperature control. When frying, the cook will (or should) watch the indicating thermometer periodically. If the temperature of the fat drops below the desirable range, the thermometer will be the warning display and indicate to the cook that the temperature needs to be adjusted.

The displays on equipment should preferably be located to the top left of center and not more than 10° above or 45° below the line of vision of the operator. The shape and design of the dial, the markings, and the pointer have a direct bearing on the accurate reading of the indicated measurements.

The legibility of dials is also dependent on the make-up of the individual numerals. The best ratio of the stroke width of the numeral compared to the stroke length should be 1/6 to 1/8. The total width to height ratio of the numerals should be 2/3. Numerals should be large enough to be easily read at the expected distance the observer is away from the dial. For a reading distance of 28 in. (711 mm), the height of the letters should be 9/64 in. (3.57 mm).

Placement of the numerals on the dial face is important from the standpoint of fast and accurate legibility. For dials that have a fixed scale and a moving pointer, the numerals should be oriented vertically and not radially.

CONTROLS

All controls should be placed within the normal reaching areas of the operator. This means the controls should be placed from 33 in. (838 mm) to 56 in. (1422 mm) above the floor, and within 16 in. (406 mm) on either side of the center line of the operator.

Emphasis should also be placed on the control-display relationship. This is the relationship, for example, between a valve and its related display such as a pressure gauge. The direction of movement of the control should be comparable to the direction of the movement of the display. If the valve is turned clockwise to increase pressure, then the gauge should also move clockwise to indicate increased pressure.

All controls on a given piece of equipment, regardless of whether they are associated with a display or not, should produce the same effect from the same type of movement. If one valve is turned clockwise to increase, then all other valves on the equipment turned in the clockwise direction should also result in an increase.

PROBLEMS AND EXERCISES

9.1. Determine the advantages and disadvantages for each of the following methods of preparation: (a) individually prepared portions, (b) small batch preparation, (c) large batch preparation, and (d) partially batch prepared items that are finished when orders are received.

9.2. Discuss the advantage of using a pressure fryer as compared to a conventional fryer for a fast-food operation.

9.3. Identify the various cooking processes that can be accomplished with the tilting fry pan.

9.4. Describe the advantages and disadvantages of the convection oven for roasting meats compared to its use in a bakeshop.

9.5. Discuss why microwave ovens are preferred for cooking small volumes of food and not suitable at all for certain types of foods.

9.6. Compare and contrast steam-jacketed kettles with steamers indicating the foods best suited to each.

9.7. Describe the operation and use of the microwave oven as compared to the infrared oven.

9.8. Identify the particular types of equipment that have a usable capacity that is less than the stated capacity.

9.9. Select one food item that can be cooked on a broiler and determine the broiler capacity needed to prepare 100 portions of that item in one hour's time. Do the same for a deep fryer, griddle, deck oven, convection oven, and a steam-jacketed kettle.

9.10. Obtain a menu from a local restaurant and determine what the equipment requirements would be for that restaurant at a chosen level of meals prepared.

BIBLIOGRAPHY

ANOFF, I.S.   1972.   Food Service Equipment Industry. Institutions/Volume Feeding Magazine, Chicago, Illinois.

AVERY, A.C.   1980.   A Modern Guide to Foodservice Equipment. CBI Publishing Co., Boston, Massachusetts.

BORSENIK, F.D.   1983.   Energy and foodservice equipment. The Consultant 16 (1), 12–20, 24.

JERNIGAN, A.K. and ROSS, L.N.   1980.   Food Service Equipment, 2nd Edition. Iowa State University Press, Ames, Iowa.

KAHRL, W.L.   1978.   Food Service Equipment. Lebhar-Friedman Books, New York.

KOTSCHEVAR, L.H., and TERRELL, M.E.   1985.   Foodservice Planning: Layout and Equipment, 3rd Edition. John Wiley and Sons, New York.

LONGREE, K. and BLAKER, G.G.   1982.   Sanitary Techniques in Foodservice, 2nd Edition. John Wiley and Sons, New York.

THORNER, M.E.   1973.   Convenience and Fast Food Handbook. AVI Publishing Co., Westport, Connecticut.

VAN EGMOND-PANNELL, D. 1981. School Foodservice, 2nd Edition. AVI Publishing Co., Westport, Connecticut.

WATTS, W.J. 1984. Energy and foodservice equipment. The Consultant *17* (1), 32–33.

WILKINSON, J. 1981. The Complete Book of Cooking Equipment, 2nd Edition. CBI Publishing Co., Boston, Massachusetts.

Equipment Selection and Design

STANDARDS

After determining the type and capacity of equipment required for a particular project, the next phase involves selecting the specific characteristics that are desired. Factors such as materials, construction techniques, special features, and consideration of maintenance are evaluated. The primary emphasis is placed on safety, sanitation, and appearance.

The selection of equipment should be guided by the minimum requirements that are identified in various standards presented by associations and agencies whose function it is to safeguard the public. Associations and agencies that prepare standards work closely with manufacturers, operators, and the public to work out problems dealing with products, equipment, and procedures. Many associations conduct ongoing research and testing of new equipment, components, methods, and operational procedures.

Sanitary Considerations

The National Sanitation Foundation is best known for the development of standards and criteria for products, foodservice equipment, and services that can have an impact upon public health. The National Sanitation Foundation Seal (NSF) is widely accepted as the sign that the article bearing it complies with public health requirements. Some of the National Sanitation Foundation standards that pertain to foodservice facilities and their operation are listed below:

Soda fountain and luncheonette equipment
Foodservice equipment
Commercial spray-type dishwashing machines

Commercial cooking and hot food storage equipment
Foodservice refrigerators and storage freezers
Commercial powered food preparation equipment (including food choppers and slicers)
Automatic ice-making equipment
Manual food and beverage dispensing equipment
Pot, pan, and utensil washers
Laminated plastics for surfacing foodservice equipment
Dinnerware
Air curtains for entranceways in food establishments
Plastic materials and components used in food equipment
Supplemental flooring

It should be stated that the National Sanitation Foundation also develops standards for areas other than foodservice facilities.

Electrical Safety

Foodservice equipment that is operated or heated electrically presents unique problems for foodservice facilities because of the need for water in close proximity. The equipment has to be designed and operated in a manner that will eliminate the possibility of electrical shocks to workers and other users. Warewashing, food preparation, and cooking areas as well as dispensing and serving facilities are examples of environments that are potentially hazardous because of water spills. Electrical equipment in all areas has to be properly installed and grounded, and operated safely in order to meet the standards of electrical safety.

The standards of Underwriters Laboratories (UL) and the National Electric Manufacturers Association (NEMA) apply to the design and operation of electric equipment. All components of the equipment, including motors, switches, overload devices, and wires, should conform to these standards. Equipment installation and devices such as lamps, bulbs, thermostats, and computer controls are also covered by the standards. The National Electric Code references the UL and NEMA standards frequently.

Gas Equipment

Standards for the design, installation, and operation of gas equipment are set forth by the American Gas Association (AGA), and AGA seals of approval are provided for equipment that has met their standards. The burners, ignition devices, and gas controls are of primary importance in the safe design and operation of fryers, ovens, ranges, broilers, and griddles. AGA also has standards for gas water heating and steam generation equipment.

Steam Equipment

Because of the special strength requirements and other safety requirements associated with the use of steam, equipment design is guided by the standards set by the American Society of Mechanical Engineers (ASME) as well as the other standards mentioned above. This is especially important for high-pressure foodservice equipment. The containment of the steam under pressure and other components that regulate and control the steam are covered by these standards. Safety devices for releasing steam pressure are particularly important to safeguard both equipment and workers.

Special Requirements

There are other associations and agencies that have standards or special requirements for certain equipment or components. For example, the American Society of Testing Materials (ASTM) can be referred to if there are situations that require certain materials that need to withstand unusual loads or stress. These standards are especially important for the design of large, heavy-duty pieces of equipment such as the heavy-duty pizza mixer shown in Fig. 10.1.

Materials

The materials that are used in the manufacture and fabrication of foodservice equipment are selected on the basis of sanitation, durability, strength, and considerations of maintenance and expected life. For many types of equipment that are expected to withstand commercial usage, the material of choice is stainless steel. Other materials, including galvanized steel, aluminized steel, other coated steels, plastics, wood, aluminum, copper, and composite materials, are used to a lesser degree or in special situations. Combinations of these materials are found in many applications.

STAINLESS STEEL

Stainless steel is an iron alloy containing minimum amounts of chromium and nickel and maximum amounts of other alloying elements such as manganese, silicon, and carbon. Its use in foodservice equipment is based on the following characteristics:

FIG. 10.1.   Heavy-duty pieces of equipment require the use of high strength materials.
Courtesy of The Hobart Corporation.

high corrosion resistance
high strength
ease of cleaning
hardness, durability, and abrasion resistance
ease of maintenance
permanence
high ductility

Types

Foodservice equipment manufacturers and fabricators usually select from the two types of stainless steel referred to as Type 302 or Type 304. These stainless steels are produced according to standards of the American Iron and Steel Institute that control the amounts of alloying materials. The amounts of the elements used in each type are shown in Table 10.1.

The corrosion resistance of stainless steel is attributed to the addition of the chromium to the alloy. Nickel lowers the thermal conductivity of the alloy and increases its coefficient of expansion, allowing it to be formed into various shapes more easily. The amount of carbon allowed is restricted so the alloy can be welded without forming chromium carbide, which lowers corrosion resistance.

Stainless steel is produced in sheets, plates, bars, wires, pipes, and tubing. Foodservice equipment manufacturers select appropriate forms to manufacture the equipment.

Finishes

A number of degrees of finishing are available for stainless steel. For stainless steel sheets, the process for producing the finishes are identified in Table 10.2. The number 1, 2D, and 2B finishes are produced by standard grinding. The number 3, 4, 6, and 7 finishes require additional polishing and buffing.

The No. 4 finish (see the fryer shown in Fig. 10.2) is the standard used for surfaces that are in contact with food or exposed to it. Nonfood contact surfaces and non-exposed supporting frames and members can have a duller finish, which is less expensive than the polished finishes.

Thicknesses

Metal thicknesses are usually designated by the United States Standard Gauge numbers. Although other gauges are manufactured,

TABLE 10.1. COMPOSITION OF TYPE 302 AND TYPE 304 STAINLESS STEELS

Element	Type 302	Type 304
Chromium	17–19%	18–20%
Nickel	8–10%	8–12%
Manganese	2% max	2% max
Silicon	1% max	1% max
Carbon	0.15% max	0.08% max

TABLE 10.2. STANDARD FINISHES FOR STAINLESS STEEL SURFACES

Finish Designation (No.)	Process
1	Hot rolled, annealed, pickled: used where smoothness of finish is not of particular importance
2D	Dull cold rolled, annealed and descaled: used in forming articles that may be polished after fabrication
2B	Bright cold rolled, receives a light cold rolled pass on polished rolls: more readily polished than the No. 1 or No. 2D finish
3	Intermediate polish, 100 grit finish: may be additionally polished after fabrication
4	Standard polish, 120 grit: most widely used finish for foodservice equipment
6	Standard polish Tampico brushed, 180 grit finish: a dull satin finish frequently used for architectural applications
7	High luster polish, 320 grit finish: used primarily for ornamental purposes
8	Mirror finish, special buffing: used for mirrors and reflectors

FIG. 10.2. Stainless steel in contact with food is polished to a number 4 finish on this fryer.
Courtesy of The Hobart Corporation.

TABLE 10.3.   ACTUAL DIMENSIONS FOR
VARIOUS GAUGE NUMBER DESIGNATIONS

Gauge Number	Thickness (Inches)
6	0.1943
7	0.1793
8	0.1644
9	0.1495
10	0.1345
11	0.1196
12	0.1046
13	0.0897
14	0.0747
15	0.0673
16	0.0598
17	0.0538
18	0.0478
19	0.0418
20	0.0359
21	0.0329
22	0.0299
23	0.0269
24	0.0239

Source: Mechanical Engineer's Handbook.

typical gauge numbers of metals used for foodservice equipment range
from 6 to 24 (6 gauge is the thickest and the 24 gauge is the thinnest).
The actual dimensions for these typical gauges are shown in Table
10.3.

Since there are different gauge standards for non-ferrous metals and
wires, it is best to always refer to thickness by the actual dimension
in inches.

OTHER MATERIALS

Galvanized Steel

Galvanized steel is produced by coating the steel with a layer of zinc.
The preferred method of producing galvanized steel is by electroplating, which gives the best bond between the steel and the zinc. For some
applications, hot-dipping the steel with zinc may be used, but the zinc
coating is not as uniform as that produced by the electroplating process. The quality of the galvanized steel is dependent upon the thickness of the zinc coating. A coating of 2 oz per ft^2 is usually used.

Galvanized steel can be satisfactorily used for foodservice equipment
where there is no food contact or where abrasion is not evident. The
zinc, although corrosion resistant, is very soft and can be easily

marred. Once the zinc coating is broken, the underlying steel will be exposed to corrosive substances and will begin to corrode. Therefore galvanized steel is usually limited in use for exterior body cover, bracing, or equipment legs. A limited number of sinks, tables, and shelving units are produced with galvanized steel. These pieces of equipment will have a much shorter life than those made of stainless steel and should be specified accordingly.

Other Coatings Used on Metals

Various materials other than zinc can be used to coat metals, especially steel. The purpose of the coatings is to give protection from corrosion and to make them easy to clean and maintain. Typical materials used for coating include aluminum, chromium, nickel, enamel, silicone compounds, and plastic compounds.

The chromium- and nickel-plated steels are used in applications where appearance is important. Plated materials should not be assumed to be as durable as stainless steel because the coating is usually very thin.

Enameled coatings may be acrylic or alkyd. The acrylic enamels give a smooth finish that resists stains and can be easily cleaned. Unfortunately, they are susceptible to some chemicals used in foodservice facilities and will abrade fairly easily. Baked alkyd finishes do have better resistance to chipping and will be satisfactory in applications that are not exposed to heavy corrosive agents.

Silicone compounds are used to create the porcelain coatings that are more durable and more mar-resistant than the enamel-coated steel. Porcelain-coated steel is widely used for ovens, refrigerators, freezers, and other larger pieces of equipment because of its relatively low cost in comparison to stainless steel.

Plastic compounds are becoming more important as coating materials since they provide desirable characteristics of food and soil release and consequently are very easy to clean. Teflon is used on oven interiors, griddle surfaces, and for coating cooking utensils.

Other Metals

There are other metals, primarily pure aluminum and copper, that find application in the manufacture of foodservice equipment.

The light weight of aluminum makes it useful for carts and mobile equipment. Aluminum is also widely used for cooking utensils and some types of cooking equipment such as griddles.

Copper has a very high coefficient of heat transmission and therefore is used in applications where rapid heat transfer is needed. The high cost of copper has limited its use in recent years, but it is still the material of choice for water pipes and electrical wires. Copper may be used for decorative effects such as in display cooking areas.

CONSTRUCTION STANDARDS

Fastening Methods

Several fastening methods are utilized by equipment manufacturers to produce the finished product. The fastening of materials in the food zone has to be capable of meeting sanitary requirements, while in non-food zones, there may be a wider choice of fastening methods. Most manufacturers follow the minimum standards set forth by the National Sanitation Foundation.

Welding

Welding is the preferred method for joining sheets of metal that cannot be formed into the desired shapes by stamping or forming. Heliarc welding is used on stainless steel if there is sufficient thickness of metal. The heliarc process utilizes an inert gas as the flux, resulting in a very smooth and strong weld. The weld can be ground and polished to the extent that the joint is the equivalent of the No. 4 finish. Whenever possible, heliarc welding should be used for foodservice equipment in all food contact zones.

Electric arc welding also has to be used on material of sufficient thickness to avoid burning through the metal. These welds do not come out as smooth or even as the heliarc welds but may be readily used in areas that are non-food contact or are not exposed.

Acetylene welding may be necessary on thin metal sheets since the electric arcs tend to burn through rather easily. There may be an increased corrosion problem with acetylene welds because of the deposits of carbon that are created. Acetylene welds also tend to distort thin metals if not done properly.

Soldering

Soldering is different from welding in that the metals to be joined are bonded rather than fused together. Soldered joints do not have the strength of welded joints and should be used appropriately in those applications that are not subjected to stress. Basic solders are mixtures of tin and lead, and the presence of lead prevents their use on joints in food contact areas. If soldering has to be used on food contact surfaces, a mixture of 95% tin and 5% silver or 100% tin may be used.

"Silver soldering" does result in greater strength than ordinary solders and is used in applications where some stress will be present. Silver solders are mixtures containing silver, copper, and zinc, which bond better than the basic tin and lead solder. Joining stainless steel to non-ferrous metals can be done with "silver soldering."

Soldered joints are checked frequently if used where vibrations and other mechanical stress is present. The joints can be re-soldered easily if the bond is broken.

Mechanical Fasteners

The use of bolts, screws, rivets, and studs is undesirable in the food zones of foodservice equipment for sanitary reasons. They may be used only in non-food zones if other joining techniques are not practical. Low profile fasteners are preferred in order to facilitate cleaning of the area where the fasteners protrude.

SPECIAL FEATURES

Edge Treatments

Exposed edges on foodservice equipment are formed to provide a safe and sanitary condition. Nosings are either open with sufficient room for cleaning or completely closed. If open edges are to be used, the National Sanitation Foundation recommends at least a ¾ in. (1.9 cm) space between the edge and the body. Several shapes for the nosings are available including the semi-roll, the bull nose roll, and die stamped shapes. Fig. 10.3 shows the edge treatments available from one manufacturer as well as other optional items for worktables.

On equipment where spillage is anticipated, such as soiled dish tables, the edges are turned up a sufficient height to contain the material.

Legs and Feet

Unless equipment is to be placed on a raised platform, sealed to the floor, or wall-hung, legs and feet may be specified for support. Tubular or square legs are usually used to raise the equipment so that the

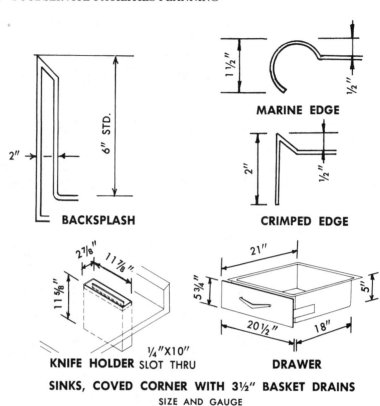

FIG. 10.3. Edge treatments and other optional items for a worktable.
Courtesy of Stanley Knight Corporation.

lowest horizontal member is at least 6 in. (15.2 cm) above the floor. Fig. 10.4 illustrates a half-size convention oven equipped with tubular legs. An example of square legs is shown in Fig. 10.5. The legs and feet should be rigid enough to support the weight of the equipment with a minimum of cross bracing. The legs are fastened to the body of the equipment in such a way as to minimize the accumulation of dirt and harborage of vermin. The feet are usually shaped to allow easy cleaning.

Gussets that are used to attach the legs to the equipment are designed to eliminate insect harborage and to be easily cleaned.

FIG. 10.4.   Tubular legs and feet used to support and raise the equipment.
Courtesy of The Hobart Corporation.

Casters and Rollers

Mobile equipment is gaining popularity in foodservice design because it provides greater flexibility to accommodate different workplace arrangements for handling changes in menu items or products. Casters and rollers are selected to assure that the equipment can be easily moved by one worker. The casters and wheels should be designed for easy maintenance and cleaning. A wheel tread that is smooth and wide enough to prevent damage to flooring materials is desirable. This is especially important if the equipment is to be moved on resilient flooring materials.

Doors and Panels

Doors that are used to enclose openings and provide access to interior areas are usually of two types, single panel or double panel. Double-

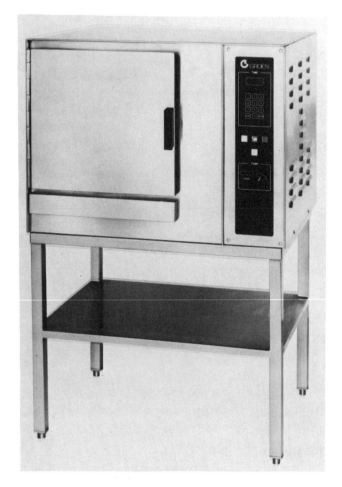

FIG. 10.5.   An example of square legs used for equipment.
Courtesy of Groen Division/Dover Corporation.

panel doors may include insulation if heat transmission is to be minimized. Double-panel insulated doors are used on refrigerators, freezers, and hot and cold food holding equipment. Hinges for the doors are
kept to a minimum because they are difficult to keep in a sanitary
condition. Sliding doors are designed to be easily removed for cleaning
purposes.

When doors or covers are used to prevent contamination from
reaching food zones, they are designed with a flange that overlaps the
opening and are sloped to provide drainage. Covers are designed to

provide sufficient clearance to prevent contact with the foods they cover. All covers should be designed for ease of removal either as a whole or in sections.

Fixed panels are fastened so that there are a minimum of protruding fasteners. Easily removable panels can be provided for equipment that needs frequent inspection and maintenance. It is best to minimize the size and weight of removable panels so that one person can handle them easily.

Drawers and Bins

Where food is to be stored in drawers or bins, special requirements are needed to assure that contamination does not occur. The drawers and bins are usually manufactured with coved construction with smooth interiors formed by welding or die stamping. Fillet material and solder are not appropriate to form the coves at angles or corners.

The drawers, bins, and drawer carriages should be designed for easy removal for cleaning purposes. Bins for storage of food items are either totally enclosed or provided with a tight-fitting cover.

FLOORS

In addition to the selection of equipment, choices must be made for flooring in every area of the foodservice facility. As with equipment, selection of materials for floors is based on minimum maintenance required to retain appearance and sanitary conditions. The main consideration for floors in kitchen areas is to provide a non-slippery surface to prevent accidents. The other factors that are considered are durability; comfort; quietness; and resistance to abrasion, grease, and cleaning compounds. Some of the most commonly used materials for floors are described below.

Asphalt Tile

Asphalt tile is a resilient tile made of asphalt, lime rock, asbestos fibers, fillers, and pigments. The tiles may be used on concrete slabs and below-grade concrete that is subject to slight moisture from the ground. Asphalt tiles are low in cost and available in a wide variety of patterns and colors. A ⅛ in. thickness is usually used for normal situations, although other thicknesses are available.

Substances such as grease, oils, acids, and solvents will soften asphalt tile. Because of these limitations, asphalt tiles cannot be recommended for kitchen or bathroom floors. They may, however, be satisfactorily used in other areas of the foodservice facility.

Carpet

Carpeting enhances the decor of dining rooms as well as providing good acoustical treatment. The wide variety of fibers used and the different types of carpet construction make the selection of carpeting a difficult process.

Among the most frequently used fibers for carpets are acrylic, nylon, polyester, rayon, and wool. The factors to consider in selecting a fiber for carpeting include cost, wear resistance, resilience, soil and stain resistance, and cleanability. Table 10.4 gives a brief comparison of these fibers.

Only commercial grade, machine-made carpets including Axminster, Knitted, Tufted, Velvet, Wilton, Loomed, and Flocked are recommended for foodservice facilities. All carpeting should be placed over a good quality pad especially in heavy traffic areas.

Ceramic Tile

There are three main types of ceramic tile used for floors: mosaic, paver, and quarry. Ceramic mosaic tiles have a very dense, fully vitrified body. They are made from natural clays or blended mixtures of clay, feldspar, and flint. Small mosaic tiles are assembled in the desired pattern and fastened together to simplify handling and installation. One method that is used is to glue the top face of the tiles to a paper base which is removed after the tiles are installed.

Paver tiles differ from mosaic tiles primarily in size. Most tiles are available in sizes from 3 by 3 in. to 6 by 6 in.

Quarry tile is an unglazed ceramic tile with a dense body that makes it resistant to abrasion and moisture. These tiles provide a better footing and are recommended for kitchens (as illustrated in Fig. 10.6) and other areas subjected to spillage and heavy wear. The initial cost

TABLE 10.4. COMPARISON OF SOME COMMON CARPET FIBERS

Factor	Acrylic	Nylon	Polyester	Rayon	Wool
Cost	Medium	Medium	Medium	Medium	Medium
Wear resistance	High	High	High	High	High
Resilience	High	Medium	Medium	Low	High
Soil and stain resistance	High	Medium	High	Low	High
Cleanability	High	High	High	Medium	High

FIG. 10.6. Quarry tile floors provide good footing and are very durable.
Courtesy of Fresh Approach Handicapped Training Center and Hamill & McKinney, Architects-Engineers, Inc.

for ceramic tiles is high compared to other flooring materials; however, the tiles are long-lasting and easily cleaned and maintained.

Concrete

Concrete is a bonded mixture of portland cement, sand, gravel, and water. The quality of concrete is dependent upon the selection of aggregates, proportioning of the mix, and the care given to pouring, finishing, and curing. Good quality concrete floors are durable, resist abrasion, and are fairly easy to maintain. Poor quality concrete, on the other hand, does erode easily and presents a bothersome dust problem.

Concrete may be finished to any degree of smoothness desired. Typical finish treatments include a float finish that gives a surface with good footing characteristics, a trowel finish that results in the smoothest surface, and a broom finish that is usually used outdoors for its skid-resistant qualities.

The relatively low cost of concrete makes it a suitable floor for storage areas.

Cork Tile

Cork tiles are manufactured by baking cork granules with phenolic or other resin binders. These tiles are usually made in thicknesses of ⅛, ³⁄₁₆, ⁵⁄₁₆, and ½ in. and may be obtained in a natural finish or a factory pre-waxed finish. Unless maintained with sealers and protective coatings, cork tiles tend to stain very easily from spills and heavy wear.

Cork tiles may be used where foot comfort and quietness are of primary importance or where it is desired for blending with other design elements used in the foodservice facility.

Linoleum

Linoleum is manufactured from linseed oil or synthetic oils, a wood flour filler, and pigments, usually with a backing of burlap or rag felt. Linoleum is available in large sheets or tiles.

Since moisture can attack the backing materials used for linoleum, it is not used on concrete that is at or below grade. Linoleum has good resistance to grease but is readily attacked by alkaline substances.

Rubber

The main use of rubber in foodservice facilities is for supplemental flooring, especially in warewashing areas. The fabrication of the rubber strips has to allow for easy cleaning and maintainance. The National Sanitation Foundation standards for material and design considerations of supplemental flooring may be consulted for details.

Terrazzo

Terrazzo floors are made of marble chips and portland cement with the addition of coloring pigments if desired. Different methods of installing the terrazzo are used depending on the expansion or movement that is anticipated. The floors are usually cast in place with metal divider strips. Precast terrazzo can be used for stairs. The use of terrazzo is mainly for its appearance and since it is stained by spillage, it is not used in kitchen areas.

Vinyl Tile

Vinyl flooring consists predominately of polyvinyl chloride with various fillers, extenders, and coloring agents. Because of the large choices of colors and patterns, vinyl tile can be used in many different types of areas. The tile exhibits good resistance to solvents, acids, and alkalis. It is also resistant to grease, oil, and many cleaning agents. Vinyl flooring can withstand heavy loads without indenting and is resilient and comfortable underfoot. Vinyl floors are somewhat susceptible to heavy foot traffic, which erodes the surface. It should therefore be protected with floor polish.

Vinyl-Asbestos

Like asbestos tile, vinyl-asbestos tiles can be installed on below grade concrete surfaces. These tiles are basically vinyl tiles with the addition of asbestos fibers. Vinyl-asbestos tiles have a duller and harder finish and consequently stand up better to heavy foot traffic compared to the pure vinyl tiles. The resistance to grease, oil, and cleaning compounds is slightly less than for vinyl tiles.

Wood

Wood floors are used primarily for their appearance and are available in a variety of forms including strips, blocks, laminated blocks, and laminated sheets. Commonly used woods are maple, beech, oak, douglas fir, and western hemlock. Wood floors are resilient but tend to wear easily and require waxing and polishing to maintain their appearance. Water is the primary enemy of wood floors.

WALLS

Wall surfaces in kitchen areas may be concrete, concrete block, or ceramic tile, described above. Concrete and concrete block walls are usually coated with paint to provide a sanitary and easily maintained surface. Other surfacing materials for kitchens include stainless steel (a very expensive wall covering), plaster, and cinder block if properly sealed and painted (primarily used in dry areas). Gypsum panels may be used on partition walls provided the joints are plastered and sealed.

Painted coatings used are glossy finish epoxy and acrylic enamels. These paints have excellent durability and are resistant to soiling.

Wall surfaces for dining rooms can include a greater choice of materials depending on the desired appearance. In addition to the above mentioned materials, wood paneling, wallpaper, and fabrics may be used. Plastic-coated materials are also being used to a greater degree in dining areas since they are available in a variety of color, designs, and textures and are easy to clean and maintain.

CEILINGS

Ceilings in kitchen areas may be plastered and painted or a dry-type construction using panels or tiles may be used. Ceiling panels and tiles are available in metal, cement-asbestos, gypsum, and fiber materials. Plastic-coated panels and tiles are preferable since they are easier to clean. Panel and tiles with acoustical properties may be used to reduce noise levels. Building and sanitary codes should be checked for acceptable ceiling materials if there is any question about their use.

Considerations for dining room ceilings are color, texture, light reflectance, flame resistance, and acoustical efficiency. Acoustical tiles are available in a variety of materials such as wood fiber, mineral fiber, cement-asbestos, or metal. The tiles may be perforated or textured.

Unique decorative ceiling may be obtained by using tin tiles that are formed into different design patterns.

PROBLEMS AND EXERCISES

10.1. Write a specification for a particular piece of mobile equipment that is to be fabricated of stainless steel.

10.2. Make a checklist of factors that should be considered in selecting a dishwashing machine. What additional factors would be added if the checklist were to be used for a glass washer?

10.3. Evaluate the variety of materials that can be used for the surfaces of walk-in refrigerators and freezers from the standpoint of cost, appearance, ease of maintenance, and insulating qualities.

10.4. Determine the square yards of carpeting that would be needed for a dining room that is 150 ft wide and 200 ft long.

10.5. Describe the type of self-dispensing equipment that you would select to place on cafeteria counters that would minimize the number of serving personnel needed.

BIBLIOGRAPHY

AVERY, A.C.   1984.   A Modern Guide to Foodservice Equipment. CBI Books, Van Nostrand Reinhold Publishing Company, New York.

HALL, C.W., FARRALL, A.W. and RIPPEN, A.L.   1986.   Encyclopedia of Food Engineering. AVI Publishing Co., Westport, Connecticut.

KNIGHT, J.B.   1986.   Successful selection of foodservice equipment. The Consultant 19 (4), 29–33.

NATIONAL SANITATION FOUNDATION   1984.   Standard Number 52, Supplemental Flooring. Ann Arbor, Michigan.

SCRIVEN, C. and STEVENS, J.   1980.   Food Equipment Facts. Conceptual Design, Troy, New York.

WILKINSON, J.   1981.   The Complete Book of Cooking Equipment. CBI Books, Van Nostrand Reinhold Company, New York.

Equipment and Facility Maintenance

INTRODUCTION

The maintenance of foodservice equipment and facilities begins with good planning. The selection of materials, design and fabrication methods all influence how easy it will be to clean and maintain the equipment. Since maintenance is primarily labor, proper planning will accomplish two things: (1) assure lower operating costs after the facility is built through reduced maintenance costs, and (2) enable high standards of sanitation to be maintained for the life of the facility. This concept also applies to selection of building features such as floor, wall, and ceiling materials and the heating, cooling, ventilating, plumbing, and electrical systems.

The primary concepts involved in the planning for ease of cleaning and maintenance are the following:

1. Minimize soil, dirt, and food buildup.
2. When buildup occurs, make it easy to remove.
3. Avoid as many soil-collecting surfaces and recesses as possible.
4. Select smooth, non-porous surfaces.
5. Provide easy access to areas that have to be frequently cleaned and maintained.
6. Streamline electrical, gas, and plumbing connections.
7. Use coved corners on equipment and building surfaces.
8. Provide adequate floor drains and clean-outs.
9. Use automated cleaning and sanitizing systems.

Well-maintained equipment and facilities will last longer and be more energy efficient. Periodic inspection and necessary adjustments form the basis of a good maintenance program. Manufacturers' recommendations for procedures should be followed. These are usually incorporated into the operational manuals supplied with the equipment. Adequate maintenance will minimize the need for repairs and minimize down time of equipment.

Stainless Steel Surfaces

Since most foodservice equipment utilizes stainless steel to some extent, general recommendation for its care and cleaning can be given. Although stainless steel is easy to clean and maintain, it nevertheless is subject to staining and requires care. In order to keep its appearance, stainless steel needs contact with air to maintain the layer of oxide that provides the shine. Thus stainless steel must be cleaned regularly.

Routine cleaning of stainless steel may be accomplished with a hot detergent solution. The washed area is then rinsed and wiped dry with a soft clean cloth. For more thorough cleaning, a paste of water and non-abrasive scouring powder may be used. The paste should be rubbed in the direction of the polish lines to avoid scratches and then rinsed and dried.

Heavy deposits of food and soil can be removed with stainless steel, wood, or plastic scrapers. Ordinary steel wool, steel scrapers or knives should never be used since particles of iron can become embedded in the surface and rust. Hard water deposits may be removed with a vinegar and water solution. The surface is then rinsed and dried as indicated earlier.

Foodservice Equipment

Since it is not practical to cover the recommended cleaning and maintenance procedures for all types of equipment available from different manufacturers, typical cleaning and maintenance procedures for the most commonly used types of foodservice equipment will be discussed. Each foodservice facility should set up its own cleaning and maintenance procedures based on the types and models of equipment that will be used. Manufacturers' manuals are the best guides to use in setting up the periodic maintenance procedures that will assure continual operating efficiency of the equipment. The training of employees who will be responsible for the cleaning and maintenance procedures is very important to the success of a preventative maintenance program. The primary purpose of these programs is to maintain a sanitary foodservice facility.

BROILERS

The basic maintenance of gas broilers includes checking the flame for proper operation and keeping the gas ports clean. A yellow-tipped flame or general yellow color indicates a shortage of air. The burners should be adjusted to give a blue flame.

The broiler grates and other removable parts are cleaned daily. Interiors may be brushed and cleaned every day to prevent the buildup of food particles. A monthly check of the pilots or ignition devices and thermostats is needed to assure satisfactory operation. Lubrication of the gas valves, if required, may also be done monthly. Periodic inspection of the gas lines and connectors is needed for safety reasons. Suspected gas leaks should be checked immediately and corrected.

The maintenance of electric broilers consists mainly of replacement of the heating elements or controls when necessary. Daily cleaning of the grates and the broiler interior is recommended. Exterior surfaces may be cleaned with a mild detergent solution and then rinsed and dried. The grate carriage and lifting mechanisms are periodically inspected for proper cleanliness and operation.

The grates and radiants of char broilers need daily cleaning. A wire brush can be used to remove heavy deposits of food.

COFFEE URNS

Proper cleaning of coffee urns is essential for top quality coffee. The surfaces exposed to brewed coffee or coffee vapor accumulate deposits that will ruin the taste of subsequent batches if not removed. Another problem arises from mineral deposits left from the water. It is good procedure to clean the coffee urn after every batch. The urn is first rinsed with water to remove any coffee and deposits that have settled to the bottom or in the spout. Then using a gallon or more of hot water, the interior should be vigorously brushed. The urn is then drained and rinsed. If the urn is not to be used immediately for another batch of coffee, a gallon or two of water may be left in the urn, making sure that it is drained before the next use.

A semi-weekly cleaning using an urn cleaner recommended by the manufacturer is needed to remove accumulated deposits. The urn is filled about two-thirds full of water and the urn cleaner is added. The urn is turned on for about an hour and then scrubbed. A long thin brush can be used to clean the sight glass and the pipe leading to the spout. Several rinsings with hot water are necessary to assure that all traces of the urn cleaner are removed. The spout valves may then be removed and cleaned. Some fresh water should again be left in the urn until the next batch is to be brewed.

Coffee urns on serving lines should be cleaned when the line is shut down to prevent customers accidentally using the urn filled with urn cleaner. "Do Not Use" signs are not always read by customers, who may be distracted by conversation or other activities.

Since coffee brewing is highly dependent upon proper temperature of the water, a good maintenance procedure is to periodically check the operation of the thermostat. Other maintenance checks for leakage at the spout, the sight glass, or water pipes can be made weekly.

DISHWASHERS

All steam, gas, and electricity as well as detergent dispensers should be turned off before cleaning the dishwashers. Scrap trays and curtains may be run through the dishwasher before shutting it down.

The tanks are drained and cleaned with a long-handled brush using a detergent recommended by the manufacturer. Wash arms are removed and cleaned. Any deposits of lime or hard water deposits are removed from the rinse jets. All interior surfaces, overflows, strainers, and filters are cleaned and rinsed.

The exterior of the dishwasher as well as the dish tables may be cleaned with a detergent solution and then rinsed and dried. Dispensers are cleaned and checked.

Typical maintenance checks are made for leakage of water from pumps, valves, or drains. Periodic inspection of the jets is recommended to make sure they are not narrowed excessively by scale deposits, which either reduce the flow of water or create uneven spray patterns. Any belts and conveyors are inspected for wear and lubricated as needed.

FRYERS AND FRY PANS

Fryers

Maintenance of fryers requires daily or twice weekly (depending on usage) cleaning. If the fryer has a removable fat container, the fat is removed and the container may be cleaned at the pot sink. Larger fryers may have siphoning attachments, come equipped with a drain, or have a central fat filtering system. After the fat has been removed, the interior of the fat container may be wiped out and then filled with water and fryer cleaner solution. The fat container is rinsed and dried after the solution is removed.

The manufacturer's recommendations should be followed for cleaning the heating elements on electric fryers. The elements should be cleaned whenever traces of carbonization are seen.

Periodic inspection of the gas flames, drain valves, lifting devices, and checking the calibration of the thermostats is essential to maintain fryers in peak operating condition.

Tilting Fry Pans

Daily cleaning of tilting fry pans may be accomplished by first scraping food residues from the surfaces and then washing down with warm water. For heavy residues of cooked or baked-on food, a recommended cleaning solution can be used to soften and help remove the food. After soaking, the pan should be rinsed thoroughly. Steel wool or abrasive cleaners should not be used.

Routine maintenance includes checking calibration of the thermostats, lubrication of the tilting gears and mechanisms, checking burners or heating elements, and periodic inspection for loose parts.

Care of Frying Fat

The most expensive part of deep fat frying is the consumption of fat by the foods. For example, french fries contain approximately 10% fat, which is absorbed during the frying process. This absorbed fat has to be continually replaced.

Fat should be strained daily and replenished with fresh fat as necessary. Fig. 11.1 shows a battery of three fryers with a central filtering system that simplifies care of the fat. A usual recommendation is to add 15 to 20% of the kettle capacity as fresh fat. For example, one would add approximately 5 lb. of fresh fat to a fryer that has a 30-lb. fat capacity. If the fryer is not utilizing at least 15% of its rated capacity through absorption by the foods, then enough should be drained off to allow the addition of the fresh fat.

Minimizing Fat Breakdown

The following precautions will minimize the costly fat breakdown that can occur:

1. The fryer should always be switched to "standby" during slack periods.

FIG. 11.1.   A battery of fryers equipped with a central fat filtering system.
Courtesy of Keating of Chicago, Inc.

2. Seasoning or salt should not be added to the foods during frying.
3. All metal components in contact with the fat should be free of carbon, food crumbs, soap, and moisture.
4. Fat level should not be topped up with lard, meat drippings, or similar fatty substances.

GRIDDLES

Regular griddle cooking surfaces should be cleaned daily or more often if necessary. During use, any particles of food that might interfere with the drainage of grease into the grease trough should be removed. The grease drawer can be cleaned at the pot sink. Depending on need, the griddle surface may be cleaned with a griddle stone, which is always rubbed with the grain of the surface. Steel wool should not be used on griddle surfaces. Season the griddle surface after each cleaning. The exterior body surfaces, control knobs, and connecting cables may be cleaned with a mild detergent solution.

Griddle surfaces are checked periodically for cold spots that would indicate bad electrical heating elements on electric models, or poor fuel-air mixtures on gas-heated models. Thermostats are also a possible cause of trouble and can be tested for calibration. Periodic visual inspection of electrical and gas connections is a good preventative measure.

OVENS AND RANGES

Conventional Deck Ovens

Proper cleaning procedures are the most important part of maintaining deck ovens. Care must be exercised when cleaning the interiors so that the thermostatic bulb and capillary tube are not damaged. Daily cleaning involves scraping burned-on particles of food from the decks and brushing the interior. Special attention is paid to the door crevices, which must be kept clean for the door to close properly. Loose-fitting doors allow too much heat to escape.

Decks may be cleaned at the pot and pan sink. Periodic cleaning of the interior using recommended detergent solutions is needed to prevent excessive buildup of food deposits. Aluminized interiors are cleaned using manufacturers' recommendations. To avoid damaging the heat reflective qualities of these surfaces, steel wool or harsh detergents should not be used.

Hardened food spillage can be removed by sprinkling with salt and operating the oven at 500° F for approximately 30 minutes. The food spillage will char and can then be removed by scraping with a blunt spatula. Exterior surfaces may be washed with a detergent solution followed by rinsing and drying. Enamel-coated surfaces may be polished with recommended polishing products. Control knobs should be given daily cleaning; otherwise excessive buildup will obscure the numbers.

Periodic inspection of burners, elements, lamps, and controls are needed to keep the deck ovens in operating condition. Thermostats can be easily checked against the reading obtained with a good oven thermometer.

Convection Ovens

In addition to the cleaning procedures described for deck ovens, the following apply to convection ovens. Interiors of convection ovens may be porcelain, stainless steel, aluminized steel, or teflon coated. Each type of interior has to be cleaned accordingly. Some manufacturers have convection ovens with removable liners to simplify cleaning.

The constant air movement in the convection oven during operation requires that the doors be kept clean so heat loss is at a minimum. Additional items that need cleaning include the fan blades and baffles. Dirty fan blades reduce the flow of air and the oven may not operate as efficiently. Fan blades are cleaned with a cloth dampened with detergent solution. Baffles can be washed in the pot sink.

Additional maintenance on convection ovens is related to the fan and fan motor. Check instruction manuals for proper lubrication requirements of these items, since some motors may be permanently lubricated while others may require periodic lubrication. Monthly inspection of oven components is suggested.

Microwave Ovens

Microwave ovens (illustrated in Fig. 11.2) are inherently much cleaner than deck or convection ovens and consequently cleaning is simplified. Normal cleaning of the interior with a mild detergent solution, with special attention paid to the door, is usually all that is required. A tight-fitting door is essential in order to minimize possible radiation leakage. Door seals should be continually inspected for bad spots. If leakage is suspected, the oven should be checked with a radiation meter. Air filters can be cleaned by soaking in a detergent solution followed by rinsing and allowing them to dry. Air inlet openings should also be checked and cleaned if necessary. Replacement and repair of microwave equipment is best left to trained service technicians.

Ranges

A typical cleaning procedure for open top ranges includes removing the burner grids and grease trays and washing them at the sink. Gas burners may be brushed and checked for cleanliness at this time.

A damp cloth dipped in recommended detergent solution can be used to clean the interior surfaces of the burner area. After the area has been cleaned, the grease trays and burner grids are replaced. It is good practice to light the gas burners to check for proper operation and adjust if necessary. Heating elements and electrical wires on electric ranges should be checked for signs of damage.

Solid top ranges may be cleaned daily by scraping burnt-on particles of food and then washing with the detergent solution, being careful not to use excessive amounts of water. After cleaning, a light coating of cooking oil may be applied to retard rusting.

FIG. 11.2.   Microwave ovens are fairly easy to clean and maintain.
Courtesy of The Hobart Corporation.

Griddle tops on ranges may be cleaned following the basic procedures given for griddles, while ovens may be cleaned using the general procedures given for deck ovens earlier in this chapter.

PREPARATION EQUIPMENT

Food Cutters and Choppers

Food cutters and choppers should be unplugged before any cleaning or maintenance procedures are performed.

The cleaning of food cutters, such as the one illustrated in Fig. 11.3, and choppers can be simplified greatly by rinsing between batches of foods. The rinsing has to be done immediately after the batch is processed, so that food particles do not dry out and adhere to the interior.

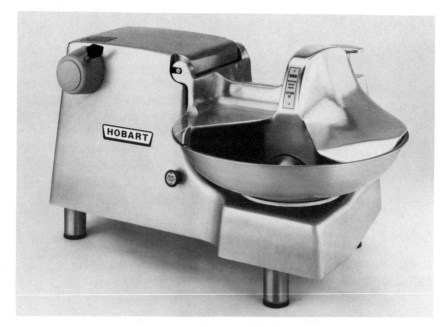

FIG. 11.3.   Food cutters are best rinsed after each use.
Courtesy of The Hobart Corporation.

Cleaning is accomplished by disassembling removable parts, including the blade, and using a mild detergent solution to wash the parts. The parts are rinsed, allowed to dry, and then reassembled.

Maintenance of cutters and choppers includes inspection of the switch and bowl-locking device and checking blades for proper adjustment and sharpness.

Slicers

Slicers should be unplugged before any cleaning and maintenance is performed.

Typical cleaning procedure for slicers (see Fig. 11.4) is to remove the carriage and blade guards, which can be washed at the pot and pan sink using regular detergent solution. These parts are allowed to dry before the slicer is assembled. Extreme caution is needed to prevent cutting the fingers or hands on the blade when cleaning the blade and shell with a cloth dipped in detergent solution. The blade and shell are sanitized and allowed to dry. Care is again needed when the carriage and blade guards are reassembled.

FIG. 11.4.   Care should be exercised when cleaning and sharpening slicers.
Courtesy of The Hobart Corporation.

Blade sharpening should be done according to the manufacturer's procedures as outlined in the owners manual. The blade should be clean before sharpening. The sharpening interval will vary with usage and the type of foods that are sliced.

Also check the manufacturer's recommendations for adjustments and lubrication of the carriage and its components.

Mixers

The mixer bowl, beaters, whips, and other accessories that have been used are best cleaned immediately after use. These items can be cleaned at the pot and pan sink with regular detergents, followed by rinsing and drying. The hubs of beaters and whips that fit over the shaft contain many irregular surfaces that require special effort to clean. The mixer body can also be cleaned with regular detergents and hot water. All surfaces are rinsed and then may be dried with a clean cloth.

Regular lubrication of the moving parts of the mixer at intervals recommended by the manufacturer should be performed, and the transmission oil should be checked periodically.

Tables

Table tops may be scrubbed with a hot detergent solution, rinsed, sanitized, and allowed to air dry. Drawers are cleaned weekly by removing the contents and washing at the pot and pan sink. They should be dried before being replaced and refilled. Any shelves at the table are emptied, cleaned, sanitized, and air dried before materials are put on them.

REFRIGERATORS

Reach-in Units

Each week, all items stored in reach-in refrigerators (Fig. 11.5) may be transferred to a walk-in unit and the entire interior thoroughly cleaned after the shelves have been removed. The interior surfaces, with emphasis on the shelf guides, can be washed with a hot detergent solution. The surfaces are rinsed with hot water and dried with clean cloths. A sanitizing solution may be used after washing. Shelves may be cleaned at the pot sink or run through the dishwashing machine if possible. Attention should be paid to the door gaskets to assure that they properly seal the door.

Periodic maintenance of the condenser coils is frequently neglected. Dirty condenser coils prohibit heat transfer and cause the refrigeration unit to run excessively. Coils can be dusted or vacuum cleaned, and if extremely dirty may be cleaned with hot detergent spray followed by a hot water rinse. Excess water is wiped up before the refrigerator is turned on.

Periodic inspection of the fan blades is needed to determine if they have become dirty and require cleaning. Blades can be cleaned in the same manner as condenser coils.

Walk-in Units

Walk-in refrigerators require complete cleaning on a periodic basis depending on usage. Heavily used walk-ins may be cleaned monthly,

FIG. 11.5.   Reach-in refrigerators are cleaned weekly.
Courtesy of The Hobart Corporation.

while less usage can extend the cleaning interval. As with reach-in units, all items should be removed and the interior cleaned thoroughly. It is a good procedure to remove all shelving units and steam clean them periodically.

The evaporator coils need to be cleaned if accumulated dirt is observed. Condenser coils are cleaned as indicated for reach-in units.

STEAM EQUIPMENT

Steam-Jacketed Kettles

Steam-jacketed kettles (Fig. 11.6) may be flushed out with warm water after making sure the steam has been turned off and the kettle has cooled down. After flushing, the kettle is filled with detergent solution and allowed to soak for 30 to 60 minutes. All interior and exterior surfaces including the cover are scrubbed, with extra effort needed around the drain. The kettle may then be drained. If the kettle is equipped with a drain valve, it should be removed for a thorough scrubbing and cleaning. All surfaces, the valve, and other parts are rinsed with hot water before the kettle is reassembled. The outlet should be sanitized with a recommended solution. The kettle may be allowed to air dry before the cover is closed.

FIG. 11.6. Cleaning of steam-jacketed kettles is done after each use.
Courtesy of Groen Division/Dover Corporation.

Maintenance of the steam-jacketed kettle includes checking the operation of the safety valve under pressure, checking for leaks from the drain valve, and checking the operation of the steam trap.

Steamers

Removable shelves should be taken out and cleaned at the pot sink. Both interior and exterior surfaces may then be scrubbed with a regular detergent solution, and rinsed with hot water. The steamer is operated for a minute or two to allow surfaces to dry. The cleaned shelves may then be replaced.

Maintenance procedures include checking the safety valve, inspecting gaskets, and checking to detect any steam leaks.

VENTILATING HOODS

Ventilating hoods over cooking equipment can become a sanitary problem because droplets containing contaminants may fall onto the foods that are being prepared. Another serious problem associated with ventilating hoods is the fire danger they present when laden with grease and dust. If the filters become clogged, they markedly reduce the air flow and impair the performance of the ventilating system.

The filters should be removed weekly, or more often if necessary, and washed in the dishwashing machine. All surfaces of the hood are cleaned with a hot detergent solution, with special attention to any ledges or joints. Cleaning of the hood and the ducts is also recommended as a weekly procedure.

Fire-extinguishing systems must be checked and serviced if necessary by qualified service personnel. Inspections should be made every six months.

WALLS, FLOORS, AND CEILINGS

Kitchen Areas

Walls may be spot cleaned as necessary to avoid drying and hardening of soils that require more effort to remove. A weekly cleaning procedure involves shifting movable items away from the walls to simplify the work. Then the walls are scrubbed from bottom to top with cleaning compounds recommended for the particular wall finish.

Tile walls with grout joints require vigorous scrubbing to remove imbedded soil. The wall surfaces are rinsed and dried and any spillage on the floor cleaned up. It is important to change the rinse water frequently.

Floors are always spot cleaned immediately whenever spillage occurs to prevent employees from slipping and falling. Wet floors can also be an electrical hazard if the grounding systems on electrical equipment fail.

For tile floors, daily care includes sweeping and either hand mopping or machine scrubbing if necessary. A weekly machine scrub is needed, especially in areas that get a great deal of usage.

If ceilings are difficult to clean, the job may be contracted out. The frequency of cleaning varies with the amount of soil buildup, but a yearly cleaning is the minimum.

Serving Areas

The cleaning of serving areas such as shown in Fig. 11.7 is critical in conveying the desired image to customers. These public areas should

FIG. 11.7. Cafeteria serving areas require constant inspection and cleaning.
Courtesy of the Michigan League; Fry Associates Inc., Ann Arbor, Michigan; and The Hysen Group, Livonia, Michigan.

FIG. 11.8. Salad bars may be cleaned daily or after each meal period as needed.
Courtesy of Cres-Cor/Crown-X, Crescent Metal Products, Inc.

be continually checked for accidental spillage by customers and users. Thorough cleaning and sanitizing of the serving counters, sneeze guards, and other equipment is necessary after each serving period (see Fig. 11.8).

Dining Areas

Each type of flooring material requires its own cleaning and maintenance procedures. A general outline of procedures for flooring commonly used in dining areas is given below:

Carpeting:

1. Vacuum lightly daily to prevent dirt and soil from becoming imbedded in the fibers.
2. Remove spots and stains as soon as they are noticed. Consult the manual supplied with the carpeting since different stains require different procedures.

3. Thoroughly vacuum all areas every week. Some areas of heavy usage may be done twice a week.
4. Shampoo carpets at least once a year—more often if necessary.

Resilient flooring (vinyl, asphalt, linoleum, and so on):

1. Dry mop or sweep as needed to remove surface dirt (it is assumed that finish coats of wax or polish have been applied).
2. Damp mop daily using a neutral cleaner and buff if necessary.
3. Apply a light coating of wax or polish to areas that appear to have lost their shine.
4. Scrub lightly when damp mopping does not provide the desired results (that is, when soil or marks remain after damp mopping).
5. Strip off old coatings once or twice a year using a stripper recommended for the floor material. The stripper is allowed to remain on the surface for about 5 minutes to soften the coating; the floor is then scrubbed and rinsed.
6. Apply one or preferably two coats of wax or polish after the floor is dry.

Wood floors:

1. Sweep or vacuum daily to remove surface dirt. A wax-treated dust mop may also be used.
2. Damp mop sealed or waxed floors occasionally to remove accumulated dirt and soil. A minimum of water is used.
3. Wax periodically to keep dirt from entering the grain crevices of the wood.
4. Buff frequently with fine steel wool to reduce the need for damp mopping.

Non-resilient flooring (tile, concrete, terrazzo, and so on):

1. Sweep with a soft broom or treated cloth daily.
2. Remove minor soils with a mop dampened with clean water.
3. Wash as necessary with recommended detergents. Wet the floor before applying the detergent.
4. Mop up after washing, rinse with clean water, and use a well-wrung mop to pick up as much water as possible from the surface.

Waxes and coatings are not usually used on non-resilient floors.

PROBLEMS AND EXERCISES

11.1. Develop a cleaning schedule chart for the foodservice equipment in a fast-food operation. Include intervals, tools, and supplies to be used.

11.2. Evaluate the sanitary conditions at a local foodservice operation and prepare a report on your findings.

11.3. Develop a sample cleaning procedure for a piece of foodservice equipment not described in this chapter, such as a toaster, paddy machine, can opener, or dough roller.

11.4. Construct an evaluation chart that would compare flooring materials according to their ability to resist grease, abrasion or wear, cleaning compounds, acids, and alkalis.

11.5. Compare wall finish materials from the standpoint of cost, appearance, ease of maintenance, and durability. Include at least paints, tile, vinyls, and fabrics in the comparison.

BIBLIOGRAPHY

AVERY, A.C. 1984. A Modern Guide to Foodservice Equipment, 2nd Edition. CBI Books, Van Nostrand Reinhold Company, New York.

GREAVES, R.E. 1984. Food Equipment Repair and Maintenance. F.E.R.M., Rochester, New York.

KOTSCHEVAR, L.H. and TERRELL, M.E. 1985. Foodservice Planning: Layout and Equipment, 3rd Edition. John Wiley and Sons, New York.

LONGREE, K. and BLAKER, G.G. 1982. Sanitary Techniques in Foodservice, 2nd Edition. John Wiley and Sons, New York.

MARRIOT, N.G. 1985. Principles of Food Sanitation. AVI Publishing Co., Westport, Connecticut.

MINOR, L.J. and CICHY, R.F. 1984. Foodservice Systems Management. AVI Publishing Co., Westport, Connecticut.

NEWLIN, D.G. 1986. Preventative maintenance—Protect your investment. The Consultant 19 (1), 34–36.

NATIONAL SANITATION FOUNDATION. 1982. Standard Number 2, Foodservice Equipment. Ann Arbor, Michigan.

Space Requirements

INTRODUCTION

Accurate determination of the space requirements for a foodservice facility is a very difficult problem, involving considerable research and computation. The space required for each functional area of the facility is dependent upon many factors which are not constant for all types of operations. The factors involved include the number of meals to be prepared; the functions and tasks to be performed; the equipment requirements; the number of employees and corresponding workplaces required; storage for materials; and suitable space for traffic and movement. The importance of accurately evaluating these factors cannot be overemphasized. Overestimating or underestimating any of them can lead to an excess or a shortage of space for the facility.

SPACE ESTIMATES

The general guides and "rules of thumb" that will be given are to be used for preliminary space estimates only. They are to be regarded as strictly tentative and subject to easy change. The "rules of thumb" are used to get a general idea of the overall size of a facility in order to make preliminary cost estimates for feasibility studies, or to determine approximate land requirements for the building. One problem with using guides and "rules of thumb" is that the figures given are usually based on existing operations and do not reflect newer methods of foodservice operation. Another difficulty is that these figures are not given for all types of foodservice operations and consequently they would be of little use for certain types of projects. Most of the figures available are for general facilities that have no unusual space requirements.

TOTAL FACILITY SIZE

Depending upon the type of foodservice to be planned, a general estimate of the total building size can be obtained by relating it to the number of seats to be provided. The estimated square footage of total space per seat is given in Table 12.1. These figures can be related to the number of meals to be prepared by considering the turnover rate for a particular meal period. A range of space estimates is given to allow for variations in the methods of operation. The smaller figures are used for limited menu and limited-space operations; the larger figures are suitable for operations with extensive menus and allow more spacious areas.

Figures for estimating the total facility size of other types of foodservice, such as tray service, car service, or take-out service, are not available because of the great variations that exist in these types of operations. The only guides available would be to evaluate similar existing operations and make adjustments as needed.

DINING AREAS

Estimating the space required for dining areas is based on the number of persons to be seated at one time and the square feet of space allowed per seat. The number of persons to be seated at one time is determined by considering the total number of customers to be served for a given time period, and the turnover. Turnover refers to seat usage and is expressed by the number of times a seat will be occupied over a given time period. Turnover is usually expressed on a per-hour basis, although it can be determined on a per meal basis.

TABLE 12.1. ESTIMATED TOTAL FACILITY SPACE FOR FOODSERVICE FACILITIES

Type of operation	Area per seat (ft²)	(m²)
Table service	24–32	2.23–2.97
Counter service	18–24	1.67–2.23
Booth service	20–28	1.86–2.60
Cafeteria service	22–30	2.04–2.79

The turnover is determined by estimating the average time a seat is occupied for the time period desired. For example, if the turnover is to be expressed on a per-hour basis and the average estimated time the seat is occupied is 20 minutes, the turnover is 3. If the average seat occupancy time is 30 min, then the turnover rate is 2 per hour. Determining the turnover rate per meal period is useful for determining the total seating capacity based on estimated sales volume.

Turnover rates are affected by the method of serving and serving time as well as by the type of customer, menu offerings, and the dining atmosphere. Typical turnover rates for some types of foodservice operations are shown in Table 12.2.

Turnover rates can be increased to some extent by many design and operational factors. This is not to suggest that all facilities should be designed for high turnover rates. However, if high turnover is one of the basic objectives, then the planner and subsequent manager can use the following to accomplish this:

Use menu items that require short processing times, or use predominately preprocessed items.

Provide ample production space and equipment to handle the peak periods.

Use well-lighted and light-colored painted areas for serving and dining.

Arrange dining tables in close proximity to each other.

Develop a somewhat uncomfortable dining seat design.

Provide sufficient service personnel so guests are served promptly after they are seated.

Provide for prompt clearing of the tables when a customer is finished with a course or the entire meal.

Make sure guest checks are presented to customers as soon as they are finished eating.

TABLE 12.2.   TURNOVER RATES FOR FOODSERVICE FACILITIES

Type of operation	Turnover rate (per hr)
Commercial cafeteria	1½–2½
Industrial or school cafeterias	2–3
Counter service	2–3½
Combination counter and table service	2–3
Leisurely table service	½–1
Regular table service	1–2½

Note that a number of factors identified above are characteristic of the management policy after the facility has been built. This again emphasizes the close working relationship that has to exist between the owner or manager and the planner during the planning process. A foodservice facility designed for high turnover must also be managed for high turnover if the anticipated volume of sales is to be generated.

The square feet of space allowed in the dining areas is governed by the amount of comfort desired. Crowding in dining areas is not desirable except in some quick-service fast-food operations. Most individuals would like to have sufficient elbow room and table space to enjoy their meal. The dining area shown in Fig. 12.1 provides ample space for the customers. Suggested space requirements for dining areas are given in Table 12.3. The figures on the high end of the range are used where ample space or leisurely dining are to be provided. The figures on the low end of the range will result in minimum space requirements.

FIG. 12.1. Dining rooms should be sized to provide sufficient room for tables and chairs without crowding.
Courtesy of Kellogg Center, Michigan State University.

TABLE 12.3.   ESTIMATED DINING AREA SPACE FOR
FOODSERVICE FACILITIES

Type of facility	Dining space per seat (ft²)	(m²)
Table service	12–18	1.11–1.67
Counter service	16–20	1.49–1.86
Booth service	12–16	1.11–1.49
Cafeteria service	12–16	1.11–1.49
Banquet	10–12	0.93–1.11

The estimates for dining areas include space for tables, chairs, aisles, and service stations. They do not allow for waiting areas, rest rooms, or other similar areas. Space requirements for these areas have to be determined separately. The size and arrangement of tables, chairs, booths, and counters selected for the dining area are important to the efficient use of the space allowed.

PRODUCTION AREAS

The space estimates for production areas include room for all the functional areas, such as receiving, storage, preparation, cooking, and warewashing, that are required to produce the menu items. Estimates for production areas for typical foodservice facilities are given in Table 12.4.

Facilities that will be processing primarily fresh items should use the higher space estimates. This allows for the additional equipment and worker space needed. The smaller figures are used for operations using preprocessed foods and require minimal production space.

A suggested percentage breakdown of the production space for general table service operations is shown in Table 12.5.

These percentage figures assume a typical operation using fresh products. Baking of rolls, pastries, and cakes are also assumed to be done in the facility.

TABLE 12.4.   ESTIMATED PRODUCTION SPACE FOR
FOOD FACILITIES

Type of facility	Space per seat (ft²)	(m²)
Table service	8–12	0.74–1.11
Counter service	4–6	0.37–0.56
Booth service	6–10	0.56–0.93
Cafeteria service	8–12	0.74–1.11

TABLE 12.5. ESTIMATED PERCENTAGE
OF PRODUCTION SPACE ALLOWED FOR
FUNCTIONAL AREAS

Functional areas	Space allowed (%)
Receiving	5
Food storage	20
Preparation	14
Cooking	8
Baking	10
Warewashing	5
Traffic aisles	16
Trash storage	5
Employee facilities	15
Miscellaneous	2

SPACE CALCULATIONS

Another approach to the problem of determining space requirements is to calculate the space needed for each of the functional areas
separately. This is done by identifying and determining the pertinent
variables involved for the different functional areas. It is assumed at
this point that the individual workplaces and pieces of equipment for
the facility have been determined and will now be grouped together.
The space required for the flow of materials and workers between the
workplaces and pieces of equipment is added as needed to develop the
space to allow for each function.

A brief discussion of some of the functional areas and the variables
affecting their space requirements will be given to illustrate this procedure. Computational examples are presented as applicable. Consideration of the traffic aisles is one of the common variables for all
areas and is therefore included.

Traffic Aisles

Traffic aisles are used for the movement of materials and workers,
and should not be confused with work aisles that provide floor space
for the worker to perform the task. The primary purpose of traffic
aisles is to allow easy movement between workplaces, equipment, and
functional areas. Since traffic aisles are not productive space, they
should be kept at a minimum both in numbers and size. Traffic aisles,
as shown in Fig. 12.2, should be just wide enough to provide easy
movement of the materials and workers required for efficient operation of the facility.

FIG. 12.2.   Traffic aisles are sized to handle the
flow of materials and workers efficiently.

In general, work aisles and traffic aisles should be separated as
much as possible. This can usually be accomplished by locating traffic
aisles perpendicular to the work aisles. In some instances, combined
work and traffic aisles may be used if the traffic is light and if they
offer a better solution to the design problem. Traffic aisles that serve
two or more functional areas will minimize the amount of space required. Placement of traffic aisles along walls and other perimeter
locations is not desirable for the same reason.

The width of traffic aisles is dependent upon the type of traffic to
be accommodated. If it consists of only people who are not carrying
anything, a minimum aisle width of 30 in. (762 mm) will allow persons to pass without difficulty. For workers who will be carrying con-

tainers and materials or pushing mobile carts and trucks an aisle width of 24 in. (610 mm) plus the width of the container or material carried or the mobile cart width will allow enough space. For example, if one worker has to pass another worker pushing a 20-in. (508 mm) wide cart, an aisle width of 44 in. (1118 mm) (24 plus 20) would be needed. The traffic aisle widths required for special types of movement such as carrying large trays have to be sized accordingly.

In those instances where a combined work and traffic aisle is needed, a minimum of 42 in. (1067 mm) is required to allow one person to pass another person at the workplace. Aisles where there are persons working in a back-to-back arrangement have to be a mimimum of 48 in. (1219 mm) wide to allow passage of people between them. An important point to remember is that the less movement required to operate the facility, the less aisle space is needed.

RECEIVING AREA

The main variables affecting the amount of space needed for the receiving function are the number, type, and size of deliveries that are to be handled at one time. Many operations can have deliveries scheduled so they will have to handle only one delivery at a time. The types of materials to be received are considered because of the variety of containers and packaging methods available. Ease of opening, checking, moving, and stackability all have a bearing on the space required.

The size of deliveries to be handled may depend on the storage space available in the facility, and is determined in conjunction with storage space requirements. Storage space in turn can be modified by the frequency of deliveries. A greater frequency of deliveries can reduce the size requirements of the receiving area as well. Therefore, storage space and receiving space requirements should be determined together after these factors have been evaluated.

Needless to say, all equipment and work areas for the receiving function must be provided for.

STORAGE AREAS

The amount of dry, refrigerator, and freezer space required for the facility is determined by the number of days of storage to be provided for. A general recommendation for dry storage of foods is to provide space for 2–4 weeks supply, depending on the availability of the food items. The total volume of goods to be stored can be estimated as follows. First determine the number of meals for which storage is to be provided. An operation planning on serving 600 meals per day and desiring a two weeks supply will need storage for 8400 (600 meals per day × 14 days) meals. Next, estimate the weight per meal of items that will be stored in the dry storage area. This calls for an evaluation of all menu items. A general estimate between ¼ and ½ lb (0.113 and 0.227 kg) per meal may be used; it is based on a total weight estimate per average meal of 1–1½ lb (0.454–0.680 kg). These figures are for full meals and adjustments for partial meals have to be made. If an estimate of ½ lb (0.227 kg) per meal is used, then the total weight to provide storage for is 4200 lb (1905 kg) (8400 meals × 0.5 lb per meal). Then the total weight computed is divided by an average density of 45 lb per ft³ (721 kg per m³), which will give the total volume of goods to be stored. In this example, the total volume in cubic feet is 4200 lb ÷ 45 lb/ft³ = 93.3. This indicates that space for 93.3 cubic ft (2.64 m³) of goods, exclusive of aisle space, will be needed.

If the goods are to be stored on shelves, the total square footage of shelving can be computed by considering the height to which the materials can be stored on the shelf. If the materials can be stored to a height of 1 ft, then 93.3 (93.3 ft³ ÷ 1 foot) ft² (8.67 m²) of shelving will

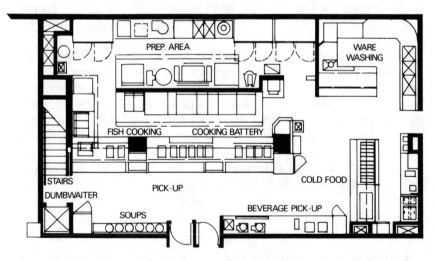

FIG. 12.3. Facilities for serving in table service operations include pick-up counters at the main cooking area.
Courtesy of Restaurant Business.

be needed. If a height of 1½ ft (0.457 m) can be used, then 62.2 (93.3 ÷ 1.5) ft² (5.78 m²) of shelving is required. The length of shelving is computed by dividing the square feet by the width of shelving to be used.

This same method of computation can be used for the refrigerator and freezer storage areas. The weight per meal of items that will be stored in the refrigerators and freezers will vary between 0.75 and 1 lb (0.340 and 0.454 kg). The average density of refrigerator items can be assumed to be 30 lb/ft³ (481 kg/m³). Items that will be stored in freezers can be assumed to have a density of 40 lb/ft³ (641 kg/m³).

The number of days of storage for refrigerator items may vary from one day to a week or more, depending on the method of operation used for the facility. Freezer items can be stored for longer periods of time and are determined by the frequency of deliveries available. An economic lot size analysis may be made to determine the optimum size of storage to provide. The analysis compares ordering, purchasing, and receiving costs to the cost of the storage.

SERVING AREAS

Serving areas for most table service facilities are planned as a part of the main cooking area and separate space determinations are not usually needed. The pick-up area shown in Fig. 12.3 is included in the space requirements for the main cooking area. Additional serving stations for table service can be considered in computations for the dining area.

Cafeteria operations require separate space for the serving function to allow room for the serving counter, room for guests, and room for servers. Variables affecting the size of the serving area are the number of people to be served and the serving time allowed. Serving line rates vary from 2 to 10 persons per minute for straight-line cafeteria counters. The serving line rate is dependent on the number of choices and the number of servers. Shopping-center counter arrangements can handle up to 20 or more persons per minute.

The length of cafeteria counters is determined by the variety and volume of food items to be displayed. Adequate space for merchandising food items, as shown in Fig. 12.4, should be allowed.

The space required for straight-line counters may be roughly estimated at 10–15 ft² (0.929–1.39 m²) of floor space for each linear foot (0.305 m) of counter. This provides room for the counters, customer aisles, room for servers, and back-bar equipment. Shopping-center ar-

FIG. 12.4.   Cafeteria counters should allow sufficient space to merchandise foods.
Courtesy of The Henry Ford Museum, Dearborn, Michigan and The Hysen Group, Livonia, Michigan.

rangements generally require 18–20 ft² (1.67–1.86 m²) of floor area for each linear foot (0.305 m) of counter.

The sizing of serving facilities for cafeterias is directly related to the capacity of the dining area. Ideal design results when the flow of people from the serving facility is balanced with the seating available in the dining room. At equilibrium conditions, the flow rate of people leaving the serving areas and entering the dining area should equal the flow rate of people leaving the dining area. In other words, the number of seats provided in the dining area has a direct relationship to the rate of people leaving the serving line for a given average eating time. This relationship can be developed from an analytical model* because certain operational characteristics of cafeterias can be easily

---

*Reprinted by permission from "An Analytical Model for the Design and Operation of Cafeterias," *The Consultant* 19 (1), 47–51, by E. A. Kazarian.

identified and described. For example, the maximum serving rate for a given type of serving area design can be estimated with a fair degree of accuracy if the variables affecting the serving rate are known. Another characteristic that is easily established for cafeterias is the average dining time for various types of customers or patrons. Although cafeterias may operate at different capacities during a meal period, a model can be developed to describe the peak period of operation since this is the most critical period for efficient design.

The following symbols and terms are used to describe the variables involved in the development of the model. Some of the variables described are not essential to the use of the model but are included as informational items which are helpful in determining operational characteristics of existing cafeterias. All terms are defined for the peak period of operation.

N_d = Number of persons in the dining room (this will be equated to the number of usable seats needed in dining room)

N_m = Total number of persons to be fed

N_{sa} = Number of persons in the serving area

R_1 = Rate of people entering the serving area

R_2 = Rate of people leaving the serving area (this is also considered to be the rate of people entering the dining area)

R_3 = Rate of people leaving the dining area

R_m = Feeding rate (number of people fed divided by the meal period)

R_s = Serving rate (number of people served divided by the serving period)

S = Total seats required in the dining area allowing for any vacancies that are anticipated

T_d = Time that a person spends in the dining area (sometimes referred to as dining time)

T_f = Time that the dining area is full

T_m = Meal period

T_o = Turnover of usable seats for the meal period

T_s = Serving period

T_{sa} = Time a person spends in the serving area

V = Vacancy ratio (ratio of vacant seats to total seats)

Basic Assumptions

The first assumption used to develop the model is that the rate of people entering the serving area is constant during the peak period of operation. This is a valid assumption if there is a waiting line of one or more persons at the entrance to the serving area during the

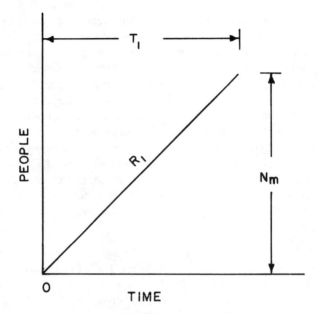

FIG. 12.5.   Relationship between the number of people entering the serving area and time.

entire peak period and no delays in service are encountered. This assumption also assures that the serving area will be used to its maximum capacity. The rate of people entering the serving area should be approximately the same as the arrival rate of people so the waiting time does not become excessive.

A constant rate of people entering the serving area (R_1) can be depicted by a straight line as shown in [Fig. 12.5]. The horizontal axis is used for time and the vertical axis is used for number of people. The line is drawn through the origin, which represents the beginning of the peak period. The line is drawn to a height of N_m, which represents the total number of persons that will enter the serving area. For a given rate, the time required for all the persons to enter the serving area is given by T_1.

The equation for the line through the origin is given by:

$$N_m = R_1 T_1 \qquad \text{Equation 1}$$

The second assumption used is that the rate of people leaving the serving area (or entering the dining area) is equal to the rate of people entering the serving area. This is shown by the line R_2 [in Fig. 12.6],

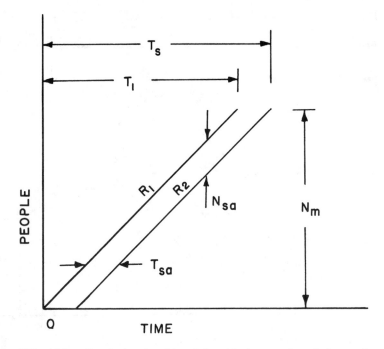

FIG. 12.6.   Graph showing the relationship for people entering and leaving the serving area.

which is drawn parallel to line R_1. Line R_2 is also drawn to a height of N_m. The horizontal distance between lines R_1 and R_2 represent the time that a person spends in the serving area (T_{sa}). The vertical distance between the lines represents the number of people in the serving area (N_{sa}).

The horizontal distance from the origin to the point where line R_2 ends can now be defined as the serving period T_s, and represents the time elapsed from the moment the first person enters the serving area until the last person leaves the serving area.

A second relationship for line R_1 can now be given by the equation:

$$R_1 = \frac{N_{sa}}{T_{sa}} \qquad \text{Equation 2}$$

which is the slope of the line. This indicates that the rate of people entering (or leaving since $R_1 = R_2$) the serving area is equal to the number of people in the serving area divided by the time that is spent in the serving area.

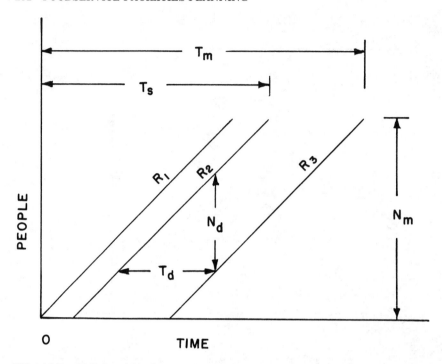

FIG. 12.7. Relationships for people entering and leaving the serving area and leaving the dining area.

The third assumption used for the development of the model is that the rate of people leaving the dining area is equal to the rate of people entering the dining area. The rate of people leaving the dining area is shown [in Fig. 12.7] by line R_3, which is drawn parallel to lines R_1 and R_2. Line R_3 is drawn to a height of N_m.

The horizontal distance between R_2 and R_3 represents the time a person spends in the dining area (T_d). The vertical distance between lines R_2 and R_3 represents the number of people in the dining area (N_d). It is important to note that the maximum value of N_d occurs in the interval $T = T_d + T_{sa}$ and $T = T_s$.

Basic Relationships

The meal period, T_m, is shown as the horizontal distance from the origin to the point where line R_3 terminates. The relationship between T_m, T_s, and T_d can be given as:

$$T_m = T_s + T_d \qquad \text{Equation 3}$$

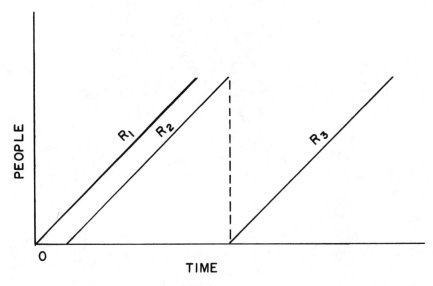

FIG. 12.8. Graph showing the furthest that the line depicting people leaving the dining area can be drawn from the origin.

At this point, the relationship between N_m and N_d can be evaluated. The turnover (T_o) in the dining area for the meal period is given by:

$$T_o = \frac{N_m}{N_d} \qquad \text{Equation 4}$$

If $N_m = N_d$, the turnover is 1, which is the lowest turnover acceptable in cafeteria design. Indeed the highest possible turnover would be desirable as a design criterion. To assure that a turnover of less than 1 is not permitted, the model will be only valid for $N_m \geqslant N_d$. The situation where $N_m = N_d$ is shown in [Fig. 12.8] and shows the furthest that R_3 can be drawn from the origin. For $N_m > N_d$, line R_3 will be drawn closer to the origin than shown in [Fig. 12.8].

The relationships for the serving rate R_s and the feeding rate R_m are described next. Using the definitions presented earlier, R_s and R_m are shown in [Fig. 12.9] in relation to R_1, R_2, and R_3. The basic equation for R_s is given by:

$$R_s = \frac{N_m}{T_s} \qquad \text{Equation 5}$$

The equation for R_m is given by:

$$R_m = \frac{N_m}{T_m} \qquad \text{Equation 6}$$

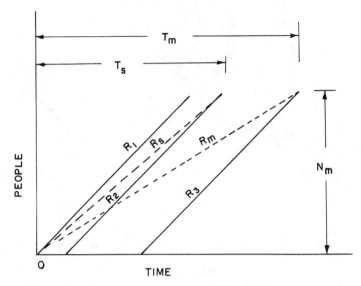

FIG. 12.9.   Relationships for determining the serving rate and the feeding rate.

These basic relationships (equations 1 through 6) were used to derive the remaining relationships for the model.

Derived Relationships

One type of cafeteria design problem exists when values or estimates of N_m, T_m, T_d, and N_{sa} are given. With this given information, the remaining characteristics of the cafeteria can be obtained by the following derived relationships.

The time in the serving area, T_{sa}, is found by determining the horizontal distance between R_1 and R_2. In terms of time values, this distance is expressed by:

$$T_{sa} = T_s - T_1; \text{ since } T_1 = \frac{N_m}{R_1}$$

$$T_{sa} = T_s - \frac{N_m}{R_1}; \text{ and since } R_1 = \frac{N_{sa}}{T_{sa}}$$

$$T_{sa} = T_s - \frac{N_m T_{sa}}{N_{sa}}$$

The equation can be rewritten as:

$$T_{sa} + \frac{N_m T_{sa}}{N_{sa}} = T_s$$

and by factoring T_{sa} gives:

$$T_{sa} \left[1 + \frac{N_m}{N_{sa}} \right] = T_s$$

and finally:

$$T_{sa} = \frac{T_s}{\left[1 + \dfrac{N_m}{N_{sa}} \right]} \qquad \text{Equation 7}$$

T_{sa} can now be found in terms of T_s, N_m, and N_{sa}.

The next relationship derived is the equation for the maximum number of people in the dining area (N_d). N_d will be considered to be the number of usable seats to provide in the dining area. The total number of seats in the dining area will be determined by using a vacancy factor to account for unused seats caused by persons occupying only a portion of the available seats. For example, when a party of three occupies a table for four, there will be one unused seat at the table. Vacancy factors are design decisions based on the type of customers, arrival patterns, and seating arrangement in the dining area. Since vacancy factors are not constant for all types of cafeterias, it is not included in the derivation at this time but will be included later.

N_d is found by determining the vertical distance between R_2 and R_3. As indicated earlier, the maximum value of N_d exists in the interval from $T = T_d + T_{sa}$ to $T = T_s$. In this interval the vertical distance is given by:

$$N_d = R_2 T_d$$

R_2 can be expressed by the slope of the line as:

$$R_2 = \frac{N_m + N_{sa}}{T_m - T_d}$$

Substituting for R_2 in the equation for N_d gives:

$$N_d = \left[\frac{N_m + N_{sa}}{T_m - T_d} \right] T_d$$

which can be rewritten as:

$$N_d = \frac{N_m + N_{sa}}{\left[\dfrac{T_m}{T_d} - 1 \right]} \qquad \text{Equation 8}$$

Equation 8 gives the maximum number of people in the dining area and is equated to the number of usable seats to provide. To allow for vacancies, the total number of seats to provide is given by the relationship:

$$S = \frac{N_d}{(1 - V)}$$

where V is the vacancy ratio expressed as a decimal.

A relationship between R_2 and R_s can be developed by using the following terms to describe the slope of line R_2:

$$R_2 = \frac{N_m}{T_s - T_{sa}}; \text{ since } N_m = R_s T_s$$

$$R_2 = \frac{R_s T_s}{T_s - T_{sa}}$$

Dividing the numerator and denominator of the right-hand side of the equation by T_s results in the following:

$$R_2 = \frac{R_s}{\left[1 - \dfrac{T_{sa}}{T_s} \right]}$$

The final relationship developed is the time that the dining room is full, as shown below:

$$T_f = T_s - T_d - T_{sa}$$

Using the Model

The equations developed may be used to make the design decisions needed in the planning of a new cafeteria, as shown by the following examples.

The first example assumes that the following information is given or estimated:

$$N_m = 200 \text{ persons}$$
$$T_m = 120 \text{ min.}$$
$$T_d = 30 \text{ min.}$$
$$N_{sa} = 10 \text{ people}$$
$$V = 10\%$$

The determination of the variables affecting the design is shown below.

$$T_s = T_m - T_d, \text{ (from equation 3)}$$

$$T_s = 120 - 30 = 90 \text{ min.}$$

$$R_s = \frac{N_m}{T_s} = \frac{200}{90} = 2.2 \text{ persons/min.}$$

$$R_m = \frac{N_m}{T_m} = \frac{200}{120} = 1.7 \text{ persons/min.}$$

$$T_{sa} = \frac{T_s}{\left[1 + \dfrac{N_m}{N_{sa}}\right]} = \frac{90}{\left[1 + \dfrac{200}{10}\right]} = 4.3 \text{ min.}$$

$$N_d = \frac{N_m + N_{sa}}{\left[\dfrac{T_m}{T_d} - 1\right]} = \frac{200 + 10}{\left[\dfrac{120}{30} - 1\right]} = 70 \text{ people}$$

$$S = \frac{N_d}{(1 - V)} = \frac{70}{(1 - 0.10)} = 77.8 \text{ or } 78 \text{ seats}$$

$$R_2 = \frac{N_{sa}}{T_{sa}} = \frac{10}{4.3} = 2.3 \text{ persons/min.}$$

$$T_o = \frac{N_m}{N_d} = \frac{200}{70} = 2.9 \text{ for the meal period}$$

$$T_f = T_s - T_d - T_{sa} = 90 - 30 - 4.3 = 55.7 \text{ min.}$$

The model can also be used to show how changes in the given data will affect the other factors. This is shown by the following example where a change in T_m from 120 min. to 90 min. is evaluated for the above problem. The results of the computations are shown in tabular form.

Given: N_m = 200 persons, T_d = 30 min., N_{sa} = 10 persons,
V = 10%

	For T_m = 120 min.	For T_m = 90 min.
T_s	90 min.	60 min.
R_s	2.2 persons/min.	3.3 persons/min.
R_m	1.7 persons/min.	2.2 persons/min.
T_{sa}	4.3 min.	2.9 min.
N_d	70 people	105 people
S	78 seats	117 seats
R_2	2.3 persons/min.	3.5 persons/min.
T_o	2.9	1.9
T_f	55.7 min.	27.1 min.

Another type of variation for the above problem can occur when a particular objective in one of the factors is desired. An illustration of a problem where the objective is to achieve a turnover of 2.5 is shown next.

Given: N_m = 200 persons, T_d = 30 min., N_{sa} = 10 persons,
V = 10%

Objective: T_o = 2.5

Computations:

$$N_d = \frac{N_m}{T_o} = \frac{200}{2.5} = 80 \text{ persons}$$

$$S = \frac{N_d}{(1 - V)} = \frac{80}{(1 - 0.10)} = 89 \text{ seats}$$

$$R_2 = \frac{N_d}{T_d} = \frac{80}{30} = 2.7 \text{ persons/min.}$$

$$T_{sa} = \frac{N_{sa}}{R_2} = \frac{10}{2.7} = 3.7 \text{ persons/min.}$$

$$T_s = T_{sa} \left[1 + \frac{N_m}{N_{sa}} \right] = 3.7 \left[1 + \frac{200}{10} \right] = 78 \text{ min.}$$

$$T_m = T_s + T_d = 78 + 30 = 108 \text{ min.}$$

$$R_s = \frac{N_m}{T_s} = \frac{200}{78} = 2.6 \text{ persons/min.}$$

$$R_m = \frac{N_m}{T_m} = \frac{200}{108} = 1.9 \text{ persons/min.}$$

Using Arrival Rates

If the arrival rate of customers to the cafeteria can be determined, it can be equated to the rate of people entering the serving area (R_1). An example of this type of computation for a different design problem is shown next.

Given: R_1 = 5 persons/min.

N_m = 300 people

T_d = 20 min.

N_{sa} = 8 persons

V = 15%

Computations:

$$T_1 = \frac{N_m}{R_1} = \frac{300}{5} = 60 \text{ min.}$$

$$T_{sa} = \frac{N_{sa}}{R_1} = \frac{8}{5} = 1.6 \text{ min.}$$

$$T_s = T_1 + T_{sa} = 60 + 1.6 = 61.6 \text{ min.}$$

$$T_m = T_s + T_d = 61.6 + 20 = 81.6 \text{ min.}$$

$$N_d = R_1 T_d = 5 \,(20) = 100 \text{ people}$$

$$S = \frac{N_d}{(1 - V)} = \frac{100}{(1 - 0.15)} = 118 \text{ seats}$$

$$R_s = \frac{N_m}{T_s} = \frac{300}{61.6} = 4.9 \text{ persons/min.}$$

$$R_m = \frac{N_m}{T_m} = \frac{300}{81.6} = 3.7 \text{ persons/min.}$$

$$T_o = \frac{N_m}{N_d} = \frac{300}{100} = 3$$

Existing Cafeterias

The model may be used to evaluate existing cafeterias, as shown by the following example. In this case the total number of seats in the dining area (S) and the size of the serving area (which determines N_{sa}) are fixed. Then for any given T_m, T_d, and V, the following calculations can be made.

Given: $S = 150$ seats
$N_{sa} = 12$ persons
$T_m = 60$ min.
$T_d = 15$ min.
$V = 10\%$

Computations:

$$N_d = S \,(1 - V) = 150 \,(1 - 0.10) = 135 \text{ people}$$

$$R_1 = \frac{N_d}{T_d} = \frac{135}{15} = 9 \text{ persons/min.}$$

$$T_{sa} = \frac{N_{sa}}{R_1} = \frac{12}{9} = 1.3 \text{ min.}$$

$$T_s = T_m - T_d = 60 - 15 = 45 \text{ min.}$$

$$R_s = R_1 \left[1 - \frac{T_{sa}}{T_s} \right] = 9 \left[1 - \frac{1.3}{45} \right] = 8.7 \text{ persons/min.}$$

$$N_m = R_s T_s = 8.7 \ (45) = 392 \text{ persons}$$

$$R_m = \frac{N_m}{T_m} = \frac{392}{60} = 6.5 \text{ persons/min.}$$

$$T_o = \frac{N_m}{N_d} = \frac{392}{135} = 2.9$$

A variation of the above example is to determine what meal period would be required to accommodate a given number of people to be fed. To illustrate, the meal period for the above problem when $N_m = 500$ will be shown. Note that the values of N_d, R_1, and T_{sa} do not change. The remaining computations are shown below.

$$T_s = \frac{[N_m + N_{sa}]}{R_1} = \frac{[500 + 12]}{9} = 56.9 \text{ min.}$$

$$T_m = T_s + T_d = 56.9 + 15 = 71.9 \text{ min.}$$

$$R_s = \frac{N_m}{T_s} = \frac{500}{56.9} = 8.8 \text{ persons/min.}$$

$$R_m = \frac{N_m}{T_m} = \frac{500}{71.9} = 7 \text{ persons/min.}$$

$$T_o = \frac{N_m}{N_d} = \frac{500}{135} = 3.7$$

The computations show that the meal period would have to be 71.9 min. in order to accommodate the 500 people.

The analytical model described for cafeteria operations is a very useful tool for planners. It allows for the manipulation of factors so that any design objective may be attained. Since the model was based on a peak period of operation, the resulting design represents the most efficient facility possible.

Operators of existing cafeterias may also use the model to describe more fully the operating characteristics of their facility. This may lead to changes that could increase the efficiency of their cafeteria.

DINING AREAS

Calculating the space requirements for dining areas can be difficult because of the many choices available. For example, the final space required for a dining room is dependent upon the following variables:

1. Types of seating to be provided:
   a. Tables and chairs
   b. Booths
   c. Counters
   d. Banquettes
   e. Combinations
2. Table sizes desired
3. Table shapes desired
4. Pattern of table arrangements
5. Aisle space desired
6. Number of service stations needed

A suggested approach that allows a planner to evaluate these variables and their effect on the dining space per seat is the modular concept. For this situation the module contains space for the table, the seats, and the appropriate share of the service and access aisles. The modular concept enables designers first to evaluate the space requirements for different choices that may be made before reaching their final decisions.

The following example will illustrate this concept for a dining room that will use tables and chairs only. The first step in the modular concept is to select the size and shape of table to be considered. This is done in relation to the customer, the menu, the type of service, and the type of atmosphere desired in the dining room. Some typical sizes and shapes of dining tables are given in Table 12.6.

TABLE 12.6. TYPICAL SIZES AND SHAPES OF DINING TABLES

Type	Shape	Minimum size (in.)	Spacious (in.)
Tables for 1's or 2's	Square	24 × 24	30 × 30
	Rectangle	24 × 30	30 × 36
	Round	30	36
Tables for 3's or 4's	Square	30 × 30	42 × 42
	Rectangle	30 × 42	36 × 48
	Round	36	48
Tables for 5's or 6's	Rectangle	30 × 60	42 × 72
	Round	48	60
Drop leaf tables	30 × 30 in. opening to 42 in. round		
	36 × 36 in. opening to 52 in. round		

The second step is to select the aisle spaces to be used. Aisle space in dining areas may be divided into service aisles and access aisles. Service aisles usually range from 2.5 ft (0.762 m) minimum for a limited menu operation to as wide as 4.5 ft (1.37 m) for a dining room featuring cart service or table side food preparation. Access aisles are provided to allow people to get into and out of the chairs easily. Thus the type of customer, size of chairs, and the desired atmosphere (crowded versus spacious) are the critical factors in selecting the access aisles. Access aisles are generally 1.5 ft (0.457 m) to 2 ft (0.610 m) wide as a minimum. Combined service and access aisles or aisles for cafeterias where people carry their own trays are usually sized from 3 ft (0.914 m) to 4.5 ft. (1.37 m).

Having selected the table size and shape and the desired aisle space, the next step is to consider possible table arrangement patterns. Square or round tables may be arranged into a rectangular or diagonal pattern, as shown in Fig. 12.10. The diagonal pattern is more efficient in the use of space than the rectangular pattern.

The module used for evaluating the factors mentioned is drawn as illustrated in Fig. 12.11. The module contains one-half of the aisle space selected. The following choices were used for the module:

1. Square table, 36 x 36 in. (914 x 914 mm), for four diners
2. 18 in. (457 mm) seating space (occupied position)
3. Combined service and access aisle of 3 ft (0.914 m)
4. Rectangular pattern of table arrangement

The module size for this example is 9 ft (2.74 m) by 9 ft (2.74 m), which results in a total area of 81 ft^2 (7.52 m^2). Considering that the module is for four persons, the space per seat for this module is 20.25 ft^2 (1.88 m^2)/seat. If this module were to be used for a dining room with 100 seats, the total area required would be 2025 ft^2 (188 m^2).

The module for a diagonal pattern of table arrangement using the same choices for the table size, seat space, and aisle space is shown in Fig. 12.12. The size of the module for the diagonal pattern is 8 ft 4 in. (2.54 m) by 8 ft 4 in. (2.54 m), which gives a total area of 69.44 ft^2 (6.45 m^2). The space per seat is 17.36 ft^2 (1.61 m^2)/seat, which is 2.89 ft^2 (0.27 m^2) less than for the rectangular pattern. For the 100 seat dining room, the diagonal pattern would require 1736 ft^2 (161 m^2), which is 289 ft^2 (26.8 m^2) less than the rectangular pattern.

Similar modules for other sizes or types of seating arrangements can be developed. Care must be taken when using different size tables so that the modules developed for each size table are compatible at

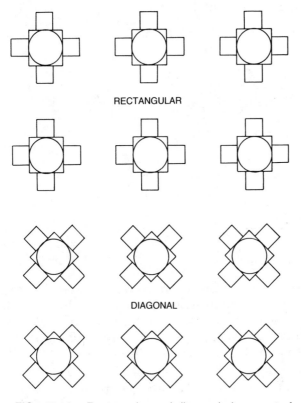

RECTANGULAR

DIAGONAL

FIG. 12.10. Rectangular and diagonal placement of tables.

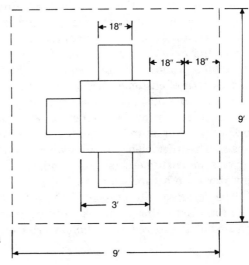

18″

18″ 18″

9′

3′

9′

FIG. 12.11. Module for a square table to be arranged in a rectangular pattern.

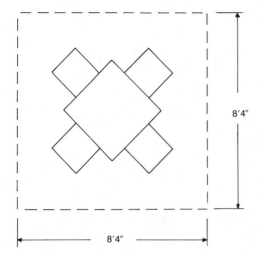

8'4"

8'4"

FIG. 12.12.   Module for the square table to be arranged in a diagonal pattern.

least on one side. For example, when tables for twos and tables for fours are to be used, the modules can be adjusted by selecting table shapes or sizes that give the same module dimension along one axis. This would allow a mixing of the tables without affecting the pattern of aisle ways in the dining area.

Maximizing Seating Capacity and Occupancy

One aspect of foodservice facilities planning that is becoming more important, especially for table service operations, is the determination of the number of each type of table to plan for the dining room. Basically this involves the determination of how many tables for two, four, six, and so on should be used in a given type of facility. In the past, this determination was accomplished by using standard guides or by providing excess seating at various sizes of tables to satisfy expected customer groups. The problem with guides is that they may not fit the pattern of customer arrival for all dining rooms. Using such guides may lead to a mismatch of seating arrangements with customer groups and result in a low occupancy of seats. A related problem that may occur by using standard guides is the inefficient use of dining room space. This inefficiency results when the percentage of tables for small groups of customers (singles and couples) is assumed to be much greater than actually occurs.

The design of dining rooms is frequently complicated by the fact that the total area allowed for the dining room is restricted. This may be caused by the increased cost of new construction as well as by the trend toward developing foodservice facilities in existing structures. As this trend continues, the design of dining rooms becomes a problem of determining the maximum number of seats to provide in a given space. However, just providing maximum seating capacity may not be the best solution if it results in a low occupancy of seats. This may occur when tables for two are occupied by singles or if tables for four or six are used to seat smaller groups. The ideal solution to the problem is to provide maximum seating capacity that matches customer group sizes and therefore results in a minimum of vacant seats.

The most important data required to solve this type of design problem is obviously an accurate knowledge of customer groups arriving for a given type of foodservice operation. For some operations, determination of the arrival of different sized customer groups for more than one meal period may be required. Although this type of data can be obtained for existing operations when a dining room is remodeled, it has to be estimated for proposed foodservice facilities. The best estimates are obtained by a careful analysis of the following factors:

1. Characteristics of customers likely to be arriving in–

Small groups	Larger groups
Professionals	Clerical and office
Retirees	Students
Higher incomes	Lower incomes
Older persons	Young to middle aged
High educational level	Low educational level
Dining out for convenience	At social functions

2. Type of menu likely to attract–

Small groups	Larger groups
A La Carte choices	Complete meals
Extensive choices	Limited choices
Higher priced items	Lower priced items

3. Type of service commonly preferred by–

Small groups	Larger groups
Counter service	Cafeteria service
Booth service	Buffet service
	Table service

4. Atmosphere likely to attract–

Small groups	Larger groups
Formal	Casual
Intimate	Bright and cheerful

5. Operational characteristics commonly preferred by–

Small groups	Larger groups
Offering breakfast	Lunch and dinner only
Take-out meals	

In some instances, data gathered from existing operations that are similar to a proposed operation could be used. The data should be in the form of numbers or percentages of customers that would arrive singly or in groups of two, three, four, and so on.

The objective of a typical design analysis is to determine the maximum number of seats to provide in a given size dining room in order to:

1. Meet customer expectations of space and comfort
2. Provide adequate aisle space in the dining room for access and service
3. Match customer group sizes to seating availability

A sample design problem will be used to illustrate a suggested procedure for finding an optimal solution. The following assumptions are made to simplify the discussion of the procedure:

1. Only tables for two and tables for four will be used. The procedure may be expanded for any combination of seating arrangements by modifying the equations that will be shown.
2. The customer demand is sufficient to fill the seats provided within an acceptable vacancy ratio.
3. Accurate estimates of the demand for various seating arrangements are available.

The solution procedure based on these assumptions for a table service operation is shown in the following steps.

Step 1. Select the size and shape of tables desired in consideration of the customer expectations and the service to be provided.

Step 2. Decide on the size of service and access aisles to be used. The usual minimum service aisle is three feet while minimum access aisles are approximately one and one-half feet. If the type of service to be provided requires special consideration, such as serving from carts, the aisle space would be increased appropriately to allow maneuvering of the carts.

Step 3. For each size of table to be used, and allowing for the aisle requirements indicated in step 2, calculate the area needed per table. This may be done by using a module for each size of table. The dimensions of the module are determined by including one-half the aisle space required to the space needed for the table and seats. For example, a 3 ft (0.914 m) by 3 ft (0.914 m) square table for four diners to be arranged in a diagonal pattern with a 3-ft (0.914 m) service aisle and a 2-ft (0.610 m) access aisle is shown in Fig. 12.13. The dimensions for this module are 7 ft 4 in. (2.24 m) by 8 ft 4 in. (2.54 m) and the area for the module is approximately 61 ft^2 (5.67 m^2). (Note that this is a different module from those used in the previous examples.)

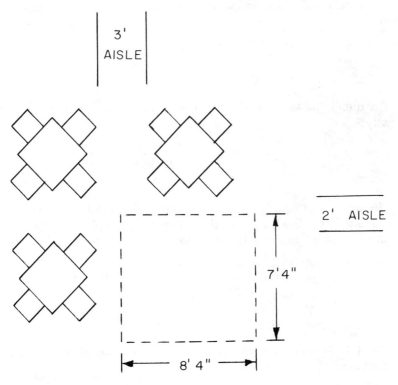

FIG. 12.13. Module for square table with a 3 ft aisle on one side and a 2 ft aisle on the other.

Step 4. Estimate the demand for each type of table to be used. This is expressed as a percentage of the total number of tables.

Step 5. Determine the maximum area available in the dining room for seating. Since the modules for the tables do not include space for serving stations, an appropriate adjustment should be made for any service stations desired in the dining room.

Step 6. The number of tables for two and for four can now be determined. The nomenclature used for the computations is as follows:

X = Number of tables for two
Y = Number of tables for four
A_x = Area of the module for tables for two
A_y = Area of the module for tables for four
A = Total area of the dining room available for seating
T = Percent demand for tables for two expressed as a decimal
F = Percent demand for tables for four expressed as a decimal

The number of tables for two can be obtained by the following equation:

$$ X = \frac{A}{A_x + A_y \dfrac{F}{T}} $$

The number of tables for four can be obtained by the equation shown next:

$$ Y = \frac{A}{A_x \dfrac{T}{F} + A_y} $$

The use of the equation for determining the numbers of each type of table will be illustrated by the following example. The data have been rounded off to simplify the presentation.

Given data: A_x = 40 ft² (3.72 m²)
A_y = 60 ft² (5.57 m²)
A = 2000 ft² (185.8 m²)
T = 0.75
F = 0.25

The data is used to solve first for X, the number of tables for two, as follows:

$$ X = \frac{2000}{40 + 60 \left[\dfrac{0.25}{0.75} \right]} $$

$$X = 33 \text{ tables for two (rounded off)}$$

Next, the data is used to solve for Y, the number of tables for four, as indicated below:

$$Y = \frac{2000}{40 \left[\dfrac{0.75}{0.25}\right] + 60}$$

$$Y = 11 \text{ tables for four (rounded off)}$$

The above solution using 33 tables for two and 11 tables for four results in a total seating capacity of 110 seats ($33 \times 2 + 11 \times 4$).

To show the effect of T and F on the total seating capacity in a given dining room, a computation using $T = 0.50$ and $F = 0.50$ with the other factors remaining constant is shown next.

$$X = \frac{2000}{40 + 60 \left[\dfrac{0.50}{0.50}\right]}$$

$$X = 20 \text{ tables for two}$$

$$Y = \frac{2000}{40 \left[\dfrac{0.50}{0.50}\right] + 60}$$

$$Y = 20 \text{ tables for four}$$

The solution shows that the total seating capacity when T and F are changed increases to 120 seats ($20 \times 2 + 20 \times 4$). This represents an increase of 10 seats or approximately 9 percent and emphasizes the importance of the need for careful analysis of customer demand based on group size.

This design procedure for maximizing the number of seats in a given size dining room in relation to customer group sizes will become very important for foodservice facility planners. Having an accurate determination of the customer group sizes that are arriving for a specific type of foodservice is the key to maximizing seating capacity and minimizing vacancies.

The possible seating configurations for dining areas are endless, and careful planning is required to make the most efficient use of space (Fig. 12.14).

These procedures illustrate the preferred method of arriving at space requirements for a foodservice facility. Each type of food facility to be planned will have differences that will result in different space requirements.

FIG. 12.14.   Efficient dining room design.
Courtesy of Ballinger Inc.

PROBLEMS AND EXERCISES

12.1. Using the rule-of-thumb average estimates for total facility space given in Table 12.1, determine the space requirements for each type of operation for 150 seats. Do the same for the estimated dining area space given in Table 12.3. Compare the two space estimates and determine how much area is allocated to the back of the house.

12.2. The turnover rate for a given type of operation is 2 per hour; determine how long it would take to serve 600 persons assuming the dining area has 150 seats.

12.3. Discuss the advantages and disadvantages of the methods used to accomplish the objective of maintaining a high turnover rate.

12.4. Using the percentages shown in Table 12.5, determine the estimated space for each of the functional areas for a foodservice facility with a total production space of 2000 ft^2.

12.5. Discuss why fast-food units with a high turnover rate differ in space requirements for functional areas from a luxury restaurant using fresh food products.

12.6. Determine the area in ft^2 of storage shelving needed for the following situation:

    a. Provide storage for 3000 meals
    b. Average weight of products to be stored is ¼ lb per meal
    c. Average density of products is 30 lb/ft^3.
    d. Height of storage on shelves is to be 1.5 ft.

12.7. Determine the rate of people that should be leaving a cafeteria serving area for a 200 seat dining room when the average eating time is 30 min.

12.8. Determine the total number of seats needed for a cafeteria operation when the rate of people leaving the serving area is 5 persons per min and the average eating time is 20 min.

12.9. Determine the dimensions of the modules for a 36 in. round dining table for four diners, using a 3 ft aisle space for both a rectangular and a diagonal pattern of arrangement.

BIBLIOGRAPHY

FRESHWATER, J.F., BOUMA, J.C. and LAMMIMAN, R.M. 1969. Labor Utilization and Operating Practices in Commercial Cafeterias. Agric. Res. Service, USDA, Washington, D.C.

GLOBERSON, S., PARSONS, R. and GOODMAN, Jr., R.J. 1985. Dining room productivity: The impact of table configurations and seating policy. The Consultant 18 (4), 54–57.

KAZARIAN, E.A. 1981. A graphical method for dining room design calculations. The Consultant 14 (4), 44–46.

KAZARIAN, E.A. 1982. Maximizing dining room seating capacity. The Consultant 15 (4), 16–18.

KAZARIAN, E.A. 1986. An analytical model for the design and operation of cafeterias. The Consultant 19 (1), 47–51.

KAZARIAN, E.A. 1981. A graphical method for dining room design calculations. The Consultant 14 (4), 44–46.

KOTSCHEVAR, L.H. and TERRELL, M.E. 1985. Food Service Planning: Equipment and Layout, 3rd Edition, John Wiley & Sons, New York.

LAWSON, F. 1973. Restaurant Planning and Design. Architectural Press Ltd., London.

MILLER, E. 1966. Profitable Cafeteria Operation. Ahrens Book Co., New York.

MUSICK, S. 1985. Loosening the storage space stranglehold. The Consultant 18 (2), 18–19.

Layout of Facilities

SPACE ARRANGEMENT

After developing the workplaces, determining the specific equipment to use, and finalizing the space requirements, the food facility designer is ready to accomplish the layout phase of the planning process. Actually, this has probably been developing in the designer's mind as the various other planning steps were being accomplished. Some of the equipment layouts for certain functions may already have been completed during the design of the workplaces. Now the designer will formalize them, first as rough sketches and ultimately in the form of blueprints.

The layout process may be described as two separate stages that occur at the same time. One stage deals with the arrangement of individual pieces of equipment, work tables, and sinks into a unit which comprise a functional area or a functional department. The term department is sometimes associated with separate rooms, but this is not necessarily the case with foodservice operations. In essence, the designer is developing an area where related functions will be performed and may include as many or as few functions as deemed appropriate for the project. To illustrate, one particular area may be developed for the functions of dessert preparation, salad preparation, and sandwich preparation, whereas another project may require three separate areas for these functions.

The second stage of the layout process involves arranging the functional areas or departments into the total facility. For example, the receiving, storage, preparation, production, and warewashing areas and the nonproduction areas, such as rest rooms, lounges, and offices, are brought together to form the basic floor plan for the facility.

There may be some question as to whether these two stages of layout are done at the same time. Even though the planner may be working on one stage or the other at any given moment, layout decisions must be considered in terms of both stages. In essence, the layout of the total facility must be considered when laying out the component areas; and in turn, the layout of the component areas must be considered when laying out the total facility.

CONCEPTS OF LAYOUT

The arrangement of facilities is best guided by the principles of layout developed by industrial engineers. The layout phase of planning is critical because it integrates most of the factors that affect the foodservice facility when it is operational. The principles of layout by various categories is shown in Table 13.1.

TABLE 13.1. CONCEPTS OF LAYOUT

A. Materials or Products
    1. The products should be designed for ease of production.
    2. The raw material used should require the minimum number of processing steps.
    3. The size, shape, and packaging of materials should be suitable to the processes to be performed.
    4. The layout should protect the materials and products from detrimental factors such as moisture, dust, vibration, and temperature changes.
    5. Provide a flexible layout to handle changes in the products or materials.
    6. The layout should provide for in-process storage of materials.
    7. Materials storage areas should facilitate taking inventory.
    8. Provide facilities for storing waste and scrap materials.

B. Machines and Equipment
    1. The equipment provided in the layout should be united to the required processes.
    2. Maximum use of the equipment should be planned.
    3. The layout should provide the required utilities to equipment and machines as economically as possible.
    4. The layout should provide for easy operation of the equipment.
    5. Storage space should be provided for hand tools and equipment.
    6. Provide for flexible use of equipment.
    7. The layout should facilitate movement of mobile equipment.
    8. Sufficient access space for equipment maintenance should be provided.
    9. Proper venting or exhausting of equipment should be provided.
  10. The layout should protect the equipment from damage.

C. Workers
    1. The layout should safeguard the workers by eliminating hazards.
    2. Adequate light should be provided.
    3. Dust, fumes, and other undesirable factors should be guarded against.
    4. The layout should be free of distracting activities.
    5. The layout should provide a productive physical environment.
    6. The design of workplaces should correspond to the height of the workers.

continued.

TABLE 13.1.   Continued

7. The layout should provide adequate working space. (Fig. 13.1 shows a well-planned working space for baking tasks.)
8. Worker-machine layouts should be based on efficient utilization of both.
9. Color coding should be used to facilitate identification of tools, equipment, or hazards.
10. The layout should anticipate crew activities and provide space for them.
11. The layout should provide adequate space for customer or patient activities.

D. Movement
1. The layout should provide for easy movement of materials and workers.
2. Provide for smooth flow into and out of workplaces.
3. The layout should prevent backtracking.
4. Cross traffic should be minimized.
5. Delays in the movement of materials should be minimized.
6. The layout should provide adequate space for movement of guests or patients.
7. Materials should be delivered to workers to minimize walking.
8. Movements should be over the shortest possible distance.
9. The arrangement of spaces should minimize movements.
10. Provide gravity movements whenever possible.

E. Building Features
1. Proper heights and clearances should be provided.
2. Plan sufficient door widths.
3. The layout should provide efficient aisles.
4. Interior walls should not impede movement.
5. Provide door locations that facilitate entry and exit.
6. Column spacing and locations should not interfere with movements or operations.
7. Receiving facilities should be located close to storage areas.
8. Building materials should facilitate cleaning and maintenance.

F. Service Factors
1. Lounges should be provided for guests and employees.
2. Space for inspection, weighing, or control should be provided.
3. The layout should provide for efficient housekeeping.
4. Space for lockers, drinking fountains, and washrooms should be provided.
5. Provide space for repair and service equipment.
6. The layout should facilitate movement of special equipment to guests.
7. Adequate utilities should be provided for equipment and machines.
8. Special needs of products or equipment such as water or steam should be provided at the point of use.

G. Waiting Factors
1. The layout should provide efficient storage for materials.
2. The quality of products-in-waiting should be safeguarded.
3. Waiting of customers should be anticipated and provided for.
4. Delays in material flow should be minimized.
5. The layout should provide for temporary delays of materials between processes when required.

FLOW

The planning of individual workplaces is followed by a logical grouping of several workplaces to develop work centers and departments. The combining of workplaces including tables, sinks, and equipment is guided by different concepts of flow. The criteria involved may include employee flow, material or product flow, customer flow, or in some cases, combinations of these. For example, the layout of a short-order cooking area to be staffed by one employee is best done by evaluating the employee's movements. This can be done by determining the frequency of movements anticipated between pairs of equipment and then placing the pairs of equipment that involve the greatest frequency of movement next to one another in the equipment arrangement. This analysis leads to arrangements that will minimize employee movement and leads to increased productivity.

In some instances it may be possible to place equipment in the same vertical plane to completely eliminate employee movements. The use of salamanders above a range or a microwave oven above a work table are examples of this concept. Consideration of combined or multipurpose equipment where appropriate is warranted.

The planning of a large dishwashing area to include a continuous dishwashing machine and where employees are primarily working in fixed areas such as the scrapping table, loading the dishwasher, or unloading the dishwasher may be guided by evaluating material flow. In this case the flow of china, glassware, and silverware is analyzed to lead to an arrangement that minimizes the material flow (see Fig. 13.1).

In some situations, the flow of two or more variables may be evaluated to determine the best layout. A salad preparation area may require evaluation of both the flow of foods and the movements of employees in order to arrive at the best layout. In most cases, arrangements that minimize the flow of materials are also those that minimize the movements of employees. This is likely when the materials are moved primarily by workers, but may not be the case if mechanical conveyors are used. If there is any doubt, both flows should be evaluated.

Regardless of the type of flow selected as the criterion for layout, the following principles can be applied:

1. Flow should be along straight-line paths as much as possible.
2. The amount of cross flow or cross traffic should be minimized.
3. Backtracking should be minimized.
4. Bypassing should be minimized.

These principles of flow, whether applied to the movement of materials or of people, can be used for all types of layout problems. The concept of keeping flow in a straight line is the most important because it results in movements over the shortest distance. To utilize

FIG. 13.1. Combining equipment and work tables into functional areas.

this concept, the designer will visualize or chart the flow involved with several different arrangements and select the one that gives the best straight-line pattern. Flow analyses for layout problems involving only a few pieces of equipment are easy to do. Layout problems involving numerous pieces of equipment or areas will require more extensive flow analysis. Some planners find flow diagrams or string charts a helpful tool in evaluating complex flow patterns.

With the great variety of materials and activities found in foodservice operations, the concept of minimizing cross traffic is important because it results in layouts that are free of bottlenecks and congestion. This concept is especially pertinent to fast-food operations, which have peak periods of flow. Cross traffic is minimized by the proper location of aisles, passageways, and doors. Some cross traffic can be tolerated if it results in shorter flow patterns. However, if the cross traffic creates a hazardous situation, it should be eliminated, even at the cost of increased distance of movement. Cross traffic between employees and guests is undesirable and should be eliminated.

Backtracking occurs when a material or person moves from one piece of equipment or an area back to the point where the movement originated. The flow is back along the same path that was just traversed. Of course, many of the tasks required in foodservice operations involve a sequence of movements that make it practically impossible to eliminate all backtracking. Many of the cooking and production tasks are of this nature. In those situations, minimizing the amount of backtracking is all that can be done. This involves evaluating several different equipment or space arrangements to find the best one.

Bypassing is the result of a material or person passing one or more pieces of equipment to get to the next piece of equipment required in the sequence of movements. Several different arrangements of the equipment or areas may have to be evaluated to determine which one results in the least amount of bypassing. As with cross traffic, it is impossible to eliminate all bypassing except in the very simplest of layout problems.

The ultimate goal of layout is to develop arrangements of equipment and spaces for the food facility that have primarily straight-line flow paths with a minimum of cross traffic, backtracking, and bypassing.

OTHER CRITERIA FOR LAYOUT

Although flow has been identified as the most important criterion of layout, other modifying considerations which may affect some layout decisions should be evaluated before the arrangement is finalized. These include the following items:

1. *Efficient use of utilities.* All equipment requiring steam, for example, may be placed together to economize on installation and operating costs.

2. *Efficient use of equipment.* Some individual pieces of equipment that will be used in two or more functional areas can be placed in central locations so they are easily accessible.

3. *Efficient use of skilled labor.* This requires arrangements of equipment that will minimize the movements of skilled personnel. This may increase the movements of other employees or increase the movement of materials. The decision may be based on an economic analysis of different arrangements.

4. *Safety.* Some layouts based on the concepts of flow alone may result in an arrangement of equipment that is hazardous. Placing a deep-fat fryer next to a sink creates a dangerous situation, and safety should over-ride flow in this case. Other hazardous arrangements may result when high-temperature equipment is placed adjacent to a traffic

aisle or near entrances and exits. If another location is not feasible, sufficient guarding and shielding of the equipment is an alternative solution.

5. *Efficient use of space.* Building configurations and shapes may require rearrangement of some layouts to make full use of available space.

6. *Environmental factors of noise and odor.* Some pieces of equipment or areas may be isolated from flow paths if they are objectionable and cannot be modified to render them environmentally acceptable. Garbage-can washers or incinerators illustrate this situation.

These modifying criteria may result in arrangements that are more expensive than those based on flow alone. They have to be used, however, to achieve many of the objectives of planning that were identified.

LAYOUT CONFIGURATIONS

The arrangement of equipment and workplaces for functional areas is usually in the form of a straight line or in combinations and modifications of straight-line configurations. The basic patterns that may be used include:

1. *Single straight-line arrangement.* This is the simplest of designs, but it is limited in the number of pieces of equipment or workplaces that can be arranged. The straight-line arrangement may be placed along a wall or take the form of an island. See Fig. 13.2.

2. *Ell-shaped arrangement.* This is a modification of the straight-line arrangement to accommodate more equipment and workplaces; it is sometimes used where linear space is limited. The ell-shaped configuration is very suitable for separating two major groups of equipment. One group of equipment would be placed on one leg of the ell, the other group forming the second leg. An ell-shaped arrangement is shown in Fig. 13.3.

3. *U-shaped arrangements.* The U-shaped configuration is ideal for small areas where only one or two employees are working. One disadvantage of this configuration is that straight-line flow through the area is not possible. A typical arrangement of equipment into the U-shape is shown in Fig. 13.4.

4. *Parallel, back-to-back arrangement.* This configuration is an arrangement of two parallel lines where the backs of the equipment and/or workplaces on each line are adjacent to each other. This arrangement centralizes the utility lines required for equipment. Some-

FIG. 13.2. Island placement of a beverage pick-up area.

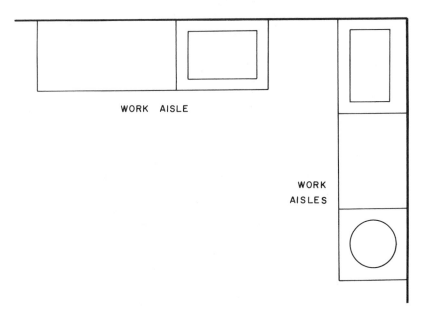

WORK AISLE

WORK
AISLES

FIG. 13.3. Ell-shaped arrangement of equipment.

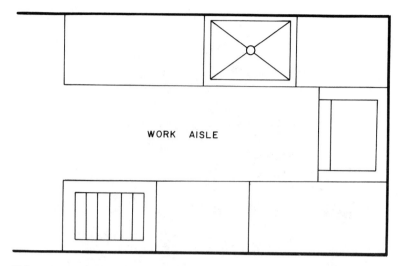

FIG. 13.4.   U-shaped arrangement of equipment.

times a short wall is placed between the two rows of equipment, in which case provision for cleaning and maintenance has to be allowed. Parallel, back-to-back arrangement of cooking equipment that must be vented is ideal because a single canopy hood can be used. The separation of major groups of equipment is easily accomplished with this configuration. Figure 13.5 illustrates parallel, back-to-back arrangement.

5. *Parallel, face-to-face arrangement.* This arrangement utilizes two straight lines of equipment and workplaces where the fronts face each other and are separated by an aisle space. This is a very common configuration that can be used in many areas of the facility. A variation of this configuration is obtained by arranging a straight line of worktables between the two rows of equipment. The parallel, face-to-face arrangement requires two separate utility lines for equipment, as compared to the single utility line used in the parallel, back-to-back arrangment. Figure 13.6 shows the parallel, face-to-face arrangement.

Modifications of any of these configurations can be used to handle special cases and problems. Tee-shaped, open-square, or other configurations should be used if they result in the best solution to the layout problem.

Curved or circular configurations are sometimes used, but they should be planned very carefully to fit straight-line configurations that may be used in the facility. Circular serving islands for shopping-

WORK AISLE

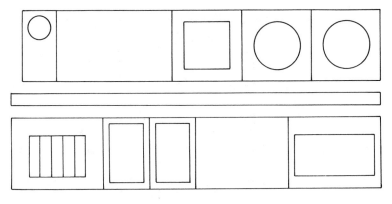

WORK AISLE

FIG. 13.5. Parallel, back-to-back arrangement of equipment.

center cafeterias and curved cafeteria counters are examples of these configurations.

The final arrangement for most facilities is usually composed of a combination of configurations of equipment and workplaces. Only the smallest of operations would use a single configuration for the layout of the facility.

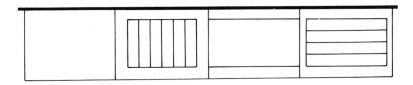

WORK AISLE

FIG. 13.6. Parallel, face-to-face arrangement of equipment.

RELATIONSHIP CHARTS FOR LAYOUTS

The consideration of flow patterns in conjunction with other criteria that may affect a layout may be evaluated by a relationship chart showing the desired degree of closeness between pieces of equipment or areas. A relationship chart is made by listing all the items or areas to be arranged for a given facility. Closeness ratings for all pairs of areas are identified in the relationship chart. These ratings are based on any number of factors including flow, efficient use of equipment, efficient use of utilities, use of labor, safety, and even the personal preferences of the planner. In the majority of the cases flow will still be the primary basis for the closeness ratings.

Closeness ratings may be expressed by a numerical scale as shown next. The ratings are used to express the desired closeness for the final arrangement of the areas.

Rating	Description
6	Closeness absolutely required
5	Closeness highly desirable
4	Closeness desired
3	Ordinary closeness
2	Closeness not essential
1	Closeness not preferred

The usefulness of the relationship chart is dependent upon the planners' awareness of the need to compromise. Indicating that all areas of a facility have to be close to all other areas negates the purpose of the relationship chart.

A suggested relationship chart of areas for one type of foodservice facility is shown in Fig. 13.7. It is important to note that other types of foodservice facilities may have a greater or fewer number of areas listed on the left side of the chart. In some cases areas may be combined as illustrated by this facility that will utilize one area for both salad and vegetable preparation. In other instances, additional areas may be designated as occurs when a separate take-out area is to be planned for in addition to the regular service area. Thus each different project to be planned requires a different relationship chart depending on the defined areas to be considered.

If the exact or approximate size and shape of each area including aisle spaces are known, a preliminary schematic can be developed from the relationship chart ratings. The relationship chart does not necessarily lead to just one layout of areas but may result in several alternative layouts. One schematic layout of the areas identified in the

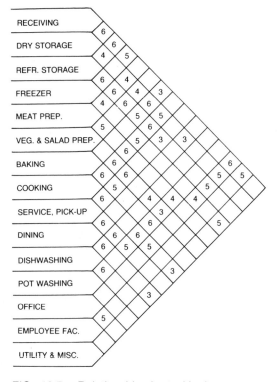

FIG. 13.7. Relationship chart with closeness ratings for a typical foodservice facility.

relationship chart is shown in Fig. 13.8. The areas and sizes of each department used to develop the layout are given in the following listing.

Department	Ft²	Dimensions
Receiving	50	5 × 10
Dry storage	200	20 × 10
Refrigerated storage	84	12 × 7
Freezer	56	8 × 7
Meat preparation	40	8 × 5
Vegetable and salad prep	117	9 × 13
Baking	93	15 × 5
		6 × 3
Cooking	160	20 × 8
Serving and pick-up	100	20 × 5

Dining	1800	50×36
Dishwashing	130	13×10
Pot washing	56	7×8
Office	50	5×10
Employee facilities	160	20×8
Utility room and misc.	104	8×13
Total	3200	

The schematic layout shows that all areas with ratings of 6 between them have been placed close to one another. An examination

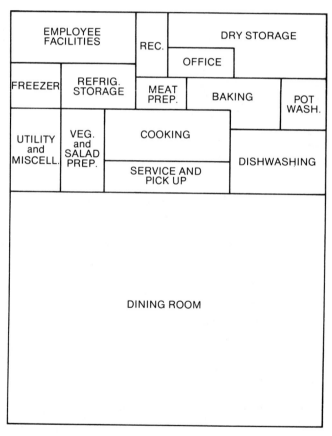

FIG. 13.8.   Schematic layout based on relationship chart closeness ratings.

of the other ratings in the relationship chart and the placement of the areas in the layout shows that the desired degree of closeness has been achieved for most departments.

The relationship chart may be used in a similiar manner to guide the layout of individual pieces of equipment in any of the departments.

LAYOUT GUIDES

The basic concepts of flow along with the modifying considerations give the planner the basic guides for laying out the facility. It is not possible to discuss the layout of all areas for all types of food facilities, but general guides to the arrangement of some areas common to most facilities will be given.

Overall design of the facility is usually based on the flow of major food items. Since most food items are received and then stored before preparation, the dry, refrigerated, and freezer storage areas should be adjacent to receiving areas and also be readily accessible to the various preparation areas. The main cooking area is so located as to receive the flow from the preparation areas and have an outlet directly to the serving area. The salad and sandwich preparation areas may be so placed that their flow of foods is directly into the serving area. Placement of the dining area adjacent to the serving area is obvious.

The flow of nonfood items is next evaluated to locate other areas. The flow of dinnerware in a repetitive route from serving areas to dining areas and then back to serving areas requires the dishwashing area to be adjacent to both. Similarly, the flow of utensils dictates placing the pot- and pan-washing section near the main cooking, baking, and serving areas.

Areas involving the flow of people are then blended into the layout in a manner that does not interfere with the flow of materials. Thus the overall layout of the facility by functional areas begins to take shape.

LAYOUT OF STORAGE AREAS

The layout of storage areas is based on convenience and accessibility. Arrangements that allow heavy and bulky materials to be moved as little and as easily as possible are preferred. Central storage facilities with several satellite locations are good arrangements for many types of facilities. The storage space in the preparation, processing, and other functional areas should be planned so they do not interfere with efficient work methods. The use of combination walk-in and reach-in storage units may increase the convenience of these areas.

It is best to plan walk-in storage areas in a manner which keeps the products at least 8 in. (203 mm) above the floor to facilitate cleaning. An alternative would be to use mobile bins and containers that can be easily moved when the area is cleaned.

Storage areas for non-food supplies may be located in the various functional areas as required. Storage space for china, glass, and silverware may be provided in serving or dining areas. Linen and paper goods used for service are also stored in or near these areas.

LAYOUT OF MAIN COOKING AREA

Laying out the main cooking area is the key to fast and efficient production of foods. The flow patterns affecting this area include inflow of foods from storage and preparation areas and utensils from the pot- and pan-washing area. Outflow of foods to the serving, salad preparation, and sandwich preparation areas is common. The cooking equipment should be arranged so that the most frequently used pieces are close to the pick-up location.

Other factors related to the design of the main cooking area include the following:

1. All heat- and moisture-producing equipment, such as fryers, broilers, griddles, ranges, and steamers, should be placed under ventilating hoods or be equipped with individual venting systems.
2. Steam cooking equipment requires special installation including depressed floors or the use of curbs.
3. Some types of equipment require air for ventilation or cooling of enclosed spaces; vents and grill openings should not be blocked by other pieces of equipment.
4. Provision has to be made to permit venting of fuel-burning equipment directly to the outside.
5. Location of the main building ventilation or air-conditioning inlets is important to effect adequate cooling of the air without cooling the cooking equipment or interfering with the equipment venting system.
6. If remote banquet rooms are to be served, methods of transporting hot foods and appropriate space for loading have to be considered.

7. The use of partially or fully preprocessed foods will increase the need for refrigerated space in the cooking areas.

Flexibility and efficient use of employees and equipment can be obtained in some operations where similiar equipment is involved in baking and cooking. In this case the baking and cooking areas are placed in close proximity so that kettles, ovens, and mixers can serve both areas. This may even result in reduced exhaust requirements.

Placing the baking and cooking areas adjacent to each other also guides the placement of the pot-washing area since these two areas generate the bulk of the soiled pots.

LAYOUT OF PREPARATION AREAS

The layout of preparation areas is fairly easy because most of the functions performed in them follow a logical sequence, and thus the equipment is arranged in the same sequence. Vegetable preparation, for example, basically involves trimming, washing, and size reduction, in that order. A straight-line arrangement of a work table for trimming, a sink for washing and draining, and equipment for size reduction becomes the layout for the area. Since the inflow of vegetables is from storage areas, the trimming table is placed close to them; consequently, the size-reduction equipment is placed near the main cooking and salad preparation areas. Provision for temporary storage of materials and removal of waste will complete the layout of the vegetable preparation area for a small facility. Larger operations will require more space and equipment such as the vegetable peeler shown in Fig. 13.9 and take longer to lay out.

Salad preparation areas are planned in a similar manner. The foods should flow in a continuous path from the start of the preparation tasks, through the various workplaces and equipment, which are arranged in the order of the steps required, and on to the serving area. Operations that prepare a large number of the same or very similar salads may be designed by the concepts of mass assembly.

LAYOUT OF BAKING AREAS

The volume and variety of baked items that will be produced in a particular foodservice operation determines the layout to be used. Operations that produce a minimum number of items such as pastries and desserts can combine the baking area with the cooking area. Em-

FIG. 13.9. Vegetable peeler used in larger operations using fresh vegetables.
Courtesy of The Hobart Corporation.

ployees' work shifts may be scheduled to avoid problems of equipment usage. Operations that will be involved in the production of a moderate amount of baked goods frequently locate the baking area adjacent to the cooking area so some equipment can be shared. Foodservice operations that will produce the full line of baked items including breads, rolls, pastries, or even specialty items may need a separate baking area in order to minimize interference between the cooking and baking functions.

Separate bakeshops allow the use of specially designed equipment such as the steam-injection oven shown in Fig. 13.10 or the spiral mixer illustrated in Fig. 13.11.

FIG. 13.10. Steam-injection oven used to produce browned crusts on baked items.
Courtesy of The Hobart Corporation.

The design of baking area layouts should follow the typical processing steps to assure a smooth work flow. For example, a proof box located near the ovens simplifies the loading of items into the ovens. Similarly, a landing table placed near the ovens simplifies unloading. Baker's tables are centrally located with easy access to storage areas, mixers, and kettles, as well as the proof box and ovens. Sufficient space is provided for mixing, cutting, panning, rolling, and finishing the baked items. Storage space for baking supplies, utensils, and tools that are frequently used are best located at the work centers.

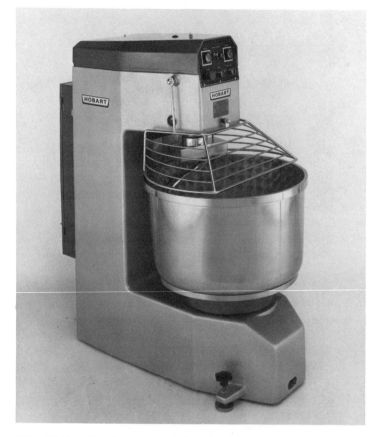

FIG. 13.11.   Spiral mixer used in bakeshop operations.
Courtesy of The Hobart Corporation.

Provision for storage of the finished baked items might take the form of mobile units for easy movement to the serving or pick-up areas. Another possibility would be to use pass-through storage units between the baking and serving areas. Special requirements such as the freezing and storage of some baked items are considered so that space for freezers is provided either in or near the baking areas. Refrigerators are required for the storage of highly perishable items such as custard-filled or whipped cream desserts.

LAYOUT OF SERVING AREAS

The layout of serving areas is based on the method and speed of service desired. Serving equipment should be arranged in the order of use, and should be located so they are easily accessible to serving personnel.

Table Service

Hot food pick-up areas are located adjacent to the main cooking battery. Provisions for maintaining the temperature of hot foods at pick-up areas should be considered. Additional serving stations or pantries for salads, desserts, rolls, and beverages are located nearer the dining area to avoid congestion. Linen, flatware, water, and butter used for setups are best placed in inconspicuous areas of the dining room. These stations may also include facilities for depositing soiled linen and tableware.

Counter Service

Most of the cooking and serving facilities in typical counter-service operations occur at the back bar opposite the dining counter. A common layout is to have a straight-line back bar with straight-line or a series of U-shaped dining counters. Some operations offering a more extensive menu may require additional preparation and cooking facilities that can be located in a separate area. An efficient layout in this case is to have the pick-up counter as a part of the back bar. This is also a good arrangement for operations having both counter and table-service sections. The pick-up area should be located for easy access to the table servers.

Cafeteria Service

Cafeteria counters are placed as close to the production areas as possible with due regard to the free flow of customers or users. The layout of cafeteria counters is based on the shape of the serving area and the anticipated traffic patterns. Counters may be arranged in a straight line, ell-shaped, U-shaped, hollow square, or combinations of these configurations, as dictated by the length of counter required.

The design of the counter should allow displayed foods that are usually selected in combination to be placed together on the counter.

Merchandising concepts call for desserts and salads to be located at the beginning of the line; hot foods should be at the end of the line to minimize cooling. Special care is needed in providing for cashiering (see Fig 13.12), since this is one of the bottleneck areas in commercial cafeterias.

The entire design of the cafeteria service system is based on volume flow, and anything that will speed service should be incorporated into the layout. Silver, napkins, water, and condiments may be located in stations away from the main counter area. Islands placed between the serving and dining areas are frequently used for this purpose. Self-dispensing equipment for beverages will also help speed the flow of people.

Cook-to-order items cause delays and are best located in a separate area where patrons can pull out of the main stream of flow to wait for their orders. This can be easily accomplished with the open square arrangement of counters.

FIG. 13.12. Careful planning of the cashiering area will eliminate bottleneck problems in cafeterias.
Courtesy of The Hysen Group, Livonia, Michigan and Hansen Lind Meyer, P.C., Architects.

LAYOUT OF DISHWASHING AREAS

The layout of dishwashing areas should follow the sequence of operations performed in washing. The arrangement has to provide for sorting, scraping or preflushing, and stacking, prior to loading the dishwashing machine. If glasses and silverware are to be washed separately, provisions for these operations have to be planned.

Preflushing of soiled dishes may be accomplished in one of two ways. One method is to use a continuous flow of water over the dishes as they are being scraped. A disposal unit is used to handle the food wastes. The other method uses an overhead spray and is suitable for dishes that are placed in dish racks. In either case, the soiled-dish table has to be designed so that water is quickly drained away. Raised edges on the table help prevent excess water spillage.

Regardless of the type of dishwashing machine used, space for loading and unloading must be arranged. Rack-type machines are frequently loaded in a straight-line flow from the soiled-dish table. Rackless or peg-type machines require space for the loader to handle the individual pieces of dinnerware.

Clean-dish areas are arranged so adequate drying time is allowed before the removal and stacking of dinnerware takes place. The flow of dinnerware through the dishwashing area is planned to be continuous and over the shortest possible distance.

The layout of other areas for the food facility should be accomplished in the same manner as given in the above examples. When all the preceding steps of the planning process are satisfactorily completed, the layout step becomes fairly easy. The final layout reflects the amount of time and care taken in completing the other steps of the planning process.

PROBLEMS AND EXERCISES

13.1. Draw a simple sketch of a kitchen facility that you are familiar with and identify its good and bad points with respect to the concepts of flow.

13.2. Determine the advantages and disadvantages of each of the following layout configurations: (a) single straight-line arrangement, (b) ell-shaped arrangement, (c) U-shaped arrangement, (d) parallel, back-to-back arrangement, and (e) parallel, face-to-face arrangement.

13.3. Discuss the differences and the reasons for those differences between the layout for a fast-food unit and a luxury restaurant that prepares most of its menu items from scratch. Include storage, cooking, preparation, service, and dishwashing in the discussion.

13.4. Give an example of how each of the following concepts can be incorporated into the floor plan for a foodservice facility: (a) efficient use of utilities, (b) efficient use of equipment, (c) efficient use of skilled labor, (d) safety, (e) efficient use of space, and (f) environmental factors of noise and odor.

13.5. Evaluate the layout shown in Fig. 15.5 for the following:

1. Material flow
   a. Foods
   b. Dinnerware
   c. Utensils

2. Employee flow
   a. Production
   b. Service

3. Customer flow

13.6. Prepare an alternative to the layout shown in Fig. 13.8 using the information given in the closeness relationship chart in Fig. 13.7.

13.7. Develop a relationship chart for a fast-food operation of your choice. Identify the functional areas and give the closeness ratings.

13.8. Refer to Fig. 15.1. and evaluate the layout using the relationship concept. How would the layout rate in terms of the closeness analysis?

13.9. Evalute the layout of a foodservice operation noting any aspects that reflect a principle of layout.

BIBLIOGRAPHY

AVERY, A.C. 1968. Simplified food service layout. Cornell Hotel, Restaurant Admin. Q. *9* (1), 114–119.

AVERY, A.C. 1980. A Modern Guide to Foodservice Equipment. CBI Publishing Co., Boston, Massachusetts.

FRESHWATER, J.F. 1971. Labor Utilization and Operating Practices in Table Service Restaurants. Agric. Res. Service, USDA, Washington, D.C.

GREEN, E.F., DRAKE, G.G. and SWEENEY, F.J. 1978. Profitable Food and Beverage Management: Planning. Hayden Book Co., Rochelle Park, New Jersey.

KAZARIAN, E.A. 1979. Work Analysis and Design for Hotels, Restaurants and Institutions. AVI Publishing Co., Westport, Connecticut.

MUTHER, R. 1973. Systematic Layout Planning, 2nd Edition. Cahners Publishing Co., Boston, Massachusetts.

STOKES, J.W. 1977. How to Manage a Restaurant or Institutional Food Service. Wm. C. Brown Co., Dubuque, Iowa.

SWART, W. and LUCA, D. 1981. Simulation modeling improves operations planning and productivity of fast food restaurants. Interfaces *11* (6), 35–47.

14

Evaluating Foodservice Layouts

INTRODUCTION

One of the most important factors to consider when improving or designing layouts for efficiency is flow. An optimum arrangement is achieved when the flow between the various workplaces is minimized. The arrangement of workplaces is relatively easy when the flow is primarily in one direction with very little backtracking or by-passing. However, when considerable backtracking or by-passing is involved, the arrangement of workplaces to minimize flow becomes difficult. The use of travel charts is a very effective technique to evaluate layouts on the basis of flow.

There are two general concepts regarding the criteria to use for travel charting. The first concept considers the movements of individuals between workplaces as the criteria to evaluate various arrangements. The second concept considers the flow of material between workplaces as the criteria to use for the travel charts. Both concepts are valid criteria to use since the movements of individuals and the flow of materials are usually related. With both concepts, considerable emphasis may be placed on weighing appropriately the desirability of forward movements against the undesirability of backtracking movements.

TRAVEL CHARTING USING MOVEMENTS OF INDIVIDUALS

For certain situations, the distance traveled by an employee is a good criterion to use in evaluating alternate arrangements of workplaces and equipment. This is especially true when the weight or volume of materials involved is not too great. When employee movements are the criteria for evaluation, the most frequent method of travel charting is to analyze workplaces that are placed in a straight line and where the distance traveled between the workplaces adjacent to one another are equal or can be assumed to be equal. The equipment bank shown in Fig. 14.1 can be easily analyzed by this method of travel charting. The data required for travel charting can be obtained from a worker process analysis.

Workplaces Placed in a Straight Line at Equal Intervals

For purposes of illustration, assume that an employee accomplishes certain tasks that require the possible use of four different workplaces. The term *workplaces* is used to designate worktables, sinks, and counters, as well as mechanical equipment. The four workplaces will

FIG. 14.1. Equipment arranged in a straight line can be evaluated by travel charting.

TABLE 14.1. SEQUENCE OF EMPLOYEE
MOVEMENTS BETWEEN WORKPLACES FOR
EACH PRODUCT GROUP

Product group	Sequence of movements
1	D A B C A C B A
2	C A C B A C A
3	A D A B A
4	D C B D A B C A
5	C A C A D A
6	B C B A
7	D C B

be designated by the letters A, B, C, and D. The tasks involve various sequences of movements between the workplaces by the employee for different product groups, as shown in Table 14.1.

For this example it was assumed that each of the product groups is made an equal number of times. In reality, certain product groups are likely to be made more frequently than others, in which case the sequence of movements should be multiplied by a relative frequency factor.

The frequency of movements between the various workplaces can be found by summarizing from the sequence of movements shown in Table 14.1. The frequency of employee movements for the seven product groups is shown in Table 14.2.

TABLE 14.2. FREQUENCY OF
EMPLOYEE MOVEMENTS BETWEEN
WORKPLACES

Workplaces		Frequency
From	To	
A	B	3
A	C	4
A	D	2
B	A	4
B	C	3
B	D	1
C	A	6
C	B	5
C	D	0
D	A	4
D	B	0
D	C	2

Constructing the Travel Chart

Construction of the travel chart for the example involves the following steps:

Step 1. Assume an arrangement using the four workplaces placed in a straight line. (Note that there are 24 possible arrangements for the 4 workplaces.) The arrangement A B C D is assumed for this example.

Step 2. Using the workplace arrangement shown in step 1, construct a chart consisting of 4 rows and 4 columns, as shown in Fig. 14.2.

The same arrangement of workplaces for the column designations must be used for the row designations. The column designations (placed horizontally across the top of the chart) are used to indicate movements "from" the various workplaces. The row designations (placed vertically at the left side of the chart) are used to indicate movements "to" the various workplaces. Since there are no movements from A to A or from B to B, etc., a diagonal line is drawn through the chart from the upper left-hand corner to the lower right-hand corner.

Step 3. The frequency of movements between the various workplaces are placed in the appropriate cells of the chart. For example, the number 3 indicating the frequency of movements from A to B is placed in the cell designated "From A" (1st column) and "To B" (2nd row). In a similar manner, the movements from A to C are placed in the cell designated "From A" (1st column) and "To C" (3rd row). The completed chart is shown in Fig. 14.2.

For the particular workplace arrangement shown (A B C D), the travel chart shows the characteristics of the various movements. The cells below the main diagonal show the forward movements. (Forward in-

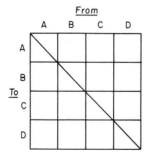 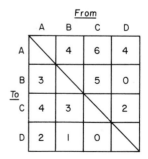

FIG. 14.2. Constructing a travel chart for four workstations, showing frequency of employee movements.

dicates movements from left to right.) The cells above the main diagonal show the backward movements (right to left). The distance of the cells from the main diagonal indicates the number of workplaces that are by-passed. The cells that are adjacent to the cells of the main diagonal of the chart (both above and below) indicate no by-passing. The cells that are separated from the cells of the main diagonal by one cell indicate that one workplace is by-passed. The cells separated from the main diagonal cells by two cells indicate that two workplaces have been by-passed.

Evaluating the Equipment Arrangement

Since the distances traveled between the workplaces adjacent to one another are equal, and the by-passing movements are indicated in the travel chart, an index of the total distance traveled can be obtained. This is done by totaling the movements (both forward and backward) according to the number of workplaces by-passed and multiplying the totals by a factor equal to one plus the number of workplaces by-passed. Thus the total movements where no by-passing is involved are multiplied by the factor one. The total movements where one workplace was by-passed are multiplied by the factor two, and so on. The grand total of the movements is the index of total distance traveled. The calculation for the example is shown below:

Type of movement		Total movements		By-pass factor		
No by-passing: 3 + 3 + 0 + 4 + 5 + 2	=	17	×	1	=	17
By-pass 1 workplace: 4 + 1 + 6 + 0	=	11	×	2	=	22
By-pass 2 workplaces: 2 + 4	=	6	×	3	=	18
				Index	=	57

The value of the travel chart is that it indicates possible changes in the arrangement of the workplaces that may reduce the index number. For example, it is desirable to get as many of the largest frequencies of movements near the main diagonal of the chart, while the smallest frequencies of movements should be furthest from the diagonal.

Another method of evaluating the workplace arrangement is to emphasize the desirability of forward movements and the undesirability of backtracking. This is done by determining the percentage of the distance moved forward. This percentage is found by dividing the index for forward distances by the index number for the total distance moved. The calculation for the percentage of forward distances moved is as follows:

	Forward movements		By-pass factor			Backward movements		By-pass factor		
No by-passing	6	×	1	=	6	11	×	1	=	11
By-pass 1 workplace	5	×	2	=	10	6	×	2	=	12
By-pass 2 workplaces	2	×	3	=	6	4	×	3	=	12
			Index	=	22			Index	=	35

$$\% \text{ forward moves} = \frac{22}{22 + 35} = 38.6\%$$

For this method of evaluation, it is desirable to get more numbers below the main diagonal of the travel chart and fewer numbers above the diagonal.

Improving the Arrangement of Workplaces

Analysis of the travel chart for the first arrangement of workplaces (A B C D) frequently gives an indication of how the arrangement may be improved. For example, the greatest number of movements (6) occurs between A and C. Rearranging the workplaces so that A and C are adjacent will move the 6 closer to the diagonal of the travel chart. Therefore an arrangement such as B A C D may be tried. The travel chart for the workplaces arranged B A C D is in Fig. 14.3. Note that the change from A B to B A changes the numbers in the first two rows and the first two columns of the travel chart.

The calculation for the various indices for the second travel chart is:

	Forward movements		By-pass factor			Backward movements		By-pass factor		
No by-passing	8	×	1	=	8	11	×	1	=	11
By-pass 1 workplace	5	×	2	=	10	9	×	2	=	18
By-pass 2 workplaces	1	×	3	=	3	0	×	3	=	0
		Forward index		=	21		Backward index		=	29

Index of total distance = 21 + 29 = 50

$$\% \text{ Forward movement} \frac{21}{21 + 29} = 42.0\%$$

A comparison of the two workplace arrangements shows:

Arrangement	Distance index	% forward movements
A B C D	57	38.6%
B A C D	50	42.0%

Thus the arrangement B A C D reduced the total distance traveled by 12.3% and increased the percentage of forward movements from 38.6% to 42.0% compared to the arrangement A B C D. Based on the criteria used, the B A C D arrangement of workplaces represents a better layout than the A B C D arrangement.

The use of travel charting for work system layouts where workplaces are arranged in a single straight line and the distances between the workplaces can be assumed to be equal is limited in its practical application. A simple modification of the technique of travel charting will allow its use in evaluating workplace arrangements where the distances between the equipment cannot be assumed to be equal. This obviously would expand the application of travel charts to more realistic situations.

Arrangement in a Straight Line with Different Distances between the Workplaces

As an example, assume that five different workplaces, designated by the letters A, B, C, D, and E, are required in the production of certain products. The sequence of movements by employees between the workplaces is shown in Table 14.3 for various product groups. The frequency of movements between the various combinations of

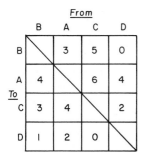

FIG. 14.3. Travel chart for improved four-workplace arrangement.

TABLE 14.3.   SEQUENCE OF EMPLOYEE MOVEMENTS BETWEEN WORKPLACES
FOR EACH PRODUCT GROUP

Product group	Sequence of movements
1	D A B C A C B A E
2	E C A C B A C A
3	E A D A B A
4	D C B D A B C A
5	E C A C A D A E
6	B C B A
7	D C B E

workplaces is summarized from the sequence of movements (Table
14.4).

For purposes of the example, assume that the workplaces have the
following length dimensions.

Workplace	Length (ft)
A	4
B	2
C	6
D	2
E	4

TABLE 14.4.   FREQUENCY OF EMPLOYEE MOVEMENTS
BETWEEN THE FIVE WORKPLACES

Workplaces		Frequency
From	To	
A	B	3
A	C	4
A	D	2
A	E	2
B	A	4
B	C	3
B	D	1
B	E	1
C	A	6
C	B	5
C	D	0
C	E	0
D	A	4
D	B	0
D	C	2
D	E	0
E	A	1
E	B	0
E	C	2
E	D	0

Constructing the Travel Chart

Step 1. Assume an arrangement using the five workplaces placed in a straight line. An arrangement of A B C D E is assumed and shown in Fig. 14.4.

Step 2. Using the workplace arrangement assumed in step 1, construct a distance chart as shown in Fig. 14.5. Note that the distances shown in the chart are for the particular workplace arrangement A B C D E and would not necessarily be the same for other arrangements.

Step 3. For the same arrangement, construct a move chart using the frequency of movements given in Table 14.4. The completed move chart is shown in Fig. 14.5. The frequency of movements as shown in the move chart will not change in value but will change position in the chart with different workplace arrangements.

Step 4. The travel chart is constructed by multiplying each entry on the distance chart by the corresponding entry on the move chart and placing the result in the appropriate cell of the chart (Fig. 14.6). The numbers entered on the travel chart indicate the total distances traveled between the various workplaces.

Evaluating the Arrangement

Since the entries on the travel chart are actual distances traveled, an absolute measure of evaluating the workplace arrangement is found by totaling all the entries. This is done by subtotaling either the rows or columns and then totaling the subtotals as shown on the chart. The actual distance traveled for this example is 272 ft (82.9 m).

Another measure used to evaluate the arrangement is to determine the percentage of forward distances compared to the total distance

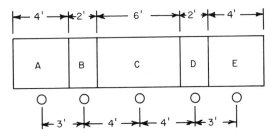

FIG. 14.4. Workplace arrangement showing different distances of movements.

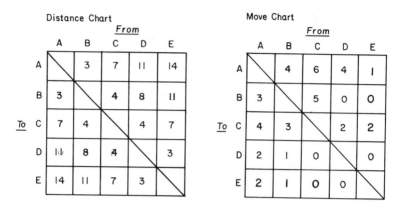

FIG. 14.5. Distance and move charts for five-workplace arrangement.

traveled. This is done by totaling the distances below the diagonal of the chart (forward moves) and dividing by the total (forward and backward) distance.

Since the entries in the travel chart are the actual distances traveled between the various workplaces, an improved layout is characterized by smaller entries in the travel chart which in turn results in less total distance traveled. Because the entries in the chart are the product of the distance traveled between the workplaces times the frequency of the movements, and since both factors of the product may vary de-

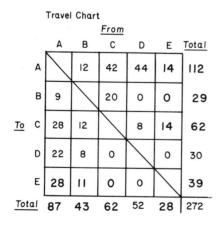

FIG. 14.6. Travel chart for five-work-place arrangement.

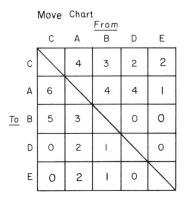

FIG. 14.7. Second workplace arrangement
showing change in distances of movements.

pending on the arrangement assumed, it becomes difficult to rationalize
an improvement in the layout. Hence the problem of trying to find
layout improvements becomes a matter of trial and error. Of course
an optimum layout can be found by trying all possible layouts and
determining the distances traveled.

A second workplace arrangement of C A B D E is assumed and is
shown in Fig. 14.7. The distance and move charts for the workplace
arrangement of C A B D E is shown in Fig. 14.8. Note that the distance
chart for the second arrangement is considerably different from the
distance chart for the first arrangement.

The completed travel chart for the second arrangement is shown in
Fig. 14.9. The total distance traveled in the second arrangement is 242
ft (73.8 m) compared to 272 ft (82.9 m) for the first arrangement. This
represents a reduction in distance traveled of 11%.

Distance Chart
From

		C	A	B	D	E
	C		5	8	10	13
	A	5		3	5	8
To	B	8	3		2	5
	D	10	5	2		3
	E	13	8	5	3	

Move Chart
From

		C	A	B	D	E
	C		4	3	2	2
	A	6		4	4	1
To	B	5	3		0	0
	D	0	2	1		0
	E	0	2	1	0	

FIG. 14.8. Distance and move charts for improved five-workplace
arrangement.

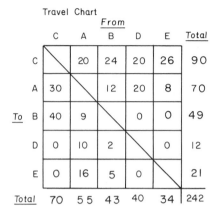

FIG. 14.9.   Travel chart for improved five-workplace arrangement.

The use of travel charts to evaluate workplace arrangement, where the distances between adjacent workplaces are not equal, uses an absolute measure of the distance traveled. Although this method of travel charting is more realistic than when equal distances are assumed between adjacent workplaces, it does not readily show how improvements in layout can be obtained. Using actual distances traveled does mean, however, that the technique is not limited to straight-line arrangements of workplaces, but can be used for any pattern.

TRAVEL CHARTING USING PRODUCT FLOW

In sections such as dishwashing areas, where large quantities of materials are handled between workplaces, product movement is a better criterion to use for travel charting. The method of travel charting using product movements is similar to the method described for employee movements. Travel charting with product movements requires information regarding the amounts of materials and the distances that the products are moved between the various workplaces. This information is readily gathered by using the product process or form process charts. The amounts of materials may be indicated by pounds, unit loads, or other suitable measurements of quantity.

Where workplaces can be arranged in a straight line, the same procedure of travel charting described with employee movements can be used for product flow. The product flow is the total amount moved between the workplaces. For example, if 100 lb (45.4 kg) are moved twice between two workplaces, the total amount of 200 lb (90.7 kg) should be indicated in the travel chart. For straight line arrangements, the desirability of flow in one direction can be emphasized by penalizing the backward movements.

A situation where workplaces cannot be arranged in a straight line will be treated here to show the differences in the travel charting method.

Workplaces Arranged at Random

As an illustration, assume that the material flow required to process several products is between six workplaces designated by A, B, C, D, E, and F. The workplace may refer to a table, piece of equipment, or storage area. The quantity of materials moved and the sequence of movements are shown in Table 14.5.

The total quantity of materials moved between the workplaces (summarized in Table 14.6) is determined by summing the quantity of materials moved between each combination of workplaces. For example, the quantity moved from workplace A to workplace B consists of 100 lb (45.4 kg) of product group 1; 300 lb (136 kg) of product group 2; 400 lb (181 kg) of product group 4; and 200 lb (90.7) kg) of product group 6; making a total of 1000 lb (454 kg). Only those combinations of workplaces that involve material flow are shown.

Assuming the workplace arrangement shown in Fig. 14.10, the distance chart showing the distances between workplaces is constructed. It should be noted that the distance chart (see Fig. 14.11) will remain constant regardless of where the various workplaces are placed. In this case an arbitrary arrangement of workplaces is selected to start the procedure. Distances are measured from the center of the locations. The distances have been rounded off to the nearest foot to simplify the presentation of the example.

TABLE 14.5. QUANTITY OF MATERIALS AND SEQUENCE OF MOVEMENTS FOR EACH PRODUCT GROUP

Product group	Quantity (lb)	Sequence of movements
1	100	A B D F
2	300	C A B C E F
3	200	B D F E
4	400	B D A B
5	100	C A C E F
6	200	C B C A B

TABLE 14.6. TOTAL QUANTITY OF MATERIALS MOVED
BETWEEN WORKPLACES

Workplace		Quantity of materials
From	To	moved (lb)
A	B	1,000
A	C	100
B	C	500
B	D	700
C	A	600
C	B	200
C	E	400
D	A	400
D	F	300
E	F	400
F	E	200

Next a quantity chart is constructed (see Fig. 14.11). The row and column designations on the quantity chart must correspond to the placement of the workplaces in the various locations. The product of the quantity times the distance is then computed and arranged into the travel chart, as shown in Fig. 14.12. The total value of 52000 lb-ft (7192 kg-m) expresses the amount of material flow for the given arrangement of workplaces.

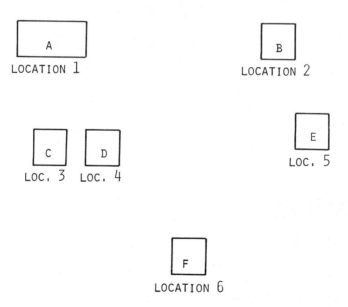

FIG. 14.10. Workplace arrangement for travel charting problem involving product flow.

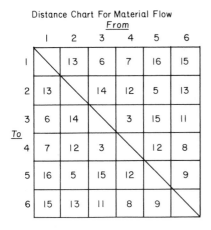

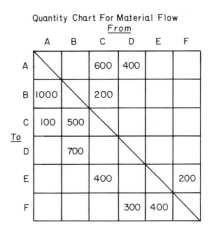

FIG. 14.11. Distance and quantity charts for material flow.

Improving the Workplace Arrangement

The workplaces should be rearranged and another travel chart constructed to see if the material flow can be reduced. Since the material flow is the product of two variables (distance and quantity) that are not constant for different arrangements, there is no general procedure that can be used to find the optimum solution quickly. The only guide that can be followed is to try to locate the workplaces involving the greatest quantities of materials close together. The travel chart for a different arrangement of workplaces is shown in Fig. 14.13. The row or column designations indicate the placement of the workplaces in

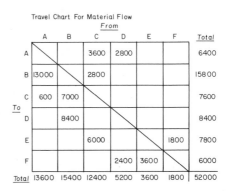

FIG. 14.12. Travel chart for material flow.

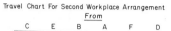

Travel Chart For Second Workplace Arrangement

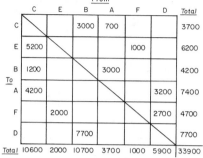

	C	E	B	A	F	D	Total
C			3000	700			3700
E	5200				1000		6200
B	1200			3000			4200
A	4200					3200	7400
F		2000				2700	4700
D			7700				7700
Total	10600	2000	10700	3700	1000	5900	33900

FIG. 14.13.   Travel chart for material flow in improved workplace arrangement.

the six locations. For example, workplace A is at location 4, workplace B is at location 3, and so on.

The material flow for the second arrangement is 33900 lb-ft (4688 kg-m) which is 18100 lb-ft (2504 kg-m) less than the original arrangement. This represents a savings of about 35% and shows that, based on material flow, the second layout arrangement is definitely better. Additional arrangements should be tried to see if further improvements can be obtained.

PROBLEMS AND EXERCISES

14.1.   An analysis of a cook's movements during a typical work period shows the following:

Movement from	Movement to	Frequency
Refrigerator	Table	10
Refrigerator	Sink	2
Refrigerator	Oven	2
Table	Refrigerator	10
Table	Sink	16
Table	Range	4
Table	Oven	8
Sink	Refrigerator	2
Sink	Table	6
Sink	Range	10
Range	Table	14
Range	Oven	4
Oven	Refrigerator	2
Oven	Table	6
Oven	Range	4

Arrange the five pieces of equipment in a straight line so that the total distance traveled by the cook is minimized. Assume that the distance moved between adjacent pieces of equipment is equal.

14.2. An analysis of several recipes shows the following frequency of movements between five workplaces designated as A, B, C, D, and E.

Movements between	Frequency
A and B	10
A and C	13
A and E	10
B and C	12
B and D	8
B and E	9
C and D	3
D and E	7

Assuming that the workplaces are to be placed equidistant in a straight line and that C must be placed adjacent to E, arrange the workplaces to minimize the total distance traveled.

14.3. The quantity of materials and the sequence of movements for four different products are shown below:

Product no.	Quantity (lbs)	Sequence of movements
1	200	B D A B C D
2	100	F E A E B D C
3	400	A C A F D C B
4	200	D A B C D B

The departments through which the materials move and their dimensions are:

Department	Dimensions
A	10 ft × 10 ft
B	10 ft × 10 ft
C	10 ft × 10 ft
D	10 ft × 20 ft
E	10 ft × 10 ft
F	10 ft × 20 ft

Arrange the departments to fit into a 20 x 40 ft rectangular configuration so that the material flow is minimized. Distances of movements are to be measured from the centers of departments over the shortest horizontal and/or vertical routes.

14.4. Using the data given in problem 14.3, arrange the departments to minimize flow given the restriction that department D must be placed at the right-hand end of the configuration.

BIBLIOGRAPHY

KAZARIAN, E.A. 1979. Work Analysis and Design for Hotels, Restaurants and Institutions, 2nd Edition. AVI Publishing Co., Westport, Connecticut.

KOTSCHEVAR, L.H. and TERRELL, M.E. 1985. Foodservice Planning: Layout and Equipment, 3rd Edition. John Wiley and Sons, New York.

PAVESIC, D.V. 1985. How to determine the most efficient layout for kitchen equipment. Hospitality Education and Research Journal *10* (1), 12–24.

15

Sample Foodservice Layouts

INTRODUCTION

The planning of foodservice facilities involves developing layouts for a wide variety of operations. Each layout should reflect the type of menu entrees to be prepared, the production processes to be used, the equipment choices, and the method of operation desired by management. This chapter presents illustrations of layouts for several different types of foodservice operations. The plans shown are examples and are not intended to represent the only layout suitable for each type of operation.

GENERAL RESTAURANTS

The Claim Company of Oak Brook*

The Claim Company of Oak Brook (Fig. 15.1) has a seating capacity of 235 and can serve 1000 to 1200 persons per day. One of the primary considerations in the design of the facility was control. Traffic flow in the kitchen and ease of movement were other important factors.

To maintain liquor control, a computerized system dispenses standard measures for drinks. Both the service bar in the kitchen and the restaurant bar dispense liquor, beer, and wine using an automatic remote system connected to locked refrigerators. Food control is maintained through several walk-in refrigerators, freezers, and storage rooms that allow systemized food handling and minimize the number of employees needing access to these areas.

The Claim Company kitchen design features separate areas for food

*Layout and description courtesy of *Restaurant Business*.

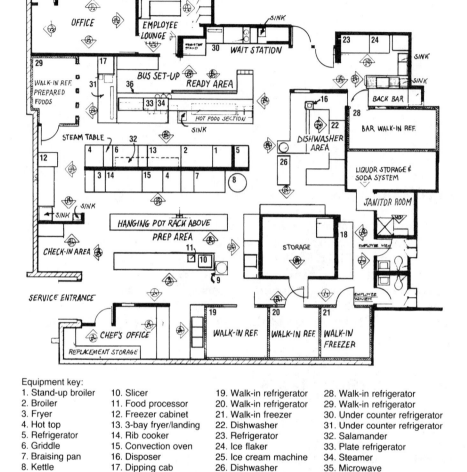

Equipment key:

1. Stand-up broiler	10. Slicer	19. Walk-in refrigerator	28. Walk-in refrigerator
2. Broiler	11. Food processor	20. Walk-in refrigerator	29. Walk-in refrigerator
3. Fryer	12. Freezer cabinet	21. Walk-in freezer	30. Under counter refrigerator
4. Hot top	13. 3-bay fryer/landing	22. Dishwasher	31. Under counter refrigerator
5. Refrigerator	14. Rib cooker	23. Refrigerator	32. Salamander
6. Griddle	15. Convection oven	24. Ice flaker	33. Plate refrigerator
7. Braising pan	16. Disposer	25. Ice cream machine	34. Steamer
8. Kettle	17. Dipping cab	26. Dishwasher	35. Microwave
9. Cutter/mixer	18. Ice machine	27. Flat top refrigerator	36. Under counter refrigerator

FIG. 15.1.   Floor plan of the Claim Company of Oak Brook.
Courtesy of Restaurant Business.

prep, cooking, serving, and dishwashing. The kitchen is designed so that service employees need never be more than a few steps from the kitchen door. For example, the service bar is located near the entrance to the dining room. Soiled dishes are dropped off at the dishwashing area, which is also located near the dining room. The pick-up area and the "waitstation" are located so the service personnel do not need to enter the main part of the kitchen during the peak hours.

The efficiency of the kitchen design is matched by an equally efficient system in the dining room. An electronic seating system provides efficient and accurate seating of guests. In addition, a computer instantly relays orders from the service employees to the kitchen.

One of the outstanding features of the design is the working environment for the employees. The kitchen is air-conditioned and provides sufficient room for easy movement. There is also an employee lounge adjacent to the office. The pleasant working environment helps reduce turnover and improve employee morale.

Group One Steakhouse*

Figure 15.2 shows the floor plan for the Group One Steakhouse. The plan was prepared by the Group One consulting firm for the National Restaurant Association's restaurant design exposition, which was developed in conjunction with the Foodservice Consultants Society International. Designs submitted for the exposition had to adhere to a fixed area of 4950 ft^2.

The Group One Steakhouse seats 84 in its dining room, 26 in a cocktail and dining lounge, and an additional 13 in a drinking and eating bar.

In the kitchen, waiters have ready access to a counter for self-dispensed soft drinks, bread, and other similar side items. The liquor service bar has an unobstructed passage from both the dining room and the cocktail lounge.

For maximum efficiency, the dishwashing and pot washing operations have been placed in one common area. Minimum work areas were planned for the receiving, production, sanitizing, and dispensing areas.

Energy conservation features for the Group One design include a "cold water" sanitizing dishwashing machine. Also, all refrigeration and ice-making compressors are remote and located in a rooftop housing that has a heat recovery system that is used to temper the make-up air. The water supply to the ice maker circulates through a coil located in the walk-in refrigerator. The lower incoming water temperature results in maximum ice production at the lowest possible cost.

The cooking battery was designed for a heavy charcoal-broiling function. The ventilator was designed to extract the heavy grease and exhaust the fumes efficiently from the char broiler. A self-cleaning mechanical water wash system was included in the ventilator design.

*Floor plan and description reprinted by permission from *Nation's Restaurant News,* September 27, 1982. Copyright Lebhar-Friedman, Inc., 425 Park Avenue, New York, NY.

Equipment key:
1. Ice
2. Mixer/stand
3. Prep table
4. Wall shelves
5. Slicer
6. Walk-in cooler
7. Shelving
8. Walk-in freezer
9. Shelving
10. Walk-in cooler
11. Shelving
12. Shelving/liquor storage
13. Shelving and dry storage
14. Waitress counter
15. Coffee urn
16. Hot chocolate dispenser
17. Refrigerator
18. Milk dispenser
19. Roll warmer
20. Juice dispenser
21. Soiled dish table
22. Rack shelf
23. Janitor's sink
24. Pot rack
25. Clean dishtable
26. Dish machine
27. Convection oven
26. Fryers
29. Spreader
30. Double broiler
31. Char broiler
32. Expando unit
33. Range
34. Hood
35. Two refrigerators
36. Sandwich unit
37. Plate dispenser
38. Grille center
39. Rotary toaster
40. Hot food well
41. Pass shelf

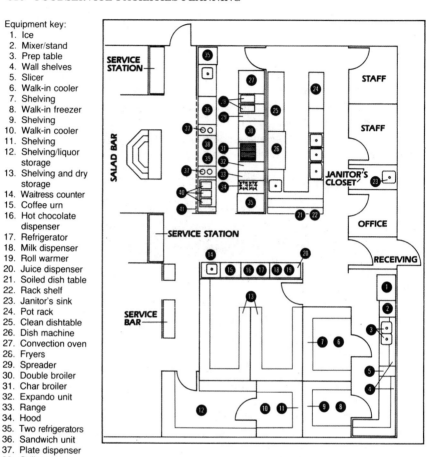

FIG. 15.2. Design of the Group One Steakhouse.
Courtesy of Nation's Restaurant News.

Van Brunt Steakhouse*

Another design from the National Restaurant Association's design exposition is shown in Fig. 15.3. This plan, for the Van Brunt Steakhouse, was developed for location in Sun Valley, Idaho. The design features several energy-saving concepts including solar panels and sunlights. All walk-in coolers, built-in refrigerators, and ice machine

*Floor plan and description reprinted by permission from *Nation's Restaurant News,* September 27, 1982. Copyright Lebhar-Friedman, Inc., 425 Park Avenue, New York, NY.

Equipment key:
1. Kitchen hood system
2. Fire protection
3. Cooking equipment (slowcook ovens; broilers; convection ovens, fryers, soup kettles)
4. Water-cooled compressors; coolers
5. Preparation area
6. Soup and salad bar
7. Service station and beverage refills
8. Bar equipment (automatic pouring system; direct draw beer and wine, post-mix soda systems)
9. Bar service station
10. Worktables
11. Ice machine
12. Cook's worktable (hot and cold holding units, plate storage, cook server sink, bain marie, garnish pan, work surfaces)
13. Salad bar
14. Dish and pot washing
15. Bar equipment
16. Offices
17. Precheck system
18. Kitchen entry and exit
19. 48-inch. wide door
20. Trash room
21. Tile surfaces
22. Ice machine
23. Employee rest rooms
24. Receiving area
25. Bar storage
26. Hot water glass washer
27. Overhead glass storage rack

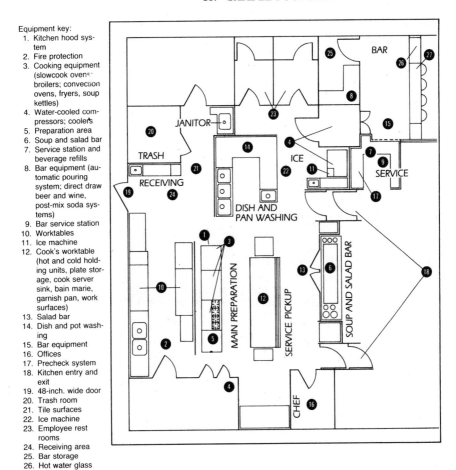

FIG. 15.3. Floor plan of the Van Brunt Steakhouse.
Courtesy of Nation's Restaurant News.

compressors are water cooled to reduce the heat load on the building air conditioning system.

The restaurant design includes such features as a salad bar that can be restocked from the back and access for the handicapped to all public areas.

Worktables include drawer and shelf storage, and all available wall space is used for dry storage shelves. The ice machine was designed to provide sufficient small cubes for the bar, the dining room, and the salad bar. The cook's worktable includes hot and cold holding units, plate storage, cook/server sink, bain marie, garnish pan, and work/

cutting surfaces. The salad bar allows for kitchen access through sliding decor panels and includes refill storage for salad items, plates, and bowls.

Storage space was minimized with daily delivery of precut and preportioned products. Reach-in coolers and automated beverage systems eliminate the need for extensive additional storage or cooler space at the bar. The pre-check pick-up area permits beverage setups and limited beverage service by the waiters.

Design features for space utilization include common wet areas for both the ice machine and the dishwashing machine. The receiving area is common to the trash room, dry storage, and dishwashing and is accessible to the refrigerated storage area. Separate bar, walk-in refrigeration, and storage areas are provided for security purposes. The employee rest rooms include change areas and locker facilities.

Aulmiller Youngquist Restaurant*

The Aulmiller Youngquist design firm developed the plan for a gourmet restaurant (Fig. 15.4) for the National Restaurant Association design exposition.

The kitchen features one main cooking line to be utilized by two or three cooks. The major cooking is done with two range ovens, an infrared broiler, and a double roasting oven. A back-up cook line is incorporated in the same area with a convection oven, range broiler, and steam-jacketed kettle. This arrangement eliminates the need for an additional exhaust hood. Reach-ins are located along the same line for easy access and minimization of employee movements.

The chef's counter is a series of modular pieces of equipment designed for easy assembly at the job site. This eliminates the need for expensive custom-fabricated equipment. On the cook's side of the counter is a large bain marie, a five-hole steam table, three cold pans with refrigerators below, soup wells, sinks, and undercounter shelving. The pick-up side of the counter has continuous open shelving for storage. An overhead display board shows daily specials and important notices.

Salad and dessert preparation was designed as an extension of the cook's line to allow waitresses to place and pick-up orders in a central

*Floor plan and description reprinted by permission from *Nation's Restaurant News*, September 27, 1982. Copyright Lebhar-Friedman, Inc., 425 Park Avenue, New York, NY.

Equipment key:
1. Freezer
2. Cooler
3. Linen storage
4. Cooler
5. Office
6. Scullery
7. Soup and sauce preparation
8. Cook line
9. Entree pickup
10. Soup and salad pickup
11. Ice
12. Mops
13. Dishwashing
14. Employee rest room
15. Lockers
16. Receiving
17. Storage
18. Women's room
19. Men's room
20. Register
21. Service station
22. Service station
23. Drink pickup
24. Bus setup
25. Service entry

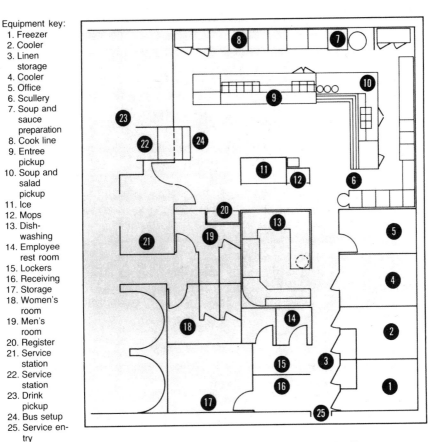

FIG. 15.4. Design of the Aulmiller Youngquist Restaurant.
Courtesy of Nation's Restaurant News.

location. The prep area's equipment includes a slicer, cutter/mixer, rolling bins, a scale, two-compartment sink, cold pans with undercounter refrigerations, and a glass-doored refrigerator case.

Dishwashing is removed from the center of activity to control noise in the kitchen, but it still is within easy access of the dining room for dropping off soiled dinnerware. The design includes a sanitizing cold water dishwashing machine to cut down on energy consumption.

The rest of the kitchen area consists of an office, walk-in refrigeration, linen storage, employee facilities, and lockers. The receiving area includes a scale and drop table. Rolling storage shelving was used in the dry storage area for more efficient use of space.

HOTEL FOODSERVICE

Garden City Hotel*

The layouts for foodservice in hotels are unique in that several restaurants have to be served simultaneously. The Garden City Hotel (Fig. 15.5) has three restaurants: the Cafe Royal, the Polo Club, and the Hunt Room. The Hunt Room is a lounge but serves a buffet luncheon at noon. The main feature of the layout is that the kitchens are in the center, unlike hotels where restaurants are located throughout the property and a kitchen is required for every restaurant.

At the Garden City Hotel, the main kitchen, the banquet kitchen, a butcher shop, a bakery, a cold garde manger station, and dishwashing facilities are all located in a 7500 ft^2 area that connects directly with the three dining rooms.

Two complete kitchens—a restaurant kitchen and the smaller banquet kitchen—are located side by side. The obvious advantage of this layout is that the smaller banquet kitchen can be closed when banquet business is light and all meals can be prepared in the restaurant kitchen.

Room service is handled from a small service area located away from the main flow. Room service meals are ordered through a computer system and are cooked in the main restaurant kitchen. The main kitchen also handles six party rooms where light food and beverages are served.

Westin O'Hare Hotel†

The Benchmark Restaurant (Fig. 15.6), located in the Westin O'Hare Hotel, features a display kitchen as a patron draw. The design is based on a European-style kitchen open to the diner's view. The display kitchen provides an elegant complement to the dining room's warm atmosphere.

The open kitchen backs up to the main kitchen (not visible to diners) where initial food preparation activities are performed. The display kitchen features the sauté and flambé stations, a mesquite grill and a European rotisserie for meats and fowl. This arrangement allows the food to be prepared much closer to the guests and eliminates many lengthy trips to the main kitchen area by the service personnel.

---

*Layout and description courtesy of *Restaurant Business.*
†Layout and description courtesy of *Restaurants/Institutions.*

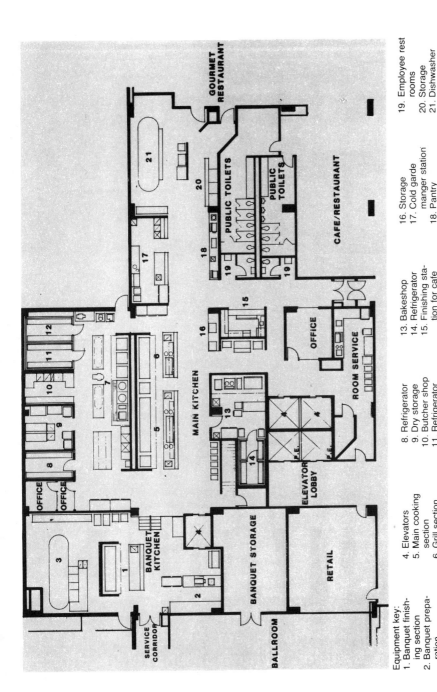

FIG. 15.5. Layout of the kitchen in the Garden City Hotel. *Courtesy of Restaurant Business.*

Equipment key:
1. Banquet finishing section
2. Banquet preparation
3. Dishwasher
4. Elevators
5. Main cooking section
6. Grill section
7. Main preparation
8. Refrigerator
9. Dry storage
10. Butcher shop
11. Refrigerator
12. Freezer
13. Bakeshop
14. Refrigerator
15. Finishing station for cafe
16. Storage
17. Cold garde manger station
18. Pantry
19. Employee rest rooms
20. Storage
21. Dishwasher

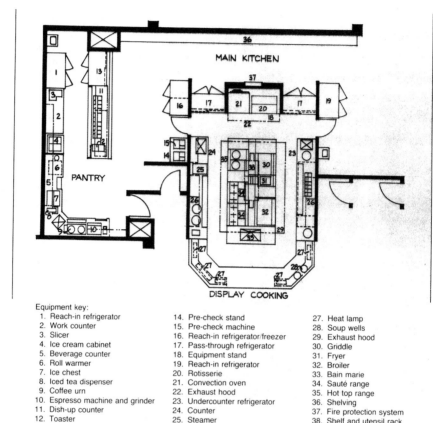

Equipment key:
1. Reach-in refrigerator
2. Work counter
3. Slicer
4. Ice cream cabinet
5. Beverage counter
6. Roll warmer
7. Ice chest
8. Iced tea dispenser
9. Coffee urn
10. Espresso machine and grinder
11. Dish-up counter
12. Toaster
13. Pass-through refrigerators
14. Pre-check stand
15. Pre-check machine
16. Reach-in refrigerator/freezer
17. Pass-through refrigerator
18. Equipment stand
19. Reach-in refrigerator
20. Rotisserie
21. Convection oven
22. Exhaust hood
23. Undercounter refrigerator
24. Counter
25. Steamer
26. Cheese melter
27. Heat lamp
28. Soup wells
29. Exhaust hood
30. Griddle
31. Fryer
32. Broiler
33. Bain marie
34. Sauté range
35. Hot top range
36. Shelving
37. Fire protection system
38. Shelf and utensil rack

FIG. 15.6. Floor plan of the Benchmark Restaurant in the Westin O'Hare Hotel. *Courtesy of* Restaurants/Institutions.

An exhibition cooking area can be created by using the variety of compact cooking equipment that is available. Custom fabrication of the display cooking area is an alternative design possibility.

FAST-FOOD OPERATIONS

Burger King*

The floor plans for two Burger King operations are shown in Fig. 15.7. The top plan shows the addition of a 42-seat dining wing that

*Floor plans and descriptions reprinted with permission from *Hotels and Restaurants International*, Cahners Publishing, Des Plaines, Illinois.

Equipment key:

BK-50 (50-seat Burger King)

1. Expediting shelf, cash drawer, coffee machine, ice tea dispenser, shake syrup tanks
2. Register stand
3. Cash registers
4. Shake machine
5. Serving counters
6. Drink prep unit, ice machine, ice bin, soda tower, cup dispenser, lid dispenser
7. Main prep board, bun steamer, condiment well, infrared heat lamp, sandwich chute, ref. meat well
8. Overshelf, infrared heat lamp, microwave oven, order printer
9. Broiler
10. Fry dump, infrared heat lamp, heat blanket
11. Fryers, thawing rack
12. Specialty sandwich table, microwave oven, reach-in freezer, pan rack, bun grill
13. Hand sink
14. Condiment sink
15. Lockers
16. Time card rack
17. Time clock
18. Safe
19. Soda factory
20. Fire extinguisher
21. Fire extinguisher
22. Office shelf
23. Storage, dry storage walk-in, walk-in refrigerator, walk-in freezer, condensing units, evaporators, heat strips, dunnage racks, steak thaw rack

DESIGNED FOR RELAXED DINING

Franchise added cozy 42-seat dining wing to 92-seat Burger King in Ansonia, Conn. Walls and booths in new wing are set at angles.

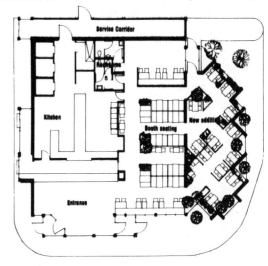

PROTOTYPE FOR PRODUCTIVITY

Computer-designed BK-50 is 32% smaller than the average 86-seat Burger King, costs 27% less to build, and can increase sales by 40%.

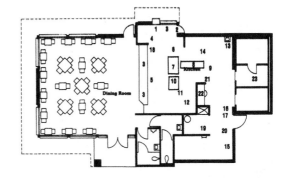

FIG. 15.7. Floor plans for two Burger King operations.
Courtesy of Hotels & Restaurants International.

was added to a 92-seat operation located in Ansonia, Connecticut. The addition was necessary to handle increased customer traffic. The interior was designed with wood-paneled walls and ceilings to give a cosy country atmosphere to the dining room. The walls and booths in the new wing were set at an angle to the existing building.

The floor plan shown at the bottom of Fig. 15.7 is the standard BK-50 design for the 50-seat Burger King operations. This design was introduced by the company's industrial engineering and operations research department. The objective of the BK-50 design is to increase profits through improved employee productivity.

To develop the BK-50, researchers collected data from more than 40 restaurants, including time-and-motion studies of the crew members. Then, using a computer, they redesigned the standard Burger King restaurant to position equipment and furnishings for maximum efficiency.

The computer-designed BK-50 is 32% smaller than the average 86-seat Burger King and costs 27% less to build.

RAX*

The design of a newer RAX facility, as shown in Fig. 15.8, is based on a flexible kitchen that can be easily modified to handle new, additional, or different menu offerings. This new design contains about 1400 ft^2 of space compared to an average size of 1000 ft^2 in the older facilities.

The concept involved in this design is that all permanently installed equipment and facilities are placed away from the center of the kitchen production area. For example, the walk-in coolers and freezers are located outside the building. If any changes are needed to increase the capacity of the walk-ins, they can be made without disturbing the interior layout of the kitchen.

Only equipment that is mobile is placed in the production center of the kitchen, so that any changes in menu offerings that require new or different types of equipment can be easily accommodated. Equipment that is electrically powered is used whenever possible since gas hook-ups and lines limit mobility. The concept of flexible design allows operators to test market new menu items without major remodeling of the kitchen. Changes that are needed can be made with minimum of interference.

EMPLOYEE FOODSERVICE

Chemical Bank†

Figure 15.9 shows the layout of the employee foodservice at the Chemical Bank in New York. The design features kitchen stations that

*Floor plan courtesy of RAX Systems Inc.
†Layout and description courtesy of *Restaurant Business*.

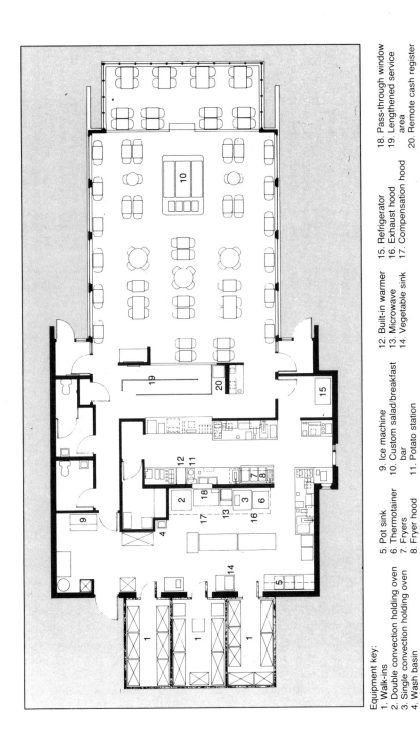

Equipment key:
1. Walk-ins
2. Double convection holding oven
3. Single convection holding oven
4. Wash basin

5. Pot sink
6. Thermotainer
7. Fryers
8. Fryer hood

9. Ice machine
10. Custom salad/breakfast bar
11. Potato station

12. Built-in warmer
13. Microwave
14. Vegetable sink

15. Refrigerator
16. Exhaust hood
17. Compensation hood

18. Pass-through window
19. Lengthened service area
20. Remote cash register

FIG. 15.8. Flexible design of the newer RAX Systems operations. *Courtesy of RAX Systems, Inc. and Restaurant and Hotel Design.*

325

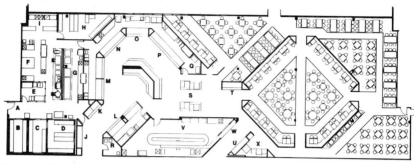

Equipment key:

A. Receiving
B. Walk-in vegetable refrigerator
C. Walk-in meat & dairy refrigerator
D. Walk-in freezer
E. Office
F. Preparation area
G. Kitchen
H. Storeroom

I. Pot washing
J. Tray pick-up
K. Display refrigerators
L. Dessert & salad counters
M. Hot food counters
N. Grill counter
O. Ice cream counter
P. Sandwich counter (three-station)

Q. Soda factory room
R. Compressor room
S. Cashiers
T. Condiments
U. Take-out
V. Dishwashing room
W. Soiled tray drop
X. Vending

FIG. 15.9. Layout of the employee foodservice in the Chemical Bank.
Courtesy of Restaurant Business.

are placed in logical sequence. For example, the refrigerators and the walk-in freezer are adjacent to the receiving area to minimize flow and to control temperatures of the foods. The manager's office is placed near the receiving area for control purposes.

The kitchen and the hot serving area are separated only by a wall with pass-thru cabinets in it. This way, small batches of recently prepared foods are kept hot and can be taken as needed by the service employees.

Customers are drawn in through a wide entrance after picking up their trays and from there go directly to specific food stations. The first stations visible upon entering are the desserts and pre-packaged foods for take-out. Desserts and salads are merchandised by positioning them at a 30 degree angle. Following sequentially are the hot food counter, grill counter, ice cream counter, and sandwich counter. Final prep is done by the service workers, relieving the back-of-the-house of some of their work and enhancing the quality image of the operation.

A visible but not intrusive tray drop-off station is located conveniently near the cafeteria exit. As trays roll into the dishwashing area on a conveyor, an employee dumps the food into a trough that goes immediately into a compacter. The belt that brings the trays in is washed by water circulating underneath, which eliminates undesirable dirt build-up. The dishes and trays run on racks through a continuously operating dishwasher.

Decor in the serving area enhances the quality image. Low ceilings are covered with long metal planks, counters are constructed of real oak, and red lettering clearly marks each station. The employees are dressed in snappy aprons with chefs' hats and bandanas.

COLLEGE FOODSERVICE

The planning of college or university foodservice facilities involves careful consideration of future needs if the facility is to handle increasing student enrollments. The foodservice operation shown in Fig. 15.10 illustrates this type of planning project. Future needs were anticipated and appropriate allowances were made for additional space and equipment.

The present facility combines a cafeteria on one side and a snack bar unit on the other. Each component has a seating capacity of 300 people. A private dining area is adjacent to the snack bar. Both units are serviced by a single 6200 ft² (576 m²) kitchen. For lunch, the cafeteria currently serves about 600 students and the snack bar serves about 900 students, for a total of 1500.

The dining schedules for the cafeteria and snack bar are arranged to complement each other. Only the cafeteria is open from 7:00 a.m. to 8:30 a.m., for breakfast. The snack bar is then opened at 8:30 a.m., and both units are used for the luncheon surge. The snack bar closes at 4:30 p.m., when the cafeteria opens for the evening meal. Then, when the cafeteria closes at 7:30 p.m., the snack bar is reopened to handle the late evening snacks. This scheduling of the units allows management to adjust the dining capacity of the facility as needed.

The cafeteria offers a multiple-selection menu with a minimum of three entrees. A great deal of the preparation, including baking, salads, and meat preparation, is done the day before and the food kept under refrigeration.

The snack bar offers the standard hamburgers, hot dogs, sandwiches, beverages, and other typical snack items.

The cafeteria unit is designed so that students can pick up condiments, trays, sugar, and napkins at a station in the dining area. The cafeteria line includes sections for hot foods, salads, desserts, beverages, and coffee, in that order. The cashier is stationed at the end of the line in the dining area. At the back of the cafeteria line are the facilities for holding hot foods, cold foods, and desserts. Equipment in

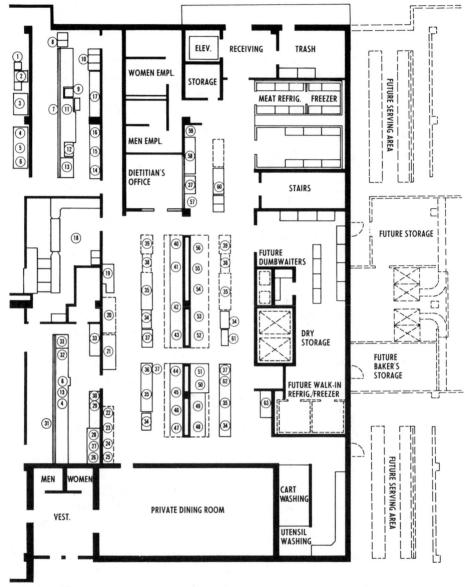

Equipment key:

1. Cream dispenser
2. Mobile undercounter coffee urn
3. Hot beverage and cashier's stand
4. Mobile cup and saucer dispenser
5. Mobile milk dispenser
6. Paper cup dispenser
7. Iced-tea urn
8. Display shelf/cold pan
9. Mobile undercounter shelf unit
10. Refrigerated cold pan
11. Sandwich, salad, dessert-serving table
12. Butter chip dispenser
13. Mobile china dispenser
14. Soup cup racks
15. Infrared warmers
16. Hot-food table
17. Hot-food wells
18. Elevated pass-through food warmer

FIG. 15.10. Typical layout for college or university foodservice facilities.
Courtesy of Kitchen Planning.

this area includes a two-section hot food pass-through unit and a three-section refrigerator. Both units can accommodate roll-racks which take standard 18 by 26-in. (457 by 660 mm) pans. The panned food is racked into the portable units and rolled into the holding units for replenishing the cafeteria line.

The kitchen plan features a double-doored receiving dock with openings to the receiving area and to the facilities for storing and washing trash cans. Three walk-in refrigerators for food storage are located next to the receiving area and also close to the vegetable preparation area. The vegetable preparation area includes a sink unit with disposals, two salad preparation tables, a potato peeler, and a cutter/mixer unit.

The meat and vegetable cooking areas are arranged back-to-back with a divider wall between them which houses the ventilation system.

The equipment for the vegetable-cooking section includes two 40-gal (151 liter) and one 60-gal (227 liter) kettle. Space for another 60-gal (227 liter) kettle has been reserved for future installation. The vegetable section also has a 60-qt (56.8 liter) mixer and two portable worktables.

The meat-cooking area includes a double-deck convection oven, two deep-fat fryers, a griddle, broiler, and range. This area is located conveniently to both the cafeteria and the snack bar. Provisions for installing additional equipment in this area were also planned for.

The back bar in the snack unit includes a sandwich work area, soft

(text continues on p. 334)

19. Table	37. Mobile parts cabinet	52. 60-gal steam kettle with agitator
20. Hot-bread well	38. 60-qt mixer	53. 3-compartment steamer
21. Salad and dessert racks	39. 80-qt mixer	54. Vertical cutter/mixer
22. Roll-through refrigerator	40. Hi-pressure steam cooker and freezer	55. 40-qt tilting kettle with table
23. Mobile dessert cabinet	41. Counter refrigerator	
24. Mobile ice-cream cabinet	42. Tilting electric skillet	56. Revolving bowl cutter with mobile stand
25. Scoop vat and faucet	43. Mobile angle ledge racks	57. Sink
26. Table with sink	44. Electric slicer with mobile stand	58. Mobile pan shelving
27. Mobile ice dispenser		59. Mixing bowls with mobile stand
28. Mobile tray dispenser	45. Mobile supply cabinet	
29. Elevated broilers	46. Mobile table racks	60. Mobile scale
30. Double-deck back shelf	47. Bain marie	61. Can opener
31. Double-deck infrared gas broiler	48. Griddle	62. Reach-in refrigerator
	49. Mobile table	63. Mobile root vegetable shelving
32. Convection oven	50. 80-gal steam kettle (⅔ jacket)	
33. Oven top range with oven		64. Vegetable peeler
34. Even heat range with oven	51. 80-gal steam kettle (full jacket)	65. Vegetable tank carts
35. Fry top range with oven		
36. Double-deck roast oven		

FIG. 15.10. Continued.

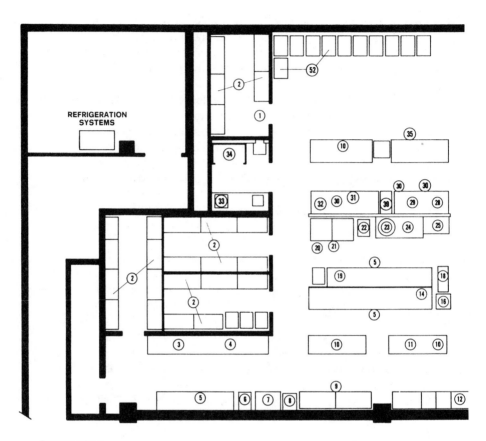

Equipment key:

1. Cold storage rooms
2. Shelving
3. Preparation sink
4. Disposer
5. Counter
6. Racks
7. Ice bin
8. Flake ice machine
9. Pot racks
10. Table
11. Food chopper
12. Pot sink assembly
13. Underliner dispenser
14. Toaster
15. Pellet heater
16. Mixer parts cabinet
17. Plate dispenser
18. Mixer
19. Slicer
20. Ventilator exhaust
21. Convection ovens
22. Undercounter refrigerator
23. Kettle
24. Steamers
25. Heated cabinets
26. Cover dispenser
27. Hot food units
28. Broiler
29. Griddle top range
30. Spreader
31. Hot top ranges
32. Trunnion kettle
33. Electronic oven
34. Freezer
35. Table w/bain marie
36. Coffee urn
37. Cup & saucer dispenser
38. Toaster
39. Fryers
40. Ice cream cabinet
41. Milk dispenser
42. Mobile carts
43. Refrigerator
44. Starter station
45. Roll-in refrigerator
46. Cash register
47. Cream dispenser
48. Hood
49. Drink dispenser
50. Heat lamps
51. Tray and silver dispenser
52. Cart

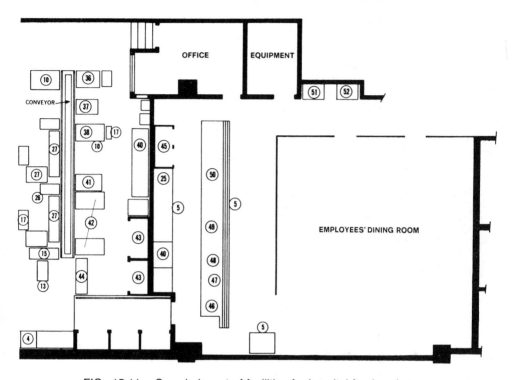

CONVEYOR

OFFICE

EQUIPMENT

EMPLOYEES' DINING ROOM

FIG. 15.11.   Sample layout of facilities for hospital foodservice.
Courtesy of Kitchen Planning.

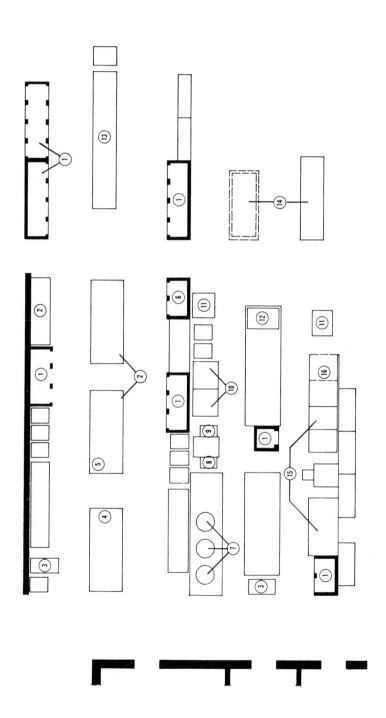

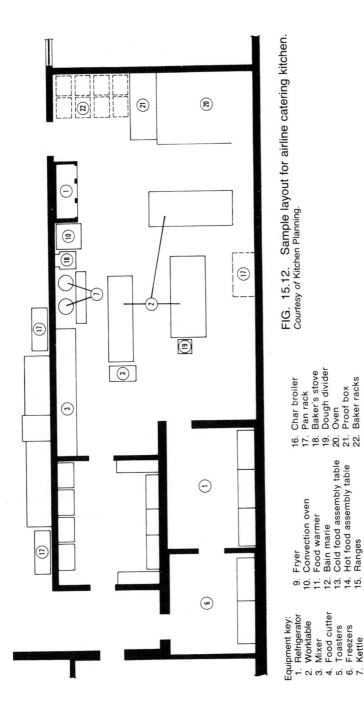

FIG. 15.12. Sample layout for airline catering kitchen.
Courtesy of Kitchen Planning.

Equipment key:
1. Refrigerator
2. Worktable
3. Mixer
4. Food cutter
5. Toasters
6. Freezers
7. Kettle
8. Steamer
9. Fryer
10. Convection oven
11. Food warmer
12. Bain marie
13. Cold food assembly table
14. Hot food assembly table
15. Ranges
16. Char broiler
17. Pan rack
18. Baker's stove
19. Dough divider
20. Oven
21. Proof box
22. Baker racks

ice-cream machine, a fry station, food warmer, and griddle. Space for additional equipment to be installed in the future has been allotted.

The snack bar is primarily self-service and the counter has a hot-food warmer with compartments for soup, sandwiches, and a single entree. A cold pan for salads and desserts and self-service beverage dispensers for juice, carbonated drinks, coffee, and hot chocolate are also on the counter. The snack bar is 100% paper service, and a paper goods storeroom is located behind the service area.

The proposed expansion of the foodservice facility is indicated by the dotted lines on the plan.

HOSPITAL FOODSERVICE

The special dietary considerations for hospitals require a wide variety of equipment, as shown in Fig. 15.11. This hospital allows the patient to choose one or more of 19 entrees, 6 cold salads, and 5 sandwiches for lunch and dinner. As food orders are placed one day in advance, adequate time exists for checking dietary requirements as well as planning the food production for the following day.

When the meals are prepared, they are placed in sealed trays to reduce heat loss. The meals are then conveyed from the kitchen to the patients' floors in specially designed electric cart lifts. On arrival at the designated floor, the lift doors open, and an automatic ejector unloads the cart without manual handling. The meals are then rolled to the rooms and served to the patients.

A typical day's production for the hospital includes 700 regular and specially prepared meals and 300 meals for the employee and guest cafeteria.

Basic equipment in the kitchen includes an ice machine, food cutter and slicer, pellet heater, two convection ovens, a steamer, griddle top range, two hot top ranges, a trunnion kettle, a microwave oven, a bain marie, and a conveyor line for the tray makeup. Additional equipment is identified in the equipment key.

AIRLINE CATERING KITCHEN

An airline catering kitchen has to be planned for the timely production of large quantities of food. The kitchen shown in Fig. 15.12 is capable of turning out 7500 meals per day for airline passengers as well as providing meals for up to 5000 diners in the air terminal's dining room, coffee shop, snack bar, and employee cafeteria. The production of meals is accelerated by (1) the use of prefabricated foods, (2) division of labor to make employees highly efficient, and (3) the use of moving-belt assembly lines.

The problems of preparing and timing meals for many different planes are numerous and complex. A highly sophisticated communications system between the various airlines and the commissary is required to make sure that the right number of meals are prepared in time and placed aboard the departing planes. Usually, three basic messages are relayed from the airlines to the commissary. The first two preliminary messages give flight information, such as flight number, size of plane, number of first and second class seats, what time the plane should land, and what time it should depart. The menu for the flight is also checked. The third message, one hour before the plane is scheduled to depart, relays the number of passengers and the section they will occupy. This message starts the production of the meals for the plane.

Frozen entrees and other items are put on to cook. An assembly line for hot foods is used to fill the plastic dishes and to package them into containers which are then placed in a hot-food holding unit. Meanwhile, employees are placing salads, appetizers, desserts, and silverware on individual plastic trays on the cold-food assembly line. Each tray that is made up is put in a chilled unit ready to be placed aboard the plane.

The kitchen layout for preparing the meals is basically straight-line configurations of equipment. One configuration is used for the preparation, cooking, and packing of hot foods and another for the preparation and production of cold foods. This type of configuration enables the commissary to utilize assembly-line concepts for the fast production of the meals.

A Glossary of Foodservice Equipment Terms*

A

Au Gratin Oven Enclosure with hinged door mounted on top of a broiler. Also called finishing oven.

B

Bain Marie Sink-like depression in a table top with a water bath heated by steam, gas, or electricity into which containers of food are placed to keep foods heated. Often used by chefs as a double boiler. Also called sandwich unit when used for refrigerated foods in sandwich preparation.

Bake Oven *See* Oven.

Baker's Stove *See* Pot Stove.

Baker's Table Table whose top has 4 to 6 in. high curbing along the rear and sides to minimize spillage of flour onto floor during preparation. Often furnished with mobile or tilt-out ingredient bins under the top.

Banquet Cart Insulated or non-insulated mobile cabinet with a series of interior shelves and/or racks to hold plates and/or platters of food. Usually equipped with an electric heating unit or refrigeration device.

Bar Workboard Equipment below the top of a bar containing sinks, drainboards, cocktail mix stations, ice storage chests, beverage coolers, glass washers, etc. Also called sink workboard.

Barbecue Grill A live charcoal or gas fired, open hearth, horizontal grill having spits set across the top of the unit with rotisserie-type drive mechanism along the front working side.

Barbecue Machine *See* Rotisserie.

Beef Cart Mobile unit, with or without bottled gas, alcohol or electric heating unit. Used for display and slicing of roast beef in the dining room.

Beer Cooler Cooler in which kegs, cans, or bottles of beer are refrigerated. The direct

*Reprinted with permission from Foodservice Consultants Society International, Washington, D.C. © Copyright 1974.

draw cooler is a low counter type with self-contained tapping equipment and dispensing head.

Beer Dispenser or **Tapping Cabinet** Refrigerated or ice-cooled insulated cabinet with beer, soda, and/or water dispensing heads, drainer plate and pan recessed flush with the bar top and a drain trough under. Usually built into a liquor bar top, between workboards.

Beer System A method for tapping beer from remotely located refrigerated kegs and transporting it through pressurized, refrigerated, and insulated lines to dispensing heads located at one or more stations in the bar and/or backbar.

Beverage Carrier *See* Carrier.

Bin Semi-enclosed, rectangular or round container, open on top, with or without lift-off, sliding, or hinged cover. Floor type bins are usually mobile, of height to roll under a table top. Bins under a baker's table may be mobile or built-in to tilt out. An ingredient bin may be used for flour, sugar, salt, beans, dry peas, etc. A vegetable storage bin has a perforated or screened body. An ice storage bin is fully enclosed and insulated with hinged or sliding insulated door at the front; it is normally stationary, and set under an ice-making machine (head). A silverware (flatware) or cutlery bin is small and mounted in a holder set on or under counter top with other bins.

Blender Vertical mixing machine with removable cup or jar, having mixing and stirring blades in the bottom and mounted on a base with a drive motor. Normally set on a table or counter top. Used in preparing special diets in hospitals, mixing cocktails in bars, as well as to whip or puree food generally at home.

Blower (Evaporator) Coil *See* Unit Cooler.

Blower-Dryer Motor-driven attachment with a blower and electric- or steamheated coil, mounted on top of a dishwasher for quick drying of ware at the end of the final rinse cycle.

Board A rectangular or round board, small for easy handling, set on a hard surface or counter top, to prevent dulling the knife blade when cutting food. It can be made of laminated or solid hard rock maple, or composition of rubber or thermal plastic material. Usually furnished with a handle or grip. Sandwich and steam table boards are rectangular and narrow; they are mounted on a sandwich unit or the corresponding section of a counter top. Also called Work Board in preparation areas of a kitchen.

Boil-In-Bag A clear plastic waterproof pouch containing foods which are heated by immersing the package in boiling water.

Bone Saw *See* Meat and Bone Saw.

Booster *See* Hot Water Booster.

Bottle Breaker Motor-driven device with revolving, horizontal, open top pan, in which empty glass bottles are safely flogged with steel bars.

Bottle Chute Flexible cylindrical tubing to convey empty bottles from bar to bottle storage bin, or breaking or crushing device. Load end is usually located at the cocktail mix station.

Bottle Crusher Motor driven device with rollers or reciprocating plate to crush bottles, plastic containers, and cans. The unit is mounted on a stand with a waste receptacle beneath to receive crushed and broken articles. The loading chute is provided with a springloaded or gravity-hinged door.

Bottle Disposer System consisting of bottle chute and storage bin, bottle breaker, or bottle crusher.

Bottle Trough Trough suspended along the front of a bar workboard, usually at the cocktail mix station, to hold various bottles of liquor or mixer used often. Also called Speed Rail.

Bowl A round bottom container open at top for mixing food. The salad bowl is a shallow type for mixing and displaying leafy vegetables. A coffee bowl is the lower of a two-piece, siphon-type coffee maker, used as a decanter.

Braising Pan, Tilting *See* Fry Pan, Tilting.

Bread Molder Machine with a series of rollers and conveyor belts to shape the ball of dough to pan bread, hearth bread, or long rolls of varied length.

Bread Slicer 1. Motor-driven machine with a multiple set of reciprocating knives in a single frame through which bread is pushed, or vice versa. 2. Motor-driven or hand operated machine with a single revolving knife to slice single slices while a bread loaf is moved along in a chute by a gear driven plate. Slice thickness may be varied.

Breading Machine Horizontal rotating cylinder, set on a base with a drive motor and filled with breading mix. Food is placed in one end, carried through the cylinder by an internally mounted auger, and discharged at the other end. Food is tumbled in breading mix.

Breath Guard *See* Display Case Sneeze Guard.

Briquette One of the coal-size pieces of permanent refractory material used in open hearth, gas-fired grills to provide radiant broiling heat.

Broiler, Backshelf Broiler with gas heated ceramic radiants or electric heating elements, having an adjustable sliding grill. The unit is normally mounted on a panel and brackets above the rear of the range. Also called Salamander Broiler.

Broiler, Char or **Open Hearth** 1. Horizontal type with gas heated briquettes under a grill at the top. 2. Horizontal type with non-glowing electric strip heaters at the top. May also be equipped with an adjustable electric grill above the top grill to broil both sides at once.

Broiler, Charcoal Horizontal type with removable bottom pan containing glowing charcoals to radiate high heat into the bottom of foods set on a grill above. Mounted on stand or enclosed cabinet or masonry base.

Broiler, Conveyor 1. Horizontal type unit with openings at both ends using a motor driven grill-type conveyor to transport food between or under gas-fired ceramics or electric heaters. 2. Horizontal type unit, open at both ends, using a motor-driven, revolving, heated griddle to transport food under gas-fired ceramics or electric heaters.

Broiler, Pop-Up Enclosed horizontal type unit with a slotted opening in the top and gas heated radiants on both sides of the cavity. Food is placed in an elevating mechanism and broiled on both sides at the same time. Similar to a pop-up toaster.

Broiler, Pork and Spare Rib, Chinese Counter- or stand-mounted, narrow depth broiler with 2 or 3 decks, each having gas burners and radiants, for cooking pork slices and spare ribs in metal platters.

Broiler, Upright Vertical type with an opening at the front, and gas heated radiant ceramics or electric heating elements at the top of the cavity. Food is placed on a sliding adjustable grill set under the radiants. May be mounted on counter top, oven or cabinet base, or stand. Often aligns with ranges. May be equipped with removable charcoal pan.

Broiler-Griddle, Combination 1. Unit with front opening with griddle plate set into top, equipped with gas heated radiants under the griddle. Radiants heat food and griddle simultaneously. 2. Unit with front opening door having gas heated radiants at the top of the cavity and food placed on a sliding or swinging type griddle plate set below.

Buffet Unit One or more mobile or stationary counters having flat surfaces, with cold pans or heated wells at the top, on which chafing dishes, canape trays, or other food displays can be placed for self service.

Bun Divider *See* Roll Divider.

Butcher Block Rectangular or round shape—6, 10, 14, or 16 in. thick—consisting of hard rock maple strips, kiln dried, hydraulically pressed together, glued and steel doweled through. Work surface of block is smoothed surface of ends of strips. Block mounted on open type wood or steel legs.

Butter Chip Dispenser Enclosed insulated unit with mechanical refrigeration or ice to hold tiers of butter pats placed on chips, and dispensed one at a time. Normally set on a counter top. Also called Butter Chip Cooler.

C

Cafeteria Counter, Serving Counter In a cafeteria, top which is usually provided with recessed cold pans, recessed pans for hot foods section, display and protector cases, and drain troughs for beverages; set on legs or masonry base with enclosure panels, semi- or fully-enclosed cabinets with refrigeration or warming units beneath; all as required to accommodate foods to be served. Unit may be equipped with tray slide.

Can Crusher Motor-driven machine with rollers or reciprocating plates or arms to crush cans and break bottles. Unit mounts on stand with space under for refuse receptacle to receive crushed articles. Also called can and bottle crusher.

Can Opener 1. Hand-operated or motor-driven device fastened to the top of a table, wall, cabinet, etc. to open individual cans. 2. Portable motor driven device capable of opening cans while still in case.

Can Washer 1. Enclosed cabinet with spray heads for washing the interior and exterior of a can, mounted on open legs. 2. Round platform with a rotating spray head at its center for washing the interior of a can, mounted on a stand with foot-operated water valves. 3. Rinse nozzle built into a floor drain and connected to a hand operated quick-opening mixing valve.

Can Washer and Sterilizer Enclosed cabinet with spray heads for washing the interiors and exteriors of cans, mounted on open legs, provided with detergent dispenser and 180°F hot water rinse or steam mixing valve for final rinse. *See* Pot and Pan Washer.

Carbonated Beverage System *See* Soda System.

Carbonator Motor-driven water pump, with tank and control valves, to combine cold water and CO_2 gas in a storage tank, producing soda water. Used for soda fountains, carbonated beverage dispensers, and dispensing systems.

Carrier A unit for carrying food, beverages, and ware by hand for short distances, furnished with grips or handles. Could be an enclosed cabinet, insulated, heated, or refrigerated; or a wire basket or rack.

Cart Mobile unit of varying structure: as an open shelf or shelves; a semi- or fully-enclosed cabinet with single or multiple compartments which may be insulated. Used for transporting food or ware, and for cleaning and storage.

Cash Drawer Shallow drawer located under a counter top at the cashier end. Often provided with removable compartmented insert for currency and coins.

Cashier Counter *See* Check-Out Counter.

Cashier Stand Mobile or stationary stand with solid top set on four legs, or semi-enclosed body open at bottom. May be provided with foot rest, cash drawer, and tray rest on one or both sides.

Cereal Cooker Rectangular shaped unit with heated water bath, having one or more openings in top with lug holders, into which pots with lugs are fitted to prevent the pot from floating. Cooker may be gas, electric, or steam heated. Unit may be floor- or wall-mounted, and equipped with water filler and gauge.

Check-Out Counter Counter located between a cafeteria serving area or kitchen and a dining room, for use by checker and/or cashier. Also called Cashier Counter.

Chinese Range Range with one or more large diameter gas burners on an inclined top, and a raised edge around each burner opening. Food is cooked in shallow bowls called Woks. Range top is cooled by water flowing from a front manifold to a rear trough, with strainer basket at one end. A swing spout faucet mounted on high splashguard at rear fills the bowl when the spout is turned 90 degrees.

Chopping or Cutting Block *See* Butcher Block.

Clam Opener Device with hand operated, hinged knife and fixed, vee-shaped block attached to a table top.

Cleaning Cart Mobile unit with one or more compartments for soiled linen, waste, and water for mops and wringer.

Coffee Filter Perforated metal container, or disposable paper or muslin bag in coffee maker or urn to hold bed of coffee grounds.

Coffee Grinder 1. Bench-mounted, hand or motor driven machine with bean hopper at the top, grinding mechanism, and discharge chute with holder for container or filter beneath. 2. Coffee grinding attachment for a food machine.

Coffee Maker 1. Hand or automatically operated, electric-heated unit in which a measure of hot water at the proper temperature is poured over a measured bed of coffee grounds contained in a filtering unit. The extracted beverage is discharged into a container and/or serving unit. 2. Hand or automatically operated, electric-heated unit in which a measure of hot water at the proper temperature is combined with a measure of instant coffee mix and discharged into a container. 3. Unit consisting of one or more sets of upper and lower bowls set on gas- or electric-heated range. The measure of water boiled in the lower bowl is forced by pressure into the upper bowl containing measured coffee grounds. When the set is removed from the heat source, the cooling lower bowl creates a vacuum, causing the liquid to flow back down through a filter in the bottom of the upper bowl. The upper bowl is then removed to permit use of the lower bowl as a server or decanter.

Coffee Mill *See* Coffee Grinder.

Coffee Percolator Covered cylindrical container with up to 120 cups capacity, electric or gas heated. Percolating device in center causes heated water to flow over measured bed of coffee grounds contained in a filtering basket at top. Unit is normally hand filled. Heating unit keeps coffee warm for serving. Bottom has draw-off faucet.

Coffee Range Counter unit consisting of one to four low rated gas or electric burners for making coffee with siphon type coffee makers.

Coffee Urn Enclosed container of water with jar (liner) set into top. Urn water is heated by gas, electric, or steam. A measure of hot water at proper temperature is poured over measured bed of coffee grounds contained in a filtering unit. Beverage collects in jar and is discharged through bottom connection to draw-off faucet. Urn water is not used for coffee making. Equipped with water inlet valve to fill urn body.

Coffee Urn Battery Assembly of units consisting of one or more water boilers and one or more coffee urns heated by gas, electric, or steam. Battery is complete with piping, fittings, and controls between boiler and urn.

Coffee Urn, Combination 1. Coffee urn with water inlet valve and additional draw-off faucet for hot water to make tea and instant beverages. 2. Pressure siphon type has sealed water and hot air chambers with piping control between water jacket and jar. 3. Twin type has two coffee jars set into top of single container. Urn body is usually rectangular in shape. 4. Automatic type has electrically operated device to pump and measure hot water at thermostatically controlled temperature.

Coffee Warmer Counter top range with one or more gas, electric, or canned heaters to maintain coffee at serving temperature; each with coffee bowl or decanter. Also called Coffee Server.

Cocktail Mix Station Section of bar workboard where drinks are poured or mixed. Usually includes open top ice storage bin and wells for mixer bottles and condiments.

Cold Beverage Dispenser or **Urn** *See* Ice Coffee/Tea Urn.

Cold Pan Insulated depressed pan set into a table or counter top; provided with waste outlet; may be refrigerated with crushed ice, refrigeration coil fastened to the underside of the lining, or a cold plate. A perforated false bottom is provided when ice is used.

Combination Steam Cooker and Kettle *See* Cooker and Kettle, Combination.

Compressor, Refrigeration *See* Condensing Unit, Refrigeration.

Condensate Evaporator Finned coil through which compressed refrigerant flows, absorbing the heat inside refrigerator or freezer.

Condensing Unit, Refrigeration Assembly consisting of mechanical compressor driven by electric powered motor with either air or water cooling device. 1. Open type unit has major components separate but mounted on same base. 2. Hermetic type unit has major components enclosed in same sealer housing, with no external shaft, and motor operating in refrigerant atmosphere. 3. Semi-hermetic type unit with hermetically sealed compressor whose housing is sealed and has means of access for servicing internal parts in field.

Condiment Cabinet Semi- or fully enclosed cabinet, mobile or stationary, having several removable or intermediate shelves to store cook's or baker's condiments and spices in the cooking or preparation areas.

Condiment Shelf or **Rack** Shelf or rack mounted above or under a table top to hold several condiment items for use by the cook or baker.

Condiment Stand Standard height mobile or stationary stand having a solid top with receptacle for holding condiment containers, and tray rest on one or both sides. May be open type with legs, enclosed type with cabinet base and shelves, or may have insulated cold pan and refrigerated base.

Confectioner's Stove *See* Pot Stove.

Container, Food and Beverage *See* Bin, Carrier.

Convection Oven Gas- or electric-heated. Heat is circulated through the oven interior with fan or blower system. Interior may be equipped with racks and/or shelves. Ovens may be stacked or set on stand. Oven bottom may be constructed as part of the platform of a mobile basket rack cart.

Convenience Food Any food item that has been processed by any method from the raw state, packaged for resale and/or further processing or use at later date.

Cook's Table Table located in the cooking area of kitchen for cook's use.

Cooker and Kettle, Combination One or more steam-jacketed kettles with one or more steam cookers mounted in top of single cabinet base or tops of adjoining cabinet bases. May be for direct steam operation, or provided with steam coil, gas or electric heated steam generator in the base under the steam cooker.

Cooker/Mixer Direct steam, gas, or electric steam-jacketed kettle, with hinged or removable agitator mounted to supporting frame or brackets.

Cookie Dropper Motor or hand driven machine used to portion and shape drops of cookie dough using dies. Unbaked cookies are dropped onto baking sheet pans or conveyor belt. Also called Cookie Machine.

Corn Popper Enclosed unit with transparent front and ends, transparent doors on the working side, electrically heated popcorn popper suspended from the top, and warming heaters for storage of finished popcorn. May be mounted on counter or enclosed base.

Cotton Candy Machine Machine with round tub and spinning unit, and electric heating unit for converting sugar into cotton candy. May be set on counter top or stand.

Creamer 1. Insulated container for cream, having ice or mechanical refrigeration, and provided with adjustable draw-off faucet for each cream measure. Often anchored to counter or wall. Also called Cream Dispenser. 2. Soda fountain unit with self-contained ice cream cabinet.

Creamer Rack Rectangular basket of wire or plastic construction with compartments to fit glass creamers, Used to wash, fill, and store creamers.

Crusher *See* Bottle Crusher, Can Crusher, Compactor, and Ice Crusher.

Cryogenic Freezer *See* Freezer (3).

Cubing Machine *See* Dicing Machine.

Cutlery Box Unit consisting of one or more compartments for storage and dispensing of flatware (knives, forks, spoons). Often set on a counter or table top, and sometimes built into the front of a cabinet under the top, or as a drawer.

Cutting Board *See* Board.

D

Deep Fat Fryer *See* Fryer.

Defrost System Refrigeration system for a freezer consisting of a blower evaporator coil, heating unit, and controls. Electric-type employs heating elements; hot gas type uses heat exchanger to remove frost from the coil and allow condensate to flow to the drain pan under the coil.

Dessert Cart Cart with several shelves for display and serving of desserts. May be equipped with mechanical or ice-refrigerated cold pan or plate, and with transparent domed cover.

Detergent Dispenser Device mounted on a dishwasher or sink for storage and dispensing of liquid detergent, or mixture of powdered detergent and water, into the wash tank of the unit through the pump manifold or incoming water line. Some units are equipped with control device, electrically operated, to detect detergent strength in tank.

Dicing Machine Bench-mounted hand or motor driven two-operation machine that first forces food through a grid network of knives in a square pattern and then slices the food the same length as the side of the square. May be attached to food mixing or cutting machine. Also called Dicing Attachment or Cubing Machine.

Dish Box *See* Carrier.

Dish Cart Cart for storage and dispensing of clean or soiled dishes. Usually of height to roll under counter or table top.

Dish Table Work surface with raised sides and end(s) having its surface pitched to a built-in waste outlet, adjoining a sink or warewashing machine. There may be a soiled table used for receiving, sorting and racking ware, located at load end of the sink or washing machine; and a clean table at unload end for draining of rinse water, drying, and stacking ware.

Dispenser Unit for storage and dispensing of beverages, condiments, food, and ware. May be insulated and refrigerated or heated. May be provided with self leveling device. May be counter- or floor-mounted, stationary or mobile type.

Display Case A semi- or fully enclosed case of one or more shelves, mounted on counter top or wall, for display of desserts. Semi-enclosed type has transparent end panels and sneeze guards along customers' side to protect uncovered foods. Refrigerated type has insulated transparent panels and doors. Heated type is usually provided with sliding doors and electric heating unit, with or without humidifier.

Dolly Solid platform or open framework mounted on a set of casters, for storage and transportation of heavy items. May be equipped with handle or push bar.

Dough Divider Motor driven floor-type machine to divide dough (usually for bread) into equally scaled pieces. Pieces are removed from work surface by conveyor to next operation. Normally used for bread dough. Also called Bread Divider.

Dough Mixer 1. Motor driven machine with vertical spindle to which various whips and beaters are attached. Bowl is raised to the agitator. Mixers of 5 to 20 quart capacity are bench-mounted. Mixers of 20 to 140 quart capacity are floor-type. 2. Motor driven, floor-type horizontal machine with tilting type bowl and horizontal agitator for a large dough batch. Also called Kneading Machine or Mixer.

Dough Molder *See* Bread Molder.

Dough Proofer *See* Proofer, Proofing Box or Cabinet.

Dough Retarder May be upright reach-in, low counter bench-type, or walk-in refrigerator with series of racks or tray slides and/or shelves, in which dough is kept cool, to retard rising.

Dough Rounder Motor driven, floor-mounted machine into which a piece of dough is dropped and rounded to ball shape, by means of a rotating cone and fixed spiral raceway running from top to bottom. See Roll Divider and Rounder.

Dough Sheeter Motor- or hand-driven machine with a series of adjustable rollers to roll dough to sheets of even thickness. Also called Pie Crust Roller.

Dough Trough Large tub with tapered sides, usually mounted on casters, for storing and transporting large batches of dough. Some troughs have gates at the ends for pouring dough when the trough is lifted above a divider and tilted.

Doughnut Fryer *See* Fryer.

Doughnut Machine Unit consisting of hand- or motor-driven batter dropper and shallow fryer. Doughnuts are conveyed through heated cooking fat or oil bath, turned over, and discharged out of bath into drain pan.

Drainer *See* Drain Trough, Kettle Drainer.

Drink Mixer Vertical counter type unit with one or more spindles with motor at top. Switch is activated by drink cup when placed in correct position. Also Malted Mixer.

Drop-In Unit Any warming, cooling, cooking, or storage unit that is dropped into an opening in a counter or table top and is fitted with accompanying mounting brackets and sized flange.

Dunnage Rack Mobile or stationary, solid or louvered platform used to stack cased or bagged goods in a store room or walk-in refrigerator or freezer.

E

Egg Boiler Electric, steam, or gas heated unit with removable timed elevating device to raise basket or bucket out of boiling water bath. Containers are lowered by hand. Ferris wheel type unit will automatically lower and raise baskets through water bath. Also called Egg Timer.

Egg Timer *See* Egg Boiler.

Electronic Oven *See* Microwave Oven.

Equipment Stand *See* Short Order Stand.

Evaporator *See* Condensate Evaporator, Unit Cooler.

Extractor 1. *See* Juice Extractor. 2. *See* Grease Filter. 3. *See* Water Extractor.
Extruder *See* French Fry Cutter.

F

Fat Filter 1. Gravity-type has disposable paper or muslin bag strainer set in holder on top of fat container. Unit is placed under drain valve of fat fryer. 2. Siphon type uses disposable paper or muslin bag strainer over fat container, attached to rigid siphon tube mounted on fat fryer, with other end of tube in fat tank. 3. Motor driven pump-type, portable or mobile, uses disposable paper strainer. Has flexible hose from fat tank to strainer. Strainer set on fat container.
Filter 1. *See* Coffee Filter. 2. *See* Fat Filter. 3. *See* Grease Filter.
Finishing Oven *See* Au Gratin Oven.
Fire Extinguisher Hand operated, sealed with chemical inside, most commonly wall-mounted and provided with control and directional hose, or horn.
Fish Box 1. Ice-refrigerated, insulated cabinet with counter-balanced hinged or sliding door at the top, and drawer at the bottom front. 2. Ice or mechanically refrigerated cabinet with tier of self-closing drawers with insulated fronts. Also called Fish File.
Fish File *See* Fish Box.
Fish and Chip Fryer *See* Fryer.
Flatware Term for knive, spoon, and fork used by the diner.
Floor Scale 1. Unit fixed in a pit, its platform flush with finished floor. May have dial or beam mounted on top of the housing at the rear of platform framing, plus tare beam. Used for weighing heavy objects on mobile carriers. 2. Mobile type *See* Platform Scale.
Food Carrier *See* Carrier.
Food Cutter 1. Motor-driven bench- or floor-mounted machine with a rotating shallow bowl to carry food through a set of rotating horizontal knives whose axis is perpendicular to the radii of the bowl. Knives are set under hinged-up cover. 2. Motor-driven, floor mounted high speed machine with vertical tilting bowl having a vertical shaft with rotating knife. Also called vertical cutter/mixer or sold under various brand names.
Food Freshener Electrically operated unit to introduce live steam to the exterior or interior of food, heating it to serving temperature without loss of moisture. Cabinet type has a hinged cover or drawer for warming the exterior of foods. Hollow pin-type heats food interior through injection.
Food Merchandiser Refrigerated, heated, or non-insulated case or cabinet with transparent doors, and possibly transparent ends. Used for display and sometimes self-service of foods.
Food Shaper 1. Motor-driven unit with loading hopper, bench- or floor-mounted. Shapes food into rectangular or round patties of varying thickness. May be equipped with paper interleaving, removing, and conveying devices. 2. Attachment to meat chopper to shape ground food into rectangles of varied thickness. Also called Food Former.
Food Warmer 1. Insulated mobile or stationary cabinet with shelves, racks, or tray slides, having insulated doors or drawers. May be electric, steam, or gas heated, and provided with humidity control. 2. Infrared lamp or electric radiant heating element with or without a glass enclosure, mounted above the serving unit in a hot food section.
French Fry Bagger Motor-driven machine to convey, measure, and insert french fried potatoes into paper bag blown open to receive product.
French Fry Cutter Hand operated or motor-driven machine, or attachment to food machine, that pushes through grid of knives in square pattern in frame.
French Fryer *See* Fryer.

Fry Pan, Tilting Rectangular pan with gas or electric heated flat bottom, pouring lip and hinged cover. Floor-mounted on a tubular stand or wall-mounted on brackets with in-wall steel carriers. A small electric pan may be table-mounted on legs. Also called Braising Pan, Tilting Griddle, or Tilting Skillet.

Fryer 1. Floor- or bench-mounted unit heated by gas or electricity with tank of oil or fat into which foods are immersed. Common type has deep tank. Special types have shallow tanks for fish, chicken, doughnuts, etc. and a basket conveyor type has a shallow tank for draining with baskets, arms, mesh type belt, or rotating auger to move foods through the bath. Pressure type has a lift or hinged cover to seal the top of the fryer tank.

Fudge Warmer Counter-mounted electrically heated insulated pot with hinged or lift-off cover and ladle.

G

Glass Washer 1. Multi-tank horizontal machine with hand activated rinse nozzle in one tank, revolving brushes in a second tank, and final rinse nozzles in a third. 2. Single or double tank doortype or rack-conveyor-type dishwasher.

Grater 1. Bench-mounted hand- or motor-driven machine in which food is forced against the face of a revolving grater plate by a pusher or hopper plate. 2. Part of vegetable slicing attachment to food machine.

Grease Filter or **Extractor** 1. Removable rectangular or round frame having several layers of wire mesh or baffles and mounted in the exhaust equipment above or behind cooking units. 2. A series of baffles mounted in exhaust equipment, from whose surfaces grease deposits are flushed with wash water into a waste outlet. 3. Manifold mounted water nozzles in exhaust equipment producing a fine spray mist which collects grease from laden air and drains through a waste outlet.

Griddle Extra thick steel plate with a ground and polished top surface, heated by gas or electricity. Surface edges are raised or provided with gutters and drain hole leading to catch trough or pan. May be set on counter top with legs, stand, or oven base.

Griddle Stand *See* Short Order Stand.

Grill Bench-mounted unit with fixed lower and hinged upper electrically heated plates. Plates have a waffle pattern for waffles, grooves for steaks, and are smooth for sandwiches.

Grill, Charcoal *See* Broiler, Charcoal.

Grinder 1. *See* Meat Chopper. 2. *See* Coffee Grinder.

H

Hamper *See* Linen Hamper.

Heat Exchanger, Steam Boiler with coils to generate clean steam with possibly contaminated house steam. Used for steam cooking units.

High Speed Cooker *See* Steam Cooker.

Hors d'Oeuvre Cart Cart with platforms on ferris wheel having several food containers on each platform. Used for display and service.

Hot Chocolate Dispenser or **Maker** 1. Counter-mounted electrically heated glass bowl with agitator, or insulated tank with agitator for dispensing premixed hot chocolate. 2. Counter-mounted electrically heated unit that combines measure of heated water with measure of chocolate mix, and dispenses mixture at touch of button.

Hot Dog and Hamburger Broiler Semi- or fully enclosed cabinet with glass doors and panels for display. An electric heater under the top radiates onto hot dogs in baskets or on pins on wheel, or onto hamburgers laid on platforms mounted on motor-driven ferris wheel. Food rotates while cooking.

Hot Dog Steamer Counter-mounted cabinet with transparent display panels and hinged covers or doors. The unit is electrically heated with a water bath and immersion device to generate steam for heating hot dogs, and dry heat for warming rolls.

Hot Food Cabinet *See* Food Warmer, Carrier.

Hot Food Table or **Section** *See* Steam Table.

Hot Plate Counter-top and floor-mounted unit with one or more open gas or tubular electric burners arranged left to right and/or front to rear. French hot plates are round or square solid steel plates, gas or electrically heated.

Hot Water Booster Electric, steam-, or gas-heated insulated tank or coil used to raise the incoming hot water from house temperature to sanitizing temperature, as required by code. Booster may be mounted inside housing or at end of ware washing machine, under ware washing table, or may be remotely located.

Housekeeping Cart Cart with one or more semi- or fully-enclosed compartments for clean linen, a compartmented tray at the top for supplies, a cloth hamper for soiled linen, and a waste receptacle.

Humidifier Electric, steam, or gas heated unit used to evaporate and distribute water inside proofing equipment and hot food warmers. May be fixed or removable attachment.

I

Ice Breaker *See* Ice Crusher.

Ice Chest *See* Ice Storage Bin.

Ice Cream Cabinet 1. Mechanically refrigerated low-type chest with removable, hinged, flip-flop covers, used for storage and dispensing of ice cream. 2. Mechanically refrigerated upright cabinet with hinged door, for storage of ice cream.

Ice Cream Display Cabinet Ice cream cabinet with sliding or hinged transparent doors or covers. Mostly used in self-service stores.

Ice Cream Freezer Floor- or counter-mounted machine with mechanically refrigerated cylinder, having a dasher to mix and refrigerate an air-and-ice cream mix to flowing ice cream. The product is then placed inside a hardening cabinet.

Ice Cream Hardening Cabinet Low cabinet with a lid or upright cabinet with hinged door, insulated and refrigerated at a very low temperature to set ice cream hard.

Ice Crusher 1. Motor-driven or hand-operated floor- or counter-mounted machine with spiked rollers, to crush large pieces of ice or ice cubes. 2. Attachment mounted between an ice cube making machine and an ice storage bin, having a damper for directing cubed ice to motor driven rollers with spikes to crush ice as required.

Ice Cuber *See* Ice Maker.

Ice Dispenser A floor-, counter-, or wall-mounted stationary ice storage bin with motor driven agitator and conveyor mechanism, or gravity feed, that dispenses a measure of ice (cubed or crushed) through a discharge chute into a container at working level.

Ice Maker Floor-, counter-, or wall-mounted unit containing refrigeration machinery for making cubed, flaked, and crushed ice. Maker may have integral ice storage bin. Larger capacity machines generally have a separate bin in which ice is received via a connecting chute. Capacity is rated in pounds of ice per 24-hour day.

Ice Maker and Dispenser Floor, counter-, or wall-mounted ice maker with storage bin and dispensing mechanism. *See* Ice Maker, Ice Dispenser.

Ice Pan, Display *See* Cold Pan.

Ice Plant 1. An assembly consisting of a large capacity ice maker that empties into a walk-in freezer or ice storage bin on the floor below via directional chute. 2. A large capacity, floor-mounted ice maker, having a small capacity bin connected to vertical and horizontal conveyors with insulated sleeves for transporting ice to large capacity bin.

Ice Shaver Hand-operated or motor-driven floor- or bench-mounted machine whose rotating plate or wheel has a sharp knife which produces ice like snow when forced against the face of a cake of ice. Also called Snow Cone Machine.

Ice Storage Bin Insulated mobile or stationary cabinet of one or more compartments with hinged or sliding door or cover. It is commonly mounted under an ice making machine, with opening in the top to receive product, and is fitted with a waste outlet in the bottom. Ice is normally scooped out of bin. Unit may be built into counter.

Ice Vendor Floor-mounted, mechanically refrigerated freezer with a coin operated mechanism to release a measure of loose or bag of ice cubes at working level.

Iced Coffee/Tea Urn Urn with stainless steel or transparent glass jar and drawoff faucet. Stainless steel type may be insulated. Glass jar may be equipped with ice compartment suspended from cover. Also called Iced Tea/Coffee Dispenser.

Infrared Heater or Warmer Unit consisting of one or more lamps or electric strip heaters, with or without protective covering or reflector, mounted in a bracket or housing. Usually set over hot food serving and display areas, or inside enclosed displays. Unit produces infrared heat to keep food warm.

Infrared Oven Oven having heat generated and radiated from electric infrared heating elements encased in a glass tube, or from an exposed quartz infrared plate.

Injector, Rinse *See* Rinse Injector.

Injector, Steam *See* Steam Injector.

Insert Rectangular pan or round pot set into the top of a steam or hot food table.

J

Juice Extractor 1. Counter-mounted motor driven ribbed cone having base with drain hole for juice. Half of fruit is pressed by hand, down onto cone. 2. Bench- or floor-mounted motor driven machine that slices fruit in half, and squeezes halves between nesting cones. 3. Hand operated bench type machine that squeezes fruit halves between inverted cones. Also called Juicer.

K

Kettle Drainer Mobile sink with screen or strainer basket, waste outlet with adjustable tailpiece, and push handle.

Kettle, Electric Heated 1. Stationary or tilting two-thirds steam jacketed, or stationary full steam jacketed kettle with electric immersion heater in water between shells. Kettle is floor-mounted inside housing or attached to housing with tilting mechanism. Tilting device may be hand or power operated. Stationary unit is provided with water filler, hinged cover, and draw-off valve. Tilting-type has pouring lip and may have draw-off valve, hinged cover, and water filler. 2. Stationary or tilting two-thirds steam jacketed kettle set into top of cabinet base with remote electric heated steam generator adjoining kettle. Kettle provided with hinged cover, water filler, and draw-off valve.

Kettle, Flat Bottom Rectangular pan with flat bottom having inner and outer shells. Live steam is introduced between shells, heating inner shell for cooking. Kettle is tilting type, floor-mounted on tubular stand, or wall mounted with brackets and in-wall steel chair carriers. Kettle front has pouring lip. Top has hinged cover.

Kettle, Gas Heated 1. Stationary full or two-thirds steam jacketed kettle with a gas burner under the bottom of its outer shell to heat water between shells. The kettle is floor-mounted inside housing, and provided with a water filler and hinged cover. 2. Stationary or tilting two-thirds steam jacketed kettle set into the top of a cabinet base with remote gas heated steam generator adjoining the kettle. The kettle provided with hinged cover, water filler, and draw-off valve. 3. Stationary floor-type direct-fired kettle with a single shell, mounted inside insulated housing, with a gas burner under bottom of shell, draw-off valve, and hinged cover.

Kettle, Steam Jacketed Kettle having live steam introduced between the inner and outer shell to heat the inner shell for cooking. Deep type kettle generally is two-thirds jacketed. Shallow-type kettle generally is fully jacketed. May be mounted to the floor with tubular legs or pedestal base, or mounted to the wall with brackets and in-wall steel chair carriers. Tilting- or trunnion-type may be floor- or wall-mounted, having a worm gear device for hand operation. The stationary kettle has a draw-off valve. The tilting kettle has a pouring lip and may have a draw-off valve. The kettle may be equipped with lift-off of hinged cover, filling faucet, water cooling system, thermostat, etc.

Kettle, Table Top Two-thirds steam jacketed kettle, tilting type, with operating lever up to 20 qt. capacity, or tilting worm gear device for 40 qt. capacity; all direct steam, electric heated. All kettles have a pouring lip. Tilting type have 20 and 40 qt. capacity with a lever handle. Oyster stewing kettle is shallow tilting type kettle.

Kettle, Tilting or **Trunnion** *See* Kettle, Steam Jacketed; Kettle, Flat Bottom.

Kneading Machine or **Mixer** *See* Dough Mixer.

Knife Rack Slotted wood or stainless steel bar set away and attached to edge of table top or butcher block. This forms a slot into which cutlery blades are inserted and held up by handles of same while the handles protrude at the top.

Knife Sharpener 1. Bench-mounted, motor driven machine with rotating stones forming a vee to grind edges on both sides of a blade. 2. Attachment to slicing machine. 3. Grinding wheel attachment to food machine having an attachment hub.

L

Linen Car Cart with several compartments for storage of clean linen. May be semi- or fully enclosed.

Linen Hamper 1. Stationary or mobile metal cabinet with hinged metal cover. 2. Stationary or mobile framework with round cloth bag or cloth sides, ends and bottom.

Lobster Tank Transparent tank open at the top, and with a water wheel at one end. Tank bottom is lined with special salt. Mounted on a stationary or mobile enclosed base with a filtering and mechanical refrigeration system for tank water. Also called Trout Tank, with salt omitted.

M

Machine Stand Mobile or stationary stand with solid or open frame top, mounted on open legs or cabinet base, with adjustable dimensions to suit a specific machine or device.

Malted Mix Dispenser Counter- or wall-mounted unit with a transparent, covered hopper, having a lever for dispensing a measure of malted mix powder.

Meat and Bone Saw Floor-mounted, motor driven band saw with upper and lower pulleys, stationary cutting table with gauge plate and movable carriage.

Meat Chopper Table- or floor-mounted, hand or motor driven horizontal machine. Food placed in top mounted hopper is led by a stomper into cylinder with tight fitting auger to drive food against rotating knife and perforated plate. Also called Meat Grinder.

Meat Grinder *See* Meat Chopper.

Meat Hook Rack One or more wood or metal bars mounted on a wall or floor stand, with fixed or removable sharp pointed metal hooks. Also called Meat Rail.

Meat Roaster, Steam Jacketed Shallow steam jacketed kettle with cover and draw-off valve.

Meat Tenderizer Counter-mounted machine having two sets of round knives with spaced cutting edges, set apart on slow speed rollers. Meats are inserted into a slot in the top, pass through the rollers and are discharged at the bottom front through which the meats to be tenderized pass.

Menu Board Sign with fixed or changeable letters, or removable lines listing the food items and prices.

Meter, Water *See* Water Meter.

Mexican Food Machine Device used to hold a vee-shaped tortilla when filling it to make a taco.

Microwave Oven Stand- or counter-mounted oven in which foods are heated and/or cooked when they absorb microwave energy (short electromagnetic waves) generated by magnetron(s).

Milk Cooler 1. Low insulated chest with mechanical or ice refrigeration, for storing and dispensing half-pint to two-quart containers of milk. 2. Counter or stand mounted refrigerator with one or more 2- to 10-gallon containers equipped with sanitary tube connections which extend through flow control handles for dispensing loose or bulk milk.

Milkshake Machine *See* Drink Mixer, Shake Mixer.

Mix Cabinet Low counter-type or upright reach-in refrigerator in which the mix for frozen shakes or ice cream is stored.

Mixer, Dough *See* Dough Mixer.

Mixer, Drink *See* Drink Mixer.

Mixer, Food Motor driven machine with vertical spindle having several speeds on which various whips and beaters are mounted. Bowl is raised up to agitator. Mixers of 5 to 20 quart capacity are bench-type. Mixers of 20 to 140 quart capacity are floor-type.

Mixer Stand Low height stationary or mobile stand with four legs and a solid top to support a mixer up to 20 quart size. May be provided with undershelf and vertical rack for mixer parts.

Mixer, Vertical Cutter *See* Vertical Cutter/Mixer.

Mixing Tank Vertical type has center, bottom or side-mounted agitator assembly. Horizontal type has end agitator assembly. All are floor-mounted and provided with removable or hinged cover and draw-off valve. Tank may be provided with recirculating pump and filtering system.

Molder, Food *See* Food Shaper.

Modular Stand Low height, open, stationary stand with four or more legs, having an open framework top, to support heavy-duty modular cooking equipment.

N

Napkin Dispenser Counter top unit for storage and dispensing of folded paper napkins. Napkins forced to head plate by spring.

O

Oven Fully enclosed insulated chamber with gas, electric, or oil-fired heat, provided with thermostatic control. Deck type units have chambers or sections stacked one above the other. Bake type decks are approximately 7 in. high inside. Roast type decks are 12 to 14 in. high inside.

Order Wheel Metal or wood spoked wheel with clips or hooks on its perimeter, located between cooks' and servers' areas, on which order slips are placed to maintain rotation and visibility.

Oyster Opener *See* Clam Opener.

P

Pan and Utensil Rack 1. One or more bars and braces suspended from a ceiling, or mounted on posts or a wall, housing fixed or removable hooks for hanging pots, pans, and utensils. 2. Upright mobile or stationary unit, open or semi-enclosed, with tiers of angle- or channel-shaped slides to support pans. 3. Heavy-duty rectangular wire basket to hold pans and utensils upright in a pot washer.

Pan Washer *See* Pot and Utensil Washer.

Pass-Through Window or **Opening** Trimmed opening between kitchen and serving areas having a shelf for a sill. May be equipped with hinged or sliding door or shutter.

Peanut Roaster Electrically heated enclosed display case with hinged cover at the top.

Peeler Floor- or bench-mounted machine having a vertical, stationary, abrasive-lined cylinder open at the top, a motor driven agitator bottom plate, and an over-the-rim water supply. Product discharged through door in cylinder side. Waste water is discharged at bottom and may be equipped with a peel trap basket that can be hung on a pipe over sink, or set inside a cabinet base under the peeler. May also be equipped with garbage disposal unit.

Peeler Stand 1. Special height mobile stand, open-type, with four legs. 2. Special height enclosed cabinet with adjustable legs, a door designed to house a trap basket, and a waste outlet.

Pellet Heater Counter-mounted, electric heated, insulated cabinet having one or more vertical cylinders in which metallic discs, inserted at the top, are heated. Discs are dispensed at the bottom through drawer type device.

Pie and Pastry Case *See* Display Case.

Pizza Oven Baking-type oven of one or more decks, gas-, electric- or oil-fired, having temperature range from 350 to 700°F. Deck(s) are of heat retaining masonry material.

Pizza Sheeter *See* Dough Sheeter.

Platform Scale Mobile unit with a dial or beam, for weights up to 1500 pounds. May be floor- or stand-mounted.

Platform Skid *See* Dunnage Rack.

Popcorn Machine *See* Corn Popper.

Pot and Utensil Washer, or **Pot Washing Machine** Machine of one or more tanks with hood or wash chamber above, inside which large ware is washed, using very big, high pressure pumps. Water is pumped from tanks and sprayed over ware placed in racks or set on a conveyor or platform. One or more final fresh water rinses sanitizes ware. Machine has a 34 to 36 in. working height. 1. Door-type, single tank machine has power wash and final rinse only. 2. Door-type, two-tank machine has power wash and power rinse tanks, and final rinse. 3. Belt conveyor machine is straight-through type machine having one to three tanks plus final rinse. Ware is set directly on a belt. 4. Revolving tray table type has two to three tanks plus final rinse. Ware is set directly on turntable platform.

Pot Filler Faucet or valve with a hose mounted at a range, pot stove, or kettle to fill a vessel direct.

Pot Stove Low, floor-mounted single burner stove with high BTU or kW rating for use with large stock pots.

Pre-Fabricated Cooler Walk-in type refrigerator or freezer having insulated walls, ceiling, and floor fabricated in a shop and assembled on the job site. The insulated floor and base of the walls may be constructed as part of the building.

Preparation Table or Counter Unit located in the preparation area of a kitchen, for cutting, slicing, peeling, and other preparation of foods.

Pre-Rinse or **Pre-Wash Sink** Sink constructed as an integral part of a soiled dish table, located near a dishwashing machine, and furnished with removable perforated scrap basket and spray hose.

Pressure Cooker *See* Steam Cooker.

Pressure Fryer *See* Fryer.

Pre-Wash Separate machine or built-in section of a warewashing machine with tank and pump or fresh water supply. Pump recirculates water over ware; fresh water type sprays over ware; before pumped wash section of machine.

Proof Box or **Cabinet** Fully enclosed cabinet with gas, steam, or electric heater and humidifier. Sometimes unit may be insulated type with thermostatic and humidity controls. Box may be mobile. Traveling type proofer has a conveying mechanism inside the overhead cabinet, as in large commercial bread bakery.

Protector Case A single shelf mounted on posts with transparent shield at the front, or front and ends. Mounted over a counter top at hot food or sandwich sections to protect uncovered food.

Pulper Floor-mounted garbage and waste disposal machine with a vertical cylinder, grinder plate and knives, and sump compartment for non-grindable matter. Waste material is ground in a deep water bath to form a slurry which is piped to a water extractor. Water from the extractor is recirculated to the pulper.

Q

Quartz Oven Oven which employs an electrically heated quartz plate or infrared quartz element inside a glass tube to generate heat. Also called Infrared Oven.

R

Rack: Cup, Dish, Glass, Plate or **Tray** 1. Rectangular or round shaped basket of wire or plastic construction, with or without compartments or intermediate lateral supports, used for washing and/or storage of small ware. Racks are self-stacking type for cups and glassware. 2. *See* Tray Rack for upright unit.

Rack Pan *See* Pan and Utensil Rack.

Rack Washer Machine of one or two tanks with hood or wash chamber over, with one or two doors, using large size high pressure pumps, and final sanitizing rinse. Steam or electric heated water is pumped from tanks and sprayed over racks wheeled onto tracks inside washer. Machine is made to recess in floor to have tracks set flush with finished floor.

Range Unit with heated top surface or burners which heat utensils in which foods are cooked, or cook foods direct. Some ranges are equipped with an insulated oven base. Hot or even heat tops, and fry or griddle tops, are gas- or oil-fired, or electrically heated. Open or hot plate tops have electric or gas burners. Fry or griddle tops are gas- or oil-fired, or electrically heated.

Reel Oven *See* Revolving Tray Oven.

Refrigerated Table Table top mounted on counter type refrigerated base.

Refrigerator Shelves Shelves of wire, solid, embossed, or slotted material with reinforced hemmed edges, mounted on tubular posts with adjustable sanitary brackets. May be in stationary or mobile sections.

Revolving Tray Oven Gas, electric, or oil heated oven with a motor driven ferris wheel device inside having four or more balanced trays. Bake or roast pans are loaded and unloaded from a single opening with a hinged down door. Steam may be added for humidity requirements of products.

Rinse Injector Device mounted to top or side of washing machine for storage and automatic dispensing of liquid water softener into the final rinse manifold.

Roast Oven *See* Oven; Convection Oven; Revolving Tray Oven.

Roaster, Meat, Steam Jacketed *See* Meat Roaster, Steam Jacketed.

Roll Divider Hand or motor operated machine that divides a ball of dough into equal pieces. Hand operated unit is stand- or table-mounted. Motor driven unit is floor mounted with a cabinet base and may be combined with a rounding device. Also called Bun Divider.

Roll Warmer 1. Enclosed cabinet with a telescoping cover, heated by pellet or glowing charcoal under a false bottom. 2. Enclosed insulated cabinet with electric heating elements, and humidity controls. The unit is provided with one or more drawers in a tier at the front; it sets on a counter top, legs or a stand, or is built into a counter. Also called Bun Warmer.

Rotisserie 1. Upright enclosed cabinet with a vertical grill having gas-fired ceramics or electric heating elements. A side-mounted motor drives revolving spits set in a tier in front of the heaters. The unit has hinged or sliding glass doors. 2. Upright enclosed cabinet containing a motor driven ferris wheel provided with food cradles or baskets passing under gas-fired ceramics or electric heating elements. 3. Enclosed, square, upright cabinet with meat suspended from top in center revolving motor driven cradle, heated by four infrared lamps radiating from the corners. 4. *See also* Hot Dog and Hamburger Broiler.

S

Salad Case Unit consisting of a refrigerated counter with refrigerated food pans set into the top, and a refrigerated or non-refrigerated display case mounted on the counter top.

Salamander A backshelf or cabinet mounted over the rear of a range or steam table, and absorbing the heat therefrom to keep foods on it warm.

Salamander Broiler *See* Broiler, Backshelf.

Saw, Meat and Bone *See* Meat and Bone Saw.

Scale *See* Floor Scale; Platform Scale.

Self-Leveling Dispenser *See* Dispenser.

Service Stand A stationary cabinet with a solid top at a working height used in a restaurant; may have shelves, bins, drawers, and refrigerated section for storage of linen, flatware, glassware, china, condiments, water, and ice.

Settee Bench Bench with upholstered seat and upholstered back.

Shake Maker Floor- or counter-mounted machine with one or two mechanically refrigerated cylinders, having dashers to mix and refrigerate an air-and-milk mixture to a flowing frozen dessert beverage. Unit may be equipped with syrup tanks and pumps, and mixing spindle to blend various flavors in shakes.

Shrimp Peeler and Deveiner Bench-mounted, motor driven machine that removes vein and shell from shrimp and prawn.

Silver Burnisher, Holloware and Flatware Machine with a tumbling barrel or vibrating open top tub filled with steel balls and compound, in which silver plated utensils are placed. Tumbling or vibrating action causes steel balls to roll down plating onto base metal. Units may be bench- or floor-mounted, or made mobile to roll under a table top.

Silver Washer and Drier Floor-mounted machine with a fixed or removable tumbling drum set inside a wash chamber with a hinged cover for washing, sterilizing, and electrically drying flatware. The removable drum has a perforated bottom and top cover. The fixed drum has a hinged cover and perforated ends. Machine has wash, rinse, and final sterilization rinse cycles. Electrically heated air is blown through wash chamber and drum to dry flatware.

Sink 1. Preparation, Cook's, or Utility: one or two-compartment type with drain-board on one or both sides, each compartment averaging 24 in. square. 2. Pot and Pan or Scullery: two, three or four-compartment type with drainboard on one or both sides, and possibly between compartments. Each compartment should be minimum 27 in. left to right, and average 24 in. front to rear.

Slaw Cutter Floor- or bench-mounted machine with revolving slicer plate and hopper. Cored and quartered cabbage heads inserted in hopper are forced against slicer plate and product discharges through chute below.

Slicer Bench- or stand-mounted machine with a stationary motor driven round knife and slice thickness gauge plate, and reciprocating feed trough or carriage. Flat trough may have hand and/or spring pressure type feed plate. Gravity trough may have hand or automatic feed plate. Trough may be hand-operated or motor driven. Slicer can be equipped with automatic stacking and conveying device.

Slicer, Bread *See* Bread Slicer.

Slicer, Vegetable *See* Vegetable Slicer.

Slush Maker Floor/counter mounted machine with one or two mechanically refrigerated cylinders having dashers to mix and refrigerate a water mixture to a flowing frozen dessert beverage.

Smokehouse, Chinese Floor-mounted, enclosed, insulated roasting cabinet with gas burners and baffle plates, hinged door, duct connection and flue at top, and removable grease pan inside the bottom. Meat, fish, and poultry are mounted on skewers inside. Interior walls and door have deflector plates to direct drippings into the grease pan.

Sneeze Guard *See* Display Case.

Snow Cone Machine *See* Ice Shaver.

Soda Dispenser 1. Part of soda making and refrigeration system: dispensing head attachment for mounting on a soda fountain, bar, counter, or at a waiter station, complete with drainer. 2. Enclosed cabinet, ice or mechanically refrigerated, to dispense pre-mixed soda or combine soda water and syrup stored in a cabinet or remote tanks. 3. Floor- or counter-mounted cabinet with a self-contained soda and refrigeration system having remote or self-contained syrup tanks.

Soda Maker Unit consisting of mechanical refrigeration system, carbonator, and soda storage tank.

Soda System Assembly consisting of soda maker, syrup tanks, syrup, soda, and refrigeration tubing, and soda dispensing heads and/or cabinet. Also known as Carbonated Beverage System.

Soft Ice Cream Maker Floor- or counter-mounted machine with one or two mechanically refrigerated cylinders having dashers to mix and refrigerate air and ice cream mix to a flowing frozen dessert. Unit is equipped with hand or foot operated dispensing head or control.

Soiled Dish Pass Window Trimmed opening in a partition between dishwashing and serving areas, having the soiled dish table as a sill. The opening may be equipped with hinged or sliding door or shutter.

Soup Station Section of cook's table or cafeteria counter with a hot food receptacle, rectangular or round, set into the top.

Speed Rail *See* Bottle Trough.

Spice Bench Table with stationary cabinet above rear or below top, or mobile cabinet under the top. Cabinet has two or more spice drawers or bins.

Squeezer, Juice *See* Juice Extractor.

Steam Cooker Enclosed cabinet with one or more sealed compartments having individual controls into which (chemically clean) steam is introduced for cooking or heating. Cooker may be direct connected or equipped with gas-fired, electric, or steam coil generator in the base. 1. A cooker with compartments in tiers cooks with low pressure steam. Each compartment has a hinged door with a floating inner panel and a sealing gasket made tight by interior steam pressure. May be floor-, counter-, or wall-mounted. 2. Cooker with high pressure has self-sealing door(s) with a gasket made tight by interior steam pressure. May be floor-, counter-, or wall-mounted. Also called High Speed Cooker.

Steam Jacketed Kettle *See* Kettle, Steam Jacketed.

Steamer, Dry *See* Food Freshener.

Steamer, Hot Dog *See* Hot Dog Steamer, Steam Cooker.

Step-In Cooler/Freezer *See* Walk-In Refrigerator/Freezer.

Stock Pot Stove *See* Pot Stove.

Storage Rack Unit consisting of one or more shelves mounted on angle, channel, or tubular posts, for storage of goods or ware.

Stove Floor- or counter-mounted unit with one or more open gas or electric burners. Also called Hot Plate.

Swill Trough 1. Depression in dish table approximately 6 to 9 in. wide, and 2 to 6 in. deep, equipped with waste outlet, strainer basket, and perforated cover. 2. Extra sink compartment of shallow depth located between compartments of pot washing sink, equipped with strainer basket.

T

Table Top with solid flat surface, mounted on floor with legs, on wall with brackets and legs, or on semi- or fully enclosed cabinet. May be stationary or mobile. May have shelves under, shelves over, and tool drawer.

Tea Maker or **Dispenser** 1. *See* Coffee Urn. Same as coffee urn with tea laid in strainer. 2. Counter-mounted unit to combine instant tea mix with heated water for hot tea or cold water for ice tea.

Tenderizer *See* Meat Tenderizer.

Timer, Egg *See* Egg Timer.

Toaster 1. Counter-mounted pop-up type having two or four slice capacity. Electric only. 2. Counter-mounted conveyor type with a motor driven conveyor carrying the product between electric or gas-fired radiants. 3. Sandwich type: *See* Grill.

Tray Make-Up or **Assembly Conveyor** Motor driven or gravity type horizontal conveyor to transport trays between various food loading stations.

Tray Rack Upright mobile or stationary unit, open or semi-enclosed, having angle, channel, or tubular posts and one or more tiers of angle or channel-shaped slides to support trays or pans. Rack may be built-in to cabinets or suspended from under table tops.

Tray Slide or **Rail** Horizontal surface to accommodate the width of a tray, extended out from, and running the length of, cafeteria counter top. May be constructed of solid material with or without raised edges and vee beads; or of several tubular or solid rails or bars. Mounted on and fastened to brackets secured to counter top and/or counter body. Also called Tray Rest.

Tray Stand Low height mobile or stationary four-legged stand with solid top. Top may have raised back and sides to prevent tray stacks from falling over.

Trough, Swill *See* Swill Trough.

Trout Tank *See* Lobster Tank.

Truck *See* Cart.

U

Undercounter Sink Workboard *See* Bar Workboard.

Unit Cooler Semi-enclosed cabinet open at front and rear or top and bottom, depending on air flow, with a motor driven fan blowing air through a mechanically refrigerated finned coil. Device is normally suspended inside a refrigerator or freezer. Also called blower (evaporator) coil.

Urn, Coffee/Tea *See* Coffee Urn.

Urn Stand Stationary stand with a solid top having raised edges all around, recessed drain trough with waste outlet, and a drainer plate flush with the top. Raised, die-stamped openings are used to connect lines to an urn. Top set on open base with shelf, semi-enclosed cabinet with bottom (and intermediate) shelf, or enclosed cabinet with bottom (and intermediate) shelf and door. May also be equipped with fold-down step.

V

Vegetable Peeler *See* Peeler.

Vegetable Slicer or Cutter 1. Hand- or motor-driven counter-mounted machine having rotating removable plates with varied knives. Product is forced against plates and knives for slicing, dicing, grating, shredding, etc. 2. Similar attachment to a food machine with rotating removable plates and knife arrangements.

Vegetable Steamer *See* Steam Cooker.

Vertical Cutter/Mixer Floor-type machine with a vertical tilting mixing bowl having a 25 to 80 quart capacity. The bowl is equipped with a two speed motor and a high speed agitator shaft at bowl bottom with cutting/mixing knife. A hand or motor driven stirring and mixing shaft is fixed to the bowl's cover. A strainer basket may be included.

W

Waffle Baker, Grill or Iron *See* Grill.

Water Boiler 1. One or more urns of coffee urn battery, heated by gas, steam, or electricity, to bring water to boil for making beverages. Usually connected to other urns with water piping and controls. Can be used separately. 2. Gas- electric-, steam-, or oil-fired unit to heat water for use in kitchen.

Water Extractor Floor-mounted machine located at the terminal of a waste pulping system. The device augers pulp in a slurry out of the tank to a pressure head at the top, extracting water which is then recirculated into the system. The pulp is discharged into a chute to a waste receptacle.

Water Heater Counter-mounted instant electric heating device with faucet for making tea and hot chocolate drinks.

Water Station Section of a counter or stand with a glass and/or pitcher filling faucet and drain trough.

Window, Soiled Dish Pass *See* Soiled Dish Pass Window.

Wine Rack Fixed or portable folding type unit with alternating stacked compartments open at front and rear to support wine bottles in a horizontal position for storage and display.

Wok *See* Chinese Range.

Wood Top Table top constructed of kiln-dried, hard rock laminated maple strips, hydraulically pressed together, glued and steel doweled through.

Workboard *See* Bar Workboard.

Work Table *See* Preparation Table.

National Sanitation Foundation Standard No. 2 for Foodservice Equipment*

SECTION 1. GENERAL

1.0 Coverage: This standard covers equipment commonly known to the trade as "fabricated food service equipment." It includes kitchen, bakery, pantry and cafeteria units and other food handling and processing equipment, such as tables of all kinds and their component parts, counters, shelves, sinks and hoods. It includes the basic principles of design, construction and performance as is necessary to achieve easy cleanability, food protection and freedom from harborages which are applicable to equipment commonly known as fabricated food service equipment and their component parts or appurtenances. This standard shall serve as a guide and in no way shall restrict new design, provided the design does not fall below the minimum specifications of this standard.

1.1 Minimum Requirements: The requirements set forth are minimum. Variations may be made when they tend to make units more resistant to wear, corrosion or more easily cleanable. Units which have component parts which are covered under existing NSF standards or criteria shall comply with the applicable requirements thereof.

1.2 Alternate Materials: Whenever specific materials are mentioned, it is understood that the use of materials proven to be equally satisfactory from the standpoint of sanitation and protection of product may be permitted.

1.3 Standard Review: A complete review of the standard shall be conducted at intervals of not more than five years to determine what changes, deletions or additions, if any, are necessary to maintain current and effective requirements consistent with new technology and progress. These reviews shall be conducted

*Reprinted with permission from the National Sanitation Foundation.

by appropriate representatives from the industry, public health and user groups. Final adoption of revisions shall be in accordance with the procedures established by the NSF Joint Committee on Food Equipment Standards.

SECTION 2. DEFINITIONS

2.0 Accessible: Capable of being exposed for cleaning and inspection with the use of simple tools such as a screwdriver, pliers or an open end wrench.

    2.0.1 Readily Accessible: Exposed or capable of being exposed for cleaning and inspection without the use of tools.

2.1 Cleaning: The physical removal of residues of foods, ingredients and other soiling materials.

    2.1.1 Easily Cleanable: Readily accessible, and of such material and finish and so fabricated that cleaning can be accomplished by normal methods.

2.2 Closed: Having an opening of not more than $\frac{1}{32}$ inch (0.8 mm) in width.

2.3 Conveyors: A mechanism for moving items from one location to another.

2.4 Cold Food Holding Equipment: An enclosed, electrically cooled device which, when precooled, is intended to receive food at not more than 45°F (7.2°C) and to hold the food at not more than 45°F (7.2°C) when connected to a power source.

2.5 Corrosion Resistant: Capable of maintaining original surface characteristics under the prolonged influence of the use environment, including the expected food contact and the normal use cleaning compounds and sanitizing (bactericidal) solutions.

2.6 Display Case: Any enclosed case used for the purpose of displaying and/ or dispensing unpackaged foods.

2.7 Electrically Operated Hot and Cold Food Transport Holding Carts and Cabinets: Enclosures designed to be connected to a power source and intended for use in the transporting of the foods in the carts or cabinets at normal room ambient, and with reconnection to a power source within a reasonable period of time.

2.8 Enclosed Food Transport Cabinet: An enclosed cabinet capable of being transported and intended for the conveyance of foods. It shall not include mobile dish or utensil storage or dispensing equipment.

2.9 Food: Any raw, cooked or processed edible substance, beverage or ingredient used or intended for use in whole, or in part, for human consumption.

2.10 Food Zone: Those surfaces of the equipment with which the food normally comes in contact and those surfaces with which the food is likely, in normal operation, to come into contact and return to surfaces normally in contact with the food or into the food.

2.11 Hot Food Holding Equipment: An enclosed, electrically heated device which, when preheated, is intended to receive food at not less than 140°F (60°C) and to hold the food at not less than 140°F (60°C) when connected to a power source.

2.12 Nonfood Zone: All exposed surfaces other than food and splash contact surfaces.

2.13 Removable: Capable of being detached from the main unit with the use of simple tools such as a screwdriver, pliers or an open end wrench.

    2.13.1 Readily (or Easily) Removable: Capable of being detached from the main unit without the use of tools.

2.14 Sanitizing: The effective bactericidal treatment of clean surfaces of equipment and utensils by a process which has proven effective and leaves no toxic residue.

2.15 Sealed: Having no openings that will permit the entry of dirt or liquid seepage.

2.16 Smooth: A surface, free of pits and inclusions, having a cleanability equal to the following: Food Contact Surfaces: No. 3 (100 grit) finish on stainless steel; Splash and Nonfood Contact Surfaces: Commercial grade, hot rolled steel, free of visible scale.

2.17 Splash Zone: Those surfaces which are subject to routine splash, spillage or other soiling during normal use.

2.18 Toxic: Having an adverse physiological effect on man.

2.19 Urn Stand: A fixed, portable or wheeled stand intended to support a coffee, tea or water urn and shall not include tables or stands on which small self-contained coffee brewers are mounted.

2.20 Wheeled Food Service Equipment: Equipment which is placed on casters or wheels and can be easily moved for auxiliary food processing or service, but shall not include licensed motor vehicles.

SECTION 3. MATERIALS

3.0 General: Only such materials shall be used in the construction of food service equipment and/or appurtenances as will withstand normal wear, penetration of vermin, corrosive action of foods or beverages, cleaning compounds and such other elements as may be found in the use environments and will not impart an odor, color or taste to the food.

3.1 Food Contact Surfaces: Surface materials in the food zone shall be smooth, corrosion resistant, nontoxic,* stable and nonabsorbent under use conditions and shall not impart an odor, color or taste nor contribute to the adulteration of food. Polyethylene shall be considered an acceptable material for ice pans or bins. Cold plates constructed integrally with ice bins shall exhibit a surface free of pits and voids and have a cleanability equal to or better than rotationally molded polyethylene.

3.2 Splash Contact Surfaces: Splash contact surfaces shall be smooth and of an easily cleanable and corrosion resistant material, or shall be rendered corrosion resistant with a material which is noncracking, nonchipping and nonspalling. Paint shall not be used except as provided in Item 4.13.

3.3 Nonfood Contact Surfaces: Nonfood contact surfaces shall be smooth and of corrosion resistant material or shall be rendered corrosion resistant or painted. Parts of the equipment directly over and adjacent to the food zone and parts having both food contact and nonfood contact surfaces shall have nonfood contact surfaces rendered corrosion resistant and, if coated, the coating shall be noncracking, nonchipping and nonspalling.

3.4 Solder: Solder on food contact surfaces shall be of such formulation as to be nontoxic under use conditions. It shall be corrosion resistant and shall be, consistent with good industrial practice in the refining of its constituent elements, free of cadmium, antimony, bismuth, lead and other toxic materials. The materials commonly used are 95 percent tin and 5 percent silver or 100 percent tin. Other solders may be accepted under the provisions of Item 1.2 if they are demonstrated to be nontoxic under use conditions.

3.5 Paint: Lead base paint shall not be used.

3.6 Plastic Resin Systems: Plastic resin systems may be used provided they meet the applicable requirements of Items 3.0, 3.1, 3.2 and 3.3.

3.7 Welding: When welded seams are used, the weld area and deposited weld material shall meet the applicable corrosion resistant requirements.

3.8 Gaskets and Packings: Gaskets and packings shall be made of materials such as resilient rubber, rubber-like materials or plastic. Such materials shall be nontoxic, stable, odor free, nonabsorbent and be unaffected by exposure to foods and cleaning compounds.

*The requirements of the Federal Food, Drug and Cosmetics Act as amended shall be used as a general guide.

3.9 Breaker Strips: Exposed breaker strips shall be made of material which is nontoxic, odor free, nonabsorbent and stable. They shall have smooth, easily cleanable surfaces with all sharp or rough edges removed.

3.10 Sound Damping: Sound damping materials shall, when applied, comply with the requirements of the zone in which used. The material shall not spall, flake or blister. Nonhardening types are not acceptable.

3.11 Scrapping Blocks: Scrapping blocks in soiled dish tables shall be of resilient, grease resistant material.

3.12 Wood-top Baker's Tables and Cutting Boards: Wood-top baker's tables and cutting boards shall be of wood having minute anatomy of between 4 and 13 vessels per square millimeter with a vessel diameter between 180 and 250 microns. The wood shall, in addition, be nontoxic and shall not impart odor, color or taste nor contribute to the adulteration of foods in contact therewith. The wood shall be kiln dried to 6–8 percent moisture content by weight after conditioning to remove stresses, case hardened and other drying defects, and shall have a weight per cubic foot of not less than 43.3 pounds (696 kilograms per cubic meter). Further, the wood shall have sufficient hardness to withstand the imbedding of a 0.444 inch (11.3 mm) ball to not more than ½ of its diameter by a force of 1200 pounds (540 kilograms) and shall have a shearing strength of at least 1800 psi (12.4 MPa) parallel to the grain.

3.13 Drawers: Drawers and containers intended only for utensil storage in fabricated food service equipment shall meet the material requirements of Item 3.2.* Drawers having food contact surfaces shall meet the requirements of Item 3.1.

---

*Material requirements for the splash zone permit the use of galvanized surfaces.

Typical Portion Sizes for Menu Items

Beverages
    Coffee   4 oz
    Tea   4 oz
    Milk   ½ pint
    Soft drinks   4 to 6 oz

Breads, Rolls, Cereals
    Bread   2 oz
    Cream of wheat   4 oz
    Hot rolls   2 oz
    Muffins   2 cakes
    Cereals, flaked   4 oz
    Cereals, puffed   2 oz
    Toast   4 oz

Casseroles, Stews, Etc.
    Baked beans   6 oz
    Chili con carne   6 oz
    Corned beef   6 oz
    Corned beef hash   6 oz
    Goulash   6 oz
    Ham à la king   4 oz
    Macaroni and cheese   5 oz
    Meat loaf   5 oz
    Short ribs   12 oz
    Spaghetti   5 oz
    Spanish rice   5 oz
    Stews   7 oz
    Stuffed cabbage   4 oz

Fruits
    Canned   4 oz
    Fresh   4 to 6 oz

Meats
    Bacon   5 oz
    Beef
        Roasts   6 oz

Steaks
    Chateaubriand   16 oz
    Filet mignon   6 oz
    Minute   6 oz
    Porterhouse   16 oz
    Salisbury   8 oz
    Sirloin   8 oz
    T-bone   12 oz
Ham   6 oz
Lamb chops   10 oz
Liver   4 oz
Pork chops   7 oz
Sausage   6 oz
Veal chops   8 oz
Veal cutlets   5 oz

Pastries, desserts, etc.
    Cakes   2 oz
    Ice cream   4 oz
    Pies, fruit   8 oz
    Puddings   5 oz

Poultry
    Chicken, fried   8 oz
    Chicken, broiled   8 oz
    Duck   10 oz
    Turkey   7 oz

Salads
    Cole slaw   3 oz
    Chicken salad   4 oz
    Mixed vegetable   4 oz
    Potato   4 oz
    Waldorf   4 oz

Sandwiches (excluding bread)
    Beef   4 oz
    Cheese   2 oz

Chicken	2 oz	Vegetables	
Ham	2 oz	Asparagus, fresh	7 pieces
Hamburgers	2 to 4 oz	Asparagus, tips	5 oz
Turkey	2 oz	Beans, green	4 oz
Seafood		Beans, lima	4 oz
Clams	12 Little	Beets	5 oz
	Neck	Cauliflower	5 oz
Crabs, soft-shell	2 crabs	Carrots	5 oz
Fish	6 to 7 oz	Corn, cob	2 ears
Frogs' legs	8 oz	Corn, kernel	5 oz
Lobster, half	12 oz	Potatoes	6 oz
Oysters	6 oysters	Peas	4 oz
Shrimp	6 oz	Spinach	6 oz
Soups		Squash	4 oz
Cup	6 oz	Tomatoes	5 oz
Bowl	8 oz		

Foodservice Establishment Plan and Specification Review Check Sheet

Michigan Department of Public Health, Division of Food Service Sanitation, Bureau of Environmental and Occupational Health

Name of Establishment _____

_____ New

Location _____ Type _____ _____ Remodeled

Owner _____ Address _____

Operator _____ Address _____

Floor Area _____ Ft² Seating Capacity _____

No. of Employees _____

Plans Received _____
 (Date)

Preliminary Review by _____ Date _____

Title _____

Final Approval by _____ Date _____

Title _____

MARK EACH ITEM IN APPROPRIATE LOCATION

S—Satisfactory U—Unsatisfactory (see remarks) NA—Not Applicable

INP—Information Not Provided on Plans or in Specifications

PART I. STRUCTURAL DESIGN AND MATERIALS
(*Indicates Sample Requested)

A. CONSTRUCTION	Floor Materials and Construction	Coving	Wall Materials and Construction	Ceiling Materials and Construction
1. Kitchen Area				
2. Dining Area				
3. Refrigeration Area				
4. Utensil-Wash Area				
5. Food-Storage (Dry)				
6. Toilet Rooms				
7. Dressing Rooms				
8. Garbage Storage (Inside)				
9. Bar Area				

REMARKS _____

B. LIGHTING   REMARKS
   1. Adequate light on all working sur-
      faces. (20 foot-candles)
   2. Adequate light on all other sur-
      faces and equipment. (10 foot-
      candles)
   3. Adequate light on all other areas.
      (5 foot-candles)
   4. Are all lights protected against
      breakage?

C. VERMIN AND RODENT
   PROTECTION   REMARKS
   1. Outer openings screened or other
      adequate controls.
   2. Outer doors self-closing.

   3. Building rodent-proof.

   4. Harborage eliminated.

PART II. KITCHEN FACILITIES AND EQUIPMENT

A. KITCHEN FACILITIES   REMARKS
   1. Food storage
      a. Easily cleanable facilities for
         storing food approximately 6
         in. above floor.

b. Accessible to delivery entrance.

c. Floor space for dry food storage equal to 0.5 ft²/meal served/day (0.5 × number of seats × number of meal periods).

d. Refrigerated storage areas equal to 0.5 ft²/meal served/day (0.5 × number of seats × number of meal periods).

e. Adequate hot foot holding facilities.

f. Proper protection from overhead leakage.

2. Adequate storage for single-service products.

3. Acceptable area for storage of poisonous and toxic materials.

4. Acceptable area for storage of bactericides and cleaning materials.

5. Adequate storage facilities for cleaned food equipment and tableware (including bar glasses).

6. Food display protection
Cafeteria ( )   Buffet ( )

7. Ice equipment (See Guidelines Relating to Protection of Potable Ice in Food Service Establishments).

a. Carbonators—out of potable ice bins

b. Cold plates—separated from potable ice

c. Ice protection
   i. No splash from beverage dispensers
   ii. Acceptable ice bin cover

   iii. Provision for storage of ice handling utensil

B. KITCHEN EQUIPMENT DESIGN, CONSTRUCTION AND INSTALLATION

REMARKS

1. Vegetable preparation sink and work area properly designed and isolated.

2. Waitress station.

3. Countertops, tabletops, and equipment stands of acceptable material.

4. Cutting boards easily cleanable and/or removable.

5. Cooking equipment easily cleanable.

6. Equipment installation
   a. Counter-type movable, sealed or elevated 4 in. above countertop.
   b. Floor-type movable, 6 in. above floor, or other acceptable installation method.
   c. Space between units or wall closed or adequate space for cleaning.
   d. Aisles—sufficient width.

7. Existing equipment.

   Specify_____

8. Clean-in-place equipment
   a. Approved design, installation.
   b. Self-draining.
   c. Floor drain and curbs installed where necessary.

C. HANDWASHING FACILITIES   REMARKS
   1. Lavoratories located within food preparation area; lavatories in or convenient to food serving and bar areas.
   2. Combination hot and cold faucets or mixing faucets.
   3. Hand cleanser provided.

   4. Acceptable hand-drying device.

D. DISHWASHING AND EQUIPMENT
   WASHING   REMARKS
   1. Dishmachine
      Make _____ Model _____
      a. Properly sized
      b. Automatic controls
      c. Gauge cock provided
      d. Thermometers provided
   2. Tableware and/or equipment washing facility.
      a. Three-compartment sink, coved corners
      b. Drainboards or dishtables
      c. Type of sanitization 170°F
         Water ____ Chemical ____

d. Approved materials _____

e. Dish baskets for hot water san-
   itization
f. Soak sink _____

g. Pre-rinse or scrapper _____

h. Garbage grinder _____

3. Janitorial service sink _____

E. VENTILATION (See Ventilation
   Standard for Food Service
   Establishments in Michigan)   REMARKS
   1. Canopy hood
      a. Length ___ Width ___
      b. Number of enclosed sides (in-
         cluding back) _____
      c. Description of side curtains _____

      d. Total proposed exhaust
         ___ ft³/min
      e. Total required exhaust
         ___ ft³/min
      f. Static pressure ___in. S.P. _____

      g. Number and size of grease fil-
         ters or extractors
      h. Adequate duct sizes and num-
         bers ___
      i. Canopy overhang _____

      j. Exhaust discharge location _____

   2. Low-side wall hood
      a. Total length ___ft _____

      b. Broiler length ___ ft × 350 =
         ___ ft³/min
      c. Non-broiler length ___ ft × 200
         = ___ ft³/min
      d. Total required exhaust
         ___ ft³/min
      e. Calculated static pressure
         ___ in. S.P.
      f. Total proposed exhaust
         ___ ft³/min

g. Proposed static pressure ____ in.
   S.P.
h. Adequate duct sizes and numbers
i. Exhaust discharge location

3. Cap-type canopy (if overhead canopy, complete as 1A)
   a. Oven length ____ ft × 100 =
      ____ or 500, whichever is less
   b. Static pressure ____ in. S.P.
   c. Total proposed exhaust
      ____ ft³/min
4. Dishmachine exhaust system
   (types):

	Pantleg Hood	Exhausted Vestibule	Canopy Hood
Total required exhaust			
Total proposed exhaust			
Total S.P. required			
Total S.P. proposed			

REMARKS ____

5. Total exhaust (cfm)

	Health Dept.	Calculations Plan #1	Plan #2
Cooking bank hood			
Dishmachine hood			
Toilet exhaust (Part III. E. 4.)			
General dining area exhaust			
Other (pizza, low-side wallhood, etc.)			
Total ft³/min			

Comments Concerning Design of Exhaust Systems ____

6. Tempered make-up air system

	Health Dept.	Calculations Plan #1	Plan #2
Total ft³/min			
Kitchen (80% min.)			
Dining area (20% max.)			
Interlocked with exhaust sys-tem			
Amount of fresh air supply through HVAC			

REMARKS _____

_____
_____

   7. Make-up air diffusers
      a. Required diffuser area   _____
      b. Terminal velocity   _____
REMARKS _____

_____
_____
_____
_____
_____

PART III. SANITARY FACILITIES

A. WATER SUPPLY   REMARKS
   1. Public ( ) Yes ( ) No   _____
   2. Private (Type _____)   _____
      a. Construction   _____
      b. Location (proper isolation)   _____
      c. Pump capacity ____ gal/min   _____
      d. Well yield ____ gal/min   _____
      e. Storage ____ gal   _____
      f. Treatment   _____
         Softener   _____
         Filtered   _____
         Chlorination   _____
         Other_____   _____
         None   _____
B. WATER HEATING EQUIPMENT
   (See Guidelines for Hot Water
   Generating Systems in Food Service
   Establishments)

Gallons	Degree Rise
	140°
	100°
	85°
	40°
	35°
	°

$$BTU = \frac{Q \times 8.33 \text{ lb/gal} \times \text{Degree Rise}}{0.70}$$

$$kW = \frac{Q \times 8.33 \text{ lb/gal} \times \text{Degree Rise}}{3412}$$

   1. Required primary heater____BTU/kW
   2. Required booster heater____BTU/kW
   3. Pipe treatment
      a. Recirculation   _____
      b. Insulation   _____
REMARKS _____

_____
_____

C. SEWAGE DISPOSAL   REMARKS

1. Public ( ) Yes ( ) No
2. Private disposal system
   a. Primary treatment
      Septic tank _____ gal
      Package plant
      Lagoon
      Other
   b. Secondary treatment
      Tile field _____ ft^2
      Dry well
      Filter
      Other
   c. Effluents discharge to
      _____

   d. Pollution control authority
      Approval obtained
      ( ) Yes ( ) No

D. PLUMBING   REMARKS

1. Complies with state and local laws or national plumbing code.
2. Potable and non-potable piping separate and identified.
3. Backsiphonage protection from: water closets, urinals, dishwashers, detergent dispenser, rinse additive injector, potato peeler, garbage grinder, hose bibb connections, steam tables, dipper wells, etc. (Note: Some refrigerated equipment may be water cooled and require backsiphonage and backflow protection.)
4. Backflow protection from: dishwashers, utensil-wash sinks, culinary sinks, refrigerators, steam tables, ice machines, ice bins, etc.
5. Floor drain located outside walk-in cooler.

E. TOILET FACILITIES

	Employee	Male Patrons	Female Patrons
1. Adequate and conveniently located			
2. Sanitary design			
3. Fully enclosed room; self-closing door			
4. Ventilation*			

* To compute ventilation requirements, utilize appropriate volume:
a. 100 ft^3/min/room
b. 25 ft^3/min/fixture
c. 2 ft^3/min/ft^2 floor area

5. Number of water closets (   ) _____

6. Number of urinals (   ) _____

7. Number of lavatories in restrooms
   (   ) _____

8. Hand cleanser _____

9. Hand-drying device _____

F. DRESSING ROOMS AND LOCKERS   REMARKS

1. Separate dressing rooms _____

2. Individual lockers _____

3. Hand-washing facilities _____

4. Ventilation _____

5. Convenient to restrooms _____

G. GARBAGE AND RUBBISH   REMARKS

1. Person responsible for disposal. _____

2. Final disposal site. _____

3. Frequency of service. _____

4. Adequate space for can storage or
   separate room. _____

5. Can washing facility. _____

6. Cans stored on concrete slab or on
   rack 12 in. high; dumpster unit
   stored on concrete slab. _____

7. Incinerator—contact Michigan Department of Natural Resources for
   approval. _____

8. Compactor. _____

Approval of these plans and specifications does not constitute endorsement or acceptance of the completed establishment (structure or equipment). A final inspection of
each completed establishment with equipment installed will be necessary to determine
if it complies with the local or State laws applying to such establishments.

Courtesy of Michigan Department of Public Health

Information for Developing a Foodservice Prospectus

A. Customer or user characteristics
  1. Identification by Occupation—indicate numbers or percentage in each category.
     Business people _____   Professionals _____
     Clerical workers _____   Retirees _____
     Craftsmen _____   Sales Personnel _____
     Homemakers _____   Service workers _____
     Laborers _____   Students _____
     Office workers _____   Others _____
  2. Income level—numbers or percentage of persons in each category.
     Under $10,000 _____   30,000–34,000 _____
     10,000–14,999 _____   35,000–39,000 _____
     15,000–19,999 _____   40,000–44,000 _____
     20,000–24,999 _____   Over 45,000 _____
     25,000–29,999 _____
  3. Age and Sex—numbers or percentage in each age bracket and breakdown by sex.

	Male	Female
Under 5 years _____	_____	_____
6–11 _____	_____	_____
12–17 _____	_____	_____
18–24 _____	_____	_____
25–34 _____	_____	_____
35–49 _____	_____	_____
50–64 _____	_____	_____
Over 65 _____	_____	_____

  4. Educational level—numbers or percentage who have completed each level.
     Elementary _____
     Secondary _____
     College (Junior or Community) _____
     University _____
  5. Motivation for eating out—indicate or estimate percentage in each category.
     Change in routine _____   Special occasions _____
     Necessity _____   Adventure _____

Convenience ———————————   Entertainment ———————————

Business reasons ———————————   To get special kinds of meals ————

Social ———————————   Other ———————————

6. Spending habits—estimate average amount to be spent for each meal; may be identified by sex, age, or income if desirable.

Breakfast ———————————   Afternoon snack ———————————

Mid-morning snack ———————————   Dinner ———————————

Lunch ———————————   After-dinner snack ———————————

7. Activities related to dining out—identify or estimate percentages.

Shopping ———————————   Entertainment events ———————————

Traveling or touring ———————————   Organized group meetings———————

Attended conventions ———————————   Social group meetings———————

Visiting ———————————   Other ———————————

Business ———————————

8. Arrival patterns—estimate percentage for each group.

Singles, male ———————————

Singles, female ———————————

Couples ———————————

Families ———————————   Average size ———————————

Men groups ———————————   Average size ———————————

Women groups ———————————   Average size ———————————

Mixed groups ———————————   Average size ———————————

9. Miscellaneous factors—identify and describe if related to a particular type of facility.

Ethnic backgrounds ———————————————————————————

Food preferences ———————————————————————————

Eating habits ———————————————————————————

Service preferences ———————————————————————————

Marital status ———————————————————————————

Means of transportation ———————————————————————————

Preferred meal periods of dining out ———————————————————————————

Preferred days for dining out ———————————————————————————

B. Menu characteristics

1. Frequency of change—indicate type for each meal period.

	Breakfast	Lunch	Dinner
Completely fixed menu	————	———	————
Fixed with seasonal changes	————	———	————
Fixed with changing specials	————	———	————
Complete daily changes	————	———	————
Cyclical daily changes	————	———	————
(Indicate length of cycle)			

Daily changes with standard
   items   _____   _____   _____

2. Type of items—indicate for each meal.

	Breakfast	Lunch	Dinner
A la Carte	_____	_____	_____
Club or complete meal	_____	_____	_____
Combination	_____	_____	_____

3. Extent of offerings—indicate number of items in each category for each meal.

	Breakfast	Lunch	Dinner
Appetizers	_____	_____	_____
Soups	_____	_____	_____
Salads	_____	_____	_____
Main entrees	_____	_____	_____
Sandwiches	_____	_____	_____

	Breakfast	Lunch	Dinner
Potatoes	_____	_____	_____
Vegetables	_____	_____	_____
Bread and rolls	_____	_____	_____
Desserts	_____	_____	_____
Beverages	_____	_____	_____
Other	_____	_____	_____

4. Typical menu for each meal—include portions size for each item.

C. Service

1. Type—indicate appropriate category.

Service units

Table service   _____
Counter service   _____
Booth service   _____
Combination table and counter   _____
Combination table and booth   _____
Combination counter and booth   _____
Tray service   _____
Car service   _____
Room service   _____

Self-service units

Cafeteria units   _____
Buffet service   _____
Take-out service   _____
Vending units   _____

2. Standards—indicate type of material and quality.

	Material	Quality
Tablecloths	_____	_____
Napkins	_____	_____
Place mats	_____	_____
Dishware	_____	_____
Hollowware	_____	_____
Glassware	_____	_____
Flatware	_____	_____
Other _____	_____	_____

3. Beverage service—indicate type and method.
    Non-alcoholic _____
    Alcoholic _____

D. Atmosphere
  1. Type—indicate.

Formal _____	Cheerful _____
Informal _____	Relaxed _____
Intimate _____	Appealing _____
	Other _____

  2. Special emphasis

Exterior _____	View _____
Interior _____	Theme _____
Location _____	Costuming _____

E. Operational characteristics
  1. Type of ownership and organization.

Independent owner _____	Proprietorship _____
Chain _____	Partnership _____
Franchise _____	Corporation _____
Lease _____	Other _____

  2. Meal periods; days and hours of operation, expected number of customers.

	Days	Hours	No. of customers
Breakfast	_____	_____	_____
Mid-morning snack	_____	_____	_____
Lunch	_____	_____	_____
Afternoon snack	_____	_____	_____
Dinner	_____	_____	_____
After-dinner snack	_____	_____	_____

  3. Procedures

Purchasing _____	Waste disposal _____
Production _____	Cash _____
Service _____	Communications _____
Warewashing _____	Others _____

  4. Regulatory considerations—check proposed project for compliance with:

Zoning laws _____	Liquor laws _____
Building code _____	Labor laws _____
Sanitary code _____	Other _____

Listing of Tasks Commonly Performed in Foodservice Facilities

I. ACCOUNTING
   A. ANALYSIS
   1. Analyzing operating data
   2. Analyzing financial data
   3. Auditing all bills
   4. Auditing all cash in the cash system
   5. Compiling financial reports
   6. Compiling financial collection reports
   7. Compiling disbursement reports
   8. Compiling reconciliation reports
   9. Compiling statistical reports
   10. Consolidating cost data
   11. Determining costs of operation
   12. Examining accounting and control procedures to determine compliance with regulations
   13. Analyzing accounting records for useful information
   14. Studying problems and recommending action
   B. BOOKKEEPING
   1. Adjusting control totals
   2. Adjusting ledger totals
   3. Approving bills and invoices
   4. Ascertaining accounts affected by transaction
   5. Assessing banquet charges
   6. Balancing control accounts
   7. Balancing disbursements
   8. Balancing ledger accounts
   9. Balancing receipts
   10. Comparing forms
   11. Correcting errors in accounts
   12. Correcting customer errors

13. Correcting vendor errors
14. Crediting accounts
15. Debiting accounts
16. Keeping records
17. Listing charges
18. Making journal entries
19. Posting bills due
20. Posting bills paid
21. Posting changes to records
22. Posting data to accounts
23. Posting supply data
24. Posting details of financial transactions
25. Posting expense vouchers
26. Posting expenses
27. Posting payroll deductions
28. Posting payroll to pay records
29. Posting revenues
30. Processing bills
31. Record financial transactions
32. Recording monetary transactions
33. Recording reservations
34. Verifying daily balances against predetermined figures
35. Verifying journal entries

C. COMPUTATION

1. Aging accounts receivable
2. Computing bills
3. Computing figures for financial reports
4. Computing financial ratios
5. Computing losses
6. Computing payroll deductions
7. Computing profits
8. Computing total costs
9. Computing total percentages
10. Computing sales
11. Computing unit costs
12. Computing unit percentages
13. Counting bills
14. Determining food costs
15. Determining maintenance costs
16. Determining labor costs
17. Determining overhead costs
18. Making out payroll
19. Preparing charts and graphs (financial)
20. Preparing daily meal abstracts
21. Preparing meal recap reports
22. Proofing computations
23. Reconciling bank account
24. Totaling accounts
25. Totaling checks

D. CREDIT
   1. Accepting payments on customer accounts
   2. Analyzing delinquent accounts and recommending action
   3. Authorizing limits and charges
   4. Authorizing issuance of credit cards
   5. Collecting funds due from employees
   6. Composing collection notes to customers
   7. Determining credit ratings
   8. Determining payment methods for accounts receivable
   9. Evaluating financial standing of credit applicants
  10. Interviewing customers to determine credit problems
  11. Issuing credit cards
  12. Issuing replacement credit cards
  13. Issuing list of lost or stolen credit cards
  14. Liaison with collection agency
  15. Maintaining credit cards records
  16. Maintaining list of lost or stolen credit cards
  17. Notifying customers of credit limits
  18. Preparing delinquency notice
  19. Presenting the bill
  20. Processing accounts due
  21. Processing credit card applications
  22. Ringing-up charges on the cash register
  23. Submitting delinquent accounts to a collection agency or attorney for collection
  24. Tracing delinquents
  25. Typing receipts
  26. Verifying accounts receivable
  27. Verifying references and information on credit applications
E. DATA COLLECTION
   1. Arranging data
   2. Comparing data
   3. Collecting specific cost-distribution data
   4. Keeping employee time records
   5. Preparing financial statement
   6. Preparing balance sheet
   7. Preparing income statement
   8. Recording data
   9. Researching outstanding accounts
  10. Compiling requested accounting information
  11. Tabulating food and beverage checks
  12. Tabulating the number of units sold of each product
F. DISBURSING
   1. Allocating funds
   2. Cashing checks
   3. Collecting parking fees
   4. Counting money
   5. Verifying accounts
   6. Disbursing funds

7. Drawing up budgets
8. Issuing refunds
9. Keeping custody of house fund
10. Maintaining bank account
11. Maintaining petty cash fund
12. Making change
13. Mailing checks
14. Mailing cash
15. Paying company expenditures
16. Paying employees
17. Preparing bank deposit
18. Preparing cash and checks for deposit
19. Preparing checks
20. Preparing payroll
21. Processing checks
22. Processing claims
23. Receiving incoming checks and currency
24. Sorting coins
25. Wrapping coins

II. CLERICAL
  A. SECRETARIAL
1. Answering letters
2. Assembling reports
3. Binding reports
4. Correcting accounts
5. Filing correspondence
6. Filing forms
7. Setting files
8. Labeling files
9. Mailing correspondence
10. Moving files
11. Proofreading
12. Scheduling appointments
13. Sorting forms
14. Stapling reports
15. Taking dictation

  B. FILING
1. Filing
2. Keeping record of calls
3. Keeping records of correspondence
4. Keeping records of long-distance calls placed
5. Maintaining files
6. Maintaining information file
7. Maintaining output records
8. Maintaining record of food items ordered
9. Maintaining record of mixed drinks ordered
10. Maintaining record of packages received
11. Maintaining record of tardiness
12. Maintaining record of uneaten food
13. Maintaining record of wines ordered

14. Maintaining capital records
15. Maintaining indebtedness records
16. Making indexes
17. Recording data on unusual occurrences
18. Retrieving requested information from files
19. Searching files for requested information

C. TYPING
1. Cutting ditto master sheets
2. Cutting stencils
3. Drafting correspondence
4. Drafting requisitions
5. Duplicating documents
6. Preparing requisitions
7. Typing correspondence
8. Typing memos
9. Typing reports
10. Typing requisitions
11. Typing schedules
12. Typing work-service requests
13. Writing accident reports
14. Writing damage reports

III. COMMUNICATION
A. GENERAL
1. Addressing envelopes, forms, and letters
2. Answering phone
3. Composing correspondence
4. Composing routine memos
5. Delivering mail to post office
6. Distributing mail
7. Drafting reports
8. Handling incoming messages
9. Handling unusual requests and inquiries
10. Issuing periodic reports of operating status
11. Issuing reports concerning financial status
12. Issuing reports of operating procedures
13. Maintaining internal communication system
14. Making daily management report
15. Making-up food and beverage report
16. Notifying employees when they must work other than scheduled periods
17. Notifying management of need for repairs
18. Opening mail
19. Picking up incoming mail
20. Preparing routine reports
21. Reporting equipment breakdown
22. Reporting maintenance needs of equipment
23. Reporting needed repairs to superior
24. Reporting unusual happenings to management
25. Reporting all accidents
26. Reporting damage
27. Sorting mail

    28. Taking telephone messages
    29. Transcribing from shorthand
IV. MAINTENANCE
  A. BUILDING
      1. Buffing floors
      2. Burning refuse
      3. Changing filters
      4. Checking for burnt-out lights
      5. Cleaning air ducts
      6. Cleaning awnings
      7. Cleaning cabinets
      8. Cleaning ceilings
      9. Cleaning counters
     10. Cleaning door glass
     11. Cleaning door ventilators
     12. Cleaning drawers
     13. Cleaning fans
     14. Cleaning marble
     15. Cleaning pipes and fixtures
     16. Cleaning storage bins
     17. Cleaning walls
     18. Cleaning windows
     19. Cleaning work areas
     20. Collecting trash
     21. Disposing of non-combustible trash
     22. Doing routine painting
     23. Doing routine plumbing
     24. Dusting
     25. Emptying garbage
     26. Emptying trash
     27. Inspecting and evaluating physical condition of building
     28. Inspecting to determine painting needs
     29. Keeping assigned area free of spilled food
     30. Maintaining hydraulic door checks
     31. Mopping floors
     32. Mopping stairs
     33. Opening clogged drains
     34. Picking up waste paper
     35. Polishing floors
     36. Removing stains from carpet
     37. Scrubbing floor
     38. Scrubbing stairs
     39. Shampooing carpet
     40. Sorting bottles
     41. Sorting trash
     42. Spraying kitchen area
     43. Sweeping floor
     44. Sweeping stairs
     45. Vacuuming floor
     46. Vacuuming stairs

47. Washing the exterior
48. Washing doors
49. Washing windows
50. Washing interior walls
51. Washing the table tops
52. Washing counter-tops
53. Washing woodwork
54. Washing shelves
55. Waxing floors
56. Waxing counters

B. EQUIPMENT
1. Adjusting sound equipment
2. Adjusting thermostatic controls
3. Assuring compliance of electrical equipment with local regulations
4. Brushing drapes, furniture, upholstery, etc.
5. Burnishing silverware
6. Calibrating equipment
7. Changing grease (fryer)
8. Checking thermostat and temperature controls
9. Cleaning artificial flowers
10. Cleaning ash urns
11. Cleaning bain marie
12. Cleaning boiler
13. Cleaning bread baskets
14. Cleaning buffet tables
15. Cleaning burnishing machine
16. Cleaning butter bowls
17. Cleaning can opener
18. Cleaning carts
19. Cleaning china
20. Cleaning chopper
21. Cleaning chopping blocks
22. Cleaning coffee urns
23. Cleaning creamer
24. Cleaning cutter boards
25. Cleaning dipper well
26. Cleaning dish-washing machine
27. Cleaning egg slicers
28. Cleaning fans
29. Cleaning filters
30. Cleaning flaming equipment
31. Cleaning food carts
32. Cleaning freezers and refrigerators
33. Cleaning fryers
34. Cleaning furnaces
35. Cleaning griddles
36. Cleaning garbage cans and trash receptacles
37. Cleaning garbage disposal
38. Cleaning grease traps
39. Cleaning grills

40. Cleaning hood
41. Cleaning ice bins
42. Cleaning ice-cream cabinet
43. Cleaning incinerator
44. Cleaning kettles
45. Cleaning light fixtures
46. Cleaning mats
47. Cleaning meat slicer
48. Cleaning milk dispenser
49. Cleaning mixers
50. Cleaning ovens
51. Cleaning pastry carts
52. Cleaning peeling machine
53. Cleaning proof boxes
54. Cleaning ranges
55. Cleaning refrigerators
56. Cleaning scales
57. Cleaning serving stations
58. Cleaning sinks
59. Cleaning steam cooker
60. Cleaning steam table
61. Cleaning stools
62. Cleaning stoves
63. Cleaning tables
64. Cleaning thermotainer
65. Cleaning toaster
66. Cleaning toilet bowls
67. Cleaning tools
68. Cleaning urinals
69. Cleaning upholstered furniture
70. Cleaning ventilator grills
71. Cleaning waffle irons
72. Cleaning wash bowls
73. Cleaning work table
74. Dusting furniture
75. Emptying ash trays
76. Filling fruit-juice dispensers
77. Filling vending machines
78. Filtering grease
79. Greasing machinery
80. Inspecting equipment
81. Maintaining refrigerating and air-conditioning equipment
82. Maintaining sound equipment
83. Making inspections of dining-room premises
84. Making inspections of kitchen equipment
85. Making inspections of store rooms
86. Moving and arranging furniture
87. Oiling machinery
88. Polishing metals
89. Removing wax

90. Scraping bakery bench
91. Scraping dishes
92. Scraping pots and pans
93. Sharpening cutting knives
94. Sorting pots and pans
95. Stocking service bar
96. Stocking vending machines
97. Vacuuming furniture
98. Vacuuming mats
99. Washing pans
100. Washing pots
101. Washing service trays

C. GROUNDS
1. Cleaning entranceways
2. Cleaning sidewalks
3. Cleaning litter outside the building
4. Picking up papers
5. Pruning shrubs and trees
6. Removing snow
7. Sweeping parking lot
8. Weeding flower beds

V. MANAGEMENT
A. CONTROLLING
1. Adjusting work loads
2. Approving service contracts
3. Approving work orders
4. Auditing beverage checks
5. Auditing food checks
6. Auditing payroll
7. Authorizing expenditures
8. Authorizing information for publication
9. Authorizing overtime
10. Authorizing payment on C.O.D. deliveries
11. Authorizing sick leave
12. Checking beverage orders
13. Checking food orders
14. Checking for adherence to control systems
15. Clearing cash registers
16. Comparing actual and budgeted figures
17. Comparing specifications
18. Comparing work performed with standards
19. Controlling costs
20. Controlling use of forms
21. Detecting employee thievery
22. Determining degree of compliance with directives
23. Determining purchasing specifications
24. Determining standards
25. Developing regulations
26. Enforcing standards
27. Establishing policy

28. Establishing standards and procedures
29. Establishing theft controls
30. Establishing wastage controls
31. Evaluating systems of internal control
32. Examining accounting records for accuracy
33. Inspecting dishes for cleanliness
34. Inspecting finished work
35. Inspecting silverware for cleanliness
36. Inspecting work
37. Installing financial controls system
38. Instituting damage controls
39. Instituting theft controls
40. Instituting waste controls
41. Making a daily report of all cash received, disbursed, and on hand
42. Preparing budgets
43. Preparing and disseminating copies of regulatory procedures
44. Proofing computations
45. Reviewing financial records
46. Reviewing operating records
47. Reviewing order to ensure accuracy
48. Reviewing proposed expenditures against budgeted amounts and report averages
49. Setting standards
50. Spot-checking entire operation
51. Standardizing recipes
52. Tasting food for palatability
53. Verifying data accuracy
54. Verifying register totals with cash turned in
55. Weighing fish
56. Weighing ingredients
57. Weighing meat
58. Weighing poultry

B. DIRECTING
1. Assigning work
2. Authorizing deviation from policy and standards
3. Coordinating work
4. Delegating work
5. Determining work needs
6. Developing methods and procedures
7. Directing activities of subordinates
8. Directing advertising campaigns
9. Directing maintenance of building
10. Interpreting policy to department heads
11. Interpreting company policy to workers
12. Planning work schedules
13. Preparing cleaning schedules
14. Scheduling periodic inspections and overhauls
15. Scheduling relief periods
16. Supervising activities of department heads

C. ORGANIZING
1. Advising employees
2. Assigning duties to employees
3. Assigning responsibilities
4. Conferring with other department heads to coordinate activities
5. Coordinating activities of department
6. Coordinating activities of workers
7. Delegating authority
8. Determining work procedures
9. Establishing operating procedures
10. Evaluating adequacy of managerial procedures
11. Evaluating adequacy of financial procedures
12. Making recommendations to management concerning accounting procedures
13. Organizing the entire operation
14. Planning administrative procedures
15. Planning production
16. Planning for surplus food utilization
17. Preparing cleaning schedules
18. Promoting unity among departments

D. PLANNING
1. Adjusting work schedules
2. Advising on methods and procedures for distributing operating costs
3. Altering policies as necessary
4. Altering goals as necessary
5. Altering objectives as necessary
6. Altering standards as necessary
7. Determining goals
8. Determining methods of collection of cost data
9. Determining methods of consolidation of cost data
10. Determining methods of correlation of cost data
11. Determining methods of data correlation
12. Determining methods of data collection
13. Determining personnel needs
14. Determining policy
15. Developing menus
16. Developing promotional plans
17. Developing security procedures
18. Developing theft controls
19. Developing waste controls
20. Establishing the arrangement for storage areas
21. Estimating costs
22. Forecasting company's needs
23. Planning advertising materials
24. Planning banquets
25. Planning personnel policies
26. Planning preventive maintenance programs
27. Planning promotional materials
28. Planning public relations program

29. Planning for expansion
30. Planning for financial needs
31. Planning operations
32. Recommending changes considered necessary to aid in more effective management
33. Reviewing menu
34. Seeking advice from vendors about new products
35. Selecting recipes

VI. MARKETING

A. PROMOTION

1. Acting as liaison with advertising agency
2. Approving advertising contracts
3. Approving advertising before release
4. Approving art work
5. Arranging for printing of menu
6. Arranging for publicity
7. Arranging food for attractiveness
8. Arranging merchandise display at counter
9. Checking advertisements when they appear in the media
10. Designing layout
11. Designing menu
12. Determining advertising needs
13. Dispersing advertising and promotional literature
14. Negotiating advertising contract
15. Preparing advertising materials
16. Preparing promotional materials
17. Preparing publicity releases
18. Procuring mailing lists
19. Promoting good will between the groups and the establishment
20. Purchasing advertising time and space as needed
21. Setting up sales displays
22. Stocking shelves at merchandise counter
23. Writing sales outlines for use by staff

B. PUBLIC RELATIONS

1. Conducting public relations programs
2. Directing public-opinion poll
3. Greeting important guests
4. Greeting visitors
5. Participating in community and civic affairs
6. Preparing company publication
7. Taking public-opinion polls
8. Writing news releases

C. SALES

1. Adjusting complaints
2. Arranging banquets
3. Arranging parties
4. Cleaning menus
5. Confirming reservations
6. Consulting with members of an organization to plan their function

7. Contacting organization heads to explain the available services and facilities
8. Determining guest satisfaction
9. Drawing-up contract for groups
10. Forecasting beverage demand
11. Forecasting food demand
12. Forecasting sales
13. Handling guest complaints
14. Organizing prospect files
15. Planning banquets
16. Planning parties
17. Planning details of group functions
18. Preparing menu boards
19. Presenting menu to patron
20. Pricing items
21. Relaying food order to kitchen
22. Relaying mixed-drink order to bar
23. Selecting markets
24. Selecting prospects
25. Setting prices for beverages
26. Setting prices for food items
27. Soliciting business
28. Suggesting desserts
29. Suggesting food courses
30. Suggesting mixed drinks
31. Suggesting wines
32. Taking patrons' orders
33. Welcoming guests
34. Writing contracts

VII. OPERATIONS
1. Assisting employees
2. Attaching bills
3. Attaching forms
4. Attaching labels
5. Checking bin cards
6. Checking breakage
7. Checking daily reports
8. Checking dining rooms for table set-ups
9. Checking doors
10. Checking drawers
11. Checking employees' work
12. Checking equipment operation
13. Checking food orders
14. Checking food quality
15. Checking inventories
16. Checking invoices
17. Checking orders
18. Checking par stocks
19. Checking refrigerators

20. Checking requisitions
21. Checking reservations
22. Checking sales
23. Checking side stands
24. Checking supplies of food
25. Checking supplies of china, glasses, silverware
26. Checking weights
27. Erecting displays
28. Getting materials
29. Getting tools
30. Listing needed supplies
31. Loading carts
32. Maintaining spare parts
33. Moving chairs
34. Moving tables
35. Operating accounting machines
36. Operating adding machines
37. Operating cash registers
38. Operating computing machines
39. Operating compactors
40. Operating copying machines
41. Operating dishwashers
42. Operating dumb waiter
43. Operating glasswasher
44. Operating mixers
45. Operating scrubbers
46. Operating slicers
47. Preparing menus
48. Preparing reports
49. Removing carts
50. Removing trays
51. Removing tables
52. Setting up menu boards
53. Setting up partitions
54. Taking reservations

VIII. PERSONNEL MANAGEMENT
  A. EVALUATING
1. Checking appearance of employees
2. Comparing work methods
3. Counseling employees
4. Determining personnel suitable for promotion and transfer
5. Evaluating employee performance
6. Evaluating supervisory and executive personnel
7. Evaluating workers
8. Examining work
9. Inspecting employees for neatness
10. Keeping personnel records
11. Maintaining personnel records
12. Making recommendations regarding promotions, etc.

      13. Observing employee performance
      14. Testing employees eligible for promotion
      15. Writing job descriptions
      16. Writing job specifications

B. MOTIVATING
      1. Authorizing pay raises
      2. Conducting time and motion studies
      3. Developing incentive programs
      4. Granting pay raises
      5. Maintaining harmony among workers
      6. Making salary adjustments
      7. Motivating workers
      8. Promoting and transferring personnel

C. NEGOTIATING
      1. Acting as liaison between labor and management
      2. Bargaining with unions
      3. Determining pay scale
      4. Developing salary and wage scales
      5. Establishing and maintaining grievance procedures
      6. Establishing pay rates
      7. Establishing pension and insurance plans
      8. Establishing workmen's compensation policies
      9. Interpreting union contracts
      10. Negotiating contracts
      11. Representing company in negotiating labor agreements
      12. Resolving complaints
      13. Resolving personnel problems at supervisory and executive level
      14. Settling arguments
      15. Settling grievances

D. STAFFING
      1. Administering aptitude tests
      2. Administering personality tests
      3. Discharging employees
      4. Determining staff requirements
      5. Establishing work schedules
      6. Hiring employees
      7. Hiring executive personnel
      8. Interpreting union policies and procedures to employees
      9. Interviewing applicants
      10. Notifying applicants of rejection
      11. Notifying applicants of selection
      12. Organizing recruiting procedures
      13. Organizing selection procedures
      14. Recording and evaluating information about job applicants
      15. Regulating workloads
      16. Selecting applicants for further consideration
      17. Testing job applicants
      18. Verifying information on job applicants
      19. Verifying references

E. TRAINING
1. Acquiring knowledge of requirements for all jobs
2. Developing training manuals
3. Evaluating performance and progress of trainees
4. Forecasting training needs
5. Informing job applicants of company and union policies
6. Interpreting standards to workers
7. Organizing training procedures
8. Orienting new employees
9. Preparing training materials
10. Revising job descriptions
11. Training employees

IX. PRODUCTION
A. PHYSICAL PRODUCT
1. Adding ingredients
2. Applying egg wash
3. Arranging cold-meat dishes
4. Baking meat
5. Baking biscuits
6. Baking bread
7. Baking buns
8. Baking cakes
9. Baking cookies
10. Baking fish
11. Baking fowl
12. Baking lamb
13. Baking pastries
14. Baking muffins
15. Baking pies
16. Baking rolls
17. Baking shellfish
18. Baking sweet rolls
19. Baking vegetables
20. Barbecuing meat
21. Barbecuing fowl
22. Batter-dipping meat
23. Batter-dipping fish
24. Batter-dipping fruit
25. Batter-dipping shellfish
26. Beating ingredients
27. Boiling beef
28. Boiling eggs
29. Boiling fish
30. Boiling fowl
31. Boiling lamb
32. Boiling shellfish
33. Boiling vegetables
34. Boning meat
35. Boning fowl
36. Braising meat

37. Breading meat
38. Breading fish
39. Breading shellfish
40. Brewing coffee
41. Brewing tea
42. Broiling fish
43. Broiling fowl
44. Broiling meat
45. Carving butter
46. Carving meat
47. Carving fowl
48. Chopping eggs
49. Chopping meat
50. Chopping fish
51. Chopping fowl
52. Chopping fruit
53. Chopping vegetables
54. Chopping nuts
55. Chopping shellfish
56. Cracking nuts
57. Creaming vegetables
58. Cutting meat
59. Cutting bread
60. Cutting fish
61. Cutting fowl
62. Cutting fruit
63. Cutting pastries
64. Cutting vegetables
65. Decorating pastry
66. Deep-frying meat
67. Deep-frying fish
68. Deep-frying fowl
69. Deep-frying vegetables
70. Deep-frying shellfish
71. Designing decorated foods
72. Designing artistic food arrangements
73. Developing new recipes
74. Dicing meat
75. Dicing fowl
76. Dicing fruit
77. Dicing vegetables
78. Dicing shellfish
79. Draining bottles
80. Draining cans
81. Drawing tap beer
82. Dusting foods with flour
83. Examining foods
84. Estimating ingredients
85. Fashioning pastry decorations
86. Fileting meat and fish

87. Filling coffee pots
88. Filling creamers
89. Filling ice bins
90. Filling milk dispenser
91. Filling sugar bowls
92. Filling vending machines
93. Filling water pitchers
94. Frosting cakes
95. Frying meat
96. Frying fish
97. Frying fowl
98. Frying vegetables
99. Frying shellfish
100. Garnishing cold-meat trays
101. Garnishing entrees
102. Garnishing mixed drinks
103. Garnishing salads
104. Grating cheese
105. Greasing pans
106. Grilling meat
107. Grilling fish
108. Grilling fowl
109. Grilling shellfish
110. Grinding cheese
111. Grinding coffee beans
112. Grinding fruit
113. Grinding meat
114. Grinding vegetables
115. Grinding spices
116. Making appetizers
117. Making broth
118. Making canapes
119. Making candy
120. Making casseroles
121. Making chili
122. Making chocolate
123. Making chowders
124. Making coffee
125. Making cold sauces
126. Making custards
127. Making desserts
128. Making doughnuts
129. Making fountain drinks
130. Making fritters
131. Making fruit salads
132. Making garnishes
133. Making gravies
134. Making gelatin salads
135. Making hot chocolate
136. Making ice cream

137. Making ice coffee
138. Making iced tea
139. Making icings
140. Making Jello
141. Making meat glazes
142. Making meat loaf
143. Making meat patties
144. Making meat pies
145. Making omelets
146. Making pancakes
147. Making pastry shells
148. Making pizza
149. Making pudding
150. Making relishes
151. Making salads
152. Making salad dressings
153. Making sandwiches
154. Making sauces
155. Making sherbet
156. Making soups
157. Making stocks
158. Making stuffing
159. Making tarts
160. Making tea
161. Marinating meat
162. Marinating fish
163. Marinating vegetables
164. Measuring ingredients
165. Melting butter and fat
166. Mixing flavored beverages
167. Obtaining supplies
168. Opening bottles
169. Packaging order for delivery
170. Paring fruits
171. Paring vegetables
172. Peeling fruit and vegetables
173. Pitting fruit
174. Placing food in pans
175. Poaching eggs
176. Portioning casseroles
177. Portioning custards
178. Portioning desserts
179. Portioning fish
180. Portioning fowl
181. Portioning meat
182. Portioning shellfish
183. Portioning soups
184. Portioning vegetables
185. Posting menus
186. Pouring batter

187. Pouring drinks
188. Preparing appetizers
189. Preparing dough
190. Preparing cake batter
191. Preparing cocktail sauces
192. Preparing cooked cereal
193. Preparing dessert fruits
194. Preparing flaming desserts
195. Preparing fountain desserts
196. Preparing fruit compotes
197. Preparing hash
198. Preparing pie fillings
199. Preparing shellfish for service
200. Preparing souffles
201. Preparing sweet roll dough
202. Preparing whipped cream
203. Removing bones
204. Removing strings
205. Roasting meat
206. Roasting fish
207. Roasting fowl
208. Seasoning food
209. Scooping ice cream
210. Scoring meats
211. Shaping fowl
212. Shaping meat
213. Shaping shellfish
214. Shelling shellfish
215. Shelling vegetables
216. Slicing bread
217. Slicing cheese
218. Slicing cold meat
219. Slicing eggs
220. Slicing pickles
221. Steaming meat
222. Steaming fowl
223. Steaming shellfish
224. Stewing fish
225. Stewing fruit
226. Stewing meat
227. Stewing poultry
228. Stewing vegetables
229. Straining vegetables
230. Stuffing celery
231. Stuffing fish
232. Stuffing vegetables
233. Tenderizing meat
234. Thawing frozen foods
235. Toasting bread
236. Traying butter

237. Trimming meat
238. Trimming fish
239. Trimming fruit
240. Trimming vegetables
241. Turning wines
242. Tying roasts
243. Washing fish
244. Washing fruit
245. Washing leafy vegetables
246. Washing shellfish
247. Whipping foods
248. Wrapping sandwiches

B. FACILITIES

1. Adjusting equipment
2. Adjusting sound equipment
3. Adjusting thermostatic controls
4. Adjusting ventilating equipment
5. Breaking-down serving station
6. Breaking-down set-ups
7. Buffing floors
8. Buffing silverware
9. Brushing furniture
10. Cleaning air ducts
11. Cleaning artificial plants
12. Cleaning ash trays
13. Cleaning ceilings
14. Cleaning condiment containers
15. Cleaning counter
16. Cleaning dining tables
17. Cleaning glass
18. Cleaning filters
19. Cleaning fixtures
20. Cleaning hollowware
21. Cleaning machinery
22. Cleaning marble
23. Cleaning out-door furniture
24. Cleaning bathroom fixtures
25. Cleaning sinks
26. Cleaning toilets
27. Cleaning upholstered furniture
28. Cleaning urinals
29. Cleaning wash basins
30. Cleaning windows
31. Clearing the table
32. Collecting trash
33. Drying glassware
34. Dusting
35. Emptying ash trays
36. Emptying garbage
37. Emptying trash

38. Fashioning table decorations
39. Filling dispensing machines
40. Folding napkins
41. Inspecting and maintaining furniture
42. Maintaining refrigerating and air-conditioning equipment
43. Maintaining sound equipment
44. Mopping floors
45. Moving tables
46. Opening clogged drains
47. Picking up and removing trays
48. Picking up waste paper
49. Polishing floors
50. Polishing glassware
51. Racking china
52. Racking glasses
53. Racking silverware
54. Removing food
55. Removing trays
56. Rinsing china
57. Rinsing glasses
58. Rinsing silverware
59. Scraping food from dirty dishes
60. Sculpturing blocks of ice
61. Setting the table
62. Setting-up decorations
63. Sorting china
64. Sorting silverware
65. Stacking dishes by category
66. Sterilizing silverware
67. Washing dishes
68. Washing glasses
69. Washing silverware
70. Washing table tops
71. Wiping glasses
72. Wiping silverware
73. Wrapping silverware

C. SERVICE
1. Answering questions
2. Arranging for credit for guest
3. Arranging for special services
4. Checking valuables
5. Discussing food courses
6. Discussing mixed drinks
7. Discussing wines
8. Entertaining
9. Ladling sauces
10. Ladling soups
11. Opening doors for guests
12. Seating guests

13. Serving breads
14. Serving beer
15. Serving butter
16. Serving canapes
17. Serving from chafing dish at table
18. Serving cocktails
19. Serving coffee
20. Serving dessert
21. Serving fountain drinks
22. Serving juices both fruit and vegetable
23. Serving milk
24. Serving salad
25. Serving sandwiches
26. Serving tea
27. Serving vegetables
28. Serving water
29. Serving wine
30. Tasting wine

X. PURCHASING
A. ORDERING
1. Authorizing purchases and expenditures
2. Collecting orders from the various departments and delivering purchases
3. Comparing orders
4. Comparing specifications
5. Compiling request for materials
6. Consolidating request for materials
7. Forwarding requests for materials
8. Ordering clean linen
9. Ordering supplies
10. Purchasing bar equipment
11. Purchasing bar supplies
12. Purchasing beer
13. Purchasing building and maintenance supplies, etc.
14. Purchasing cleaning equipment
15. Purchasing clerical supplies
16. Purchasing dairy products
17. Purchasing dining-room equipment
18. Purchasing dining-room supplies
19. Purchasing kitchen equipment
20. Purchasing kitchen supplies
21. Purchasing linens
22. Purchasing liquor
23. Purchasing meats
24. Purchasing non-alcoholic beverages
25. Purchasing produce
26. Purchasing staples
27. Purchasing wines
28. Requisitioning supplies and services

B. RECEIVING
    1. Examining incoming orders for quality
    2. Moving containers, opening containers
    3. Receiving clean linen supplies
    4. Receiving clean uniforms from laundry
    5. Unpacking items
    6. Verifying incoming orders of supplies

C. STORING
    1. Inspecting food supplies
    2. Inventorying bar equipment
    3. Inventorying bar supplies
    4. Inventorying beer
    5. Inventorying cleaning equipment
    6. Inventorying cleaning supplies
    7. Inventorying clerical equipment
    8. Inventorying dairy products
    9. Inventorying dining room supplies
    10. Inventorying fish
    11. Inventorying fruits
    12. Inventorying kitchen equipment
    13. Inventorying kitchen supplies
    14. Inventorying vegetables
    15. Inventorying linens
    16. Inventorying liquors
    17. Inventorying meats
    18. Inventorying non-alcoholic beverages
    19. Inventorying shellfish
    20. Issuing linens
    21. Rotating stock
    22. Storing bar equipment
    23. Storing bar supplies
    24. Storing beer
    25. Storing cleaning supplies
    26. Storing clerical supplies
    27. Storing dairy products
    28. Storing dining-room supplies
    29. Storing fish
    30. Storing frozen foods
    31. Storing fruits
    32. Storing kitchen supplies
    33. Storing vegetables
    34. Storing left-overs
    35. Storing linens
    36. Storing liquors
    37. Storing meats
    38. Storing non-alcoholic beverages
    39. Storing poultry
    40. Storing shellfish
    41. Storing uniforms
    42. Storing wines

XI. REPAIR
   A. BUILDING
      1. Painting ceilings
      2. Painting walls
      3. Painting woodwork
      4. Preparing surfaces for painting
      5. Refinishing floors
      6. Removing wall paper
      7. Repairing carpets
      8. Repairing drapes
      9. Replacing broken tiles
      10. Replacing faucet washers
      11. Replacing floor tile
      12. Scraping paint
      13. Varnishing surfaces
   B. EQUIPMENT
      1. Repairing electrical fixtures
      2. Repairing refrigerating and air-conditioning equipment
      3. Repairing silverware
      4. Repairing sound equipment
      5. Repairing thermostats
      6. Replacing bearings
      7. Replacing silverware
      8. Reupholstering worn or damaged furniture
XII. TRANSPORTATION
   A. NON-VEHICULAR
      1. Delivering messages
      2. Removing empty bottles
      3. Removing garbage
      4. Removing trash
      5. Transporting foods from storage area to production area
      6. Transporting food to serving counters
      7. Transporting supplies from storage to production area
      8. Transporting used utensils from dining room to washing area
      9. Transporting utensils to serving counter

Index